Also by Andrei Amalrik

Will the Soviet Union Survive Until 1984?

Involuntary Journey to Siberia

Nose! Nose? No-se & Other Plays

Notes of a Revolutionary

NOTES OF A REVOLUTIONARY

by Andrei Amalrik

Translated by Guy Daniels

With an introduction by Susan Jacoby

Alfred A. Knopf   New York   1982

Translation Copyright © 1982 by Alfred A. Knopf, Inc.

Library of Congress Cataloging in Publication Data

Amal'rik, Andrei, 1938–1980.
Notes of a revolutionary.

Translation of: Zapiski dissidenta / A. Amalrik.
1. Amal'rik, Andrei, 1938–1980.   2. Political prisoners—Soviet Union.
3. Dissenters—Soviet Union—Biography.   I. Title.
HV8959.S65A4513   1982   345.47'0231   81-48120
ISBN 0-394-41756-9   347.05231   AACR2

Manufactured in the United States of America

FIRST EDITION

I wish I were an ancient master of the elegaic hexameter that I might in two or four chiseled lines imperishably commemorate the passing of Andrei Amalrik. Fate was never more malevolent than in decreeing that he, who had survived Siberian prison camps, should come to a banal end in an automobile accident on his way to the Helsinki treaty conference in Madrid.

May this indomitable young man's abrupt extinction serve at least to call sharper attention to the Soviet Union's open violation of its Helsinki obligations in the treatment of his fellow dissidents. Amalrik will live in his country's memory with the Decembrists and Herzen and Tolstoy and our own time's honored Sakharov to inspire the continued struggle, though it often seems hopeless, for a free Russia.

I. F. Stone
Washington, Nov. 17, 1980

Letter to the Editor, the *New York Times*

"Ask them if they know how a person should act, according to Christ's teachings, when he is offended by another."

Nekhlyudov translated the Englishman's question.

"Tell the chief, so he can look into it?" one of them said uncertainly, with a sideways look at the imposing jailkeeper.

"Give him a good beating, and he won't treat you bad again," said another.

Some chuckles of approval were heard. . . .

"Tell them that according to Christ's teachings, a person should do just the opposite," said the Englishman. "If someone strikes you on one cheek, turn the other cheek to him." And he made as if to offer his own cheek. . . .

Loud, irrepressible laughter rang through the cell. Even the man who had been beaten laughed through his blood and snot.

Tolstoy, *Resurrection*

Contents

Introduction

No. I was never anyone's contemporary.

—OSIP MANDELSTAM

Andrei Alekseyevich Amalrik was a man who stubbornly refused to fit any of the categories usually assigned to Soviet dissidents. He was a participant in what came to be known as the "democratic movement," but it would be more accurate to describe him as a movement of one. He did not take part in the small number of public demonstrations by dissidents in the late 1960's, nor did he sign the collective protests that appeared more and more frequently as the present Soviet leadership intensified its efforts to halt the process of de-Stalinization begun by Nikita Khrushchev. He irritated some of his fellow dissidents by his pessimism about prospects for changing the Soviet system from within, but that pessimism did not alter his determination to act, speak, and write as a free man. His books—the products of a skeptical, abrasive, and witty intellect—were his form of dissent. After he nearly died of meningitis in a Siberian prison, his wife, Gusel, told me, "In spite of everything, he is freer inside himself in jail than any of us who are walking around on the streets."

Andrei was born in Moscow in 1938. When the Nazis invaded the Soviet Union in 1941, his father, then completing his history studies at Moscow State University (MGU), returned to his duties as a lieutenant in the Red Army. Unfortunately, he made the mistake of remarking in the presence of several fellow officers that Stalin's purges were responsible for the lack of military preparedness that had allowed the Germans to advance so swiftly during the early months of the war. He was arrested and sentenced to eight years in camp. In 1943, however, like many imprisoned soldiers, he was pardoned in the interests of filling the army's desperate need for officers during the siege of Stalingrad.

Like his father, Andrei became a student of history. His first open clash with the political authority that governs every Soviet institution came in 1960, when he submitted his diploma dissertation to a senior professor at MGU. His paper, which dealt with the ninth-century state of Kievan Rus, concluded that Norman traders had exerted a significant influence on early Russian civilization. Despite the remoteness of the subject matter, the dissertation was politically unacceptable; it contradicted the official historical position that Russian culture and civilization were produced by Slavs alone. Andrei's professor told him the research was brilliant, and that the dissertation would be accepted if he would simply leave out his conclusion. Andrei refused and was expelled from the university.

After the expulsion, Andrei attempted to send his paper to a distinguished Danish professor of Slavic languages who shared his views and with whom he had been corresponding. Assuming that the dissertation would be confiscated if he attempted to post it through the open mail, Andrei asked the Danish Embassy in Moscow to pass the paper on to the professor. The embassy, however, without informing Andrei, turned the dissertation over to the Soviet Ministry of Foreign Affairs, which handed it on to the KGB. And so Andrei had his first official "conversation" with the secret police.

The incident is important, because it typified the behavior of a number of western diplomats and correspondents in Moscow. Some foreigners were as bewildered as Soviet officialdom by the spectacle of a man insisting on his freedom in an unfree environment. As Andrei would later write in *Will the Soviet Union Survive Until 1984?*, an act like sending a scholarly paper to a foreign professor falls within a "gray belt" of activities which are permitted in theory but are forbidden in practice to most Soviet citizens.

Under Soviet law, there is no explicit prohibition against sending a scholarly paper abroad—just as there is no formal ban on the activities in defense of human rights that have caused even so eminent a figure as Andrei Sakharov to be stripped of everything but his dignity. The fact that most Soviet citizens do not engage in such activities is part of an unwritten contract of fear that was established in Stalin's time.

In the early sixties, before the courageous acts of a small band of dissenters became known in their own country and in the West, many foreigners in Moscow regarded the behavior of Amalrik as the rash actions of a lunatic at best or as a trap set by a KGB provocateur at worst. This attitude was not unknown among western correspondents a decade later, when I was living in Moscow and working on my first book. My former husband, then the correspondent of the Washington *Post*, was among the minority of journalists who were willing to meet with dissenters. Most of the press corps was content to get its "unofficial" news secondhand, from less timid colleagues. Andrei Amalrik, who was a reliable source of news about official persecution of other dissenters, was the first—and for many years the only—Russian dissident to discuss publicly what he considered to be the inadequacy of western news reporting from Moscow.

From the day when he refused to censor his own dissertation, Andrei's life can only be understood as one man's refusal to be bound by the old terms of the contract of fear.

In the early sixties, Andrei lived with his father, who was partially paralyzed and needed regular care. He took part-time jobs that left him time to look after his parent, wrote plays (unpublished and unperformed, naturally), and began collecting the sort of unofficial art once characterized as "dog shit" by Khrushchev. It was this involvement in the unofficial art world that was responsible for his early contacts with the foreign community in Moscow.

All of these "gray" activities played a role in his exile to Siberia as a "parasite" in 1965. His father's fragile health gave way after Andrei was forced to leave Moscow; he received a telegram about the illness and obtained permission to return home for eighteen days—but his father had already died by the time the message reached his remote Siberian collective farm. While Andrei was in Moscow arranging the funeral, he married Gusel, a talented artist and a remarkable woman whose ability to create a private world of beauty in the grimmest surroundings was itself an act of resistance that matched her husband's determination.

It was through Gusel that I first "met" Andrei four years later, when she was commuting between Moscow and Siberia for the second time in their married life. Before she left to visit Andrei in camp, we gathered a number of items he might be able to use, including a tube of toothpaste and dozens of Swiss bouillon cubes. The bouillon cubes failed to pass inspection; Andrei had explained that you dissolved them in water to make soup, but the guards examining them used cold rather than hot liquid. The cubes simply fell apart, and the authorities assumed Andrei had been lying and might be concealing some mysterious message. When he saw Gusel, Andrei was concerned because her hair had begun to fall out as a result of emotional stress. He wrote her not to worry about the loss of the broth. "One lock of your hair," he said, "is dearer to me than any number of bouillon cubes." His letters were the means by which I felt I had come to know him; we were not to meet face-to-face until he and Gusel were allowed to leave the Soviet Union six years later.

Andrei wound up in Siberia again because he began writing books as soon as he and Gusel returned to Moscow in 1966. His experiences during his first exile formed the core of *Involuntary Journey to Siberia*, one of the most insightful pieces of reportage to emerge from the literature of dissent.

Andrei's eye (and ear) for detail produced a rare account of the harsh existence on a Soviet collective farm—a world as alien to urban Russian intellectuals as it is to Westerners. *Involuntary Journey* also provides a memorable catalogue of the police system's homelier details. We meet a police inspector who spied a nude Matisse drawing on Andrei's wall and volunteered the information (in the midst of an official search) that he could only be sexually aroused by fat women. Then there is the ex-director of a wallpaper factory who received a six-year camp sentence for embezzling only 400 rubles—a small sum at the time. Andrei asks an interrogator why the man received such a heavy sentence, and the police official replies: "Four hundred rubles is what he was *caught* with, but he must have stolen much more."

After his return from exile, Andrei also wrote *Will the Soviet Union Survive Until 1984?*, a theoretical essay challenging the then-prevalent notion that the growth of an educated middle class would create strong pressure for democratization of the Soviet system. "In any country," he argues, "the stratum of society least inclined toward change or any sort of independent action is that composed of state employees. . . . In our country, since all of us work for the state, we all have the psychology of government workers."

The book also challenges the idea that consumerism and foreign trade would lead to liberalization of Soviet society and that "foreign tourists, jazz records, and miniskirts" would hasten progress. "It is possible that we will indeed have a socialism with bare knees someday," Andrei declares, "but not likely one with a human face."

The pessimism of this essay was strongly influenced by the tightening of internal repression in the wake of the Soviet invasion of Czechoslovakia. By early 1970, both books had been published in the West. In May of that year, Andrei was arrested and charged with spreading "falsehoods derogatory to the Soviet state." He was sentenced to three years in a labor camp and re-sentenced in camp at the end of his term in May 1973. Possibly in response to international protests focusing on Andrei's ill health (after his near-fatal bout of meningitis, he was classified as an invalid entitled to be excused from hard labor), the sentence was eventually commuted to exile in the frigid northeastern city of Magadan—a town heavily populated by an earlier generation of camp survivors from Stalin's day. When Andrei's term of internal exile expired, the Amalriks applied for permission to emigrate to the West; they left their native land in 1976. For most survivors of the "democratic movement," emigration had become the only alternative to either silencing themselves or spending the rest of their lives in jail.

Andrei began work on *Notes of a Revolutionary* soon after his departure from the Soviet Union. In his preface he describes the theme of his memoir as "the conflict between the individual person and the system in a country where the individual is nothing and the system is everything."

That description is too modest. (Uncharacteristically so—humility is not ordinarily an accompaniment to Andrei's brand of moral resoluteness. The phrase "humble as Amalrik" became a standing joke among his friends.)

Notes of a Revolutionary is a personal memoir, but it is also much more—just as Nadezhda Mandelstam's *Hope Against Hope* is much more than a personal account of her life with a great poet doomed by his inability to adapt to the Stalinist state. Amalrik's book begins at approximately the point where Madame Mandelstam's ends. It constitutes a thorough cultural history of the period between 1966 and 1976, when the forces of democratization and dissent, set in motion during the brief period of "de-Staliniza-tion," came into inexorable conflict with a state determined to restore the status quo ante (not the status quo of Stalinism, but that of the period before Khrushchev). The book combines the keen powers of observation displayed in *Involuntary Journey to Siberia* with the more speculative bent of *Will the Soviet Union Survive Until 1984?*

Andrei was killed in an automobile accident near Madrid in November of 1980, while on his way to testify at an international conference set up to examine compliance with the Helsinki Accords. At the time of his death, he was hard at work on a biography of Rasputin; in the West, he had elected to pursue the scholarly vocation that had been interrupted twenty years earlier by the KGB. Andrei Amalrik's readers are fortunate that the Soviet state was unable to prevent him from recording his life and times.

SUSAN JACOBY

New York, December 1981

Preface

After my longtime negative attitude toward the word "revolution," I became a participant in what is perhaps one of the most significant radical changes of our times. No one yet knows whether this agonizing attempt to create a new ideology will succeed, or whether it will end in a blind alley. The crisis of Christianity gave birth to the Enlightenment, and the crisis of the Enlightenment engendered Marxism. But can we yet affirm with confidence that Marxism's crisis will be solved by a transformation of the "person" from an element in the "system" into a true person? The philosophy of totalitarianism is still spreading through the world. But in the land where it first triumphed, the process of overcoming it has begun, not "from the right" but "from the left," in a movement that gropes its way along but in a forward direction.

The theme of these memoirs is the conflict between the individual person and the system in a country where the individual is nothing and the system is everything. I have not written the history of an idea or of a movement—merely my own personal story. I have tried to tell that story artlessly and honestly; hence I have not written merely about what I like to recall. The logic of events sometimes comes into conflict with the logic of their narration; and it would be hard to separate what is "important" from what is "secondary." Alas! Life consists mostly of "secondary" things; and if one's selection is too strict, the pungency of reality is lost.

The title of this book is of course intended to evoke the memoirs of Prince Peter Kropotkin.

ANDREI AMALRIK

Genthod, Switzerland

PART ONE

MOSCOW (1966 – 70)

C H A P T E R   1

Artists and Collectors

"An English journalist recently came to Daniel's wife and left his address," Alexander Ginzburg said to me in December 1966. "You know how to socialize with foreigners. Couldn't you put that journalist in touch with me?"

Only four months before, I had returned from exile in Siberia. Most of what I knew about the trial of Andrei Sinyavsky and Yuri Daniel I had read in the Soviet newspapers. I had heard vaguely about the demonstration and letters in their defense; and that Ginzburg had almost finished compiling a "White Paper"—a collection of documents on the trial—and wanted to set up a press conference. Once when I was sitting on a broken-down sofa at his place, he told me his manuscript was directly under me. But I never asked him to let me read it, partly so that if an investigator asked me if I had seen it, I could say I knew nothing about it. I figured the authorities would not stand upon ceremony with either Ginzburg or me. And apparently Ginzburg had the same idea, which might explain why he didn't risk going to see the foreign correspondent. Or perhaps he thought the latter would be frightened if he came to see him. Because in those days, all of us were a little afraid: afraid of the regime; afraid that people who feared the regime would take us for provocateurs; and afraid of provocateurs.

Nonetheless, I agreed to put the correspondent in touch with Ginzburg and thereby took upon myself a role that I played until the autumn of 1969— a role that involved me, to some extent, in what was later called the Democratic Movement. Even now I have a clear remembrance of Tverskaya-Yamskaya Street buried in snow, the street lamps spaced at long intervals, and the empty sentry box in front of the apartment house—empty because too few foreigners lived there to justify keeping a policeman watching it around the clock. I remember, too, the correspondent's wife, her face framed by long, straight hair, and her somewhat bewildered expression as I tried to explain what I wanted. (This difficulty was due to the fact that, despite my ability to "socialize with foreigners," I could speak only Russian.)

Ginzburg met with the journalist at our place. Since my wife and I had no curtains for our windows, we came up with a naïve conspiratorial stratagem just in case someone tried to photograph us from outside: we covered the windows with paintings. The three of us agreed to meet again on January 17, 1967. But that day, it turned out, was when a search was carried out at Ginzburg's home from morning until night.

Sometime afterward I saw Ginzburg at a showing of works by "unofficial" artists at the Druzhba (Friendship) Club. The exhibit was closed after only one hour. But during that brief time, both rooms were so full of people that you could hardly make your way through them. Across one of the crowded rooms, I glimpsed Ginzburg's face. His expression was lively, but the imprint of doom was already visible: it was clear to everyone—and especially to Ginzburg—that he would soon be arrested.

Even after the showing had been closed, KGB officers kept wandering through the rooms, looking at the paintings with interest, and saying to the artists: "We're not against this exhibit. The order came from the *raikom*."*
And in the corridor, a gray-faced man, indicating a group of artists, was telling a younger man: "Go ahead! Go and hang around them!"

Both the first search made at Ginzburg's home and his arrest on January 23 coincided with meetings I had arranged; and I had the heavyhearted feeling that there might be informers among his friends and that I might be suspect. Today, however, I am inclined to think that Ginzburg was about to be apprehended anyway.

My meetings with Ginzburg and his friend Yuri Galanskov the previous autumn had made it plain to me that a moral, if not a political, opposition to the regime already existed. Galanskov was already talking about forming a party. I was ready to help both of them; but I didn't want to get tied in too closely.

I had always been in opposition to the regime; in fact, as a young boy I didn't even join the Pioneers.† But that opposition was, more than anything else, a personal rejection of something I felt unable to change. Essentially, I was looking for a niche where I could live and carry on my work: I was trying to find a kind of coexistence with the regime. But that scheme—one to which

---

*An asterisk in the text refers to the Glossary section at the end of the book. A dagger (†) indicates a text footnote; a number refers to a citation note, found in the Notes section at the end of the book.—Trans.

†The Soviet youth organization for young children (i.e., not yet of an age to join the Young Communists' League).—Trans.

I returned again and again—was not feasible. Of course, many people *have* found their own sort of niche in the Soviet Union; any private life there is a "niche." The regime, however, exacts a rather high price for the right to stay in that corner. Not only that, but sooner or later everyone is asked whether he is for the regime or against it. The regime is not content that anyone simply be "not against" it: everyone must be "for" it and must demonstrate this from time to time.

A second obstacle was the fact that I had always wanted not so much to adapt myself to the world as to change it. For a long time I did not realize this, but it was the source of many conflicts. Besides, I wanted to return blow for blow. Thus, during the first days of my exile in Siberia, I began thinking of how I would write a book about it and in that way get at least some revenge on the people who had treated me so outrageously. What I found myself faced with, however, was not individual persons but a system; and under the circumstances, I don't see how I had any hope of coexisting with it.

At the time, my wife, Gusel, and I were living in a large communal apartment on Vakhtangov Street, in the heart of the Arbat district. From the entrance hall, where a dim bulb burned (except when our neighbors turned it off for reasons of economy), a long hallway in the shape of a capital L led past a steamy kitchen where laundry was hung up to dry and old ladies with weary faces stood at their tables; past the bathroom where another neighbor— with her head bent down over the tub and her enormous rear, swathed in blue cotton slacks, protruding into the hallway—was doing her laundry; past an area concealed by a curtain with suitcases and trunks sticking out from under it; past big doors and little doors; past chests of drawers standing along the wall; and ended up at the door of our room.

When you opened the door, you ran smack into a grand piano that took up half of the room. Neither Gusel nor I could play it. I had inherited the instrument from an aunt who had been a singer, and for me it was like an elephant for an impecunious Hindu. Besides, it was completely out of tune. Only rarely was it played—by two madcaps, Gusel's sister and the painter Anatoly Zverev, both of whom somehow managed to extract lovely sounds from it, Zverev sometimes even using his head for the purpose.

Some people—especially foreigners—used to laugh at us, because while we didn't even have a table to eat at, half the room was occupied by a useless grand piano. But its very uselessness and beauty, together with the paintings, the old books, the grandfather clock, and the withered, spidery plants on the sideboard, made our room look like something out of a fairy tale.

The communal apartment was a microcosm of the Soviet world. The room next to the entrance was occupied by an elderly Jewish couple. The husband, a major, worked at some vague institution. He was given to expressing his admiration for Israel, although in guarded terms. His wife, whose chief concern in life was preparing dinner for her husband, was deferential toward those neighbors who had influence, and showed goodwill toward others.

Next door to them lived an old Communist, squat as a mushroom, with a squeaky voice, who seldom left the room, and his tall, sturdy wife, who held sway in the communal kitchen. She stressed her devotion to the Soviet regime, and was very proud that her son was a prosecutor,† although he had been removed from that office for graft. When you went past their room, you could hear the BBC, the Deutsche Welle, or the Voice of America, because the old man felt one must "know the enemy." (Also, listening to foreign radio stations is the favorite pastime of retired people in the Soviet Union.) But this business turned out badly for him. He had heard on the radio that various dissidents had been arrested, or confined in a psychiatric hospital, or expelled from Moscow; and when he was being moved to his dacha for the summer by his wife, he suddenly got it into his head that he was being expelled from Moscow. He began weeping and repeating: "They're doing this to *me*—to a man who has honorably served the Soviet regime all his life!" He died not long afterward.

Across the hall there were two women: an old lady with a caved-in mouth and her forty-year-old daughter. The old woman had come to Moscow from the country long before, but she still had some rural ways about her. The daughter managed a bakery.

Further down the hall lived a sour-faced woman of seventy, the widow of a colonel. She was very rank-conscious, and as a result the apartment became a field of battle to determine who was more important: the colonel's widow or the major's wife (although only a major, he was alive); the bakery manager or the prosecutor's mother. Even though he was only an ex-prosecutor, for his mother he was still a prosecutor.

The room next to ours was occupied by two women, neither of whom had any social inferiority complex whatsoever. Forty-five-year-old Olya, haggard and bony, worked as a charwoman at a movie theater and lived with her aunt, whom she called "Grandma." Olya's minor son was in prison for the gang rape of a girl who was also a minor. When Olya got drunk, which was almost every night, she would put a tape on her recorder full blast, pound her fist on the table, and shout: "Grandma, I'm drinking! I'm having a ball!"

Toward the end of the tape, the music would be muted a bit, and a hearty male voice, imitating a radio announcer, would be heard saying: "This music

---

†Throughout this book I have used the term "prosecutor" rather than the less familiar "procurator," although in fact the latter has broader powers.—TRANS.

was recorded for Olga Vorontsova by the senior projector operator of the Cadre Movie Theater."

"Listen, Grandma! That music is for me!" Olya would shout.

Grandma's response was blunt: "Blah, blah, blah!"

Gusel worked at her painting, slapping a shoebrush against her canvas so hard that the chair shook. She developed her own style, in some ways following her teacher, Vasily Sitnikov, and in other ways Vladimir Veisberg. But in terms of design and her sensuous perception of nature, she was closest of all to Modigliani and Van Dongen. Since the authorities rejected non-conformist art and there were only one or two Soviet collectors, the foreign colony in Moscow was our major market.

The low prices in Moscow made paintings accessible to people who could not afford the work of good artists in their own countries. Many of them wanted to acquire, in a foreign country, something that was typical of it and yet rather rare, and unofficial art that contained an element of protest and yet was permitted by the regime corresponded well to the foreigners' hopes for the "liberalization" of the Soviet system.

Then of course there was the desire, common to all times and the people of all countries, to ornament one's home. I recall how astounded an American was when she saw the walls of our room covered with pictures; they created their own kind of magnetic field. So long as a person lives in an atmosphere of beauty, it alleviates such feelings as envy and spite. I agree, indeed, that "beauty will save the world"; but we are now moving away from beauty rather than toward it. In the past, even peasant utensils were art objects. Today, however, many paintings have the look of factory products. The flourishing of totalitarianism in political and socioeconomic life has coincided with the flourishing of functionalism in architecture and design.

Among the foreigners—more accurately, the quasi-foreigners—in Moscow, some realized (or perhaps it was suggested to them) that collecting the work of unofficial artists and acting as middlemen between the new Soviet art and the old Western market might prove to be profitable. There was a Russian-American couple whom I shall call Richard and Lidia. They had married before the war. Later, Lidia went with her husband to the U.S., where she studied history at an American university. Then, in the mid-1950s, they settled permanently in Moscow.

When I met them in 1964, they were living in a large private house with pictures, most of them by young painters, hung in almost all of the rooms. But when I came back to Moscow in 1966, I saw almost no pictures at their place, because Lidia had taken most of them to the U.S. and sold them there. She had wanted to be the only broker offering unofficial Soviet art to the U.S. market; and her eagerness to act as go-between reached a ridiculous extreme.

When artists and buyers were at her home at the same time, she would literally shove them into different rooms; and on one occasion she even locked up Vasily Sitnikov in the toilet. The collector Armand Hammer came to her place when the artist Dima Plavinsky and a friend were already there, so drunk that Lidia couldn't drag them off to another room. Hammer couldn't believe that it was possible to drink that much, and decided that Lidia had invited two actors trained in the Stanislavsky method to impersonate drunken Russian artists. Nor, I feel, did Stanislavsky fail in Hammer's eyes, because I once had to drag Plavinsky's friend by the legs along the hallway described above, past all my shook-up neighbors, and shove him down the stairs. He tumbled down head over heels, and when he reached the bottom he shouted: "I dare you to come down here!" To this, Plavinsky responded with the words of Lenin: "We'll go by another route!"

In spite of Lidia's wealth, which was quite conspicuous when contrasted with the marginal life-style of most people in the Soviet Union, one sensed in her and in her home a kind of unhappiness. I remember one late afternoon when she was trying to show me a Japanese movie camera and kept taking one camera after another out of a box, some of them without lenses, others without cranks, and still others with all the parts missing, a whole row of crippled cameras. The room was already in semidarkness; and when, glancing at her from the side, I noticed the taut wrinkles on her face and neck, I suddenly realized how unhappy she was.

Once when Zverev, Plavinsky, and I were visiting Richard and Lidia's home, there were two girls and a young man (an albino with a face impossible to recall) sitting in one corner of the living room, while Richard stood in the middle, and the three of us were seated on the other side. (According to Plavinsky's strategic plan, we had occupied the corner nearest the bar.) The expressions on the faces of both trios seemed to say: "We have our little group, and you have yours."

"But where is Lidia?" Plavinsky asked amiably.

"At this very moment," Richard replied with equal amiability, "Lidia is lying on an operating table. She broke a leg and went to America for an operation."

We sat there for a while with sad faces. Then suddenly a door was thrown open and in came Lidia, all in black, with one leg in a white plaster cast, carrying a black umbrella.

Going up to the young albino, she shouted: "How many times have I told you not to show up here!" Whereupon she whacked him on the rear with her umbrella. He ran for the door, and the girls followed him, squealing, as we froze in our chairs.

"Lidia! Lidia!" Richard exclaimed, making a helpless gesture with his hands as though in feeble defense of the albino.

"This is a whorehouse! A whorehouse!" Lidia shouted. It was plain to see that she was glad to have an audience.

When Lidia told about finding a naked girl in the bedroom, Richard offered the explanation that the girl was a talented violinist who had no place to practice (she did in fact have a violin with her), so he had allowed her to perform in the bedroom. It seems that she played in such self-oblivion and so passionately that she got into a terrible sweat and had to take off all her clothes. While he was talking, Lidia proceeded to pick up the girl's panties, brassiere, and other apparel and throw them out the window. They caught in the branches of a cherry tree in the garden, where they hung like some kind of fabulous fruit. Richard was too fat to climb the tree, so the poor girl had to go outside stark naked and climb it herself. It must be said to Lidia's credit that she didn't throw the violin out too.

The Soviet authorities are stern. They don't like girls' panties hanging on cherry trees, Russians going as guests to the homes of Americans, or foreigners buying and selling paintings. And above all, they don't like it when foreign correspondents stay in Russia too long; because the longer a correspondent lives there, the better he understands the situation. But Richard lingered in Moscow for more than three decades.

Ever since my student years, I had been seeking out friends and acquaintances among foreigners. It was not that I had practical aims in mind: to buy a book, to sell a painting, or to pass on a manuscript—although I shall have something to say of such matters later on. The main thing for me, as for many others—I daresay even for the young people trading in blue jeans—was to find some almost metaphysical way out of the world around us. The authorities tried to make us believe that the Soviet world was a closed sphere, that it was the whole universe. But those of us who were making holes in that sphere, however little, could breathe a different kind of air. Sometimes it was even bad air; but even so, it was not the thin air of totalitarianism.

Although I have increasingly become involved in other things, relations with artists have always meant a lot to me. Anatoly Zverev used to come to our place sometimes—that is, until we quarreled over who should lead in a card game. I fear that in the history of Russian art, Zverev's works will occupy a humble place; the finest of them have simply got lost among all the trash he produced. But that is not the only thing. In the West, even his best paintings have not aroused interest. They have proven too reminiscent of the lyrical impressionism of the twenties and thirties—as if the development of Russian art were being revived, going back for a starting point to the moment when it was artificially cut off.

Unshaven, in dirty, hand-me-down clothes with his cap pulled down low over his eyes, Zverev provoked disgust in many people. At the same time, he himself was terribly squeamish. For instance, he never ate a piece of bread with the crust still on it. Instead, he would dig out a chunk from inside the loaf, scattering crumbs all around him. He drank straight from the bottle, since he didn't want his vodka soiled by a glass; and he was so sensitive about it that his lips never touched the neck of the bottle. His notions of how one should drink, and how much, were very far from the norm, even in Russia. Once at breakfast he drank about a liter of vodka while I was consuming one small glass of it. Next we split a bottle of champagne. Then Zverev said: "A little beer would go well right now."

He was forever getting into strange adventures. At one time he was living in a basement room with an elephantine poetess who wrote children's books. Their favorite pastime was to make up rhymes. His friend would say a word, and Zverev would instantly think up a rhyme for it. Then he would say another word, and she would create the rhyme.

"Salmonella," the poetess would say.

"Sol on Ella," Zverev would promptly respond.

"Argentina."

"Arch on Tina."

And so on, until either his or her imagination was exhausted. But the poet once chanced to come up with such bad rhymes that Zverev lost his patience. With a curse, he threw a smoldering match at her mass of curly, fluffed-up hair.

"You bastard!" she screamed, grabbing at her flaming hair. "That's enough! I'm going to tell the KGB that you sell paintings to foreigners!" And she ran out of the room, locking the door behind her.

Terrified, Zverev started pounding on the door, which caused the man in the next room, a war veteran with one leg, to come hopping out to see what the trouble was. Wanting to help, he tried to undo the tight latch by sticking his finger in the notch. But Zverev's fear of the KGB was so great that without waiting for the door to be unlatched he broke it down, thereby tearing off the finger of his deliverer.

"I was in such a hurry that I didn't even beg his pardon," Zverev later told me sorrowfully. He was feeling really bad about it, since he ascribed great importance to matters of *politesse*.

It turned out that his poet friend, instead of going to the KGB, was at a hairdresser's getting what was left of her hair fixed up. But the KGB *did* get a complaint—from the veteran. He wrote that it wasn't enough that he had lost a leg fighting in a war to defend the radiant future of the younger generation; that younger generation had now torn off his finger.

Zverev had a habit of striking up conversations with women on the street. And if any of them, frightened by his absurd appearance and strange way of talking, appealed to a passerby, he would say in an aggrieved tone: "Comrade, that woman has been pursuing me for a whole month, now. And what can I do? I have a case of impotentization.''

Much of his behavior could be ascribed to his pathological cowardice. For instance, his constant dread made him incite quarrels between people who admired his work. He had been discovered by Alexander Rumnev, a dancer and producer; later, the collector Georgi Kostaki had become very interested in his work. One night when Zverev was dining at Kostaki's home, he said: ''There are some bad people in this world, Georgi.''

''What do you mean, Tolechka?'' Kostaki asked, somewhat disquieted.

''Well, take Alexander Rumnev, for example. He's a man people respect. But he said things about you that I'm ashamed to repeat. He said you were a black-assed little Armenian faggot.''

''*Wha-a-at*?'' exploded Kostaki. ''But he himself has Armenian tendencies.''

The next evening, while dining at the home of Rumnev, Zverev began: ''There are some bad people in this world, Alex . . .''

And later he told me: ''For some reason, Rumnev doesn't like you. He said straight out to me: 'Don't you dare go to see that old whore, Amalrik.' ''

I can just imagine what he told Rumnev about me.

By the time we met, Zverev's fame had given him a certain amount of self-confidence. But his childhood and youth were horrible. As he himself wrote: ''For me, the only stars were sketching, checkers, and poetry.''

CHAPTER 2

The Novosti
Press Agency

I had to think about getting a regular, official job. Already I had been visited
by an obese district police inspector and a *gebist** in plain clothes with a
typical surly smile on his face that reminded me of a piece of boiled meat in
sour sauce. These officials had hinted that if I didn't find a job, I might soon
be going back to Siberia. Unexpectedly, an aunt of mine told me that another
nephew of hers was working at the Novosti Press Agency and that she would
ask him to see what he could do by way of "mutual assistance" between
nephews.

A few days later, I was on my way to the Novosti building in Pushkin
Square. In the outer office, three doorkeepers were on duty: one in the vesti-
bule, one at the telephone, and one by the door leading into the inner offices.
The expression on their faces left no doubt as to what organization they
belonged to. I was met by my cousin, Boris Alekseyev, a tall fellow some
five years older than I. His face seemed to be manly, yet had a kind of jellylike
mobility: one felt that he was very much a mamma's boy. I had the impression
that in agreeing to this interview he was trying to show respect to his aunt
without doing anything of practical consequence. But then we were joined by
his girlfriend, a young blonde woman with rather sharp features and a vigorous gait. It was Ira who suggested my first assignment: interviewing theatrical
set designers. Articles had been commissioned, but the journalist hadn't
written anything. So she thought: Why not let this young man do it? Unlike
Boris, she had carved out her own career; and such people like to sponsor
others. For her, my exile had endowed me with a kind of romantic halo.
Besides, my sentence had been set aside by the Supreme Court.

The Novosti Press Agency was created in the last years of Khrushchev's
regime. It was chiefly designed to send propaganda abroad, although Soviet
newspapers also subscribed to the service. Like any Soviet agency involved

in foreign operations, Novosti collaborated with the KGB and served as a "cover" for its agents abroad. Later on, the fact that I had worked for Novosti was cited in the West as evidence that I was a KGB agent. Not only Novosti, but the Union of Soviet Writers, publishing houses, and other Soviet institutions have ties with the KGB. Indeed, from a metaphysical viewpoint, all Soviet citizens work for the KGB.

There were quite a few KGB agents employed by Novosti, either on the regular staff or as stringers, but most of the reporters had no direct relations with the KGB. As for me, I was in no sense a regular employee of Novosti. I was just one of the thousands of writers to whom the agency gave free-lance assignments. Of course, even the free-lancers were carefully chosen. Thus the agency kept a special file on me, with my address, education, place of permanent employment, etc. Ira and I took special pains to make sure nothing suspect showed up in it, and I put down "student" as my occupation.

I had no idea how to interview artists. Finally, I arranged to see Boris Messerer. His father had been a choreographer and his mother a ballerina; Boris himself designed sets for ballet productions. In his studio I was greeted by a woman who struck me as very beautiful. This was his former wife. (There is a certain type of beauty found only in ballerinas that is always recognizable—although of course not all ballerinas are beautiful.) She picked up a dancing doll in a glass case and wound it up. "That's me!" she said, pointing to the doll. Then she went out.

Messerer, a short, totally bald man of about forty, asked me to sit down. So I did, and he did; and we both sat there in silence, giving each other looks full of deep meaning. He was waiting for me to ask him a question, and I had no idea what to ask. Finally I said, "How amazing! You're still young, yet you're completely bald."

Despite that shaky start, I interviewed several set designers, some of whom were gifted. Yet I got the impression that there is no such thing as a person with a vocation for designing sets; all of them are easel painters manqué. For that matter, the better they understood the space of the stage, the worse was their easel painting.

When I turned in my article, I made my first acquaintance with what is called "editing." The passages I thought were the best were deleted and replaced by questions like: "What are your fondest dreams and plans?" But the article was accepted, and was even commended.

For Novosti I wrote mostly about the theater—the thing that interested me as a playwright. (It was partly on account of my plays that I had been exiled to Siberia.) The first director I interviewed was Valentin Pluchek. I went to see a play he was directing (a good one). Then I asked Ginzburg— just a few days before his arrest, as it happened—what background reading he thought I should do on Pluchek. Ginzburg said his advice was not to read anything but to peruse the *APN Herald* (for which I was going to write) to find out how their articles were written. The interview with Pluchek began, quite by accident, with some talk about painting, and he eagerly questioned me about the show at the Druzhba Club that had been closed down so abruptly. But the moment we got on the subject of theater, something in him seemed to click off, like a switch, and he started talking in bland, banal phrases. Even his voice changed. Then, as soon as I stopped taking notes, he went back to talking in a human voice.

In general, the names of Soviet theaters have a solemn ring: the Moscow City Soviet Theater, the Lenin Komsomol* Theater, the Soviet Army Theater. And their artistic directors are more like generals than directors. But I got a rather different impression from Leonid Varpakhovsky. Like Pluchek, he was one of the last pupils of Vsevolod Meyerhold.

For all Varpakhovsky's success and prosperity, I had the feeling that something in him had broken. He had spent many years in the Kolyma camps and then was director of the theater in Magadan, the capital of the Kolyma Territory. (Of course I had no notion that I would be visiting that theater myself six years later.)

Varpakhovsky was very friendly toward me and praised my play *Is Uncle Jack a Conformist?* Since there was no possibility of mounting it in a Soviet theater, he suggested that I adapt a story of Gogol's for the stage. (I chose "The Nose.") But when the KGB decided to expel me from Moscow and began to ask questions about me among theater people, Varpakhovsky immediately returned the play to me—not personally, but through his wife.

At some of the plays I attended when I was young, there were more actors on the stage than there were people in the audience—especially if it was a play about the Revolution with a cast including "the popular masses." But now, for many performances, it was impossible to get tickets. Although Khrushchev had been overthrown, the momentum of liberalism had not been brought to a halt.

It seemed that the achievements of Russian dramatic art in the first quarter of this century had not died out completely but had merely been smoldering, like coals under a layer of ashes, and were now ready to flare up again. Anatoly Efros was being talked up as the best of the young directors. And yet in 1967, when the authorities launched their counterattack on the theater, it was with him that they began. His dismissal as artistic director of the Lenin Komsomol Theater provoked a protest and was an example of the cultural dissent developing in parallel to political dissent, and therefore seemed all the more dangerous to the authorities. Many actors left that theater immediately after his dismissal. And when the new director said pathetically, at a meeting, "The Party sent me here," people in the audience shouted: "Go back to the ones who sent you!" But the contending forces were unequal, and the Party won, as usual.

I met Efros when he had already been assigned, as an ordinary director, to the Malaya Bronnaya Theater; he still possessed strong feelings about the struggle he had recently experienced. A year and a half later, he seemed to be a completely different person. His shoulders drooped; he was unsure of himself.

The authorities' attack did not stop with Efros. A number of plays were taken off the boards, including Tvardovsky's *Tyorkin in the New World* as mounted by Pluchek, Sukhovo-Kobylin's *The Death of Tarelkin* as staged by Petr Fomenko, and Mark Zakharov's production of Ostrovsky's *A Lucrative Position*.

Zakharov's career was not ruined in those embryonic purges. On the contrary, a few years later he was appointed to the position Efros had occupied at the Lenin Komsomol Theater. The fact that he had a Russian name may have played some part in this, although in fact he is half-Jewish.

I very much fear that since 1967, this criterion has been the basic one when it comes to replacing and appointing directors. Tatyana Shchekin-Krotova, secretary of the Frunze *raikom** in Moscow, where there are many theaters, told me they finally were about to dismiss Boris Lvov-Anokhin, their last Jew. They fired him just when he had suggested that I adapt for the stage Kazakevich's story "The Blue Notebook," which deals with the period when Lenin was living in a hut with Zinoviev and writing *The State and Revolution*. One could have made an absurdist play out of that story.

Among people in the arts in Moscow—especially among those with some talent—the number of Jews was great, and anti-Semitism was extensive. It seems to me that the exceptional role played by Jews in Soviet culture could be ascribed to a good many causes, both historical and biological. As a rule, the Russians, often very talented, lack both culture and the ability to develop their talent. From among the directors of that period, only Yury Lyubimov is still carrying on. I am convinced, however, that despite all his virtues, if his name had been Tsirlin or Tsipelzon, nothing would be left of his theater.

Directors are no doubt the most likable people in the theater. As for actors, I have always found them hard to take; the way they have of being "on" actually repels me. After all, it's frightfully burdensome always "playing" someone other than oneself; and those re-creations must destroy a person. It's hard to leap over the chasm between the stage and real life. Once when I went backstage, I saw in a hallway an actress I had just watched on stage, and I felt as embarrassed as if I had seen her naked.

Those "people in the arts" who had the approval of the authorities were rather outspoken. Thus I interviewed Ekaterina Belashaya, head of the Union of Soviet Artists, without saying a single word; I simply took down almost everything she said. Later I showed the manuscript to her. She looked through it, made one slight correction, and sent it back to me. It was published in the magazine *Soviet Sport* under the title "Artists in the Main Ranks."

While interviewing Rodion Shchedrin, head of the Union of Soviet Composers, I asked him what he thought of the future of Soviet music. He replied that a congress of composers would soon be held, and then he would find out what he thought, but for the time being he preferred not to think. While in his apartment, I noticed that some beautiful things Marc Chagall had given his wife, Maya Plisetskaya, were hung alongside some terrible junk. (On my way back home, my boots suddenly fell apart. I had no money to have them repaired; and because of that I felt a surge of irritation toward Shchedrin, something he in no way deserved.) Later, when I was in Sverdlovsk Prison, I heard his ballet *Carmen Suite* over the radio and enjoyed it very much. He had reworked Bizet's opera for his wife.

While it wasn't my cousin Boris who gave me my first assignment at Novosti, he did commission the two strangest ones I worked on. The first was to write a series of articles about art collectors in Moscow. A Collectors' Club had just been founded at the Moscow Artists' Palace, but in general, collecting was regarded as a shady business. Thus when Andrei Gromyko, the Minister of Foreign Affairs, asked his deputy, Vladimir Semyonov, to show him his collection of Russian paintings from the early twentieth century, his words were: "Show me what kind of anti-Soviet stuff you've hung in your home." One exception was a Russified Greek, Georgi Kostaki. (He too was an official in the Ministry of Foreign Affairs, but at a lower level than Semyonov.) Kostaki used to collect young painters at a time when there were hopes for the future. Most of his collection consisted of works from the first third of the twentieth century, and I believe it was the best one of its kind in Russia. He started it in the days when paintings by Chagall and Malevich were being used to stuff up holes in broken bathroom windows. Dima Plavinsky gave a really hilarious account of how Kostaki would go about buying pictures from young artists.

"A beautiful picture," he would say, having as a rule chosen the best one. "How much do you want for it?"

The artist would hesitate. On the one hand, he didn't want to scare Kostaki away by asking too much. On the other hand, if he asked too little, he would be demeaning himself as an artist. Finally he would say something like, "Oh, I'll take a hundred rubles."

"*One hundred*?" Kostaki would exclaim. "Only a hundred for a picture like that? It's worth at least two hundred. Let's agree on two hundred. In the meantime, here's twenty-five in advance."

Then they would part company, each pleased with himself. Certain artists who had made this kind of deal with Kostaki would later keep reminding him of the money he owed them, but by no means all of them did so. In any case, Kostaki performed a great service; he saved many paintings from destruction and many artists from oblivion.

An even more interesting collection was the one assembled by Felix Vishnevsky, a marketing expert in the match industry. He bought Western European and Russian paintings, furniture, porcelain, and jewels. He always wore a threadbare jacket and, unlike the imposing, loud-voiced Kostaki, was self-effacing. He had begun collecting when he was very young; and I remember his telling me how in the twenties he was sent to Suzdal to "combat religious prejudices." That kind of combat meant taking an ax to old icons and burning them in a stove. "I wept and chopped," he told me, "then burned and wept." But I trust he saved something for his collection. On several occasions, everything he had collected would be confiscated; and each time he would start again from scratch. He spent several hours showing me around his house, and I even saw a Cranach the Elder he had hung in his bedroom. All in all, he had scrounged quite a few interesting things from among the many paintings the Soviet generals had brought back from Germany. He also had a collection of works by Russian serf artists, especially Tropinin. He offered to give the State both the house and a large part of the collection so as to found a Tropinin Museum, with himself acting not even as director but as assistant curator. But the State flatly refused to accept his gift, since a new museum would mean new worries: assembling a staff, including it in the plan, etc. Then in 1970 the KGB sealed up his collection, called him in for interrogation, and threatened confiscation: the State was determined to take by force what had been offered to it voluntarily.

In the spring of 1968, I was asked to write a series of articles about the unofficial Soviet artists—written in such a way that "it was plain that nobody was harassing them; that they were living and working in peace." Up to that time, whatever articles Soviet reporters may have written about the unofficial artists were published under titles like "Trash Heap Number Eight" or "The High Price of a Mess of Pottage." It was my hope that I could write objectively, even within the restrictions that would be imposed on me, and that my articles might be of some use to the artists.

My first choices were Anatoly Zverev, Vladimir Veisberg, and Oskar Rabin. I thought they exemplified very well the different trends and methods prevalent in unofficial art; and each of them, in his own way, had had a strong influence on me. Unfortunately, I later had a falling-out both with Zverev and with Veisberg. Each of them was afflicted with serious mental disturbance; Veisberg suspected I was visiting him in order to learn his artistic secrets and pass them on to my wife. Yet he was one of the most interesting and cultivated artists I knew.

When Veisberg was teaching painting, a student said that in her opinion one should teach artists in such a way as to develop their individuality. He nodded in polite agreement. Then five minutes later he remarked: "You know, there are women who have everything—a husband, a sofa, a television set. But along with all that, they want individuality! Take Sisley and Pissarro. They were both fine artists, but you can't always tell a Sisley from a Pissarro. Individuality is rarer than talent!" And he concluded in a fit of temper: "I teach painting, not individuality!"

Novosti gave a lot of attention to the projected series on unofficial artists. The idea had "come down from above," as I was told by the section chief, who wanted to become acquainted with me. He bad-mouthed the style of the Soviet newspapers, calling it antediluvian, and said we should learn from the English. Our foreign propaganda should not be as crudely direct as that meant for home consumption. Everything must be more subtle, more finely drawn.

In general, the Novosti people treated me well. And it was there that my career reached its peak; in various sections, positions were being offered to persons without a degree in journalism; they suggested that I register for an extension course in journalism and wrote up a fine character reference. But to everyone's amazement, I declined. I was subjected to all kinds of arguments and even indignation; I realized that, for me, upward mobility in the Soviet system was out of the question. Of course I could have gone along with it out of curiosity, but I didn't want to bring harm to people who wished me well. Because those who had recommended me would soon get into trouble for having done so.

Relations among Novosti personnel seemed unconstrained and friendly. But that was only on the surface: one felt that deep inside they mistrusted one another and were fearful of saying too much. These journalists were also actors playing the role of ordinary men and women on one level, while on another they were "stalwart, uncompromising workers on the ideological front." Yet inwardly they were not really like that, so that their lives became a kind of game in which their own personalities were gradually lost. When a person takes up such a career, he is still a whole personality and may feel he is happy. But as the years go by, even though he is outwardly successful and self-confident, he becomes a spiritual wreck—provided, of course, that he has an immortal soul. Many party and KGB officials, on the other hand, seem to have no soul, so that they suffer no torments, either overt or latent.

C H A P T E R   3

Monologue
from a Gagged Mouth

One day I noticed, hanging around my house, a citizen who had the look of
an investigator. (You can spot such people, even in a crowd.) And that same
day, when I came back from taking a walk, I couldn't find the page on which
I had drawn up the outline of *Involuntary Journey to Siberia*, although I had
checked the outline that same morning. (I had already sent two copies of
the book abroad.) Everything else was untouched.

I wouldn't bet my life on it, but I think it quite possible that the KGB
found out about my book. Vera Lashkova was working as a typist for Ginzburg
and Galanskov when two agents entered her home under some pretext and
stole several pages of manuscript. The KGB often knew that a book—from
their viewpoint, a "criminal" book—was being written or typed up, but
they did nothing until it was completed, so that they could have, so to speak,
an "accomplished crime" to deal with. The KGB needs to have several cases
"in their vest pocket," as they say, in case the Party leadership needs an
"ideological trial." Since a trial of that kind (that of Ginzburg and Galanskov) was already being prepared, my own case could be postponed "for
later." Or perhaps it wouldn't be needed at all. (But of course that didn't
mean they would leave me in peace.)

Does this not mean that it is better to do nothing and in that way deprive
the KGB of any work? Does it mean that the absence of opposition would
have eliminated the activities of the political police? Even if that were the
case, I would still prefer to be gagged by the police than to gag myself. The
need to change the outside world through one's own creativity is greater than
the need to adapt to it. If a person refuses the opportunity to judge the world
around him and to express that judgment, he begins to destroy himself before
the police can destroy him. In any case, the lack of real opposition does not

mean that the political police will cease their activity. To the contrary, they will become more vigorous, because they will have to dream up opposition. As the criterion for opposition is eroded, the machinery of destruction expands. (The terrorism under Stalin was a good example.) The moment real opposition appears, the terrorism narrows its scope. And the further the opposition advances, the better it secures its rear area.

History shows that the more stubborn the ruling circles are in resisting any kind of change, the more extreme will be the forms of struggle against them. To a considerable extent, the authorities themselves determine the style of the opposition; and once the slaves have triumphed, they begin to repeat the worst practices of their former masters. If one were to ask who should bear the guilt for the postrevolutionary horrors that Russia has gone through, and is still going through, I would be inclined to blame, first, Nicholas II and then Lenin. I invoke these names in a collective sense, as an expression of what they embodied.

Continuing to play the role that Ginzburg had proposed for me before his arrest, I became a kind of link between his mother and the foreign correspondents, who were following his and Galanskov's case as a continuation of the Daniel and Sinyavsky affair. Ludmilla Ginzburg was petite, a bit hunchbacked, and always very lively. In her youth she must have resembled a squirrel; in her later years she looked like the American writer Lillian Hellman, whose works Zhdanov had recommended to Akhmatova. It seems that it was Ginzburg himself who gave his mother the nickname of "the old lady," although she really wasn't all that old; almost everyone called her that behind her back. But she herself also used the nickname, in the third person. "They invited the old lady," she would say with approval. Or, with disapproval: "They didn't invite the old lady." Her two rooms—one of them large and hung with pictures, the other small with books everywhere—became a kind of club for the emergent Movement. It was there that I met on several occasions a tall young man whose face suggested he had been a former Komsomol member. Ludmilla Ginzburg had earlier told me with an air of some importance that she received regular visits from the grandson of Maxim Litvinov, the late People's Commissar of Foreign Affairs. And I learned with amazement that the young man in question was in fact that grandson.

In retrospect, it may be said that there were two currents in the Opposition Movement. First, there were those who from early youth had understood rather clearly the nature of the Soviet regime. Most of them regarded it as a regrettable necessity and tried to adapt to it, either by finding some niche or other, or (in the case of the most cynical) by becoming its functionaries. But when it suddenly turned out that resistance was possible, some of them began gradually to adhere to the Movement. Second, there were people who since youth had believed in the ultimate rightness of the regime. Then, little by little, as they became aware of the gap between its ideals and its practices, that awareness engendered in them an urge to help actively in "improving the regime" and brought many of them into the Movement. Some of them remained Communists inwardly (although they had been expelled from the Party) and defended "socialism with a human face." Others gradually abandoned the Communist ideology, having found that the embryo of totalitarian violence was to be found in that ideology itself.

One might also distinguish two generations of oppositionists, using the word "generation" in the philosophical rather than the chronological sense: the generation of 1956 and that of 1966.

The "generation of 1956" was influenced by de-Stalinization, by the disturbances in Poland, and especially by the Hungarian uprising in October 1956. I recall my impatience while waiting for the news from Hungary. If at that time there had existed some organization that asked me to take up arms against the regime, I would have agreed without giving it a second thought. But there was no such organization.

The "generation of 1966" was formed under the influence of the Sinyavsky-Daniel trial of 1966, the Czechoslovak reforms of 1967–68, and (finally) the Soviet invasion of Czechoslovakia in 1968.

The "generation of 1956" was one of "dropouts." I use the word in quotes, because it is the Soviet press's favorite epithet for us. It can, however, also be used without quotes, because in fact we began our protests at such an early age that we were not allowed to complete our education. Galanskov, Ginzburg, Vladimir Bukovsky, myself, and many others were expelled from universities on several occasions; in some cases, expulsion was either preceded by arrest or followed by it.

By contrast, the "generation of 1966" consisted of "establishment" people. Instead of half-scholars, it included doctors of science; instead of poets who had never published a single line, it included longtime members of the Union of Soviet Writers; instead of "persons with no specific occupation," it included old Bolsheviks, officers, actors, and artists. For many of them, the years 1953–56 had also been decisive. But they had still had hopes for improvement; and it was not until the unmistakable regression toward Stalinization in 1965–66 that their inner dissent was strengthened and their protest provoked.

In the case of my contemporaries—both those whose attitudes toward the regime were determined in the late fifties and those whose views were developed in the late sixties—the formation of our character coincided with de-Stalinization. It coincided with liberation, although only partially, and with a struggle, although unsuccessfully. And that is no doubt why it gave us a belief—though not always a conscious one—in the possibility of struggle and ultimate victory. In 1975 Nadezhda Mandelstam, the widow of the poet, told me: "I've heard you wrote that this regime will not survive until 1984. Nonsense! It will last for another thousand years!" The poor old woman, I thought to myself. It's plain to see that this regime has really fooled her for sixty years, if she believes in its eternal existence.

Quite apart from the grudges that the authorities held against both the dropouts and the "establishment dissidents," there were special reasons for exasperation in each case. With respect to the latter, the attitude was: "What more did they want? After all, those doctors of science and members of the Academy enjoyed benefits unavailable to the average 'Soviet man.' " The motives of the dropouts were more understandable to the authorities: "They're embittered because of their own failure." And yet: "How dare they? Who do they think they are?" It was especially intolerable when a dropout became famous. In Russia, in order to become somebody, you must gain recognition "from above," as Solzhenitsyn did. It was due to a mistake on Khrushchev's part, but nonetheless he got it. But just who is Amalrik? How did he dare to become famous? The authorities couldn't get over the fact that I became a "writer" without their approval, without following the rules they had laid down.

Pavel Litvinov belonged to the "generation of 1966." For him, the first decisive impetus was the trial of Daniel and Sinyavsky. His "baptism of fire" came with the trial of Khaustov and Bukovsky, and by 1968 he had become a key figure in the Movement. As a college teacher and (most important) a grandson of Maxim Litvinov, he was a valuable asset to the open opposition from the "representatives of the establishment." The fact that he was Maxim Litvinov's grandson was endlessly repeated in radio broadcasts from the West. In those days, it was constantly being emphasized that such-and-such a person was the son or grandson of somebody-or-other, as if to say that the dissidents were not just "anybody."

In the autumn of 1967, Pavel Litvinov was summoned to a KGB office, where the agents told him they knew about the collection of documents he had put together under the title of "The Demonstration on Pushkin Square" (dealing with the trials of Khaustov and Bukovsky). They "advised" him to destroy the manuscript and said that if he preserved it or circulated it, he would be prosecuted. From the KGB's viewpoint, it was a rather mild warning. But it had an unexpected result: Pavel recorded the conversation in writing and circulated it. It was published abroad; the BBC even broadcast a dramatized version of it to the USSR.

Gusel recalled how Pavel first showed up at our place one night; and how, sitting there at the table with the air of conspirators, we exchanged certain documents. "A Conversation at a KGB Office,"which was broadcast that same night, made a tremendous impression on me—and not just on me, I suspect. It was not only the conversation itself, of course, since there had been plenty of such conversations and warnings, but the fact that Pavel had recorded it and made it public. In so doing, he had thrown out a challenge not only to the KGB but to one of the most important unpublished laws of Soviet society: a kind of agreement between cat and mouse to the effect that the mouse will not squeak if the cat starts to eat him. This strongly reinforced my conviction that it was possible not only to refrain from being part of the system but to offer resistance to it.

But what kind of resistance? On the occasion of a gathering at Ludmilla Ginzburg's home in November to honor the birthday of her son, who was then in prison, I noticed that a piece of paper was being handed around—one that each person signed after having read it. Finally Pavel passed it to me, saying, "Here, sign this." It was a statement addressed to the USSR Prosecutor's Office and the Supreme Court demanding that any trial of Galanskov and Ginzburg be an open one and that the signers of the statement be allowed in the courtroom. It was not the first statement of its kind, and certainly not the last.

The practice of addressing group appeals to the authorities—to the Central Committee, to the Presidium of the USSR Supreme Soviet, to the General Prosecutor's Office, to the Supreme Court—dated back to 1966, after the arrest of Daniel and Sinyavsky. At first the tone was timid and suppliant, then it became more and more demanding. The earliest statements were written by people whose names would (so they hoped) make an impression on the authorities. Later a broader public became involved, so that for a time there were two types of petitions, differing both in style and in signatures. One would be signed: "I. Ivanov and P. Petrov." The other would be signed: "I. Ivanov, Honored Artist, and P. Petrov, Doctor of Technical Sciences." Ludmilla Ginzburg once said, jokingly, but with a touch of vanity: "Our petitions are being signed by professors, and Galanskov's by janitors." Later on, though, these two currents merged into one.

Petitioning the authorities is a form of protest typical of authoritarian regimes. The French revolution of 1830 began with petitions to the king; the movement that overthrew the Ethiopian monarchy in 1975 had its beginnings in very timid petitions. So the development of a "campaign of petitions" in the USSR might presumably have been regarded as a potential transition from totalitarianism to authoritarianism.

But of course such considerations never entered my head at the moment

I took the piece of paper Pavel handed me. Frankly, I was reluctant to sign it. I feared that the most likely result would be the harassment of the signers rather than their admission to the courtroom. Moreover, it had been only a year since I had returned from exile, and I could still feel it in my bones. Former exiles would be given shorter shrift than anyone else. Finally, on the basis of my experience and my way of thinking, I was not ready to take part in group actions: my form of protest was my books. Yet to refuse to sign would have been interpreted either as an acknowledgment that I was afraid (something always distasteful to young people) or as an indication that I was not really that concerned about the fate of my friends in prison. So, without saying a word, I signed.

A few days later, however, when I got a copy of the letter from Ludmilla so that I could pass it on to some foreign correspondents, my signature wasn't on it. "I deleted it," she explained. "I told the others: 'Amalrik is the only one doing the job for us. Why take risks with him?' " (By "the job" she meant my role as "liaison officer.") From that time until my own arrest, I didn't sign any more group appeals.

I don't mean to exaggerate my own fear—or, to put it more mildly, my caution. Although that was my first reaction, it wasn't really very strong or long-lasting. The fact is that I didn't sign petitions later on, even when I had nothing to lose. I have an instinctive dislike for collective actions. Because of my staunch individualism—the kind that Soviet indoctrination vigorously combats—I have always been repelled by the necessity of marching under one banner. All group actions based on the imitation of some people by others, be they reasonable or not, contain an element of psychosis.

Even the style of the open letters sometimes struck me as false, and often as simply ridiculous. In 1975 I was infuriated by the first lines of an appeal in defense of Sergei Kovalev: "Outstanding biologist, defender of human rights . . ." I insisted it should begin: "Outstanding defender of human rights, biologist . . .," because whether he was a biologist or a geologist, outstanding or mediocre, was of secondary importance—a mere curtsy to the position he held in the Soviet system. He was arrested because he was a defender of human rights, and that's the most important thing.

One of the chief reasons for the petition campaign was the belief that the authorities would give some weight to this show of public opinion and at the least evince some flexibility. The trial of Galanskov and Ginzburg was not the only issue and really not the main one: that trial was a symptom of the regime's pressure on society, just as the Sinyavsky-Daniel trial had been. But I had no faith in the practical results of the petitions. It wasn't hard to predict that the regime's first reaction would be: "We'll show 'em!" And if the authorities did display some flexibility, it was only in the different kinds of harassment: arrests, dismissal from employment, stripping a person of his academic degrees, beatings, murder, confinement in psychiatric hospitals, and (later) the maximum display of flexibility: expulsion from the country.

No wonder that the flow of petitions began to dry up. And it was not until eight years later that it got started again. The kind of petition for which in 1968 one could gather three hundred signatures would, two years later, be signed by only five or six persons. Some withdrew their signatures and publicly "expressed their regrets." Others simply expressed their regrets while staying home, although these were not the majority. On the other hand, those whose signatures had special significance in view of their status, and who were not threatened with arrest, would say: "I could sign this letter, but it wouldn't do any good. Besides, I'd like to complete this research project before they take my lab away from me." Or: "I want to finish this film I've been working on for several years." And one can understand such people. Incidentally, it is not so much fear as the realization that nothing will be changed in any case, that so often paralyzes any actions in Soviet society.

Within the opposition, the petition campaign was later attacked from two sides: from the viewpoint of Marxist economics and from that of Christian ethics. The liberal Marxists believed that the campaign had no positive program, that its methods were romantic, and that it was an objective provocation, since the gathering of signatures only provided the KGB with a list of the malcontents. The best thing was to not rock the boat, to think up socioeconomic programs, and to rely on the process of objective development, because *that* wouldn't let you down. The criticism from the viewpoint of Christian ethics boiled down to the contention that the campaign had no other aim than to "improve" Soviet socialism and restore Khrushchev's reforms; hence it was not real opposition to the inhumane foundations of the Soviet system.

I cannot in good conscience completely support either of these criticisms, although I may give the impression of a rather negative attitude toward the campaign. But even in those days, I was ambivalent. If I had felt the campaign was a mistake, I would not have helped to get those letters sent abroad. I now feel that the petition campaign, although it did not achieve the specific results it was aimed at, restrained the process of re-Stalinization; that without it, things would certainly have been worse. Back then I realized we had found an important means of acting on public opinion, and even of creating it. Each signature on a letter helped to convince people that opposition was not something practiced only by loners, not a social anomaly. And this conviction was strengthened by the fact that Western radio stations promptly broadcast, in Russian, summaries of many such letters, or even their full text.

And there was something else: in putting his signature on a public document, a person was taking a step toward self-liberation; and for many people, that step was decisive. One signature may make no difference at all in the nation's political situation, but for the signer himself it may be a kind of catharsis, a breaking away from the system of doublethink in which "Soviet man" has been indoctrinated since childhood. In essence, the dissidents accomplished something that was simple to the point of genius: in an unfree country, they behaved like free men, thereby changing the moral atmosphere and the nation's governing tradition.

The regime had destroyed many humanistic ideas, and the dissidents had to restore them, displaying courage not with the sanction of society but in the face of its indifference, and even its opposition. When I wonder how the phenomenon of dissidence could have arisen in a closed society, and what were its roots, I think first of all of the role played by Russian literature, which has had a strong influence on the formation of every educated citizen. Although the regime did for a time ban the books of Dostoyevsky and many works of Tolstoy, it did not totally proscribe the literature of the nineteenth century. And that may have been a mistake, since that literature is passionate in its defense of the individual against the system. The soil from which our Movement grew was nineteenth-century Russian literature, not at all the Western influence that KGB officials and Western Sovietologists like to talk about. Our strongest Western teacher was Martin Luther King and his campaign against violence. But King learned from Gandhi, and Gandhi learned from Tolstoy, whose ideas returned to Russia like a kind of boomerang.

Yet we did not uncritically accept either the ambivalent teachings of Tolstoy as an evident precursor of the Revolution or the lesson of Russian literature in general or the experience of the prerevolutionary social movements. One of the dominant ideas of the prerevolutionary opposition was the readiness to sacrifice one's "I" for the sake of the general public; and in that way everything was lost. But how to replace that senseless sacrifice, not with the idea of narrow selfishness, but with the value of one's "I" in the universal sense—how, in the words of Nikolai Fyodorov, to live not for oneself alone and not just for others but with all and for all—that was the search that underlay our Movement, and it created real bonds among human beings.

I began to feel apprehensive that the protests, which were becoming more and more routine, would elicit less response each time. When I said as much to Victor Krasin in the spring of 1969, he replied, "But it's also important that not a single crime committed by the regime escape open public protest." As for sending the authorities letters dealing with basic problems, the objection was raised: Was a dialogue with the regime possible or even necessary? I got into an argument with an old priest, Sergei Zheludkov, saying that we should address the authorities only on matters of a formal and legal nature but not on ideological matters. I said we could not discuss our ideas with those who put you in prison for them. And I almost convinced Zheludkov I was right—only to have doubts about it myself later on.

Almost all of the dissidents, I believe, made some attempt to have a dialogue with the authorities: to "convince" them of something by means of a gesture, a letter, or just by talking to them. Ivan Yakhimovich tried to use suasion on his investigator and was put into a psychiatric hospital. Solzhenitsyn wrote his "Letter to the Soviet Leaders" and was soon expelled from the country. Later I shall tell of my own attempts, which were equally pathetic. Essentially, this "dialogue" is a monologue that at any moment can be broken off by the gagging of the speaker. Yet may it not be that the old priest, with his Christian readiness to turn the other cheek, was right after all? If we did not try to persuade the authorities to listen to us—"us" in the broadest sense of the word—if we did not persist in reaching out a hand to them (a hand they will bite!), sooner or later all our problems would be "resolved" in a sea of blood.

C H A P T E R 4

The Trial of the Four

The trial of Galanskov and Ginzburg began on January 8, 1968, after they had been under detention for a year. Also accused were Vera Lashkova, their typist, and Alexei Dobrovolsky, who had played the pathetic role of provocateur.

A detail of police and some *druzhinniks** from the security squad wearing red armbands were stationed at the main entrance to the Moscow City Courthouse; only those with passes were allowed into the courtroom. The defendants' friends and relatives and foreign correspondents were not permitted to go beyond the dimly lit corridor leading to the offices in the left wing. Along the wall stood some young people with indifferent expressions and roving eyes. One of them came up to me and, acting as if he had just showed up at the courthouse by chance, began asking me if I knew the defendants and why we were being photographed. On the stairs, amid another throng of *druzhinniks*, stood a photographer who kept taking snapshots of us, one after another—a scene that was later repeated at all political trials. Even before I could reply to the first youth, some of our people shouted at me: "Who are you talking to?" My questioner was of course an informer. But we couldn't entirely ignore the informers. From time to time there would be exchanges of curses. Our women, especially, kept trying to outdo the informers in saying offensive things. One of the latter complained to another: "Some clients we got this time!" Every now and then the two sides would get into more or less theoretical arguments, about the Cultural Revolution in China, for instance. And one of the *druzhinniks* said, "You're always putting down China. But at least there the people have a hand in running the State."

At about ten o'clock, a tall, broad-shouldered, older man in a long, dark overcoat showed up. He had an air of authority about him—the kind of facial expression one acquires from years of command—and with his cane he brushed aside the informers who were in his way. A typical Stalinist, I thought: he must be the judge. But Pavel Litvinov, with a smile, came up to greet the "judge," who turned out to be General Petr Grigorenko. Or, more accurately, ex-General Grigorenko, since he had been reduced to the ranks.

At a Party conference in 1961, when he was department head at a military academy, Grigorenko raised the question: "Is everything possible being done to prevent a recurrence of the cult of personality?" He refused to recant. And then, strictly by virtue of his sincere Communist convictions as a genuine Bolshevik, he decided to combat "bureaucratic degeneration" in the Bolshevik manner, by setting up an underground "union" to struggle for the restoration of Leninism, and by distributing leaflets. The "union" was discovered, and Grigorenko was confined to a psychiatric hospital. After the overthrow of Khrushchev he was discharged.

There was a sudden commotion, and the reporters rushed toward the door. Alexander Esenin-Volpin had been arrested! And in fact, the police were escorting down the hall a man with a tousled beard and wild, staring eyes. It turned out that Esenin-Volpin, quite by chance—and no doubt through absentmindedness—had mingled with the police as they were changing the guard.

Esenin-Volpin, mathematician, poet, and son of the famous poet Sergei Esenin, had since the late 1940s spent many years in prisons and psychiatric hospitals. He was the first to realize that an effective method of opposition might be to demand that the authorities observe their own laws. The concept of the law as something binding upon everyone, in general a very weak concept in Russia, had been replaced by the notion of "expediency." The laws were framed to serve the interests of the rulers, but even so they were sometimes burdensome for the authorities; and behind the demand that the laws be observed loomed the dangerous idea of the rule of law.

A bit later, I struck up a conversation with a tall foreigner. He asked me for my opinion about the trial, and I replied that as a "Soviet man" I would find out what my opinion was from the latest edition of the newspapers. Standing beside him was a rather colorless professorial type who had been listening closely to our conversation without saying anything himself. This was Karel van het Reve, correspondent for the newspaper *Het Parol* and a professor at the University of Leyden. We later became friends, and it was he who first published my books abroad. He recalled that at the trial, I was wearing a dark overcoat of the style worn in Holland before the war and looked very much like a schoolteacher.

The night of the gathering at Ludmilla Ginzburg's home, I had made an agreement with the correspondents that I would question the witnesses and relatives who were allowed in the courtroom and later at my place I would recount what they had told me. When I left her apartment after the first day of the trial, I noticed that two cars were waiting near the building. As I boarded a bus, one of them started up to follow me. Galanskov's wife, Olga, who had been drinking, was so sick of being tailed that she calmly went up to the car and began to unscrew the license plate. The tails have orders not to talk to the people they are following, so instead of chasing her away, the driver began slowly to move off. Olga ran after him, but slipped on the ice-covered pavement and broke her leg.

I was not so resolute. I simply jumped off the bus at the next stop, dashed into the crowd at the subway entrance, and took a train to the Arbat Station. I couldn't detect anyone shadowing me, and, breathing heavily, I leaned for a moment against a newly whitewashed arch. Then suddenly I saw a young man wearing the light-blue tabs of the KGB coming toward me from somewhere off to the side. I was still hoping that he would pass me by; instead, he tapped me on the shoulder—politely but firmly. Well, that's it, I thought, with a kind of indifference.

"You've got some spots on the back," the officer said considerately, and brushed the traces of whitewash off my schoolteacherish coat.

When I got home, the Reuters correspondent was waiting for me.

That night, lying in bed, I could see before my mind's eye the hallway whose floor had been worn down by so many scuffling feet, the faces of the stoolies, Kalanchevskaya Street lined by trees covered with hoarfrost, the gloomy crowd outside the courthouse—and at certain moments it seemed that an icy hand was touching my heart.

The next day the corridors outside the courthouse offices were also closed, and the public had to stand in the street near the entrance. The courtroom audience consisted of *aktivsts** from the *raikom* and KGB agents. They whistled, stamped their feet, made noise generally, and interrupted the witnesses, the defendants, and their counsel. To objections, the judge would reply: "The public is expressing its opinion. You say you're defending free expression of opinion, so there's no reason for you to object."

Although it was against the law, the witnesses were taken out of the courtroom after testifying; even Galanskov's sister was removed. Such things made the atmosphere very tense. On the fourth day, near the courthouse, Larisa Bogoraz and Pavel Litvinov handed out to correspondents their statement: "To the World Public." That declaration was drafted in strong language. It demanded "condemnation of this shameful trial," "release of the defendants from armed custody," and "stripping the judge of his judicial powers."

In one leap we had overcome a difficult barrier. We had addressed ourselves to public opinion rather than to the regime; and we had spoken up in the language of free persons, not in that of loyal subjects, thereby overcoming a centuries-old complex: the idea that no Russian—and least of all, a Soviet

Russian—should address appeals to foreigners. ("We are we, and they are they." "Don't wash your dirty linen in public." "It's better to get a blow from your master's club than a piece of bread from a stranger.") That same evening, on the BBC, we heard the statement translated back into Russian. Esenin-Volpin, sitting with the text in his hands, kept repeating: "Right! That's it! Exactly!" Huddled around the radio, we resembled a painting we had been familiar with since our youth: *Behind the Fascist Lines, Members of the Young Guard Listen to Radio Moscow.*

The importance of the statement was understood in the West. It was reprinted, fully or in part, in many newspapers, and *The Times* of London devoted an editorial to it. The flow of statements and appeals that followed it during the next two months raised hopes that a social movement of sorts had surfaced in the USSR and that something would happen at any moment. It was rather like the hopes raised in 1956 by the theory of liberalization known as "The Thaw."

But months and years went by, and nothing happened except more and more political trials. Disappointed in their expectation of immediate results, Western observers advanced a theory that there was no social movement in the USSR. There were perhaps a few high-minded but naïve individuals who, in accordance with Russian tradition (and it wasn't the West's business to change it), were constantly being imprisoned, individuals with whom one could sympathize in a human way. But they were not people one could really take seriously. However, although "reform from above" had not resulted in the creation of a liberal Soviet society, still the system had softened as compared to the Stalin era. Likewise, the social movement may not have achieved a democratic system in ten years, but the moral atmosphere of Soviet society had changed.

The proceeding against Ginzburg and Galanskov had been conceived as a show trial. While continuing the policy laid down for the Sinyavsky-Daniel trial, the authorities wanted to demonstrate that they were trying not writers but young men with no regular occupation who, moreover, had ties with the émigré organization known as the NTS (The People's Labor Union). It was emphasized that the NTS was subsidized by the CIA and that its aim was to overthrow the existing system in the USSR. The NTS theme was sketched out in the pretrial investigation and vividly brought out in the indictment; it loomed larger than anything else in the verdict and sentence.† The contents of Ginzburg's "White Paper" and Galanskov's *Phoenix* were played down.

---

†In Soviet legal proceedings, the verdict (decision) and sentence together make up one document called a *prigovor*, usually translated by experts on Soviet law as "judgment."—TRANS.

What was considered most important was that both books had allegedly been put together on instructions from the NTS and conveyed to it for publication.

This scenario was built on the testimony of co-defendant Alexei Dobrovolsky, who had already served several sentences in labor camps and been confined to psychiatric hospitals. During the pretrial investigation he "cracked" almost immediately, and his eagerness to collaborate with the KGB exceeded all bounds. It was proposed that he speak on television, so as to warn young people against "anti-Soviet" activities. And he was supposed to tell where Ginzburg had allegedly buried the "White Paper," along with other treasures. The KGB dug up the entire park around the building where Ginzburg lived to no avail, but no television appearance was arranged for Dobrovolsky. Apparently the opposition had not yet merited such an honor; indeed, it was not until five years later that the first "recantation" was televised.

The search of Dobrovolsky's home was the only one that turned up NTS materials. He testified that Galanskov had given them to him and told of his own and Ginzburg's contacts with the NTS. An emissary of the NTS, Nikolas Broks-Sokolov, appeared in court. Broks-Sokolov had no connection with the defendants. He had come from France, at a time when Galanskov and Ginzburg had already been in prison for some months, with instructions to hand over to a certain person (not named at the trial) a package containing 3,000 rubles and a hectograph. He was also supposed to mail five envelopes that had already been addressed. But since these envelopes turned out to contain postcards with photographs of Galanskov, Ginzburg, and Dobrovolsky, the KGB figured that was quite adequate for propagandistic effect.

Later, we were able to examine the materials in the file. The KGB had no proof of any connection between Galanskov or Ginzburg and the NTS, and it was rather easy to see that Dobrovolsky had lied. This does not mean, however, that there were no ties between Galanskov and the NTS. It is senseless to say that he received orders from the NTS, or even that he had an agreement with it to publish *The Phoenix*. (It was not published.) But Galanskov was in fact visited by NTS emissaries, and he even asked me if they could come to my place and leave some literature. He had the idea of buying a printing press so that he could publish a magazine himself. And he could obtain the money from the NTS, although the deal was very complicated, involving both dollars and rubles. A few years later, the NTS Council stated that Galanskov had been a member of the organization. Bukovsky told me this was not true; and that at a time when it was not known whether he himself would get out of prison, NTS members began to hint that Bukovsky too had joined the group before his arrest.

I first saw an NTS publication in 1962. Then, some fifteen years later, I met some of its members abroad. The history of NTS is part of the problem—

one becoming increasingly important—of relations between resistance within the USSR and émigré political forces. The People's Labor Union—or, as it was then called, the National Labor Union (of the Younger Generation)—was founded in Belgrade in 1930. It represented the reaction of the younger generation of émigrés not only to the triumphant ideology of bolshevism but to what they regarded as the bankrupt ideology of their "fathers": conservative monarchism and democratic liberalism. Under the circumstances, it was only natural that they should have been most strongly influenced by what was then the most dynamic ideology in Europe—nationalism, or national socialism. The NTS had a noble slogan: "Our names may perish, but Russia will be glorified." Behind it, however, one could sense another famous slogan: "You are nothing, but your nation is everything."

The NTS wanted to influence events in the USSR; and many young lives were sacrificed when its members were sent into Russia and perished there. When war came, it seemed to many in the NTS that there now was an opportunity to create an alternative force. But this involved an irreconcilable contradiction: How could one count on a rebirth of Russia while acting under the control of people whose announced aim was to destroy Russia? This was clearly evident in the movement led by General Vlasov, which was supported by NTS. Whatever Vlasov's intentions, he was a puppet controlled by the Germans; and even when his comrades were prepared to resist, he yielded to the Nazis. It's a painful admission to make, but the fact is that in those years Stalin became a symbol of national resistance, thanks to the insane policy of the Germans. The war enabled Stalin and his heirs to consolidate Soviet society. Even today, Soviet propaganda keeps hammering on the theme of the war, as if it happened yesterday.

By the war's end, many NTS leaders were in German prisons, which enabled the organization to save face. Its ranks were swelled by former Soviet citizens. The lessons of the war and its orientation toward the West compelled the NTS to revise its program, combining notions of national solidarity with those of liberal democracy. I hesitate to say just how far this revision has succeeded, because it is still my impression that liberalism fits the NTS pretty much like a second-hand suit of clothes.

Of all the prewar and postwar associations of Russian émigrés, the NTS is the only one to survive, and it is still trying to extend its activities to the USSR. It indulges in a good deal of wishful thinking, and the literature it sends into the USSR often indicates a lack of contact with reality. Back in the late 1960s, I chanced upon a bundle of NTS leaflets bearing the notation: "Read and pass on to someone else." I simply didn't know what to do with the stuff, or whom to pass it on to. But just to destroy it struck me as somehow cowardly. So I decided to behave in a completely anti-Soviet manner: I dropped the leaflets into mailboxes—not out of sympathy with the NTS but in order to bug the authorities just a bit. (Incidentally, the NTS publishing house, Posev, does not merely put out propaganda: it has published quite a few good books, and many people in Russia can be grateful to it.)

The rise of a democratic opposition in the USSR prompted the NTS to alter its policies and to try somehow to alter those of the opposition. Naturally, nothing could come of this—and not just because the dissidents feared the reputation of the NTS or didn't want to take on the burden of its past. There were simply too many differences in aims and methods. The opposition's aim is the gradual democratization of the Soviet system by open and lawful means, while the NTS goal is its violent overthrow, and nationalism. But whenever I hear them being abused by newly arrived émigrés, I reply that the NTS has existed for almost half a century, and nobody yet knows how long *we'll* last. In the event of any upheavals in the USSR, and of an opportunity to shift the NTS's activities there, that organization—small but disciplined, with slogans the people can easily understand—may play a significant role.

The trial was concluded at 5:00 P.M. on January 12, just four days after it had begun. It was already getting dark, and the weather was quite cold. More than two hundred people were gathered outside the courthouse; dissidents, reporters, and the policemen at the entrance were stamping their feet. Soon the "public" began to emerge: plainclothesmen with lowering expressions on their faces, as if they themselves had been convicted, hurried toward their cars. When asked what kind of sentences had been given out, many of them replied: "Too short! Too short!"

I was amazed at their hostility. Later I realized how much hatred must be felt—especially by veteran gebists—toward a crowd that has so freely assembled on a Soviet street. Pavel Litvinov and Sasha Daniel carried out Olga Galanskova, with her leg in a cast. Galanskov's mother came out, weeping loudly. Carnations were presented to the lawyers, and everyone began to disperse. Galanskov had been sentenced to seven years in a labor camp, Ginzburg to five years, Dobrovolsky to two, and Lashkova to one.

Of the seven years to which he was sentenced, Yuri Timofeyevich Galanskov spent in prison and camp five years and seven and one-half months. On November 2, 1972, at the age of thirty-three, he died in a Mordovian camp as a result of an operation performed belatedly by an unqualified surgeon. Permission was given to put a cross on his grave and to inscribe his name on it.

Of the four persons convicted, Galanskov struck me as the most tragic figure. I didn't know him very well, although during the last few months before his arrest we met frequently. His habitual expression was very serious, even gloomy; and in conversation, the great importance he attached to simple things seemed to me a sign of limited intelligence. As for his poems, they appeared to be a kind of journalism in rhyme. Through all this, one could glimpse something childlike. Once he showed me the rough draft of his "Open Letter to Sholokhov," in which he abused him roundly. Yet in the middle of the letter he kept repeating, "And so, Dear Reader," or, "As I said, Dear Reader."

"Yuri," I told him, "what this adds up to is that while you despise Sholokhov as a writer, he's still dear to you as a reader."

Later, that letter served as one of the main charges in his indictment. Mikhail Sholokhov, the Nobel laureate, not only demanded that Sinyavsky and Daniel be shot; the death of Yuri Galanskov is also on his conscience.

I could glimpse in Galanskov another trait for which I can find no other name than "saintliness." Or, more simply, a certain *yurodstvo* (behaving like a Fool of God) in the highest sense of the word. (Later, I noticed something similar in a man who in many respects was very different from Galanskov: Andrei Sakharov. I have in mind his willingness to help people and his ability to experience another's misfortune as his own.) Yuri Galanskov either had little understanding of people or else he felt that there was something good in everyone. Dobrovolsky took special advantage of this characteristic. He would send notes from his prison cell to Yuri in his cell, with the idea that Yuri should take all of Dobrovolsky's guilt upon himself. Which Yuri did. And he became so confused in his testimony that he had to change it four times. Likewise, two vagrants he had sheltered and fed testified during the pretrial investigation that he had given them dollars for exchange. By their testimony, a man who would give you the shirt off his back became a calculating speculator in foreign exchange. Apparently, he intended to use the dollars to buy a printing press. But when the exchange was made, the con men palmed off on him a packet of mustard plaster instead of rubles. How the gebists in the courtroom laughed when they heard that. They also had a good chuckle when they heard how Yuri scrubbed the floor for Ginzburg's sick mother, when Ginzburg was serving his first term in prison. Unfortunately, not everyone who spoke out for Ginzburg did the same for Galanskov. Ginzburg himself asked in his final plea to the court that he be given a sentence no shorter than Galanskov's—whereupon some people in the courtroom shouted: "Longer! Longer!"

Galanskov's father was a lathe operator, and his mother a charwoman. She was a thickset, plain woman with a coarse voice who loved her son very much and enjoyed the respect of his friends, who called her "Mama Katya." The investigator in charge of the case, in an attempt to frighten her, read her the most incriminating excerpt from his writings, then commented: "Just look at what your son writes!"

"He writes just fine—very well," Mama Katya said to the amazed investigator. "It goes right to your heart."

"And what did he read to you?" Ludmilla Ginzburg asked later.

"Nothing that I understood," replied Mama Katya. "Something about a coffin and a grave—some kind of nonsense."

Galanskov called himself a proletarian democrat and a pacifist, and for him every foreigner was a potential friend of freedom. In 1966, when American forces landed in the Dominican Republic, he put on a one-man demonstration in front of the U.S. Embassy in Moscow. (I very much doubt whether, during his own trial, anyone in the Dominican Republic demonstrated against it.) Judging from his letters, during his imprisonment he became more and more interested in Christianity.

The accounts of the trial that appeared in the Soviet press were written in the style used by fishwives when trading insults. Also, they contained a good many inaccuracies, or, to put it bluntly, a lot of slander. So I proposed to Ginzburg's mother and Galanskov's wife that we three hold a press conference for foreign journalists—Soviet reporters would also be free to attend if they wanted. The idea seemed very bold: it would have been the first meeting between Soviet citizens and foreign correspondents that was open and not planned "from above." I made arrangements with the journalists and asked them not to spread the word in advance, but I failed to take into account their habit of phoning one another and asking: "Are you going to something?"

The conference was set for 11:00 A.M. on January 19 at Ludmilla Ginzburg's apartment. I arrived toward 11:00 and found both Ludmilla and Olga Galanskova in great dismay. A half-hour earlier, a deputy of Smekalkin, the raion* prosecutor, had come to the apartment and told them that private persons were not allowed to hold press conferences in their homes and that if they wanted to talk to the journalists they would have to go out into the street. So they were getting dressed with that in mind. I told them, however, that they should in no case go out, because it was an obvious trap. Recently a law had been passed setting a penalty of up to three years in a labor camp for "disorders associated with disrupting traffic." It would be easy for several agents to get a crowd to gather around the two women and the journalists as they were talking, then stop a couple of cars. And quickly the police would arrive and arrest them for a "disturbance on the street."

At eleven o'clock sharp, the first correspondent arrived. His appearance struck me as odd. Although his clothes were of foreign make, his face was unmistakably Russian, even with something of the Soviet official about it. And on his hand I noticed a tattoo that read: "Vasya," or "I'll never forget my dear mother," something of that kind—and in Russian, of course. But he repeated that he was a foreign correspondent invited to the press conference. I asked for his credentials, and he turned out to be Vasily Gritsan, on special assignment with the Associated Press as a newspaper photographer.

Since he had come alone, I had no doubts as to why he had been sent, and told him to leave, saying there wasn't going to be any press conference. He was overjoyed at this. (I don't know who he took me to be, a cautious friend of Ginzburg's or the prosecutor Smekalkin.) He said he had in fact come to suggest that the press conference not be held, and that now we could jointly hammer out a few little phrases that he would hand out to the journalists. I said that nobody had any need of his suggestions and that he should leave. Which he did.

When none of the regular journalists showed up, we began to get very nervous; toward noon I asked Olga to phone the Reuters bureau. The Reuters correspondent explained that they had all been warned by the MID* press section that if they came to see us, "very unpleasant" consequences would follow. That vague statement sufficed. None of them showed up, or even warned us. This made possible Smekalkin's and Gritsan's provocations, which might have turned out badly for both women. A few other correspondents the press section had not managed to warn did drive up to the apartment house, but they were turned back by KGB agents with the same vaguely threatening phrases.

This would have been the first press conference of its kind; and it seemed to the authorities that if it took place, something terrible would happen. (Later, of course, press conferences held by dissidents became a regular occurrence, and the regime did not collapse.) The Moscow bureau of UPI reported that the press conference was barred by the authorities in accordance with a decree of 1947 that prohibited the socializing of Soviet citizens with foreigners, and that the law was the law. We promptly looked up the decree. It spelled out the procedure for relations between official Soviet institutions and those of other countries and had absolutely no bearing on our situation.

It's hard for me to figure out why Henry Shapiro, chief of UPI's Moscow bureau, stretched that decree to such an extent. Shapiro was such an expert on Russia that when he received a copy of a letter written by Ivan Yakhimovich, chairman of a Latvian kolkhoz,* supporting the statement issued by Litvinov and Bogoraz, he said that Litvinov was the true author of the letter, since no kolkhoz chairman could write like that. But being a reporter in Moscow for forty years does something to a man. When Shapiro got a copy of Sakharov's article "Progress, Coexistence, and Intellectual Freedom," he hid it in his desk, saying nothing should be written or said about it, since it might bring "very unpleasant consequences." When he retired, he said: "A person who believes in propagandistic journalism should not work here. If you take someone's side, you become emotionally involved, and you cease to be a reporter." It's hard to believe that Shapiro himself was emotionally involved. But he was *involved*.

By birth a Rumanian Jew, Shapiro was taken to the U.S. as an adolescent, and was naturalized eight years later. Often a person belonging to an ethnic group that has been persecuted for centuries, a person with the psychology of an exile, who is compelled to pull up his roots from one place and put them down in another, is guided by an attitude of adaptation at any price. (The Russians have evolved several good sayings for such a situation. One is: "When you're living with wolves, howl like a wolf.") And since such a person frequently carves out a good professional career—he may head up not only the foreign bureau of a press agency but the State Department of a great country—he leaves the imprint of his own approach to life on the institution he directs.

No foreign journalist in the USSR can really feel and believe that he is a "noninvolved" chronicler "looking upon both good and evil with indifference,"[1] primarily because he himself is an object of manipulation by the Soviet system. Naturally, the authorities realize they cannot manage the foreign press as they do the Soviet media. But to some degree they are able to control the information that foreign correspondents send abroad from Moscow. This is accomplished in two ways: by isolating the correspondents and by employing the stick-and-carrot policy.

The very fact of living in Moscow—with a good salary, a housemaid, a secretary, and a chauffeur—is a privilege for some journalists. For them, returning home would mean reverting to a more modest scale of living, rather like coming back from a colony to the mother country. Also, some Western reporters take advantage of the difference between rates of exchange and the price difference between Soviet and foreign goods. And some even receive direct subsidies from the Soviet authorities. Thus the correspondent for *L'Unità* complained to me that the Soviet government paid him his subsidy mostly in rubles rather than in convertible foreign currency. (Incidentally, that was before the era of "Eurocommunism." It may be that today they don't pay at all; or else they pay in foreign currency, because of the Italian Communist party's distinct independence of Moscow.) There are also less direct and more professional incentives, e.g., access to information the correspondent is interested in—or often merely the promise of such access.

As for the stick, it is graduated like a yardstick. At one end is the polite warning. And at the other end the journalist can be brought to trial, as happened with the correspondents of the *New York Times* and the *Baltimore Sun* in 1978. This is done as a warning to other reporters, some of whom respond to such warnings very well. Thus in 1975 the correspondent of *Der Spiegel* publicly assured the *Literaturnaya Gazeta* that he would never, ever interview a dissident.

The role played by foreign journalists in the USSR as a source of information has been, and still is, crucial. And many journalists, despite all the difficulties, have resisted blackmail—a fact confirmed *inter alia* by the long list of correspondents expelled from Moscow in the past fifteen years. Yet most have no sense of solidarity. Up to now, no club or association of journalists has been formed in Moscow, although if the reporters acted in concert, the authorities would make concessions, since they themselves fear isolation. As for the Western embassies, they act as a restraining force, trying to persuade the journalists not to write anything that would displease the Soviet authorities. The editors back home, too, are often prepared to beat a retreat, arguing that otherwise the Moscow bureaus will be closed down.

At one time I wanted to write a story, rather in the manner of Gogol, about a foreign correspondent who was summoned to the MID press section, where he was given a flogging by way of a strict warning. Not knowing how he should behave under such circumstances, he consulted with other journalists, bureau chiefs, and the ambassador. They all said, in effect: "Yes, it's quite unpleasant to be given a whipping, but one must take into account Russia's national customs and long traditions." They went on to say that he himself had not always been moderate in his articles. Also, that if he protested, the Russians would be offended. They are very sensitive about interference in their domestic affairs and might in a fit of temper flog a few other journalists. Moreover, from a legal viewpoint the case was not clear-cut. After all, a journalist does not have diplomatic immunity; and his rights and duties are not clearly defined. Besides, presenting one's naked posterior as evidence is rather awkward. The journalist's position was understandable, but so was that of the MID. One should not, moreover, be carried away by emotions arising from buttocks made hot by flogging but should weigh everything with a clear and cool head. One must see not only the negative but the positive side of things. And the journalist understood all that. Indeed, he felt it at the very moment he was being birched.

I didn't write the story, but in the spring of 1970 I composed an article called "Foreign Correspondents in Moscow," and my lawyer later told me that was the straw that broke the camel's back. For a long time the article was passed around among the correspondents as a specimen of "samizdat."* No one wanted to send it abroad and thereby refute my claims as to the lack of solidarity among them. Finally it was published in the *New York Review of Books,* with ellipses substituted for Henry Shapiro's name.

I realize how complex the situation is for a foreigner who is not altogether sure of his own security, finding himself in a strange country with a system based on different principles. It is a condition in which he himself must ascertain what he can and cannot do. The Soviet authorities refuse to issue press regulations, since vagueness serves their purpose. As for the Western governments, not only do they not insist on these measures but they refuse to draw up, for their own citizens, suggestions for their conduct in the USSR based on international accords, published Soviet laws, and the experience of correspondents and diplomats with service in Russia.

A journalist has a duty toward those for whom he is writing to provide objective information. But the kind of duty he has toward people *about* whom he is writing is moral rather than professional.

Foreigners are fond of quoting the Marquis de Custine's comments on Mother Russia. He once wrote:

> In the eyes of that oppressed multitude, every foreigner appears to be a savior, because he personifies truth, open discussion, and freedom for a people deprived of those blessings. . . . Everyone who does not protest with all his might against a system which makes such incidents possible, is to some degree its accomplice and fellow-conspirator.

CHAPTER 5

A Warm Spring, a Hot Summer

After the trial, I was introduced at Pavel Litvinov's home to a man of rather short stature (or so he seemed next to Pavel) with dark eyes and, as I recall, a small, dark moustache. After so much time, I cannot picture his features in detail. But I do remember that I was put on my guard by something about him—that kind of sweetish quality that I never believe is entirely genuine. This was Victor Krasin; and I was a bit disgruntled when, later, Pavel brought him to our home when Karel van het Reve was there. But that feeling was soon dissipated by a lively conversation, which over the inevitable bottle of vodka soon turned into purely Russian talk about whether one can "understand Russia with one's intellect"[2] and whether one should be cordial and kind. There was no question but what Krasin was in favor of cordiality; but much to Gusel's disappointment, I was skeptical of that cordiality.

Later I started going to Krasin's "Wednesdays" or "Thursdays." He lived on the outskirts of Moscow in a lean-to that he himself had built as an addition to a wooden house. Its only furnishings were a table, some shelves full of books (all photocopies of foreign editions, which he willingly lent out), and a folding cot covered with sheepskin. He had only contempt for bed linen and made much of his low regard for any kind of convenience or, God forbid, luxury. When he was at our place he would tramp across the carpet in his muddy boots, much to Gusel's dismay.

Krasin had a lively mind, plus a good sense of humor; and his boldness and readiness to work vigorously for the cause had put him in the first ranks of the Democratic Movement. Also, like Petr Yakir, he had the charisma of a person who had spent many years in the labor camps because of his convictions. In the late 1940s, when he was in his second year at the university, Krasin had been sentenced to a penal camp because he belonged to a study group whose chief interest was Oriental philosophy. His original sentence was eight years, but he got another four because, so he told us, he made an unsuccessful attempt to escape. All in all, however, he served only six years. The process of de-Stalinization had begun; he was rehabilitated with respect to his first trial and pardoned in connection with the second one. He then completed his university studies and began to work as an economist at a research institute. When he heard about Pavel from a radio broadcast, he immediately sought him out.

Inwardly, Krasin was never able to come to terms with the regime. Even before he joined the Movement, he had formed a small group from among the friends he had made in camp.

Pavel also began holding weekly gatherings at his place, which I shall call "Fridays." The room would be packed with people, standing in little clusters and talking. But they were mostly busy passing typescripts to one another and reading them right there on the spot, so that the rustling of paper could be heard throughout the room.

It would not be true to say, however, that all the evenings at his place were spent reading documents. For one thing, we celebrated birthdays, including those of people in prison. In later times the investigator Akimov, a specialist in dissidents, told one of his friends: "Don't get the idea that they're all saints. They drink vodka, and they have women."

It was at Pavel's that I got to know the Crimean Tatars. In 1944 their entire civilian population was deported to Central Asia on a charge of "collaborating" with the Germans. After the war, demobilized Tatar soldiers were sent to the same area. In 1956 a decree was promulgated rehabilitating the Tatars; but, unlike some Caucasian peoples who had also been deported, they were not allowed to return to their homeland. No doubt one factor in this was opposition from the Ukrainian Party leadership, on whom Khrushchev was then relying in his struggle for power. Also, unlike the Caucasians, the Tatars did not get into motion spontaneously but instead waited for a while. In general, they are more industrious and peaceable than, say, the Chechens, so that the Uzbek authorities in Central Asia had an interest in keeping them.

The Crimean Tatars were carrying on their struggle by peaceful means. They would go to the Crimea, where they were caught and deported. They would hold orderly demonstrations, which were broken up by troops. Acting as loyal citizens, they would file petitions replete with phrases like "the great Party of Lenin" and "the Leninist policy toward national minorities"— petitions that were not answered. I was amazed at their patience. It seemed likely to me that if some of the Crimean Tatars converted to terrorism—to hijacking airplanes, for example—the authorities would make concessions to them, just as they authorized Jewish emigration only after the attempted hijacking by Edward Kuznetsov and Mark Dymshitz in 1970.

Among the guests who began to show up at Pavel's home were people
who served as a kind of link between the dissidents and the Zionists. The
movement for Jewish emigration had existed since the founding of Israel. But
that existence had been a miserable one until it was given a new impulse by
the Six Day War of 1967 and the rise of the Democratic Movement in the
USSR in 1968. I have a vivid memory of the gray-haired, bustling Julius
Telesin, who photocopied and circulated samizdat, including everything from
foreign editions of Solzhenitsyn's novels to transcripts of his own interrogations by the KGB. When one reads these transcripts—and Telesin distributed
a huge number of them—one cannot help but feel sorry for those poor investigators. He assigned numbers to all of his own statements, to the interrogations, to the investigator's questions, and to his own replies. For example, the
investigator would ask: "Did you give your Statement #3 to anyone to read?
And if so, to whom?" To which Julius would reply: "My Answer #7 suffices
as a reply to your Question #9." So that by the end of the interrogation,
neither the investigator, nor Telesin, nor anyone reading the transcript could
tell what was an answer to what.

When the Moscow Zionists drafted a letter in 1969 demanding free
emigration to Israel, they at first collected thirty-nine signatures. But apparently they wanted a round number; and at this point someone thought of
Telesin. Having taken part in the Democratic Movement, he had already
signed so many petitions that one more (or one less) made not the slightest
difference to him. But to his amazement—and the indignation of the veteran
Zionists—a few days later *Izvestiya* published an article calling Telesin the
leader of the Zionists. (Soon thereafter, he became one of the first to get
permission to emigrate to Israel.)

Pavel Litvinov was not a good organizer. But because of his goodwill,
openness, common sense, boldness, and freedom from vanity, he brought
together people of seeming incompatibility: individuals of different ages,
outlooks, experiences, and interests. It would not be true to say that we all
shared a negative attitude toward the regime. What we did have in common,
although it was not yet clearly formulated, was a belief in human rights and
in the worth of the individual. The experience of the disciplined Communist,
General Grigorenko, had brought him to that belief; and the experience of the
individualist writer, Amalrik, had led him to the same belief. But we still
needed someone we could all regard as one of us, and that person was Pavel.

In April 1968, when the tide of petitions had begun to ebb and the tide
of repressions had begun to rise, Pavel brought me a few cigarette papers with
a faintly typed text. This was the rough draft of the first issue of the magazine
Human Rights Year in the Soviet Union, subtitled *A Chronicle of Current
Events.* In time, *Chronicle* became the title of the journal, with "Human
Rights Year in the USSR Continues" or "The Struggle for Human Rights in

the USSR Goes On" as its motto, like *Pravda*'s "Workers of the World,
Unite!" or the *New York Times*'s "All the News That's Fit to Print." Con-
sciously or unconsciously, that title was taken from the BBC's Russian-
language broadcasts: they have a daily program called "A Chronicle of Current Events: The View from London." Our *Chronicle* was conceived as a
bimonthly report of incidents involving violations of human rights: trials,
arrests, searches. I told Pavel I thought the idea was very good, but I suggested a tone that was less emotional and less judgmental: let the facts speak
for themselves. And with rare exceptions, the *Chronicle* has kept that quality
through all these years.

In 1972 the KGB announced that after each new issue of *Chronicle*
appeared, they would arrest one person—not necessarily someone associated
with the particular issue. Publication was suspended, but it was resumed
eighteen months later. And at that time, the editors wrote: "Continued silence
would mean supporting, howbeit indirectly and passively, 'the tactic of taking
hostages'—which is incompatible with the law, with morality, and with human dignity."

The first issue of the *Chronicle* carried a report on the Leningrad trial of
members of the VSKhSON.* It was in this way that we first learned of an
opposition whose aims and methods were completely different from our own.
The VSKhSON was a conspiratorial organization whose aim was to seize
power in fifteen or twenty years and set up a theocratic state on a Christian
foundation. In 1977 I met Evgeny Vagin, who headed the Union's "ideological section" and who had spent eight years in prison. When I asked him what
he intended to do with the Moslem peoples of Russia, he only shrugged.
When both of us were questioned about our nationalities, I explained at some
length that one of my forebears was French, another Russian, another Ukrainian, another Swedish, and still another a gypsy. But Vagin just replied curtly:
"I'm Russian Orthodox."

The same kind of confusion between "nation" and "religion" can be
found, I think, in the group that took shape around the journal *Veche*. I met
the future editor of that journal, Vladimir Osipov, when he returned from a
seven-year term in the labor camps. (Right now he is back in a penal camp
serving a term of eight years.) His methods, unlike those of the VSKhSON,
were legal and open; and he impressed me as a very decent person. But when
he suggested that I write an article for his "Christian patriotic magazine," I
replied that in my view, Christianity and patriotism were incompatible concepts. Christ did not say: "I am a son of the Jews," or, "I am a son of the
Russians." He said: "I am the son of Man." The notion of "The God of the
Russians" is more reminiscent of Judaism than of Christianity; and the bed-
rock of the Russians' hostility toward the Jews is the feeling that there is not
room on this earth for two messianic peoples. Those same "Russian patriots"

who see that, however much Christianity is Russified, its relevance to all mankind cannot be eliminated have begun to talk of a return to Russian paganism, calling Christianity the "[bathhouse] dressing room of Judaism."

When one is presented with a philosophy whose aim is not merely to explain the world but (in Marx's phrase) "to change it," when one witnesses the creation of a social program capable of embodying a more or less vague future, it is always interesting not only to examine that program as a thing in itself but to see which of its aspects, when they come up against crude reality, have a chance of success and which will never be realized. The Slavophile philosophy, which was based on very noble ideas, degenerated in practice into "The Union of the Russian People," with its narrowness, its reactionary program, and its pogroms against the Jews. In the course of this kind of development, the Slavophiles were able to distort the peasant reforms so that the *obshchina* (peasant commune) was not destroyed and the peasant remained a half-person—which accounts for the horrors of the peasant rebellion. I very much fear that "neo-Slavophilism," in all its moderate and extremist varieties, will follow the same route. Because the mass of people, the nation, or history—call it what you will—will select its own degraded version of the lofty theory presented to it.

I am not against religion or nationhood. But for me, religion is the relationship between man and God, and not an ideology or political philosophy. Religion can, of course, influence society by setting a moral example. But the moment a church tries to become a political party, whether it be the only party or just one among many others, it ceases to be a church. As for nationhood, belonging to a people and a national culture and having an awareness of one's ties with one's own country is such a natural thing that very little is conceivable outside of it. But when "nationalism" changes from a natural feeling into a political category, it leads directly to authoritarian and totalitarian regimes. No longer are you simply a Russian or a German by birth and culture, you are a member of the Russian nation or the German nation. The nationalism of small peoples is understandable as a means of self-defense, although even here nationalism can sometimes take on repulsive attributes. But the nationalism of a very numerous people is, as a rule, not a means of defense but one of pressure, from both within and without. And nationalist slogans are sure to be popular, since all they require of you is to follow the path of least resistance. By the mere fact of having been born a Russian or a German, you can identify with the all-conquering political doctrine and in this way ascribe some importance to yourself.

The emergence of the VSKhSON, with its rejection of both Marxist totalitarianism and liberal parliamentarianism, makes it plain that after a period of paralysis, social thought in the Soviet Union is running up against the same problems that faced the Russian émigrés in the first years after the

Revolution. In both cases one can note a striving for a new ideology—a realization that since Marxism arose as a reaction to Western liberalism, it is hardly possible to overcome Marxism merely by a return to the ideals of liberalism. But what strikes me as equally important is another question: not where Marxism arose as an ideology, but where it was really embodied; namely, in societies with strong vestiges of feudalism. Bolshevism was a very Russian phenomenon, and not an accidental one. So that in their reliance on nationalism, both the NTS and the VSKhSON, while striving to move ahead, have actually been regressing. In certain respects they have been moving toward a really new ideology; but their sense of nationalist justification has led them in another direction. It would seem that in order to formulate a new ideology one must find the proper balance among the inalienable rights of the human individual, the social group, the nation, and all mankind.

Foreigners stress the Russians' strong attachment to their country—their demonstrative patriotism. Thus unlike the English, we don't say "this country" but "the motherland." My own reaction to this kind of display is distrust. Experience has shown that those who make a display of their love for the motherland or their belief in God, as if it were a medal worn on their chest, often prove to be unreliable. One element of Russian patriotism is not so much a feeling of tranquil pride in the country and of self-respect because we are Russians but rather a feeling of wounded vanity. Yes, to be sure, we are backward, poor, unfree, coarse, dirty, barbarous, etc., etc. But on the other hand:

> *Weary from the burden of the Cross,*
> *The King of Heaven, like a serf,*
> *Has trudged thy length and breadth,*
> *O Land of Russia, blessing thee.*[3]

We have brought, or we are bringing, to the rest of the world our great spiritual values; and whether this messianism is Russian Orthodox or Marxist-Leninist is a matter of indifference. So much for that side of things. On the other hand:

> *From the Urals to the Danube,*
> *To that mighty stream,*
> *The regiments are moving, swaying,*
> *Their bayonets agleam.*[4]

We are that force. You can despise us as much as you like. You live better than we. But we'll show you. We'll crush you with our might—and might always makes right.

The isolation of a people makes not only for solidarity but for xenophobia as well; and it is not always easy to draw the line between natural xenophobia and the artificial kind inculcated by the regime. The regime sees to it that the people draw a line between "us" and "them"; but the paradoxical thing is that the people's attitude toward the regime is also one that distinguishes between "us" and "them." And there come times when the ambivalence of a patriotism based on an awareness of one's strength emerges into the clear: the regime loses its power, and love of country is weakened. Because it turns out that the loyalty was to the regime and not to the country.

Two typical examples may be cited here, both of them involving the Germans. The first involved the mass desertions and the opening of the Russian front to the Germans in 1917–18. In effect, the entire rank and file of the armed forces—i.e., the people—showed they did not want to defend Russia, since its regime was no longer a force. The second example included the mass surrenders to the Germans in 1941–42, the hospitality shown them, and the collaboration by millions of people with an enemy who did not for a moment conceal his aim of destroying the nation. (At the time it seemed to many people that the regime was not strong enough to resist the Germans.)

The two "we and they" concepts—the Russians as against foreigners and the people as against the regime—also come into conflict with regard to the Russian dissidents. Dissidents, from Prince Kurbsky to Solzhenitsyn, make their appeals to foreign countries, or via foreign countries, or from foreign countries.† The incumbent regimes have always tried to emphasize this; but it is plain that on the whole they have suffered defeat. Lenin is a typical example: not only did he live abroad for many years and make appeals to foreign countries, he openly despised Russian patriotism, wanted Russia to lose the war with Germany, took money from the Germans, was described in the Russian press as a "German agent," and concluded with Germany a most humiliating peace pact. Yet he became for many years a symbol of Russia's national greatness, and his prestige among the common people is still very high.

Today the Soviet regime is trying to portray the dissidents either as foreign agents or simply as vain, rather stupid people who are being used by the foreigners, but this tactic is failing with respect to the Democratic Movement. I have sometimes encountered hostility because I was a dissident, but only rarely. Much more often, the reaction has been one of interest and sympathy.

"You're wasting your time," a police officer once told me. "You can

†Prince Andrei Kurbsky was one of Ivan the Terrible's most capable generals who in 1564, after losing a battle to the Lithuanians, defected to their side. He is chiefly known for his ensuing mutually vituperative correspondence with Ivan.—TRANS.

see for yourself that people easily soak up Soviet propaganda and accept everything as the way things should be."

"Well, if that's the way it is," I replied, "they will just as easily accept everything that comes from us."

The people's hostility toward foreign countries is largely based on the fear that foreigners are contemptuous of Russians. And the fact that the dissidents have found a common language with foreigners improves the chances of success for the Democratic Movement.

According to the KGB, the term "Democratic Movement" was dreamed up by the NTS and "dropped" (parachuted) into the USSR. Pavel Litvinov told me on one occasion that I myself had proposed the name early in 1968. Also in use for a time was the phrase "The December 5th Movement." It was suggested by Esenin-Volpin, one of the organizers of the first demonstration in Pushkin Square on December 5, 1965, with the slogan: "Respect the Constitution—the Fundamental Law of the USSR!"

In 1973 Andrei Sakharov said that in effect there was no Movement, since there was no political goal, no struggle for power. On the one hand, that opinion met his inner needs: he wanted to protest against unfair trials and help the victims of unlawfulness independently of any movement. But on the other hand, it was voiced at a time when the Movement was undergoing a crisis, and it was said in conversation and not in an article, in which he would have been able to weigh each word carefully. But the fact that one has no political goal does not mean that there is no movement: it merely means there is no *political* movement. If a group of people sets up common goals (and such goals have been well formulated by Sakharov himself: political amnesty; freedom of speech, of assembly, of association, and of entry into and departure from a country), utilizes common methods to achieve those goals, coordinates its activities, and in so doing expresses the interests of a part of society, then one can say that a moral movement exists. In 1973 it began to be called the Human Rights Movement—a more accurate designation at that time.

Since 1968 the dissidents have split (although the line is not always clearly drawn) into the "politicals" and the "moralists." The former are those who think of the Movement as the embryo of a political party and want to work out a program of political, social, and economic reforms. The latter are those who refuse, on moral grounds, to accept or take part in the evil done by the totalitarian regime. But the division is of course an arbitrary one, since every person is to some extent both a moralist and a politician. Even Sakharov, in his appeals to the authorities, proposed a program of socioeconomic changes; and later he criticized détente, so he was in fact playing a political role.

In speaking of a "party" and a "program," I do not mean that the "politicals" have proposed the immediate founding of a party and the formal adoption of a program. Yet there is a felt need in society for an ideological alternative. People in the Movement are constantly being asked: What is your program? What kind of society do you think we should have? (Pavel Litvinov laughingly told us that a worker once asked him: "What are you going to do with the factories?") Of course you can reject such questions, since the task the Movement has set for itself—that of restoring to people a sense of their own dignity—is a prerequisite for a just society. Still and all, it is plain that if we don't answer the question as to what kind of society we should have, it will be answered by those who want to drag us from one totalitarian pitfall into another.

The watershed between the "politicals" and the "moralists" is a division between those who do not believe in the stability of the system—who feel that sooner or later it will collapse and that we must give thought to means of restructuring it—and those who believe that the system is stable, that it will exist for a good long time, and that in the best case moral resistance (which is first and foremost an act of personal nonparticipation) will soften it. One's view of the possibility of a Russian opposition flows from one's general view of Russian history. Even when examining the subject most critically, I do not regard the Russians as a hopeless people for whom slavery is a natural mode of existence, an assumption shared by Senator Fulbright and Professor Kissinger. If I held that opinion, there would be nothing left for me to do but to keep quiet or disown myself as a Russian. But I can see that in the authoritarian stream of Russian history there is an undercurrent, sometimes strong, of a sense of law.

Another question is whether our Movement should take on organizational forms. Any organization would mean a transition to a new stage and, at the same time, a challenge to the authorities. Krasin, on one occasion, said it would not be worthwhile to assemble some kind of committee, all of whose members would promptly be arrested. I replied that most probably the authorities would ignore it; then in due course its members, one after another, would end up in prison under various pretexts. And it turned out that I was right.

In early July, Krasin, Petr Grigorenko, Larisa Bogoraz, Anatoly Marchenko, Pavel Litvinov, Petr Yakir, and I went to Aleksei Kosterin's dacha to discuss this question. Kosterin had spent twenty years in prisons and labor camps. His career behind bars began even before the Revolution, since he was already a member of the Bolshevik party, but most of the time he served was during the Stalin era. It was hard for me to judge how much bolshevism was left in him after all he had seen and experienced.

The visit at his dacha was the first time I had ever talked to Kosterin, and it was also the last: he died four months later. Before his death he had been ejected from the Writers' Union and from the Party because, after the Soviet invasion of Czechoslovakia, he had demanded Brezhnev's expulsion from the Party.

I also met other old Bolsheviks who had spent many years in the camps— not the kind who kept insisting that the Party never made a mistake but those who wanted to help bring about democratic changes.

At our meeting I suggested forming a Committee to Defend the Soviet Constitution, because the hypocritical Stalinist Constitution did contain articles on freedom of speech, of assembly, of demonstration, etc., and hence could serve as juridical cover for the committee. (This idea of using "from below" something that "from above" was regarded as merely window dressing was realized seven years later when the Helsinki Watch Group was founded to promote observance of the Helsinki accords.) I further proposed a structure something like a three-layered cake. The middle layer would consist of the best-known members of the Movement, such as Grigorenko and Litvinov, who would serve on the committee. The top layer would be made up of those academicians, writers, and directors who sympathized with our cause and were not yet frightened. They would not be members of the committee but would lend their prestige to its founding. The bottom layer—obscure members of the Movement—would do a good part of the practical work and would serve as backups for committee members in case of their arrest. This was nothing more than a formalization of the situation that already existed; but it posed the problem of working out and announcing some kind of program. The disputes that followed were lengthy, and no resolution was passed: it was hard to overcome the fear of the word "organization" that the Soviet regime has bred in its citizens.

In March, those who had signed the letter in defense of Galanskov and Ginzburg began to be dismissed from their jobs and the Party, and were condemned at public meetings. The signers said they had acted out of humanitarianism. But at a Moscow Party conference the writer Sergei Mikhalkov gave a new definition of that concept. To applause from his audience, he declared: "Hating the enemy indefatigably—that's humanitarianism!" At the same conference, Brezhnev stressed that "the renegades cannot count on going unpunished." The authorities had now clearly gone on the offensive. The initiative, however, remained with the dissidents. True, there was a sense of confusion, and it wasn't clear what should be done. But the Movement had as its background the Prague Spring, and so long as the process of liberalization was going on in Czechoslovakia, we lived on hope. The authorities realized this very well. The newspaper articles became more and more threatening; and when a brief item reported the alleged discovery of a cache of

German weapons in Czechoslovakia, anyone with a clear head could see that intervention was inevitable. Still, it was not easy to bury one's hopes.

In late July, Kosterin, Sergei Pisarev, Grigorenko, Ivan Yakhimovich, and Valery Pavlenchuk—all five of them Communists, the first having joined the Party in 1916 and the last in 1963—issued a statement welcoming the developments in Czechoslovakia and stating that Soviet intervention was not feasible. As a former general, Petr Grigorenko naturally regarded intervention as possible; but he counted on the resistance of the Czechs. "I know our troops," he said. "They'll head straight for a mountain pass, and they can be held up there for a long time." But things turned out quite differently.

Grigorenko and Yakhimovich (who had come down from his Latvian kolkhoz) decided to transmit this statement to the Czech Embassy. Since Grigorenko was wearing his decorations, the counselor of the embassy took him to be a Stalinist (as I had on a previous occasion). "Don't worry," the counselor told the general, "the Czech Republic is still Communist and true to its friendship with the USSR." To which Grigorenko replied: "Don't you worry, either. We're on your side." Then he proffered the statement, which the overjoyed counselor accepted, along with an open letter by Anatoly Marchenko warning that Brezhnev intended to occupy Czechoslovakia to make sure that developments there would not infect the USSR.

Grigorenko and Yakhimovich left the embassy as they had entered it— without hindrance. Several inconspicuous plainclothesmen were already lurking behind the trees, as though the whole thing were a stage set.

"Are you in the service?" asked one of our group.

"Yes, sir!" one of them replied eagerly.

A few days later, Pavel Litvinov phoned me and asked me to go right away to Larisa Bogoraz's home. It seemed that Anatoly Marchenko had been arrested. For the regime, the waiting period was over.

CHAPTER 6

August 21, 1968

We had been sending our declarations and articles to the outside world because that was the only way we could make them public without censorship. Our aim was to give the world a better idea of the state of affairs in the USSR and to reach the Russian people via Western radio. And in that we succeeded. The number of listeners to foreign radio broadcasts increased several times over. We could not, of course, instruct the Western papers and radio stations how to publish and broadcast our material. And sometimes they wrote and broadcast the opposite of what we wanted people to hear.

Before Pavel Litvinov's mail was put under surveillance, he received many letters from Soviet listeners, some of which were put directly into his mailbox. The ratio of favorable letters to unfavorable responses was about three to one. Soon, however, the KGB wised up: they not only confiscated letters to well-known dissidents but instructed the information bureaus not to give out their addresses. And at least one of the letters left in Pavel's mailbox was a KGB forgery, a clumsy imitation of a statement by a "group of students" about the founding of a new political party.

We prepared a collection of these letters—so far the only such compilation of the reaction of ordinary Soviet citizens to the Movement—and the manuscript was published in several languages.

Pavel received several letters with abusive language. One of them—which, judging from the official postmark, was from the KGB—began: "Why are you disgracing your grandfather's memory, you lousy kike?" Since the letter was anonymous, Pavel didn't know to whom he should reply, saying that he was a "lousy kike" precisely because his grandfather was a "kike." Then there was a very amusing letter from a retired gebist who wrote: "Just who are you people saying 'We demand'? You're nothing more than insects;

but even insects can stink." And he went so far as to mete out a sentence to Pavel: twelve years.

When Karel van het Reve looked over the manuscript, he asked why there were so many ellipses. I said they stood for unprintable words. "But we're getting out a scholarly edition," Karel said, "and not a single word should be left out." So I had to go over the manuscript again and restore all the words we had deleted.

Ginzburg's "White Paper" had begun a tradition of compiling collections of documents on political trials. Next, Pavel and Natalya Gorbanevskaya put together a collection dealing with the trials of Bukovsky and Khaustov, which we likewise passed on to Karel. It seemed important to assemble a similar compilation on the trial of Galanskov and Ginzburg, and Pavel began to collect the materials. It is difficult to reconstruct a trial, since no stenographic record is kept, and notes taken in the courtroom by relatives and witnesses are likely to be confiscated. Galanskov's father even concealed his notes in his felt boots. Since he was thought to be an illiterate, he was not frisked when he left the courtroom.

I was apprehensive of searches and arrests and urged Pavel to make haste. In June I lent a hand in the work, starting to systematize and retype the materials, writing introductory articles, and drawing up an index of names. I used a variety of typewriters and even changed the typeface of one of them so that the KGB couldn't use it as evidence against me. When Karel found me working on the index, his usual remark was: "I always knew you were working for 'the organs'!"*

Pavel was arrested in August, and in October I completed the work. I was helped very much by Marusya Rubin, who retyped part of the manuscript, and by Julius Telesin, who gathered articles from Soviet papers. But I encountered opposition from Arina Ginzburg, Alexander's wife, Olga Galanskova, and Natalya Gorbanevskaya. Arina was afraid that publication of the collection would jeopardize contact with her husband, now in a labor camp. Olga was afraid for herself, a feeling I should say was entirely natural. And Natalya was apprehensive that publication would adversely affect Pavel.

I thought it would be best to credit Pavel as editor of the collection, but I decided that if he refused, I would put the book out under my own name. He gave his agreement, however, from Lefortovo Prison, where I had managed to query him. Later, when he was in Siberia, I sent him a copy to look over, then forwarded the book to Karel in Holland, having given it the title *The Trial of the Four*. So far as Pavel was concerned, I turned out to be right: there were no bad consequences for him.

Of the manuscripts that I sent abroad, the most important was one I got from Pavel in late June: Academician Andrei Sakharov's "Progress, Coexistence, and Intellectual Freedom." Sakharov wrote the article in early 1967 and then for the next year and a half kept going back to it. Apparently it was not easy for him to take the decisive step of publishing it in samizdat. It meant a break with the scientific establishment and with the entire system of which that establishment is a part.

Many scientists have taken part in the Human Rights Movement in the USSR. This is because a scientist is inclined to subject facts to objective analysis and not get caught in the mythological traps that snare the average "Soviet man." In his own work, a scientist depends very little upon the State's ideology; but the State is directly dependent upon the results of the scientist's production. This does not mean that the majority of scientists are dissidents, not even secretly. The predominant attitude is apolitical: "You do what you want, and I'll work at science." This allows scientists to be manipulated when it serves the purposes of the State. For example, signing a letter *for* Sakharov is a political act, while signing a letter *against* him is an apolitical gesture. The argument employed to persuade scientists is: "If you sign the letter against Sakharov, you'll get imported equipment for your laboratory." And the scientist, as he signs, thinks to himself: "Let the equipment be used for science. If I didn't sign, somebody else would. My refusal would not save Sakharov, and the equipment might go to some scoundrel." Most scientists are pragmatists. If things change for the better, they are likely to support that change. But there is little hope that they themselves will show any initiative, or that they will take ethical values into account when they act.

There has been a gradual change in the breed of scientists. The old generation was the product of an academic milieu. They lived according to the prerevolutionary traditions of pure science, the scientific ethic, and the moral principles handed down by the Lord God. Of course, during the eras of Lenin and Stalin, that ethic got some pretty rough treatment. But with the first relaxation, those scientists tried to return to the old principles; e.g., Academician Mikhail Leontovich, who signed several letters in defense of convicted persons. The new breed, however, is the product of a scientific-bureaucratic milieu. They live in symbiosis with the Party bureaucracy; they make a career not so much *in* science as *through* science. One example is Academician Nikolai Shilo, who will make a later appearance in these pages.

The thing about Sakharov's article that most shook me up was not *what* had been written but *who* had written it. Sakharov should have belonged to the second breed, not only by reason of his age but because of his special kind of scientific career in the development of the hydrogen bomb. And the fact that he did not belong to it was a miracle. But was it not also a miracle that a major general heading up a department at a military academy (General Grigorenko) became the most vigorous of dissidents? This fissure in the establishment—and I have cited only two of the most striking examples—was an indication of deep geological faults in the Soviet structure.

That summer of 1968, most of my friends were concerned only with what was happening in Russia and Czechoslovakia. As for me, I was following the events in Africa with mounting bitterness. It had become obvious that Biafra's war for independence would end in defeat. I have always felt stirred to rebellion at the sight of a majority imposing its will upon a minority. A small people's right to self-determination seemed to me more important than any geopolitical considerations, artificially drawn borders, or imperialist interests. Gusel and I were terribly depressed to learn that because of the blockade in Biafra, three thousand children were dying every day. Both the USSR and Great Britain were supporting Nigeria; for me that was just one more example of how Soviet communism collaborates with Western reactionaries to maintain the seeming status quo in the world.

Both Gusel and I wanted to protest to Britain's Prime Minister Wilson and the head of Nigeria's military government, General Gowon. I suggested the two of us demonstrate in front of the British Embassy in Moscow, following the example of Yuri Galanskov, who three years before had picketed the U.S. Embassy. At the same time we wanted to show those dissidents imbued with a respect for group actions that you don't necessarily have to have five hundred or even fifty people to carry out a political action. I punched out fifty leaflets on my typewriter, and we made two placards in Russian and English: "Gowon Is Killing Children!" and "Wilson, Don't Help Gowon!" (Today, General Gowon has long since been overthrown, and those who overthrew him have been overthrown, while he himself is studying at an English university, which does him honor. Perhaps he is really not so bad as we thought at the time.)

That morning, as we approached the British Embassy on the Sofiyskaya Quay, opposite the Kremlin, my heart was beating fast. But when, only a few paces from the embassy, we unrolled our placards and held them up, I quickly calmed down. The day before, I had carefully looked over the site and had asked some English journalists to be there in the morning. And sure enough, several people with cameras were standing on the parapet of the embankment. A few days later, a frightened Boris Alekseyev came from Novosti with a brief UPI item. "When I saw the name 'Amalrik,' " he told me, "I even started trembling."

Gusel and I began by handing out leaflets to the policemen on duty in front of the embassy. A young sergeant took a leaflet and started to read it. Another, a middle-aged major, refused to accept one and dashed off to a telephone to ask for instructions. The passersby took them willingly. Encouraged by the journalists, we entered the courtyard of the embassy—the confused policemen were standing idly by. At the elegant entrance to the mansion there appeared a dignified, monumental gentleman, looking every inch the ambassador. But he merely stood there making helpless gestures, just as the major was doing, and the journalists whispered to us that he was nothing more than a doorman. At that point two long-haired young men who looked like bureaucrats came out, and each of them took a leaflet from us.

We picketed the embassy for about an hour. Then the major, who had finally received his instructions, told us: "All right. You've put on a show for the journalists, and they've photographed you. Now it's time for you to go home."

A bus full of English tourists drove up, and the Russian girl serving as their guide asked us in some excitement: "What organization are you from?" When we replied that we were representing only ourselves, she said: "That's incredible! That's really incredible!"

Later, Larisa Bogoraz told us: "Look what you've done. Now the English will think that people are free to hold demonstrations in this country."

Our demonstration was held on July 16. On August 14, a smiling sergeant brought us a summons to the local police precinct. The next morning we were awakened by a knocking sound, as if someone were hammering on the ceiling. We figured they were bugging our room (although that is usually done with a certain pretense at being inconspicuous), and we decided that I would go to the police station alone while Gusel remained at home. She wasn't feeling well anyway.

Captain Dosuzhev, second in command at the precinct, greeted me politely, saying he had received a report that I was not employed anywhere, so that he would have to interrogate me. It looked like a repeat of 1965, when I was exiled to Siberia for two-and-a-half years for leading a "parasitic way of life." I told Dosuzhev that, in the first place, I was working for Novosti, and in the second place, the RSFSR Supreme Court had ruled that my ill health exempted me from the decree on compulsory employment.

"That's fine," said Dosuzhev. "Just write an explanation and submit the appropriate documents, so we can close the case."

But I knew that this was the usual kind of trap: they needed the documents and the explanation so they could properly prepare a case against me. The best tactic was to explain nothing, submit nothing, and just drag out the proceedings.

Dosuzhev did not show me the report about me, but later I got a look at it. It was dated August 7 and was handwritten:

To the Chief of the Sixth Police Precinct:
I hereby inform you that Andrei Amalrik, thirty years of age,

has for a long time been leading a parasitic way of life, and has no job . . . . In 1964 Amalrik was sent to prison for speculation and parasitism. Yet since his return from there he has continued the same way of life, and has no job. . . . At present some woman, allegedly his wife, is living in his home without a residence permit. No one knows where she came from, but one thing is clear: she is just as much of a parasite, and doesn't have a job. In her home she does paintings of some kind, and they are sold to private persons. I entreat you to look into this matter and compel these healthy young people to get work in a factory.

Deponent

Across the top of the page was written the decision of L. Dobrer, the precinct chief: "To Comrade G. M. Dosuzhev. In collaboration with the district commissioner, please check on Amalrik's way of life. Find out where he works, and the identity of the woman living at his home without a residence permit. August 12, 1968."

"Where is your wife?" Dosuzhev asked me. "I sent that summons to both of you."

"She's sick."

"I'll clear up this matter with my superior right now," Dosuzhev said, and got on the phone, trying to show that he was only carrying out orders. His "superior" turned out to be none other than the mysterious "deponent," KGB Captain Denisov, who was heading up the operation.

Later I said to Dosuzhev: "Your superior is Dobrer. Yet a KGB captain gives you orders, and you obey them with no questions asked. How come? Is there some directive saying the police have to follow the orders of the KGB?"

"I never heard of any such directive," he replied. "But you know, for example, that if a wolf meets up with a bear in the forest, he always shies away." (The police harbor a noticeable envy toward the KGB, just as domestic KGB agents do toward their colleagues working abroad.)

The result of clearing up the matter with Dosuzhev's "superior" was that I was detained, and Gusel was brought to the station with a police escort. They even called a doctor from the raion polyclinic—an old woman who was more frightened than Gusel herself—in order to get certification that Gusel was in good health. Even though Gusel was running a high fever, the doctor certified her as well.

After repeating to both of us what he had said before, Dosuzhev released us. When we got home, I noticed there was no one in the communal apartment. The KGB had decided to kill two birds with one stone: to start proceedings for expelling me from Moscow and at the same time to bug our room. I went up to the room above ours, from which they had installed the listening device, to complain about the hammering; but the woman living there wouldn't let me in.

On August 21, Anatoly Marchenko was tried on a charge of "violating the internal passport regulations," and was given a sentence of one year, the maximum for that violation. (Subsequently, while in prison camp, he got two more years for "circulating fabrications defaming the Soviet system.") Passport cases are nonpolitical, so the trial was open. Half of the people in the courtroom were gebists, of two categories: old ones (pensioners) and young ones ("apprentices"). Later I saw many of the same agents at other trials. Flanking the judge were the people's assessors, two intelligent-looking women who sat there looking unhappy.† I was astounded that there were no foreign correspondents in the courtroom. But I found out why during the recess, when someone came up to me and said: "Have you heard the news? Our troops have gone into Czechoslovakia."

The moment the trial was over, the judge and the gebists rushed off: meetings were being held all over the country to approve the incursion by our troops. It can hardly be said, however, that the approval was unanimous. I am not referring to the dissidents, who, in Moscow, at any rate, were to be found at many meetings, but to the kind of person who in the West is called "the man in the street." To be sure, one heard statements like, "We'll show 'em!" or "If we didn't go in, the Germans would!" Such pronouncements came down "from above," but they were easily accepted below. (One blue-collar worker explained to me: "What kind of government is it if they're afraid of me, a poor workingman? I'm the one who should be afraid of the government.") Even so, I would not say that was the general opinion of the people. I met people from all walks of life who regarded the Czech invasion as a tragedy. Later I got to know an orthodox Party woman and was amazed to learn that on August 21 she had wept. And when I was in prison camp, a quarrel broke out between two working-class men. One of them said, "We saved them from the Germans in the war, and just now they tried to disown us!" The other retorted, "Listen, if you saw a girl drowning and saved her, would that give you the right to fuck her the rest of her life?" Since the first man was serving time for rape, he had no comeback.

Directly after our summons to the police precinct, Gusel and I had decided to go away for a while; it was only because of Marchenko's trial that we had delayed leaving. I figured I would certainly be sent to prison sooner or later, and when I got out I would not be able to get a residence permit for either Moscow or the Moscow region. Therefore, I wanted to make advance

---

†At lower court trials in the Soviet Union, "the bench" usually consists of one judge and two "people's assessors," laymen who are supposed, on principle, to represent "the people."—TRANS.

preparations by buying a peasant cottage somewhere south of Moscow. In that way I would not again find myself homeless, as I had when I came back from Siberia. Meanwhile, we could spend the summer and fall in the country.

One of our neighbors had given us his sister's address in the Ryazan Oblast.* The train was a long one, with very old cars, and was almost empty. We spent an entire night on it, as it huffed and puffed its way along. In the morning we switched to a bus. At a bus stop we met a young shepherd who kindly offered to take us to our destination, although he had said he was going to visit relatives in another village. On the way, Gusel ingenuously told him that we wanted to buy a house and asked if he knew of anything suitable.

I cannot truthfully say that we were joyfully welcomed by the young man's sister, a saleswoman in a local store. Several times she asked me if I wasn't the friend of her nephew, who had either just got out of prison or was still there. She would not let us sleep in her house, so we spent the night on the hay in a little barn. But we did eat supper with her, and in order to ease the tension, I took a bottle of gin out of my knapsack. The sight of that bottle, however, *really* upset her. ("They got hold of a bottle from a foreign country, and poured Russian vodka into it!" she told people in the store the next day, misled by the fact that gin is colorless, like the vodka she was familiar with.) In the morning she said she hoped we wouldn't take offense, but she would have to ask us to leave.

I walked around the village, prettily situated on a bank of the Vozha, and looked at one house. But the locals eyed me suspiciously. One peasant, saying we wouldn't find anything here, suggested we go a mile or so farther down to Akulovo. Under a scorching sun, we followed a path through a dry plowed field, through a field of rye stubble, through a strange village past empty, boarded-up houses that reminded me of the abandoned villages in Siberia, and finally came to a brick house that stood on the edge of a stream in the shade of some lime trees. After the heat, we liked this spot so much that we immediately decided to buy the house—and it was for sale.

We spent a few days in the house, waiting for the return of the owner, who had gone off to visit her son, and listening to the radio. Broadcasts had been jammed since the time the troops were sent into Czechoslovakia, but outside the city one could get good reception. On the evening of August 25, the Voice of America reported that a group of unknown persons had tried to stage a demonstration in Red Square and that they were promptly arrested. I had no doubt that this was the demonstration Pavel Litvinov had mentioned to me before Gusel and I left Moscow. But why call the demonstrators "unknown persons"? After all, many of the dissidents were well known. And the Voice of America had broadcast in detail, stressing its significance, every statement issued by Litvinov himself.

The next morning we left for Moscow, where I learned that seven per-

sons had taken part in the demonstration: Pavel Litvinov, Vladimir Dremlyuga, Victor Feinberg, Konstantin Babitsky, Vadim Delone, Natalya Gorbanevskaya, and Larisa Bogoraz. Bogoraz had notified the foreign correspondents
that the protest would begin at 11:00 A.M., but the group did not assemble at
the Lobnoye Mesto† in Red Square until noon, by which time all of the
correspondents but one had left. That one journalist watched as a group of
people at the far end of the square displayed their placards and were promptly
overwhelmed by policemen and agents in plain clothes. The agents created
the appearance of an agitated crowd, and at the trial it turned out that most of
them belonged to the same unit of the internal security forces. All of the
demonstrators were detained except Gorbanevskaya, who was released because she had two small children.

A few minutes after the demonstrators had been taken away, the Czech
delegation, headed by Alexander Dubcek, emerged from the Kremlin.

It seemed to me at the time that the demonstration was a tactical mistake.
I felt that if the Movement concentrated on domestic problems it would gain
broader support, and the authorities would find it harder to represent us as a
handful of renegades. And at a time when matters were nerve-racking for the
authorities, a demonstration like this would lead to the arrest of all the partic-
ipants and thus deprive the Movement of its leaders and most active members.

I now believe I was wrong. It would have been very sad indeed if a cry
of protest, however feeble and despairing, had not come from Russia itself.
It was historically indispensable—and that is more important than tactical
considerations—that someone say an emphatic No to Russian imperialism.
Perhaps in the final accounting that resolute No uttered by seven persons in
Red Square will have more weight than the indifferent Yes of 70 million
people at "meetings of the toilers."

I wanted to get the demonstrators' names and other details to the foreign
correspondents right away, but to use the telephone to talk about what had just
happened seemed not yet feasible. I therefore decided to go directly to the
New York Times correspondent, Raymond Anderson. One or two policeman
were always stationed at the gate in front of his house, and plainclothesmen
were always strolling about in the vicinity. I told Gusel she should dress as
elegantly as possible, so that she might be taken for a foreigner. I have always
felt oppressed by the humiliating procedure involved when visiting foreigners
in Moscow, especially when they asked us to speak English when we came
through the gate, so the policeman wouldn't take us for Russians. More than
once I have argued with policemen, maintaining that I had the right to go

---

†"Place of Execution," or Golgotha, where the decrees of the tsars used to be read to the
public.—TRANS.

where I wanted in my own country. But this time it seemed better to slip in without being conspicuous, and fortunately, no one detained us at the gate.

A few days later, Gusel and I returned to Akulovo, where we bought the house and lived happily for two weeks. An old stove maker built us a stove, while expressing his opinion that you could always oppose craftiness to sheer strength, so the Czechs would outwit the Russians. We received a visit from the chairman and *partorg** of the kolkhoz and solemnly submitted a request that we be authorized to live on the territory of their kolkhoz.

"It's your place to ask, and ours to decide," the chairman said. But since we were just then celebrating the purchase of the house with a large quantity of vodka, the matter was settled. When Gusel asked whether kolkhoz workers were getting decent pay, the partorg said the pay was good but there was nothing to buy.

One day when we were standing by the well, a short, swarthy, agile young man appeared from somewhere in the direction of the field that extended for a good distance behind our house. He came up to us, hands outstretched, and said: "So that's what you look like!"

He went on to say that he had come from Moscow to visit an uncle of his. The next day he returned with a duck and a bottle of liqueur; and at dinner he voiced some opinions that were rather critical of the government, if not actually anti-Soviet. Gradually it dawned upon me that the KGB had been playing cat and mouse with us during our stay in the country. Of course we had been careful while in Moscow not to say a single word to each other about buying the house, knowing our room was bugged. But at the time I didn't feel that the matter of the house had to be kept secret.

The trial of the demonstrators was held in the center of Moscow, not far from the Kotelnicheskaya Quay. It was in that time of October when the sunlight is especially clear; and in the little park across from the courthouse the leaves on the trees had turned a beautiful yellow. The side street was crowded with the friends of those on trial, with foreign correspondents, and with a large number of informers. To an outside observer, the whole thing might have looked like a folk festival. But what the KGB had arranged was not a folk festival but a display of "folk wrath." From nearby factories they had recruited workers to be on hand at the trial. Just to make sure that high spirits prevailed (and also to make sure that the workers didn't simply take off), tables laden with bottles of vodka were set up in the basement of a building on the next side street. A great many drunks were jostling their way through the crowd and muttering: "They're all kikes! They're fascists! They oughta be strangled!" A middle-aged workingman, already very drunk, came staggering up to the wife of an Italian correspondent and said over and over again: "Czechoslovakia! Czechoslovakia! How about you and me having a little tête-à-tête about American aggression in Vietnam?" Then he loudly hiccuped in the face of the bewildered woman.

None of this gang set upon us directly. But they did snatch a security druzhinnik's camera, so that the other druzhinniks had to rescue one of their own people from their own people, so to speak. But the police were the most exasperated by the drunken workingmen. They were used to dragging them off to the drunk tank without further ado, and now they found themselves in the role of allies, as it were. When someone complained to a police major about the drunks, he replied in great irritation, "What can I do? They're drunk even when they're on the job in the factory."

During the trial of Galanskov and Ginzburg, and at other trials since, I noticed a young black-bearded leader of the security druzhinniks named Aleksandrov. From the bloodthirsty tone of his talk, I figured he must be a Party fanatic. But General Grigorenko, who was much more experienced in Party matters than I was, said he was an ordinary careerist. Usually, any remarks exchanged between dissidents and gebists at trials boil down to mutual insults. But as a writer, I was interested in finding out what kind of people these were. Whenever I chanced to have anything resembling a human conversation with a young gebist, he would always try to stress that his motivations were strictly lofty. To which I would reply that it's hard to draw a line showing where a person's convictions do not conflict with his career.

On this occasion, Aleksandrov looked as if he would welcome the chance for a talk, so for a rather long time we strolled along the quay together, under the anxious gazes of both the dissidents and the gebists. I asked Aleksandrov if he realized that he, too, was taking a risk. I said that the situation at the top was unstable, that someone might die or simply be overthrown; then one fine day it might be declared that the incursion into Czechoslovakia was a "mistake," that the trials were "excesses." If so, the kind of person who had been sitting in an office and passing resolutions would simply switch over to the new policy. But people like himself, who had been "ordered to do their job in public," would become the scapegoats. Aleksandrov said he realized that and never again did I see him at a trial.

Nor did the wrathful folk ever again appear at a trial. Either the authorities decided that their effect was the opposite of what they intended or they figured: "Today we sic the workers on them; tomorrow the workers will go after us." A few months later, at the trial of Irina Belogorodskaya, who was charged with circulating an appeal in defense of Marchenko, the official "public" consisted of languid young men and women in Western-style sheepskin coats. They didn't hector anyone and listened politely to the dissidents' speeches. Every now and then, one of them would say to another, with a sigh: "The sooner this is over, the better."

Owing to the peculiarities of Soviet jurisprudence, none of the authors of the Marchenko appeal was brought to trial, summoned as a witness, or (naturally) allowed in the courtroom as a spectator. The practice of handpicking the "public" for political trials serves two ends: it reduces leaks of "uncontrolled information" to a minimum and it puts more psychological strain on the defendant, because he doesn't see support coming to him from anywhere.

The haste with which the investigation and trial of the Red Square demonstrators were carried out showed that the authorities did not want to keep them in remand prison* too long but preferred sentencing them to exile. (One day in prison is equated with three days of exile—hence the haste.) As a matter of fact, even though all of them held their heads high and not a single one pled guilty, Babitsky, Bogoraz, and Litvinov each got five years of exile; Delone and Dremlyuga were sentenced to three years in prison camp; and Feinberg, previously found mentally incompetent, was committed to a psychiatric hospital. Gorbanevskaya, as I mentioned earlier, was not brought to trial.

A Cold Autumn,
a Bitter Cold Winter

It was one o'clock in the morning. Without looking to one side or the other, I was walking along the dark, empty streets of the Arbat section and had almost reached the Arbat itself when I was stopped by a policeman and asked to show my papers. With some inconsistency, he explained that a suitcase like the one I was carrying had been stolen at the Kazan Station.

At the next corner was a car that had chanced to pull up and stop there. The driver was tinkering with the motor, and another individual was loitering nearby.

"Can you take us to the precinct station?" the policeman asked.

"Oh, all right," the driver said, feigning reluctance.

At the familiar Sixth Precinct Station, I opened my worn suitcase unprotestingly and showed the desk sergeant its contents: a portable typewriter and a bundle of papers.

The sergeant, sitting behind a partition with a little window in it, reached out his hand for the papers. I said they were my personal papers, and I wouldn't give them to him; but of course he took them with no great effort. While he leafed through them, I was made to sit down on a bench next to a petty thief who had been picked up for stealing a television set. "The things they do!" he said to me, in an appeal for sympathy. "I didn't steal that TV set. I just took it to have a look."

After a few minutes the desk sergeant poked his head through the little window and announced on a note of triumph: "We're going to pass on these papers of yours to our colleagues at the Committee of State Security. They're not for us to deal with."

The TV thief recoiled from me. And almost immediately, as though they had been waiting outside the door to hear the sergeant's announcement, two plainclothesmen appeared. They took the papers from him and, without saying a word, vanished into the depths of the building.

An hour later I was escorted to a small office on the third floor for interrogation. I was feeling very dispirited: it wasn't hard for them to see that the materials were intended for the collection we were going to publish, *The Trial of the Four*. Is it really that simple to get seven years, I wondered, remembering Galanskov's collection.

One of the investigators was a tall man named Vasily Ivanovich or Ivan Vasilyevich. The other, who was in charge, gave his name as Captain Smelov or Sedov. "You're thirty years old," the captain said to me, "and I'm forty-five. We're not that far apart in age, so why play tricks with each other?" Both were gebists of the old breed.

Then two younger men came in. One of them, wearing a fashionable scarf, began to go through the papers, using a plastic penholder instead of his fingers so as not to leave fingerprints. But Vasily Ivanovich grasped the paper with all five fingers, showing both his young colleague and myself that veterans like him could dig into a file without any newfangled refinements. It was what one might call a conflict between fathers and sons.

Their questions were pretty much as follows: Where do you work? So you're not on the staff at Novosti? You do free-lance hack work? How do your associates at Novosti feel about that? Why do you have all these documents? Who gave them to you? Where were you taking them? Were you going to keep them and then distribute them? Etc., etc.

I replied that I had obtained them from friends whose names I would not reveal; that I intended, merely out of curiosity, to look them over, and then I was going to destroy them.

"But who *did* give them to you? You'll have to tell us."

"I'll have to if you hang me up by the feet and torture me."

"We don't do things like that these days."

"Then I won't have to tell."

"It's true that your name isn't signed to any of this slanderous stuff," said Sedov-Smelov. "But I myself wouldn't soil my hands with papers like these. It looks as though you are envious of the fame of Galanskov and Ginzburg. Well, I've seen them many times, and they're just ordinary people."

"Wanting to become famous"—this seems to have been the authorities' standard explanation for the activity of dissidents. Later on I got into the habit of responding to it by just saying calmly: "Well, there's no harm in being famous."

Meanwhile, it was becoming clear to me that "our glorious organs" had made a mistake. Apparently, an order had been issued to seize the transcripts of the trial of the demonstrators, whereas what I possessed were letters that had already been published. So they didn't really know what to do with me. They just waited for instructions, and in the morning I was released—to the great joy of Gusel, who hadn't slept at all that night.

The next day, however, I was again brought in to the same precinct station. (By this time I refused to go on my own in response to a summons.) The police officer Dosuzhev and the KGB captain Denisov spent a long time rehearsing the incident of the day before and tried to get something out of me. Then they gave me a formal warning that I must find regular employment within a month. And if I didn't find a regular job, I could, after one more warning, be sent into exile or incarcerated for two years.

When I asked about the papers and the typewriter, Denisov and Dosuzhev said they knew nothing about them.

But the gebists who had detained me had overlooked one thing. Being security agents who were not accustomed to observing formalities, and not having legal training, they had made no record of the confiscation. So I promptly filed a complaint with the City Prosecutor's Office, claiming illegal detention and the misappropriation of my typewriter and papers. I encountered hostility from that quarter; but the complaint went through, and on October 30, Dosuzhev returned my typewriter and papers to me. Among the latter was a document, mislaid by someone, written in the familiar hand of "deponent": Denisov's decoding of unclear passages. An accompanying statement from the prosecutor's office amounted to more or less the following: Your typewriter and papers have been returned to you; you were detained so that your documents could be checked; just be glad that everything turned out well. And I *was* glad.

I soon sent *The Trial of the Four* to Holland. And I had the pleasure of seeing Vasily Ivanovich again—at the appellate hearing for the demonstrators. I was talking to a French journalist in a hallway at the courthouse, when I spotted him coming our way.

"Vasily Ivanovich?"

"That's right."

"KGB agent?"

"Yes, KGB agent," he said, with growing irritation.

"Okay, run along now," I told him, waving him away, and with a hangdog look he went off. I had only wanted to have a little fun at his expense.

When the trial was over, and the "public" began to come out of the courtroom, I received quite a jolt: I had never before, nor have I since, seen such a motley assembly. Each one of them had some unpleasant physical defect or discernibly vicious trait. I couldn't imagine how they had managed to get all of them together on this occasion. (Not that all gebists are disgusting; I have even seen some of attractive appearance.)

As might have been expected, the verdict against the demonstrators was upheld.

Although I had won the battle of the typewriter, the struggle to avoid being sent into exile was more difficult. I wrote letters to the police, the raion prosecutor's office, and the journalists' union, enclosing lists of my interviews for Novosti, extracts from the Supreme Court's decision in my case, etc. This gave the KGB and the police more work to do, but I knew it couldn't save me: I had to find a regular job, if only for a short time.

Boris Alekseyev phoned me to say that he would have to return the articles I had written; Novosti would not be commissioning any more work from me. He did not, however, return the pieces I had written about the artists, saying they were in the hands of the "top bosses." A year later, when I visited him at the Novosti building, he told me nervously that "they'd thrown that trash in the wastebasket." He added that he had never accepted any articles from me. Finally he said he had had lots of trouble and therefore didn't want to see me or hear from me anymore.

A young woman who had just brought in a piece on ballet asked with a terrified look: "Could the same thing happen to my article?"

"Throw that slanderer out!" came a shout from behind a partition. The shouter was the section chief, who had in times past praised my "subtlety."

"You're a slanderer!" came the echo from Alekseyev, who by this time was all worked up. "You write denunciations of the Soviet regime."

"Denunciations are exactly what I *don't* write," I said. Then, after cursing all of them out roundly, I went home to write a denunciation of Alekseyev to the editorial board of Novosti. I received no reply—nor did I get back my articles.†

So, the KGB had decided it was preferable to have me sent into exile as a "parasite" rather than to set up a political trial. They had deprived me of my work for Novosti, and they saw to it that I couldn't get work anywhere else. All they had to do was keep track of where I was trying to get a job, then phone the chief of personnel and tell him not to hire Amalrik. Every day, beginning at eight in the morning, they staked out my apartment building. But I had noticed an announcement from the local post office saying people were needed to deliver letters and newspapers, beginning at 6:00 A.M. I went there at 6:00 the next morning and was joyfully received—and hired, since not many people wanted to work for twenty-six rubles a month. I would

---

†Incidentally, the KGB did not find the articles to be incriminating, and after my trial, the investigator returned the confiscated copies to Gusel.

deliver the papers rapidly, then get back home before eight, leaving the KGB under the illusion that I wasn't working anywhere.

During the first month I was on probationary status and could have been dismissed summarily, so I had to conceal the job from the police. They gave me my last warning, but then discovered the truth. The prosecutor's office sent them a reprimand (although a rather gentle one) for having issued a warning to a person who had a job. One police officer complained bitterly to Denisov: "I did my best for the KGB, and the result was a reprimand!"

I couldn't be put on the regular payroll until I submitted a reference from my place of previous employment. At Novosti they at first refused to give me a reference, but I got into the chief accountant's office and said I wouldn't leave until I was given a reference. The accountant's instinctive fear of any disturbance prevailed, and he wrote out the reference. He added a note saying it was "not valid for purposes of receiving a pension"; but I didn't give a damn about any pension. Finally, the personnel department of the raion administration of communications made an entry in my workbook.†

I promptly filed a complaint with the raion prosecutor, Fetisov, about the warning from the police; I even went to visit him. It had been three years since I had seen Fetisov, who in 1965 had signed the order for my arrest. Either he had become dispirited since that time or I had become more high-spirited. In any case, something about him struck me as pitiable.

"What do you want?" he asked, scowling down at his desk.

"I have three questions to ask in connection with my complaints," I began, opening my portfolio. The sight of the copies of complaints affected him as a red flag does a bull.

"You should be working, instead of writing complaints!" he barked, giving me a look of sheer abhorrence.

"There's no point in bellowing at me," I told him. "You sent me into exile. As you can see, I've come back; and I'm sitting here in front of you alive and well. As for you, if you go swelling up with anger until you're red in the face, you'll soon drop dead from apoplexy."

He leapt to his feet and began shouting something unintelligible. I left his office very pleased with myself, hoping he really would have an apoplectic fit. But I didn't want to rely on that alone; so I wrote a complaint to the *raikom* of the Communist Party of the Soviet Union, saying that the prosecutor shouted, foamed at the mouth, and stamped his feet. I said that this looked not only strange but comical, and that in doing these things he was "lowering the dignity of a Communist and a prosecutor." I requested, however, that in view of his past services, he not be punished but merely be given a "well-

---

†Every Soviet citizen is required to carry a workbook with a record of his employment.—TRANS.

deserved rest." (It was my fond hope that that last phrase would particularly enrage him.)

Some two months later, I was called in by Tatyana Shchekin-Krotova, the *raikom* secretary, who conversed with me politely and with a certain amount of curiosity. It was plain to see that for her the prosecutor was small fry, and I had noticed some chiefs sitting in her waiting room with the look of guilty schoolboys. Being experienced in bureaucratic work, however, she thought that I had other accounts to settle with Fetisov, since in and of itself, "a tongue-lashing doesn't cause pain."

I told her I was defending myself against exile. Further, I had concluded that the KGB could not function effectively either under conditions of lawfulness, since they did not know or understand the laws, or under conditions of disorder, since at the first show of resistance against them, they lose their heads. And I still believe that in the event of mass disturbances and revolts, the KGB will malfunction, even though preparations have been made to deal with such outbreaks. Thus, in 1968 orders were drawn up specifying that in the event of disturbances, all power in each raion was to pass to a troika consisting of the first secretary of the *raikom*, the chief of the *raiotdel** of the KGB, and the military commissar. In rural areas, kolkhoz chairmen were issued weapons, and telephones were installed in their homes.

"What did you do?" asked Shchekin-Krotova, "when you found out that your home had been bugged?" (I wouldn't rule out the possibility that even her own office was bugged.)

"What could I do? I climbed up on the grand piano and shouted obscenities at the crack in the ceiling, until I got tired of doing it."

Captain Denisov and Colonel Dobrer, disenchanted with their deputies, went to the post office. But it wasn't all that easy to get me fired. At the post office, where the supervisors more or less realized what was going on, they treated me well. For my part, I also worked well. Then in March 1969, when I felt that the danger had passed, I quit.

During those months my understanding of how the apparatus functioned had been broadened. I now realized that while the powers of the KGB are great, they are not without limits; that the KGB must observe certain formalities; and that if one understands how the bureaucratic machine works, one can throw a monkey wrench into the wheels.

On November 10, 1968, Aleksei Kosterin died.

On the day of the funeral the coffin was put in the first of two buses unexpectedly rented by the Writers' Union; Kosterin's family and close friends took their seats in it, while the rest of us got into the second bus. When we had gone about half the distance to our destination, Krasin discovered we were being taken in the wrong direction. Passengers starting shouting and pounding on the windows; and the driver, frightened, turned the vehicle around and headed for the crematorium. (The Writers' Union later refused to pay the bill for the buses.)

In the gloomy main room of the crematorium, Kosterin's coffin was set down to the right of the entrance, behind some columns. In the center of the room a kind of funeral service was being held; and the man pronouncing the eulogy, a colleague of the deceased, kept using the word "finished": at such-and-such a time he had finished school, then his military service, then his education at some institute, then his doctoral dissertation, and now he had finished his glorious life. At this point the speaker himself finished, and it was our turn.

The big room was full of people. They included not only Moscow dissidents and Kosterin's family but writers, Crimean Tatars, Chechens, and Ingushes who had managed to get there, along with various other persons who had come to offer their sympathy, some foreign correspondents, and of course a good many gebists. (There must have been at least ten gebists for every correspondent.) Some embarrassment arose when girls from our group, who were passing out black-and-red ribbons, by-passed the informers, so that the sheep were separated from the goats. After those who had received mourning ribbons had pinned them on, no one looked anyone else in the face but instead scrutinized the next person's coat lapel to see whether he or she was wearing a ribbon.

The organist played something by Bach. Then Petr Grigorenko mounted the rostrum. "Comrades!" he began, and at that very moment the microphone was switched off. But Grigorenko's voice, a real general's voice, carried well. He began with some warm personal remarks about Kosterin, saying how much the man had meant to him, how he had transformed Grigorenko himself from a mere rebel into a fighter. And then he went into the kind of struggle Kosterin had waged: "The destruction of the bureaucratic machine must begin first of all with a revolution in the way people think—in their consciousness. . . . The most important task today is an uncompromising struggle against totalitarianism concealed under the mask of 'socialist democracy.' And that is what he gave all his strength to."

Gusel said later that she was watching the organist and saw his facial expression change. At first, apparently, he simply wasn't listening. Then his face fell, his mouth gaped, and his expression was one of extreme bewilderment. No doubt he had never heard anything like Grigorenko's eulogy in all his career at the crematorium. For that matter, nothing like it had been heard by anyone for several decades: a political speech had been delivered, quite openly, in Moscow before a gathering of several hundred people.

The gebists were totally at a loss. Should they rush toward the rostrum, overturning the coffin, and drag off Grigorenko? Or should they listen to the end? The general's speech was interrupted twice by a voice saying (via the reactivated PA system): "Your time has expired!" but he went on talking, and ended with the words: "Don't sleep, Alyosha! Fight on, Alyosha Kosterin! We, your friends, will not lag behind you! Freedom will be ours! Democracy will be ours!"

Kosterin's death was a heavy blow for Grigorenko. The "Communist cell" of our Movement, which on the eve of August 21 came out in support of the Czechs, thinned out rapidly: Pavlenchuk and Kosterin died, and Pisarev fell seriously ill. Most of those in the Movement took a rather dim view of communism and Marxism; the only one with whom Grigorenko could find a common language in all matters was Ivan Yakhimovich, who was arrested in March 1969. He had become famous the year before because of a letter he wrote to Mikhail Suslov about the necessity of circulating information freely and discontinuing political trials. A few years earlier, *Komsomolskaya pravda* had published a long article about him as an outstanding kolkhoz chairman.

I had no doubts about the sincerity of his belief in communism. He would say things like: "Love for the people, the idea of equality, fidelity to the ideals of the Revolution: if we don't return to those ideals, a new revolution is inevitable."

"Do you know how that revolution will happen?" I once asked Yakhimovich. "By that time you'll already be in prison. Then one day, in your own Kraslavskiy Raion, people will go to the store for sausages and find out that there aren't any sausages. And even though there had been no sausages many times before, even though some people had even forgotten what sausages were like, on that particular day some cog in the machine will break, and it will go out of commission. The people will riot, and shout: 'Where's the sausages? There's nothing to eat!' They'll start to break windows, and they'll head for the *raikom*. The terrified officials will flee. And the mob, drunk on its success, will get the idea that it's not just sausages they should be demanding but freedom, equality, and brotherhood. They'll march on the prison shouting: 'Free Yakhimovich!' You'll be released, and from a balcony you'll make a speech to the people. Then they'll disperse to their homes, only to discover the next day that the stores are lacking not only sausages but bread besides."

In the course of the pretrial investigation of his case, Yakhimovich made revolutionary speeches to the investigator and even hoped to win him over. He was declared mentally incompetent and shortly thereafter he recanted. He was released and, like Alexander Dubcek, got a job as a forester.

The degree of resistance put up by a person after arrest and while incarcerated depends on his personal traits and not on his political views.

And even though Marxism tends to justify recantation as a tactical maneuver, I can name several Marxists who were not broken in camp. For that matter, a person who does break down can find justification in any philosophy. If he's a Christian, he can say: "Don't sin, and you won't have to repent. But if you don't repent, you won't be saved." And if he's a liberal humanist, he can say that in saving himself, he is saving a human individual, and that's the most important thing. In general, I have found that the more a person huffs and puffs in his eagerness to fight, the less reliable he is.

The school of thought represented by Yakhimovich, Grigorenko, and other opposition Marxists wanted to return to "true Leninism." It seems to me that this trend involved a paradox. Both in theory and in practice, bolshevism was broader than Leninism; and it was only gradually that Leninism gained the upper hand within bolshevism and that it developed logically into Stalinism. And although our "true Leninists" swore fealty to Lenin on every convenient or inconvenient occasion, what they were actually trying to do was to revive a non-Leninist trend in bolshevism.

One may regard bolshevism and Menshevism not only as political doctrines but as political temperaments in every social movement that sets out to change the existing system. From this viewpoint, the scientist Valery Chalidze and Pavel Litvinov, with their legalistic doctrinairism, and Roy and Zhores Medvedev, with their Marxist doctrinairism, are typical Mensheviks; while Alexander Solzhenitsyn and Petr Grigorenko are Bolsheviks. And I'm afraid I am more at home with the latter two, since for all my liberalism, I am not without my violent tendencies.

Grigorenko suggested organizing a committee in defense of Yakhimovich, which again raised the question of organization. But Krasin and Petr Yakir had serious doubts as to whether we should found a committee on the basis of one particular case. They said that if one were to be founded, it would be better to start with a Human Rights Committee; I agreed with them. We managed to convince the others to hold it down to a declaration in defense of Yakhimovich, something that Grigorenko long held against us.

Boris Zuckerman had been invited to the discussion so that he might explain the legal aspects of founding a committee. (Although physics was his specialty, he was—along with two other scientists, Valery Chalidze and Alexander Esenin-Volpin—one of the Movement's three experts in legal matters.) But the more he explained, the less understandable everything became. A quiet and stubborn type who spoke slowly and boringly, he had written and filed many intricate briefs against various government organizations. When it became the practice to deport dissidents, Chalidze, Volpin, and Zuckerman were among the first to go—the best testimony to the importance of their work.

As a Nominalist, I believe that for something to exist, it must be named. So I suggested we announce the establishment of the Soviet Democratic Movement (SDD); briefly set forth its basic ideas and methods; and propose that anyone who shared them could regard himself as a member of the Movement. I thought that if such a declaration were broadcast over the radio and widely distributed in the form of leaflets, it would enable many people who were currently isolated to identify themselves with the Movement and create a broad base for it. Krasin said rather evasively that it was something we should think about. But the reaction of the others—especially Grigorenko— was negative. The abbreviation "SDD" was suggestive of a political party; the text set forth ideological goals; and the majority wanted to remain a "human rights movement." But merely defending those people who were in prison because they had supported the rights of others imprisoned before them had made the Movement hermetic and severed it from the interests of the greater part of society.

The question of organization was settled in the summer of 1969, when fifteen persons founded the Initiative Group for the Defense of Human Rights in the USSR and sent a letter to the United Nations. When the group was formed, I was not in Moscow. It was essentially the creation of Yakir and Krasin. Litvinov told me later that several persons had been included in the group without their consent, but I heard no such complaint from any member. As I had predicted, they were not arrested right away, and the authorities did not set up a show trial; instead, they pretended to ignore the group's existence. But in time, all its fifteen members were either arrested or confined in psychiatric hospitals or expelled from the country. A psychological barrier, however, had been overcome; and after that, various groups and committees were established within the framework of the Movement.

In that cold spring of 1969 we often met with Anatole Shub of the *Washington Post*, who tried to convince me that the USSR would soon have to make some changes, however slight, in order to find a common language with the West. But Shub, as an American, had too much faith in common sense. The Soviet system is basically senseless. Like a paranoiac, it *behaves* logically; but since its premises are senseless, the same is true of the results.

Even if there were pragmatists "at the top" who wanted reforms, they certainly weren't setting the stage for them. Indeed, the domestic situation indicated just the opposite. It had seemed to Shub that this veering toward the West would make for more liberal domestic policies. He was rapidly disillusioned, however, and reached the conclusion that "Russia is turning the clock back." In 1972, when détente was in full swing, even I had hopes for liberalization, although after having been kicked in the rear for fifteen years, I should have known the Soviet regime better. Rather than adapt itself to the

West, it compelled the West to do the adapting. Since its own economic difficulties had been alleviated by means of favorable Western credits, Western technology, and Western grain, what need was there for reforms? The Soviet incursion into Czechoslovakia frightened the West and prompted it to move toward détente. If the USSR was indebted to the use of force for détente, why should it refrain from a further show of force? As the saying goes among criminals: "Beat up your own people so the others will be afraid."

I felt that because of the sluggishness of the Soviet leadership, the USSR would sooner or later undergo the same kind of crisis as the Russian Empire had in 1904–18, with China now playing the role of Japan and Germany. As early as 1967, I had written something to that effect, in cautious terms, to two Soviet newspapers and had even received replies—meaningless, but polite. And during a talk with Shub I set forth the idea to him, saying I was thinking about writing a book called *Will the USSR Survive Until 1980?* One can imagine my astonishment when Shub brought me a copy of the *International Herald Tribune* for March 31 with an article by him titled "Will the Soviet Union Survive Until 1980?" He had led off, in that article, by saying that a Russian friend of his intended to write such a book. After that, there was nothing I could do but sit down and start to write it.

"Why '1980'?" asked Vitaly Rubin. " '1984' would be better."

He of course had in mind George Orwell's novel, a book that I read only five years later, while in exile in Magadan. I was amazed by Orwell's perceptiveness and glad I had taken part of my title from such an outstanding book. But I had given the regime four more years of life only in the hope that I would get four less years when I was tried. (Under Article 70 of the Criminal Code, the maximum sentence is seven years, whereas under Article 190-1 it is three.)† I realized that I would be arrested for writing the book, but I figured that in any case I would be arrested sooner or later, so it was all the more urgent to get as much done as I could.

It was time for me to come out and say what I thought about the disgusting regime. And in particular, I wanted to say one simple but important thing: that for all its might and all its boasting, the Soviet empire was not going to last forever. I felt like the little boy in Hans Christian Andersen's fairy tale when he was about to shout: "But the Emperor doesn't *have* any clothes on!"

The people in the press section at the MID told Shub that his Russian friend was a bottle of vodka he had talked to, after emptying it. But the KGB

---

†Article 70 covers "anti-Soviet agitation and propaganda," which is considered an especially dangerous crime against the State; Article 190-1 has to do with "circulating libelous information known to be false, which defames the Soviet system," considered a crime against "the established order."—TRANS.

decided not to rifle Shub's wastebasket looking for the empty bottle: they would use other means to locate his Russian friend.

In April I got a phone call from a French correspondent who said he was writing a book about Moscow artists and that Boris Alekseyev of Novosti had suggested he get together with me. The reporter said he would like to buy some materials from me for his book. I replied that the two of us could sign a contract with his publisher.

"No, I think you should deal directly with me," he insisted with considerable fervor. "I'll give you lots and lots of dollars, and the whole thing will be between just the two of us."

I said that was precisely what I wanted to avoid. The next day he brought me his own materials on Russian painting. They turned out to be two or three photographs of sculptures by Ernst Neizvestny and, most important, snapshots of himself with Sophia Loren and Marcello Mastroianni, which he said proved he was a man *comme il faut*. Then, dropping the subject of artists, he showed me Shub's article, asking whether I had read it, whether I knew Shub, and who the "Russian friend" was. The reporter, needless to say, wanted to meet that friend so he could give him "lots and lots of dollars" for his future book. I said that to my deep regret, I did not know the identity of the person in question.

As he was leaving, he asked me to go outside with him because he wanted to show me his car. As we came up to it, he touched it here and there rather gracefully; and I had the feeling that someone was watching us and taking movies of us.

C H A P T E R 8

A "KGB Agent" vs. a KGB Agent

Gusel and I were eating dinner when suddenly we heard the tramping of many footsteps in the hall. I jumped up and locked the door. A moment later there was a loud knock, and someone pulled at the doorknob. "Open up! There's a summons for you from the house manager's office."

"Shove it under the door," I said.

There was some whispering outside in the hallway, and threats were shouted at me. Then they tugged at the doorknob some more. But apparently they didn't intend to break in, and after a while we could hear them leaving.

Gusel went out to have a look around, and I began burning papers I didn't want to fall into the hands of investigators. Then the doorbell rang several times, and again we could hear the tramping of feet.

"They say they've come from the prosecutor's office to make a search," said Gusel, who was still outside in the hallway.

"How many are there?"

"Lots of them—the hallway's full of them."

"Tell them to show you their search warrant," I said, stalling for time.

"They have one," Gusel replied.

At this, a half-dozen men came rushing into the room. "Did you have a fire in here?" one of them asked, smelling the burning paper and seeing charred scraps wafting about.

"Why didn't you break in the door?" I replied. "Have you lost the kind of self-confidence they had back in '37?"

It's hard to describe just how humiliating a search can be. I have undergone many of them: frisking and general searches, in prisons and in camps, and while riding from one place of confinement to another. But there is nothing so demeaning as a search of your own home. You feel that you have no home—that nothing is really yours.

The report of the search stated that it had been made "with a view to finding and seizing documents and valuables with a bearing on the case." The investigator explained that the "case" was that of Grigorenko. But he didn't say, when I asked him, whether Grigorenko had been arrested or not. Officially, the search was conducted by a senior investigator from the Moscow Prosecutor's Office. This was a man named Polyanov, about fifty years old, who was every inch the bureaucrat and seemed totally indifferent to the results of the search. The others did not give their names. One of them, a bit older than the rest, told Polyanov what to seize, and the latter would bring the item to him for inspection.

The report of the search gave the names and addresses of the two witnesses. In political cases—with only rare exceptions—these witnesses are also KGB agents. Victor Krasin once gave an amusing account of how, during a search of his home, the investigator and the witnesses pretended not to know each other. Then, when they went to search his mother's home and noticed a familiar car at an intersection, the witnesses shouted joyfully: "Ivan Ivanovich, our people are coming!" The investigator just shook his head sorrowfully, and said to Krasin: "You teach them over and over again, and they never understand anything!"

There was nothing in our home that had any bearing on Grigorenko's case. But they confiscated my manuscripts, books of mine that had been published abroad, typewriters, and checks from the Foreign Trade Bank that Gusel had received for her paintings. That's why the word "valuables" had been used in the report. So there was good reason why we had recently been visited by a connoisseur of art who had offered to buy "all the paintings."

What I most resented, however, was that they seized the manuscript, which I had just started working on, of *Will the Soviet Union Survive Until 1984?* Was that not perhaps the purpose of the search?

We had been making preparations to leave for the country the next day. Scattered over the floor were boxes of groats and sugar, cans of meat, bottles of sunflower-seed oil, etc. (We had laid in supplies for six months, since in the country you can't buy anything.) To all this was added the disorder of the search. Then some friends came to say good-bye to us, an MID official was sent to keep an eye on the foreigners, and more gebists arrived as reinforcements. As a result, the gebists, guests, other people, groats, flour, meat, books, manuscripts, and overturned pieces of furniture were so mixed up in our room that the total effect was quite bewildering. I took advantage of the confusion: at a moment when none of the gebists was watching me, I grabbed the portfolio containing my manuscript and quickly shoved it into a pile of papers they had already gone through and set aside as of no use to them. When the book was published, I said in my foreword that I felt pleasantly obliged to thank the KGB agents and the prosecutor's office for not having confiscated my manuscript. But my little joke at the expense of the KGB boomeranged: some people in the West took my expression of gratitude seriously.

The behavior of gebists during searches varies in accordance with their personal traits and the immediate situation. But it can be said for them that they try to pretend that nothing unusual is going on, as if to say: "We're doing a job together: you're being searched, and we're doing the searching." It's as though we were on opposite sides in a card game; and it's in our common interest to avoid quarreling and get the thing over with as quickly as possible. And in this case, things did go off without any harsh words, with one exception. When I was standing in the doorway, Burakov of the MID told me to come into the room. *"What?"* I exploded. *"You're* inviting *me* into my own room? This is my home. You're not from the KGB, and you can't order me around!"

Burakov made no reply. And I must say that to some extent I was venting on him my impotent rage at the humiliation of the search.

Gradually, I got the impression that I wouldn't be arrested. Toward ten o'clock the search was completed. Almost immediately afterward, Yakir and Krasin showed up, excited and talking loudly. All their noise affected Gusel nearly as badly as the search. "This is not right," she said to me quietly, "not at all right." General Grigorenko had been arrested that morning in Tashkent, where he had gone to the trial of the Crimean Tatars. Several searches had been carried out in Moscow at the same time, but more than likely his case was only a pretext for them.

The general was a disciplined member of the Movement, perhaps just because he was a general. When we brought him a public appeal for his signature, he would read it, frown, and say that he didn't like it; but since it had been decided that he should sign, he would of course sign. In the case of the Crimean Tatars, no matter how much we insisted that he shouldn't go, he was totally obdurate: the authorities had warned him that he would be arrested in Tashkent, and he refused to give in to blackmail.

Someone phoned him from Tashkent, saying a friend of his had urgently requested that he fly there, which he did. But it turned out that none of his friends had called. The day before he was to return to Moscow, he was arrested.

He was held in confinement until June 1974, first spending several years in prison, then several months in psychiatric hospitals. The next time I saw him was in the summer of 1975. His mind was still sound; but he spoke with difficulty, he could scarcely read, and could hardly write at all.

The search of our home had been carried out on May 7, and the next day we left for the country, where we spent seven months of happiness. I cannot believe that during that period the KGB forgot about us; but from time to time we did forget about the KGB. In Russia, a dacha is a form of escapism: you seem to have got far away not only from city life but from the Soviet regime.

In the country I noticed the same thing as in Siberia: drunkenness is the commonest form of escapism and apathy among the people, even though the standard of living has risen. Once when I went to a tractor driver's home, I saw a little pig taking a shit under a big television set. (Apparently it hadn't occurred to his owner to provide heat for the pigsty.) Near the pig was a hole in the floor, one he would fall into sooner or later.

"Why don't you repair the hole?" I asked.

"What for? I'll be moving to another village in a few years."

Then there was the stableboy from the kolkhoz who twice brought some brushwood for our stove. But the third time he showed up he was empty-handed. "Can you give me three rubles in advance?" he asked "I'll bring the wood tomorrow."

I gave him the three rubles. But Lord, what that got me into! Naturally, he never brought us anything more—which was no great loss, although we needed the wood. And of course he never returned the rubles—an even lesser loss. But he spread the word that I was a man who for nothing at all would give you three rubles. From that time on, our house was besieged by peasants asking, begging, and demanding that I give them three rubles. And lots of them muttered threats as they went away, because I wasn't handing out money any longer.

On sunny days I worked in the garden or orchard, and when it was raining I got back to my book. Its apocalyptic tone was due, at least in part, to my anticipation of being arrested, the disillusionment I felt when the Prague Spring was brought to an end, and discouragement because of the repressions. To some extent, I had conceived of the book as an answer to Sakharov, and it is interesting to read the two books in succession. The fact that Sakharov had been a part of the establishment, had not been persecuted, had been educated in a scientific milieu and worked in science, and believed in man's innate nobility was reflected in his essay to the same degree that social alienation, the experience of exile, poetic intuition, a skeptical attitude toward the social role of science, and an awareness of human imperfection were reflected in my book.

There was neither electricity nor a desk in the house, so I wrote by candlelight on a board set on two packing cases—like Marshal Lavout when he signed Pierre Bezukhov's sentence.[5] By the end of June I had completed the manuscript, and went to Moscow to give it to Henry Kamm of the *New York Times*.

When he saw the title, he was astounded. "What do you think you're doing? They'll most likely put you in the loony bin."

"They won't put me in," I said. "I'll stress the fact that I got—and want to get—as much money as possible from the book. And from the viewpoint of our authorities, a love of money is the best sign of common sense." The regime has managed to indoctrinate "the new man," whose entire understanding is on the level of his belly's needs.

As for those who knew nothing of my royalties, their first thought was: "Have you been examined by a psychiatrist?" It is quite possible, however, that the higher-ups regarded me as normal, because just at the time I was writing my book, they were in fact—if one can trust the memoirs of H. R. Haldeman—planning a nuclear strike against China.

I heard of the book's impending publication via Radio Liberty. A few days later I had a letter from the indefatigable French correspondent saying that he had read about my book in the *New York Times* and offering his help in connection with its publication. He was even ready to come to my country home. I did not answer his letter, but as soon as I was back in Moscow, he called me. And even after my arrest he came to see Gusel—but she did not let him in.

The Frenchman's letter was not the only indication that we had not been forgotten. Our neighbors in the country told us that the previous autumn some plainclothesmen had come to the village, given our house a careful look-over, and said of us: "You won't be seeing them anymore." And every evening, now, in the vicinity of our house, figures would make their appearance, and then scurry away at my approach. In October, two cars drove up, and my first thought, as always, was: They've come for me. But the people in the cars turned out to be the director of the *sovkhoz** (our kolkhoz had been transformed into a sovkhoz with one stroke of the pen), the chief of the Raion Agricultural Administration, and a third party who said he was his "brother." The director found it hard to look us straight in the eye, and the chief of the administration also seemed uncomfortable. The "brother," however, was plainly in high spirits. They stayed about five minutes—just time enough for a drink. As they were leaving, the "brother" said: "We'll be seeing you again, Andrei Alekseyevich." Two days later the director sent me several sheets of roofing tin as a kind of compensation for having brought "Big Brother" to my house.

That summer we had heard that the Soviet writer Anatoly Kuznetsov had vanished in London. Shortly thereafter, the whole story came out. He had gone to England in connection with a novel he was writing about Lenin; once there, he had requested political asylum. He wrote quite frankly about the reasons for his defection, about literary conformism, and even about how he had become a KGB agent. The tenor of Kuznetsov's articles was that he was given no other choice. But he *did* have a choice.

Coercion is possible wherever there is a readiness to submit to it; but if a person begins to resist, coercion gradually comes to an end. Naturally, the question as to the degree of resistance is by no means simple, human nature being imperfect. For example, when I replied to the investigator that I would tell him from whom I got the typewriter and papers if they hung me up by the feet and beat me, I realized there was a limit to my capacity for resistance. One thug used to tell how, at the police station, they had hung him up by the heels and beat him so he would identify his accomplices. "I would have told them long before that," he said. "I didn't give a damn. But I got mad at the guy who was beating me, so I kept mum." Once a person has reached a certain limit and passed through the crisis, he can find new strength in himself.

But where is the limit? For the majority of the intelligentsia, the desire to live without complications is sufficient grounds for serving the regime unquestioningly. Yet there is a line that every honorable person not only can but must draw: the line of nonparticipation. If you can't be against the system of coercion, at least don't be for it! I know of several cases when venerable Doctors of Science, who would never sign a letter in defense of Sakharov, nonetheless resorted to all kinds of subterfuges—even going off to harvest rotten potatoes—simply in order to avoid signing a letter condemning Sakharov.

Kuznetsov, it would seem, was looking for sympathy, and he probably resented the fact that many people in the West reacted coldly to his complaints. I wrote him: "The more calmly and objectively we set forth the situation, and the less dramatically we point out to the 'progressive Western public' its dishonesty toward us, the sooner we shall be able to destroy that false reputation which our regime has managed to make for itself abroad."

Some people interpreted my letter as a reproach to Kuznetsov, not for his philosophy of impotence but for his defection—the truth is I viewed his defection as the only act in which he showed strength of character. "If," I wrote him, "you as a writer could not work here, or publish your books in the form in which they were written, then it was not only your right but, in a sense, your duty as a writer to leave."

"They'll be put behind bars! Now they'll be put behind bars!" exclaimed Ilya Glazunov when he showed another artist the issue of *L'Express* with a summary of *Will the Soviet Union Survive Until 1984?* This meant that the enraged authorities would imprison not only me but just about anybody. It was the first reaction of the establishment. But even certain dissidents had bitter feelings about my book and resented my fame as "unmerited." One of them, who had recently emigrated, wrote to me: "Your little book has nothing unusual about it, except that for all enemies of the Soviet Union it has created the pleasant illusion that maybe the regime will in fact soon collapse. . . . Thanks to that pleasant illusion, your little book was publicized in the West, and later they acclaimed you as a celebrity."

I began to receive visits from strangers, sometimes from the provinces, who had read the book in samizdat or had heard excerpts on the radio. The visits showed me that samizdat had a wider scope than I had realized. I must say that I never took any of these uninvited guests to be agents; and I was not mistaken.

Also, some curious things happened. The doorbell rang, and there at the door was a biologist whom I had met both at Grigorenko's home and at Esenin-Volpin's. "Ah, so you're the one who lives here," he said, rather disenchanted. "I wanted to see Amalrik."

"I *am* Amalrik."

To which my guest replied, with an important air, "But I wanted to see the *historian* Amalrik."

For a long time, the staff of Radio Liberty was opposed to broadcasting excerpts from my book on the ground that it was "anti-Russian." As I heard it, the matter was settled when, during one of the discussions, a "Russian patriot" dashed in with a photograph of me, exclaiming: "I *told* you he was a Jew!" After that, the American management of the station came over to my side.

Certain Sovietologists seemed to be annoyed that a young nobody with no education or knowledge of foreign languages should suddenly and unexpectedly emerge, like an imp from a bottle, and begin to refute theories that had been nurtured over many years—to refute them by the very fact of his existence. Of course, there was the explanation that the whole thing could not be so simple; that it was some kind of clever plot. One version had it that I was a KGB agent; another, that the KGB had used me without my knowing it. An explanation was found for the strange prophecy of the USSR's collapse by 1984: the KGB wanted to dull the vigilance of the West. Since in any case the USSR would soon collapse, it wasn't worthwhile (so these people said) to spend money on defense. Then there was the story that my ties with the KGB would give the book much more value, since it raised doubts as to the Soviet leadership. It seems to me, however, that if my book actually had been the work of the KGB, its value would have been lessened. I wrote it as an honest analysis; if done by the KGB, it would have been an attempt at "disinformation." Even though I realize that such rumors were inevitable, I found it very annoying to be regarded as an agent of that system I was combatting— precisely because I *was* combatting it.

The suspicion that one is an informer or provocateur is a kind of rust eroding Soviet society. In fact, many provocateurs *do* work for the KGB. But mutual suspicion is the worst provocateur. The only way to combat it is to refrain from accusing anyone of being a KGB agent, merely on the ground that he *might* be one. A provocateur may be betrayed by his eagerness to urge you on to hazardous acts. Thus in 1968, a person who suggested hijacking an airplane was thought to be a provocateur. But on the other hand, that kind of eagerness may be evidence not of provocation but of decisiveness, or of a failure to understand the principle of nonviolent action. The venerable writer Vera Panova regarded Boris Pasternak as a dangerous provocateur because he had written *Doctor Zhivago* and thereby stirred up the authorities' wrath against the intelligentsia. And some members of the intelligentsia look upon the Democratic Movement as a provocation by the KGB—or at least a subconscious one. In the opinion of some Western observers, the samizdat phenomenon is a provocation by the KGB to mislead foreigners. I should note in passing that every "suspecter of provocation" is inclined to overrate the importance of the clan to which he himself belongs and against which the provocation is supposedly being set up.

Of course, intuition sometimes tells you unerringly that a particular person is an informer. In that connection, I recall an episode that occurred when I was twelve. At school I heard that we were living in the happiest and freest society in the world, and nothing I saw contradicted that. I still didn't know that an uncle of mine had been shot thirteen years before, or that my father had been sent to a prison camp nine years before. Nor did I know that a year later another uncle would be sent to a labor camp. One day, cheerful and happy, I was strolling along Tversky Boulevard; since at the time I was interested in world politics, I used my pocket money to buy a copy of *Britanskiy soyuznik* ("Our British Ally"). (A month later it would be closed down "at the request of the workers"; but that was something else I didn't know at the time.) Then I sat down on a bench to read about the war in Korea. The next thing I knew, a very affable citizen in a dark overcoat and a cap (they all wore them in those days) sat down beside me and started talking as if I were an adult—which was supposed to flatter me, I guess. He asked what I thought about the war in Korea and how come the reportage in the paper I was reading was completely different from what was being reported in the Soviet papers.

I was already well known for my tactlessness. At school I declared, to the teacher's horror, that I didn't want to be a Pioneer. But that day on Tversky Boulevard, I realized (by what instinct?) that despite the man's encouraging smile, I must not say anything to him. I realized it so clearly that after muttering something unintelligible, I got up and left.

Another incident may provide a rational explanation for the above one. When I was eight or nine, there was a shortage of space in the school buildings, so we went to classes in shifts. One evening when I was coming home from the late shift (it was already dark in Khlebnyi Lane, and there were occasional yellow patches of light on the snow from the street lamps swaying on their wires), I noticed a little knot of people on the corner, looking frightened but curious. Some policemen and others in black clothing were putting a man into a dark car—he looked like a workingman and was also wearing black. I remember that everybody waited a few minutes, until the car drove away. I had often seen policemen pick up drunks on the street. Sometimes it was very funny: the drunk would be shouting nonsense, the onlookers would laugh, and even the policemen would smile good-naturedly. But this time I felt that something horrible was happening, that the police were not picking up a drunk or that, even if he were drunk, they weren't picking him up for that reason. Perhaps because someone in that miserable-looking bunch of witnesses made a remark about it, or because I somehow realized what was going on, I understood that they were picking that man up because he had just said something. And I also realized that they would not let him go the next morning, after fining him, like a drunk. I had the heavy-hearted feeling at that moment that they were taking the man away forever.

Intuition, however, must also not be overrated. You may feel a dislike for a person not at all because he is an informer but because he has a disgusting way of blowing his nose or spitting, or because he perhaps doesn't believe in your ideas.

Intuition, however, is always infallible in identifying an outsider. An outsider does not share your values, he follows a different mode of behavior, and he is inclined to think he is better than you. No question about it: for any society, an outsider is a dangerous phenomenon. "Beware of the man you don't understand!" one Marxist said. And everyone does just that. It's more understandable (but also more unpleasant) if someone seems to be conde-scending to you. Even something so easily understandable as the hostility of the poor toward the rich is due, in my opinion, not so much to the former's envy of the latter's wealth as to the poor man's apprehension that the rich man will look upon him with contempt.

I was an outsider in the Movement, just as I was in school, at the university, and in prison camp. My tendency to mock at others just a bit—to make them look silly—was of course not direct evidence that I was a KGB agent. It did, however, fit well with the image of me as a cynic for whom nothing was sacred.

The foreign correspondents had simpler motives for suspecting me. They took it for granted that Russians were afraid to socialize with foreigners and that the KGB would send agents to contact them. From this it followed that a Russian who held no official position and yet was so manifestly willing to meet with them must—or could—be a KGB agent. There was nothing illog-ical in that view. But it was so exaggerated both by fear and by an overesti-mation of my own importance, that it kept them from realizing a simple fact; namely, that some Russians wanted to grow out of their fear and their isolation.

Finally, my behavior was a challenge to the Soviet "liberals"—to those whom the authorities had to whip up, while at the same time tightening the reins on the "conservatives," so that the team would pull evenly. Even more than the Western journalists and Sovietologists, the "liberals" regarded the Soviet system as built on fear; and the emergence of individuals who seemed disdainful of that fear struck them as personally insulting. The fact that a young man who did not belong to their circle had written a book like *Will the Soviet Union Survive Until 1984?* was a challenge to those who had accepted the idea that the regime would exist forever.

Little by little, one argument superseded all others: he still hasn't been arrested. For the West, it posed something of an analytic problem. But for Russia it was a moral one: if a person can write something like *that* and still remain at liberty, does it mean "we" have been keeping silent for nothing? For this, there could be only one explanation: he is a KGB agent!

C H A P T E R 9

Waiting

Another problem was that of getting my royalties. It turned out to be rather a complex one for me. Soviet citizens are forbidden to hold foreign currency. If they do receive some dollars or marks, they are required to exchange them for rubles.

In the Soviet Union, which has completely done away with social inequality, there are five kinds of domestic currency that I know about. First, ordinary rubles. Second, the blue-banded certificates of Vneshposyltorg.* Soviet citizens can get these in exchange for the currency of the Socialist countries. Third, the yellow-banded certificates, which can be obtained in exchange for currency from the developing countries. With these two kinds of certificates, you can purchase some things on sale in the foreign-currency stores, but not all of them. Fourth, the unbanded certificates, which are exchangeable for currency from the capitalist countries; i.e., for freely convertible currency. Fifth, the Series D notes from the USSR Foreign Trade Bank. Foreign diplomats and correspondents, along with Soviet diplomats, can have these notes in exchange for freely convertible currency. The fourth and fifth types of currency are the most valuable, since with them you can buy anything available in the foreign-exchange stores.

Monies received from abroad are classified in three categories: (1) inheritances, (2) gifts, and (3) royalties. I don't know what the tax on estates was, but on gifts it was 35 percent, and on royalties—if I remember correctly—30 percent. In October the Dutch magazine *Tirade* published the first chapter of *Involuntary Journey to Siberia,* and I asked that my small royalty payment be sent to me through the USSR Foreign Trade Bank. In a short time I had a letter from someone at the bank saying that they had received some money for me from abroad (the figure was not named) and that I could come and get it on such and such a day at such and such a time. But every time that I or Gusel went to the bank, the same conversation took place.

"Some money from abroad has come in for you. From whom were you expecting it?" (It was the same kind of question they ask you in prison, when a parcel or money order comes in for you.)

"But that's just what I wanted to find out from you."

"You should know who's sending you the money."

Next there would be a long argument, which would endure until the clerk finally said (or you yourself gave up): "Money is money, whoever sent it."

Then you'd be told the amount, and it would be suggested that you either take it in Soviet rubles or transfer it to Vneshposyltorg, with the bank getting 2 percent in either case. Considering the real value of the ordinary ruble and of the certificate, I'm quite sure no one took rubles. But in 1975 a new system was introduced in order to deprive Jews and dissidents of monetary aid from abroad. Anyone without special authorization from the USSR Ministry of Finance had to take rubles, with a tax of 30 percent.

The first time I uncomplainingly collected my royalties as a gift. Later it was explained that I had to submit a document confirming that the monies were in fact royalties. So I asked my American and French publishers to mail me letters confirming that the money they were sending represented an advance on a book.

"Royalties? Or a gift?" the girl in the teller's cage asked me curtly.

"Royalties!" I said proudly.

"Show me the statement." The girl took the letters and, looking at me as if I had gone out of my mind, she said: "We need a Soviet document."

"But it's not Soviet publishing houses that are sending the money."

"We need a letter from the Soviet institution through which your manuscript was sent abroad," she explained to me, as if to a child. Nonetheless, she referred the matter to her supervisor, and we went through the same conversation. With the chief of Vneshposyltorg, the conversation was just the same.

"If we don't have a statement, we can't pay out royalties. That's what our instructions say."

"May I see the instructions?"

"No. We can't show them to you. You say you yourself sent your manuscript abroad. What article or book was it? What was the title?"

"Will the Soviet Union Survive Until 1984?"

When these fateful words were uttered, we both gazed at each other long and attentively. The chief knew from everything in his experience that the author of a book with that kind of title—who, moreover, had had it published abroad—should by now have disappeared without a trace, rather than be boldly demanding money. Since the whole thing was monstrous and went far beyond the framework of his common sense, he sought some deeper meaning in it, something that did not run counter to his experience.

"Well, what did you write?" he finally asked.

"Show me your instructions, and I'll show you my book—tit for tat."

"Ha, ha! That's a good one. The fact is that we're essentially a commercial establishment, and certificates are the commodities we handle. We can sell them if we want to, or we can hang on to them."

"What that really means," I said, "is that you're an anarchist. 'I want things this way, I want them that way.' But Soviet law is the same for everyone." After pausing to see how he would react to my charge of anarchism, I added: "The only Soviet institution interested in my book is the KGB, and I seriously doubt whether they'd provide you with a report on it."

Evidently I had uttered the magic phrase, the same one he had been turning over and over in his mind. Like lots of other people, he no doubt concluded that if I was still at liberty, it was because of some secret operation of the KGB, and he must not take a false step. I also figured that if he had come to such a conclusion, he would rashly give me the money. And once it had been paid out, there'd be no getting it back.

In a pleasant tone of voice he said he would call the ministry. He made the call, then put down the phone with a helpless gesture, with every show of sympathy. "Unfortunately, without a report they won't authorize us to make any payment. I suggest you have a talk with the Copyright Administration at the Writers' Union."

The administration's offices were located on the first floor of the famous building in Lavrushinskiy Lane where Bulgakov's Margarita had broken the windows on her way to the ball being given by Satan. Here I went through the same routine again. First I talked with the section chief, a thin and reserved woman named Gorelik, then with the chief of the administration, a fat and good-natured gentleman by the name of Albanov.

After Albanov looked over my papers, he said pleasantly, "Well, the question of royalties is hard to deal with. I remember when Solzhenitsyn was sitting here in my office." And he pointed to the armchair in which, I suppose, Solzhenitsyn must have loomed like a monument to himself. "From the viewpoint of the USSR Constitution, you're absolutely right. But you're treading a difficult path."

As far as I could gather, neither he nor the administration wanted to follow me along that difficult path. At his suggestion, I corresponded with the Ministry of Trade and the Ministry of Finance—all in vain.

I wanted to make a symbolic gesture to honor the memory of my father, and I decided to send the royalties from his book, *In Search of Lost Civiliza-*

tions, to the city of Florence, which had suffered damage from a flood, before that civilization, too, vanished for good. The bureaucratic merry-go-round was set in motion. The MID sent me to the USSR State Bank; the State Bank forwarded my letter to the Foreign Trade Bank; and the Foreign Trade Bank passed it to the Foreign Exchange Administration of the USSR Ministry of Finance, from which I received the following reply: "It does not appear feasible to grant your request."

Written replies from Soviet institutions are laconic, with no superfluous salutations like "Dear Sir." Also, they contain an element of mystery, since nowhere do they explain exactly why a thing is "not feasible."

In this case, the mystery was rather transparent: the authorities did not want to exchange Soviet rubles for convertible currency. But I still went on writing letters, receiving identical replies from different individuals. For that matter, we were, so to speak, playing blindman's buff; nobody was even interested in whether the royalties were large, and I myself still don't know.

Finally, after I had written to the chairman of the Council of Ministers, I was asked to see Moshkin, chief of the Foreign Exchange Administration.

I asked him, "Why is a Soviet citizen not allowed to make a contribution to the noble cause of aiding Florence?"

"Because," the chief of the administration replied, "your money is more or less paper. Within this country we can assure its circulation, although it's difficult. But outside the country it's worth nothing." And even though our talk had been amicable, I went out of his office shouting: "No! I can't live this way anymore!"

"Yes, you can," Moshkin and his deputy shouted after me. "After all, we're living!"

A year later, a KGB agent who was trying to catch me out for dealing in paintings demanded that I draw up a report of my earnings. He said ironically: "Andrei Alekseyevich, you're earning twenty-six rubles a month at the post office. You and your wife live on that money, yet you have still managed to buy a cottage in the country. How can you explain something so amazing?"

"You can chalk it up to the power of our Soviet ruble," I told him, remembering my talk with the chief of the Foreign Exchange Administration. "Obviously, if I had got only mangy dollars instead of rubles, I wouldn't have seen hide nor hair of our cottage."

"You wouldn't talk like that to the American Internal Revenue Service," the gebist replied, plainly irritated. In general, these people have an inferiority complex vis-à-vis the U.S. In America, the bugging and wiretapping techniques are better; the police are paid more; and you can't get the IRS off your back so easily.

By late 1969, then, I was involved in two disputes with the Soviet authorities about money. First, I wanted to send my own money abroad, and they wouldn't permit it. Second, I wanted to receive the money sent me from abroad, and they wouldn't permit that either. I decided I could at least berate them publicly, so I sent letters to several European and American newspapers, insisting on my right to publish without prior censorship and to receive royalties. I wanted, I said, "publicly to shame the Soviet government for its stinginess and pettiness. Stalin would have had me shot for publishing my books abroad, but the best his pathetic successors can do is to try to get part of my money. This merely confirms the opinion I expressed in *Will the Soviet Union Survive Until 1984?*—that the present regime is degraded and enfeebled."

There were some people who didn't believe in the authenticity of my letter—especially those who knew very well that Stalin would in fact have had me shot and were amazed that Brezhnev had not yet done so. But that letter, which may well have seemed an act of desperate boldness, was more like the result of a calculated risk.

My basic assumption was that since my status in the Soviet hierarchy was the lowly one of a "dropout," the authorities, being compelled to struggle with me openly—openly, because my book had already been published and caught the attention of the foreign press—the authorities would according to their own logic have to belittle me. They had to show that a dissident of my low standing aroused nothing more than contempt in them. Naturally, there was no hope that they would ignore me. But there *was* something I *could* hope for: that they would not charge me under Article 70, which carries a penalty of up to seven years' incarceration and five years' internal exile, but under Article 190-1, which carries a penalty of no more than three years. I figured that the more sharply and insultingly I attacked the authorities, the more they would want to stress my insignificance, and the greater the chance that I would be indicted under Article 190-1. ("The man is so no-account, it's a shame even to bring that light charge against him.") My reckoning proved to be correct, but only in part.

If my case were unknown, the authorities would not have hesitated to give me at least seven years. I therefore wanted, especially in my letter about the royalties, to keep my name in the public eye so that they could not take advantage of any lull. My general policy was to meet danger head on, not to flee from it. Also, I was feeling "up." The unexpected success of the book, and the euphoria I experienced at the freedom to say and write whatever I was thinking, seemed to lift me right off the ground.

As for the money due me, I did not want to accept it as a gift, so I sent it back to the foreign publishers, a gesture gratifying to my proud spirit. But Gusel and I, our flesh being weak, needed something to eat every day, and later I asked the publishers to send the money back in Gusel's name as a "gift." Between the two of us, we decided to regard it as a gift from husband to wife.

In the midst of the battle for the money, I learned of the arrest of Victor Krasin. He had been hiding, but one day when he went to see his sister, the police showed up—literally minutes after he arrived there—broke in the door, and dragged him out of the bathroom. Within five days he had been sentenced to five years of internal exile as a "person refusing to perform socially valuable labor." (It was the same kind of sentence they gave me in 1965 and tried again to give me in 1968.) The prosecutor and the judge also declared that he had neglected his family. In particular, he was charged with, and convicted of, having failed to visit his son on the latter's birthday. The KGB was angry that Krasin had not shown up for his son's birthday because they had counted on arresting him that day: they staked out the house, but all in vain. And now they were reminding him (while at the same time showing their fondness for children): If you don't visit your son on his birthday, you get time behind bars.

The day after Krasin's trial, I received a telephone call that Natalya Gorbanevskaya's home was being searched. I went there immediately, since we always tried, whenever we managed to learn about a search, not to leave our comrades alone with the searchers. I didn't know the person who opened the door for me; but he was plainly so glad to see me and invite me in that I knew for sure a search was in progress.

One of my pockets was bulging as if stuffed full of papers, and the gebists were already rubbing their hands at the sight of a new prospective victim. But the paper in my pocket was nothing more than the wrapping for sandwiches Gusel had fixed, thinking I might get hungry before the search was concluded. For my part, I had only wanted to stir up the wrath of the gebists; and they were in fact furious that anyone should show up at a search and bring along his lunch, as if going to a picnic.

When I first entered the room, my attention was caught by three men. One of them, short and fat with sharp features, was busying himself at a desk with a pile of documents on it. The second was standing in the middle of the room and gesturing like a hospitable host. The third was sitting on the bed, an expression of philosophical melancholy on his face. There were also some young men "on standby," but I paid no attention to them.

"You," I said to the fat man sitting at the desk, "are from the prosecutor's office." And to the man in the middle of the room I said: "And you are from the KGB." Then I turned to the third man: "And you . . ." But I couldn't imagine where he was from. There was nothing of the policeman about him, so I couldn't figure out who he was.

As it turned out, the first man, whose name was Shilov, *was* in fact a senior investigator from the prosecutor's office; and the second, Sidorov, *was* from the KGB. (Although he was really running the show, he identified himself as a police captain, presumably sent to protect Shilov against any attack by Natalya Gorbanevskaya.) But the third man had no connection with the KGB whatsoever: he was the philosopher Boris Shragin, who had come there with the same purpose as I had.

While continuing with the search, Shilov began discoursing on how life was getting better from one day to the next (slight consolation for Natalya, whom they were preparing to incarcerate for several years). I asked him if that meant that things were better now than they were twenty years ago.

"Of course!" he exclaimed.

"So things were worse under Stalin?"

Shilov fell silent. And Sidorov, who had been going through papers and books, left off for a moment and drew himself erect. For the past three years a current of Stalinism had wafted down from "above," and I suspect it was felt more strongly in "the organs" than anywhere else. For that matter, if Shilov had said that things were better under Stalin, I had another question ready for him: So you don't like Brezhnev? But after thinking it over a long time, he replied: "Maybe things are a little better now." And then they ejected me from the apartment.

I didn't see Natalya Gorbanevskaya until six years later, in Moscow. And it wasn't until seven years later that I again saw Shragin, in New York. But unfortunately I was to meet up with Shilov and Sidorov again within two months. (As I was leaving, Shilov told me I could have been a good investigator, which I suppose was a great compliment.)

After *Will the Soviet Union Survive Until 1984?* was published, I gave my first interviews to American correspondents: to James Clarity of the *New York Times* and William Cole of CBS. Clarity spoke Russian correctly, but very slowly. Cole was rather dry, fidgety, and nervous: life in Russia was not easy for him, because he took everything too much to heart. And he didn't speak Russian.

We established good relations with both of them and were invited to their homes on several occasions. American hospitality (and Western hospitality in general) is a kind of smoothly functioning mechanism with no touch of Russian improvisation. After the cocktails came dinner—but without vodka, which is also very non-Russian. The dinners served by Americans are sometimes pretty good, but never really first-rate. I recall that once we had pumpkin pie. Russians ate pumpkins only in wartime; and in my mind, pumpkin porridge has always been associated with the most desperate poverty and hunger. I remember how greedily, after that pumpkin pie, I consumed American boiled ham, an unforgettable symbol of lend-lease.

I regarded the interview with William Cole as very important, since it was the first TV interview with a dissident, and millions of people would be able to see and hear me. It was a terrible blow when I learned that the videotape had been confiscated at Sheremetovo Airport. (It was shown at my trial as one of the most damning pieces of evidence.) I thought that Cole would be mortally frightened by all this, but he suggested that we repeat the interview. I agreed, with the proviso that he not try to get the videotape out of the country himself. This time I invited Petr Yakir to take part, and he invited Bukovsky; and a taped talk by Ginzburg was smuggled out of his prison camp.

Yakir and I hoped that the first interview from Russia would be a sensation. But I was told later that CBS was reluctant to broadcast it at all, because we talked in Russian, and the American TV networks don't want interviews in foreign languages, figuring that if the viewer doesn't hear people talking directly in English, he will get bored. In this way, of course, the Americans lose the opportunity to acquire firsthand information about the rest of the world.

After this incident I realized why many people don't like Americans. I used to think that the chief reason for this dislike of Americans was envy of their wealth and, for Europeans, the fact that their dependence on the U.S. in matters of defense was humiliating. But there is a much more profound reason: the Americans' confidence, on a subconscious level, that they can get along without the rest of the world. The average American—and in America everything is designed to please the "average American"—simply fails to realize (not in his mind, of course, but in his heart) that there are other worlds besides America. Hence he is willing to accept only what fits into the framework of his culture. The result is not contempt for a foreign language—there is no question of contempt—but a lack of interest. True, Americans travel all over Europe with cameras hung around their necks, but this kind of interest is like a curiosity about the ruins of the palace at Knossos. It is not that lively feeling of interdependence that makes peoples and cultures pleasurable to one another.

After the arrests of Litvinov, Grigorenko, and Krasin, Petr Yakir remained the most prominent and active member of the Movement. In the winter of 1969–70 I was often a guest at his home. He had no "Wednesdays" or "Thursdays" for receiving visitors, because for him the entire week was one big "Thursday." He lived in a two-room apartment with his mother and his wife, whom he had met in prison camp. Between them they had spent more than a half-century in confinement; and the effect of this was especially noticeable in the case of Yakir's wife, whom I never once saw in gay spirits.

Yakir himself made quite the opposite impression: he was a merry man. What with his curly black hair and ample belly, Gusel called him "Bacchus."

He would sit there, glass of vodka in hand, surrounded by women, at a table spread with food and, belly protruding from his unbuttoned shirt, would shout good-naturedly at his provincial relatives crowded together at the other end of the table: "Quiet, you Jews!" Thanks to his name, he had entree into establishment circles, but he preferred people in the Movement, people with whom he could relax.† Some of his visitors were rather odd. I recall in particular one man who, on the eve of the centennial of Lenin's birth, walked all the way from Moscow to Vladimir, where he asked the warden of the prison to show him the cell once occupied by Lenin's teacher, Fedoseyev.

Yakir was a typical hothead: energetic, lacking in depth, easily excitable but liable to become dispirited at the first real tribulation. His excitability required constant "fixes," including the consumption of huge quantities of vodka. A certain biologist with a worldwide reputation had decided to join in the struggle for human rights. As a conscientious scientist, to study the tactics of the struggle, he went to see Yakir as a student might visit a professor. Yakir, when he received his visitor, was drunk and wearing only his shorts; and in lieu of the booklet *What Is to Be Done?*[6] he proffered him a glass of vodka. The bewildered scientist drank the vodka, had a bite to eat, listened to Yakir's mumbled discourse—and never came to see him again.

Yakir's dissolute reputation was linked to the Movement as a whole, to the joy (*and* through the efforts) of those who disliked the Movement because it was a challenge to their bad consciences—of those who figured that playing up to the authorities would soften them and lead to "liberalization," whereas resistance would anger them and lead to Stalinism.

Unfortunately, Yakir's and Krasin's table talk with foreign correspondents involved such questions as: "Who, in your opinion, is taking part in the struggle?" and such answers as: "Only us." In that "us" they also included those Russians who happened to be at the table with them at the time. Although not the chief cause of it, this kind of thing helped to foster the theory that there really wasn't any Movement—just a few desperate intellectuals who could be disregarded. In the case of Yakir and Krasin themselves, this "only us" led to a theory of total permissiveness: everything was permitted to the person who risked his life in the struggle while the others vegetated in a state of cowardice.

I defended Yakir up until the last day. While I didn't approve of his drunkenness, his life-style, or his way of handling things, I bore in mind that he was one of the first openly to oppose the system and that he had waged a struggle against it (howbeit in his own, Yakirian way), whereas many of his

---

†Yakir is the son of General Iona Yakir, a hero of the Russian Civil War who was executed in Stalin's purge of top-ranking officers in 1937.—TRANS.

critics saw in his drunkenness a justification for their own "soberness." But much in Yakir that was bad was superficial; I thought that when put to such a severe test as arrest, his best traits would emerge. For me, the fact that he had served time in prison camps was important. (Since I had not yet been in camp myself, there was a lot that I didn't understand.) But I did not deserve the description of my character that Yakir gave to the KGB under interrogation, when he said I was "calculating, reserved, and arrogant."

As in my case, Muscovites were wondering why Yakir had not yet been arrested. There's something amazing about a country where society decides whom the political police should arrest, and when; and then gets nervous if the police are dilatory. It's a kind of social pressure on the KGB. On stage, a tragic struggle was being waged between the loners and the system. In the wings, a chorus was singing: They are noble, but naïve. Why beat your head against the wall? Why tease the cat?

The first hypothesis put forward was that if Yakir himself was not a KGB agent, then they were using his home as a trap. It was assumed that the authorities were giving consideration to Yakir's mother, the widow of General Yakir. Khrushchev had known Iona Yakir very well and had tried to do something for his family. In my opinion, the authorities postponed Yakir's arrest partly because they feared Khrushchev's reaction. They were afraid that there would be one more, extremely prominent, dissident; that the further his authority receded into the past, the more liberal Khrushchev would become. According to Yakir, Khrushchev was attracted by Populist ideas, and Stalin once jokingly called him a *Narodnik* (Populist)—yet one more demonstration of "Stalin's acuteness of insight." Before I was arrested, Yakir and I had made arrangements to go together to visit Khrushchev. I would have been very interested to learn whether he had read *Will the Soviet Union Survive Until 1984?*

Yakir also called himself a *Narodnik*, although he had no general or clear conception of anything much: he was quite simply animated by a revulsion against Stalinism. He had no definite tactics and did everything impulsively. I recall telling him that at the time no open appeals would provoke any response, that it was more important to devote all our efforts to our *Chronicle of Current Events* and to samizdat as a whole. He willingly agreed.

On February 21, our room was searched again, with Shilov and Sidorov once more in on the act. (Sidorov took offense at the fact that I didn't recognize him.)

The search was not a thorough one. They didn't even look at the books on the shelves; and all they took was my typewriter and a few foreign magazines with excerpts from my book. Sidorov spread out the magazines and the checks from the Foreign Trade Bank on my desk and took movies of them. They didn't photograph either Gusel or me, but they were very energetic when it came to checking out the friends who came to our room during the search.

A few days before, we had invited the *New York Times* correspondent, Bernard Gwertzman, and his wife to dinner that evening. (Since the KGB had a tap on our telephone, I suspect they knew the Gwertzmans would be there and decided to film the event as conclusive evidence of our contacts with foreigners.) Gwertzman was really frightened. The investigator asked who he was, and I replied that he was a friend who had come to dinner. In using the word "friend," I had no intention of foisting my friendship on Gwertzman: I only wanted to make it plain that he had not come on business but as a guest. He seemed afraid of getting a reputation as a friend of a dangerous dissident, so he said "friend" was not the right word. It would be better, he said, to say simply "a person." But the incident caused no bad consequences for him, and for a journalist to work in Russia without experiencing a search is like visiting Spain without witnessing a bullfight.

(The next day Gwertzman sent James Clarity to our place on a reconnaissance mission. Clarity had dinner with us, showing not the slightest sign of nervousness, and afterward he went outside with Gusel to throw snowballs. But none of this allayed Gwertzman's anxiety; and he was unwilling to print one line in his newspaper about the search.)

Hardly had Gwertzman left the premises when our drunken neighbor, Olya, whose son had just returned home after serving time for rape, appeared. "Where are the KGB men?" she shouted from the doorway. "Arrest my son! Put him in prison! He hit his own mother!"

"Disorderly conduct! You have to call the police," said the gebists, who only a short time before had assured me they were policemen and not from the KGB. Of course, what really bothered them was not that Olya's son had hit her, but that the smooth course of the search had been disturbed in such a scandalous manner.

Just as I was showing Olya out of the room, the lights went out because of a short in the wiring. The gebists, however, figured I had rigged up a special device for turning off the lights and was taking advantage of the darkness to shift something from one hiding place to another. By the end of the search I had driven Shilov up the wall—so much so that he refused to leave a copy of the search report with me.

It was at this time that I tried to take the counteroffensive. I began by demanding the return of the possessions that had been seized from me in May. I received replies with different (illegible) signatures but the same content: "Your complaint has been forwarded to the Moscow Prosecutor's Office with the *suggestion* that you be informed of the decision taken." But the

Moscow Prosecutor's Office let six months go by without sending me an answer. From time to time the district inspector would bring me a summons to the precinct station, but I never responded. I was holding in reserve an affidavit stating that I was working as a reader for a blind man, but intended to use it only in case I got a final warning. (When I was arrested, the blind man suddenly regained his sight—at least so far as I was concerned—for the KGB can work miracles.) I realized that while they were keeping hands off me, everything depended on the turn things would take "above."

In the spring of 1970, the crisis in the government became evident even to an outside observer, and there were rumors that Brezhnev would soon be overthrown. But he prevailed, and it meant that a definite policy had been decided on. I believed that my arrest was imminent. I have never understood the notion that Brezhnev is a "liberal," or what meaning his admirers attach to that word. After each crisis resulting in more power for Brezhnev, I was arrested. I was taken in after he became First Secretary in late 1964, after he prevailed in the crisis of 1970, and after he triumphed over his opponents in 1972–73 in the matter of détente. Of course, there were many others involved besides me; it's just that each of my arrests was a symptom of increased repression. Likewise, the constitutional crisis of 1977 ended in a victory for Brezhnev and the arrest of members of the Helsinki Watch Group.

It was expected that the arrests would start after the celebration of two anniversaries: that of Lenin's centenary, in late April, and the twenty-fifth anniversary of the victory over Germany, in early May. As for me, I noticed that I was now being tailed. Friends advised me to disappear for a while, and one even conceived the romantic scheme of hiding out in the caves of Dagestan. But I decided to stick to my policy: to see to it that everything I did was legal, so that I had no reason to hide from anyone.

In late April we went for a week to Leningrad, Tallin, and Riga, because I wanted to show Gusel those beautiful cities before I was arrested. Leningrad, which I used to visit quite often, has always made a strange impression on me: the decor of the imperial capital has never had any affinity with everyday life in a provincial Soviet town; and I suspect that Leningraders themselves have been aware of this great gap. Also, in Leningrad one feels particularly oppressed by that gloominess and lack of freedom that generally characterizes Soviet society. In the spring of 1968 in Moscow, one Leningrader said to me: "I feel as if I were in a free city." As I was walking down Nevsky Prospekt in Leningrad, I constantly had the feeling that the place was a mirage; that if I turned off the boulevard, the city would cease to exist right then and there, would dissolve in the fog, in the vapors from the swamps—and there would be only moss, lichen, and an endless expanse of marshland with no trees.

Totally different is the impression one gets from Tallin, whose "Old

City" strikes me as one of the most beautiful in the world. Tallin is a genuine capital: the small capital of a small country, but a city that is plainly what it gives itself out to be. In the center of Tallin on a curb, we saw a cat tranquilly eating a fish that had been wrapped in paper—something impossible in Russia, where a citizen would promptly have given the cat a kick. The Estonians are reserved and polite. During the time we spent there we saw only two drunks—both Russian, alas! In between obscenities, each was assuring the other of how much he respected him.

We shared our compartment on the trip from Leningrad to Tallin with two young men. We talked about Yudenich, the White Russian general, who in 1919 launched an attack on Petrograd from Tallin—one that proved to be unsuccessful. For that reason, one of the young men called him a "failure." I said it was hardly accurate to label as a failure a man who, in any case, had become a general; and they both agreed with me. Plainly, they were much concerned with the matter of rank.

In mid-May we went to our cottage in Akulovo. The day we got there I saw some "summer people" strolling through the village and noticed that they were constantly running their hands through their hair in a professional gesture that was very familiar to me. I was still hoping, though, that they were only checking to see whether I was there. I knew my arrest was inevitable; yet in some strange way I felt safer in our country cabin than in Moscow. I rationalized that feeling with the saying, "Out of sight, out of mind." In other words, since I wasn't making myself a nuisance to the KGB in Moscow, they had forgotten about me.

Two of our friends spent a week with us; and on May 20, I drove them to the station. Later, in prison, I recalled that trip: the horse trotting slowly along, the squeaking of the cart's wheels, the coppices, the fields, and the little red brick houses seeming to have grown up out of the earth.

TOWARD THE PLACE FROM WHICH NO ONE RETURNS (1970–73)

C H A P T E R   1 0

Arrest

On the morning of May 21, when I was working in the garden, the sovkhoz engineer's van drove up and stopped behind the house next to ours, where an old man lived alone. I wondered briefly why the engineer wanted to see him, then forgot about it. But no sooner had we sat down for coffee than Gusel, looking out the window, saw two people walking toward our house: the old man and another fellow with the face of a gebist.

When I met them at the door, the old man didn't say a word. His manner was uncertain, and he stood there shuffling his feet. But the other one asked, in the most friendly way, where we were going to vote—there or in the city—since the elections were imminent.

We had never taken part in that farce. But in order to avoid any needless explanations, I said we were going to vote in Moscow, so there was nothing for him to be concerned about. Instead of leaving, however, he loitered in the hallway and asked the same question again.

"So you're an '*agitator*'?"* I asked, nudging him toward the door.

"Yes, in one way I am, but in general I'm not."

"Then just who are you?" At that moment everything literally went dark before my eyes: a crowd of men in black suits suddenly dashed from the street onto the terrace, jostling one another like people in a subway at the rush hour.

One of them, a robust fellow with features that were roughhewn but not mean-looking, shouted at me almost joyfully: "We've come to make a search, Andrei Alekseyevich—on orders from the Sverdlovsk Prosecutor's Office." And as I stared in amazement, he added: "Your writings have shown up even here—in Sverdlovsk."

I wanted to finish drinking my coffee, and they let me do so, watching me intently and enviously.

"You may despise us," one of them said, "but you could at least ask us to sit down."

"You're the masters here," I said. "You can sit down wherever you want to."

They demanded that I go to Moscow, saying that they would search our house in the presence of my wife. I told them my wife had no connection with any of this, and they could go ahead and make the search in my presence.

We argued for a few minutes, and then the investigator from Sverdlovsk said, "In that case, we'll have a different kind of talk." And he produced a warrant for my arrest. Although I had been expecting to be arrested, the realization that the process was now irreversible hit me very hard. It made me feel better, however, to note that the warrant was signed by an investigator from the prosecutor's office and not by the KGB, which meant Article 190-1 and a sentence of three years.

When I had examined the warrant, I said: "This has nothing to do with me. It is made out for Andrei Alekseyevich Amalrik, born in 1939. Of course my last name is Amalrik too; and my first name and patronymic are the same. But I was born in 1938." (They had been pursuing me for years and still hadn't managed to get my birthdate right!) This rather upset the investigator, who had to return to the prosecutor's office while the gebists made the search.

I refused to leave before the search, so they grabbed hold of the armchair I was sitting in and carried me like a Chinese emperor. At the doorway, however, they dumped me disrespectfully into the hall, since the chair was too wide to get through the door. In the hallway, a regular brawl began. Two or three stalwart men could have dragged me out of the house with ease. But there were too many of them; and each one, eager to make a show of zeal, rushed forward to grab me, getting in the way of the others. In this way, a huge ball of human bodies took shape, with me at its center, floundering helplessly. This ball finally rolled out into the street, where several Volgas were waiting. When they started shoving me into one of the cars, my old friend Captain Sidorov displayed unusual vigor, huffing and puffing and swearing obscenely.

Once I was inside, he climbed in after me and asked: "Well, have you calmed down now?"

"Oh, yes," I replied. And I was in fact calm, since I had merely wanted to put up token resistance.

Gusel came to the car and, weeping, handed me a pair of warm socks. (Why had she thought of socks at that moment?) We kissed, not knowing when we would see each other again; then Sidorov ordered the driver to get going.

The gebists had come in four or five cars to the sovkhoz administration building, where they had boarded the engineer's van so they would not attract my attention when approaching our place. Then they had sent the phony agitator on ahead, fearing that if I saw a gang of men coming through the village, I would manage to hide or (once again) burn some papers. And I must admit that their plan proved successful.

The investigator, Ivan Kirinkin, sat in the front seat next to the driver. In the back, I had Sidorov on one side of me and, on the other, a young gebist. About halfway to Moscow he began to nod, and I gave Sidorov a look as if to say: "The young fellow is letting you down."

When Sidorov gently reproached him, he sighed: "I can't help it. On my schedule, I'm used to sleeping at this time of day." (And indeed, he had the look of an athlete who kept himself in shape.)

I didn't speak a word, although Kirinkin tried several times to start up a conversation. As for Sidorov, the success of the operation had put him in a lyrical mood; every now and then, as we were going along a side road, he would exclaim, "I'd sure like a drink of fresh milk from the village."

But he wasn't in charge, so he didn't get his drink of milk. We did, however, stop at a shabby restaurant upon getting a signal from the second car in the procession: it was time for the gebists to eat, according to their schedule. They invited me too, but I refused.

During the stopover, a man I recognized from trials I had attended passed by me once or twice. It wasn't difficult to remember him, because in one way he resembled a toad covered with warts and in another way he looked rather like Henry Kissinger. He was in charge of the whole operation; but, like a great strategist, he did not take part in the actual fighting.

When we stopped in front of my home on Vakhtangov Street, the athletic gebist got my overcoat out of the trunk and hurried after me up the stairs. It was plain that he was a man with a sense of dignity, who felt humiliated at having to carry the coat of somebody who had been arrested. Realizing how sensitive his feelings were, I hastened my steps.

As it turned out, we were late: the specially designated "search witnesses" had left. Since by law they could not begin the search until the witnesses were present, I insisted that they wait in the communal kitchen. There was a parcel on our shelf in the kitchen, but I hoped that area would not be searched. The gebists finally called in two young passersby with no involvement in the proceedings. Both were very timid and took no part in what went on. One of them, however, when a mattress was being searched, exclaimed in admiration: "That's a fine mattress!"

"Everything Andrei Alekseyevich has is fine," Sidorov said venomously. "It's all foreign stuff."

"Do you really mean everything foreign is fine?" I asked. "It's our Soviet stuff that is fine." At this, Sidorov fell silent.

Apparently, it was felt that six men were not enough to deal with me, because a seventh soon arrived. He apologized for being late and started shaking hands with everybody. He held out his hand to me too, evidently taking me to be one of the investigators.

"You've made a mistake," I said with a laugh, not taking his hand.

The search didn't last long, but it was a distressing experience for me. On the day we left for the country, I had been expecting a courier from Karel van het Reve. The courier never showed up, but other people did: our driver, and several acquaintances. With them there, I couldn't hide my manuscripts securely, so I had left everything where it was, pending my return to Moscow. And now that return had taken place.

I had decided that I would not voluntarily leave the apartment house until Gusel came, but by the time the search was over, she had arrived. We embraced by way of farewell and didn't see each other until eight months later.

As they were taking me through the hallway, a woman who lived in our communal apartment rushed up to us from the kitchen shouting: "Here is a parcel for you!" The gebists eagerly seized the parcel from the U.S. and opened it. It was an edition of the New Testament in Russian. After hesitating for a moment, Sidorov said magnanimously, "Leave it!"

The warrant for my arrest was originally dated May 15, which confirmed rumors that the arrests were scheduled to begin that day. Then it was redated May 19, and finally May 20. It may be that the authorities had been waiting until our friends left our place in the country: if they had taken something away with them, they could then be charged in the same case.

Among the documents seized was a photocopy of a *Pravda* article about Karel. And they also confiscated a typewritten copy of a chapter from Marx's *The History of Secret Diplomacy*. As Sidorov explained it: "Marx, too, carelessly wrote a lot of stuff like that—stuff that makes you liable under Article 70."

I was taken, not to Lefortovo, but to Butyrki, a prison of lower rank, just as Article 190-1 ranks below Article 70. So my plans had worked out, as it were. The tension I had felt during the waiting period, my arrest, and the searches left me; I even began to feel cheerful. Sidorov and Kirinkin were glad to see me in a good mood.

"Andrei Alekseyevich is an intelligent man," Sidorov would say. "He won't be behind bars for long—a year at the most."

My intelligence troubled him. "You, now—you're an intelligent man.

But your wife is . . ." I thought he was going to say "stupid," but he went on: ". . . a naïve person. Now she'll start rushing around seeing foreigners and make trouble for herself."

As we were standing in the prison yard, Sidorov said to me: "It's because of capitalist encirclement that people have to be put behind bars, Andrei Alekseyevich."

I shrugged. "People will always be put in prison."

"But not people like you!" he objected with considerable feeling. In effect, he was giving me to understand that I was made for better things than vegetating in prison.

"Stand right where you are, and keep your hands behind you!" shouted the officer on duty. And the iron door clanged shut behind me.

Just how a person feels when he gets put into prison is something that has often been described—most strikingly, I should say, in Solzhenitsyn's *The First Circle*. I myself tried to depict that experience, at this very prison, in *Involuntary Journey to Siberia*. And now, five years later, I was again being taken into that same waiting room at Butyrki Prison, with the same sign over the door leading to freedom: To Freedom, with a Clear Conscience! And once again I was put through the routine: registration, photograph, finger-prints, relieving of my valuables, shaving my head, a bath, prison things issued. Then I was taken to my cell—a procedure that for me had lost the charm of novelty.

I was registered by an elderly top sergeant seated behind a wooden partition with a little window in it. From time to time, as he wrote down my answers to his questions, he would look at me through the window. He kept an air of great solemnity throughout these proceedings.

Meanwhile, two woman employees behind the partition and invisible to me, were commenting on my answers. When I was asked what kind of work my wife did and replied that she didn't work, one of the women exclaimed in amazement: "Just look at him! His wife doesn't work."

"Why should she work?" said the other. "You get only kopecks for working, but he was getting rubles." Then, with less condemnation than envy in her voice, she explained, "He worked for American intelligence."

They put me in a "box"—a tiny cell in which I could not lie down or walk but only sit or stand—and kept me there for a day. I suppose their intention was to make me realize from the very start just what prison was: the more pressure you put on at the outset, the sooner the willpower breaks down.

When the time came to take me to the bathhouse, an argument broke out between my two warders (or, as they are now being called, "controllers").

"This one will have to be taken there strictly apart from the others," said the sergeant who had interrogated me.

"No, he can bathe along with all the rest of them," said the other, who obviously didn't want to make two trips to the bathhouse.

As I was being taken through the main yard, I noticed that a new block had been put up in the area where, five years before, there had been exercise yards. At almost all the prisons I inhabited later on, new blocks had been built.† The old buildings, moreover, were jammed full of prisoners. I don't see how one can reconcile this with the official statements that the crime rate is dropping.

I was apprehensive that I would be put either in solitary or in a big cell with forty other prisoners. But my fears proved unjustified; I was placed in a cell with only two other prisoners, who gave me a warm welcome. They were astonished at my air of well-being, because most new prisoners are much more upset. But I had prepared myself, so for me it was easier. And the first thing I did after entering the cell was to drink heartily from the faucet, since during my day in the "box" I had been tormented by thirst.

One of my cell-mates, a physicist by the name of Alexander Bork, had been convicted of taking bribes to pass students on their entrance examinations. He was facing from eight to fifteen years of incarceration and had a wife and young son on the outside. The dryness and reserve of the scientist were apparent in his features.

The other man, a ski instructor named Ilya Romanenko, was doing time for concealment of stolen goods. It seems that two young men, one of them an inventor, had decided to build a small submarine to escape to a foreign country. But they needed money to build the sub, so they held up a store and committed a murder in the process. At the request of the inventor, Romanenko hid some of the stolen goods at his home.

I'm sure, now, that Romanenko was an informer. He was expecting a three-year sentence, and he could count on its suspension and his immediate release on probation. I suspect that he played an unenviable role in the case of his two friends; for that matter, he extracted a good deal of information from Bork. As for myself, I was not in the same cell with him long enough to be done any damage. To the contrary, he taught me to exercise and dash cold water over my face every morning—things that helped me during my years in prison, and still do.

We spent our time pleasantly, reading books and carrying on lively conversations; I even began to give lectures on the history of the Democratic Movement, which I continued at Harvard University eight years later. Roma-

---

†I say "prisons," although the official name for places like Butyrki is "investigative isolator," meaning a place where persons are detained during their pretrial investigation and until such time as their sentence enters into legal force. Strictly speaking, a "prison" (*krytka*, in prison argot) is a building or block of buildings for confining persons who have been sentenced.

nenko listened to me eagerly, excited by the thought of how much material I would give him for the security officer.† Three days after I had been assigned to the cell, I received a parcel from Gusel; that made our meals more enjoyable. For his part, Romanenko kept his own goodies for himself. (At night you could hear him unwrapping chocolate bars, which he claimed his lawyer had sent him.) And when I was transferred from the cell on May 25, his parting words were: "Don't divvy up your food parcels too much." In his own way, he showed good feeling toward me, and along with the good advice he gave me a chocolate bar "for the road."

When I was taken out of the cell, the duty officer wanted me handcuffed, but Kirinkin and Sidorov objected and brought me safe and sound to the investigative section of the USSR Prosecutor's Office. There, I was charged with having written *Will the Soviet Union Survive Until 1984?* and *Involuntary Journey to Siberia* as well as an article titled "Russian Painting of the Past Decade," along with my interviews with Clarity and Cole. Kirinkin had forgotten my "Letter to Anatoly Kuznetsov," which was the only one of my writings to have been discovered in the Sverdlovsk Oblast, and the only peg they had for conducting proceedings there.

Anyone charged with having circulated his own opinions or those of others has a choice of tactics during the pretrial investigation and the trial. First, you can admit that the writings are anti-Soviet, admit that you circulated them, and recant. This tactic is, of course, the one the investigator prefers. But there are different varieties. You can go along with the investigator and yet admit only what he has already proved against you—things that he already knew before your confession. Or you can tell him everything you know indiscriminately—"spill your guts," as they say in underworld slang.

Second, you can admit that you circulated the writings and acknowledge that they are anti-Soviet, but instead of recanting, say, "I consider my views anti-Soviet, and will not disown them." In general, this tactic also makes the investigator's work easier, and it may create serious problems for others involved in the case.

Third, you can admit that you circulated the writings but deny that they are anti-Soviet or slanderous, emphasizing that, on the contrary, they are strictly lawful and that prosecution for them is illegal. This is the tactic that has been used by most of those in the Human Rights Movement. It rules out giving the investigator information he does not already have or testifying about others.

Fourth, you can deny the "facts" or incidents. In this case the person under investigation says, "No, I did not say or write that. No, I did not give

† *Oper,* the officer in charge of security at a penal camp.

that manuscript to the person who claims the contrary: he is either mistaken, or he is slandering me." As for the appraisal of the writings as anti-Soviet, you can agree with it, disagree with it, or do neither.

In my case, I chose a fifth tactic. I told Kirinkin that in my opinion there was nothing either anti-Soviet or libelous in my writings, and that I would give no testimony during the investigation. Even before my arrest, I had decided to take that approach under any circumstances, regardless of what kind of indictment was brought against me. I would neither affirm nor deny incidents or the interpretation put upon them, but rather deny the right of the court and the investigative organs to prosecute people for their views, be they true or untrue.

Kirinkin gave me a melancholy look and said, "In that case, we'll charge you under Article 70." I merely spread my hands, indicating resignation to my fate. But I didn't for a moment take the threat seriously. I assumed that Article 190-1 had been decided on by higher authorities, and that there was little likelihood they would switch to another article because of my behavior. Under that article I would in any case get the maximum of three years. (I could get a one-year sentence only if I fully recanted and humiliated myself.) Again, taking that position enabled me to avoid the fuss of admitting one thing and denying another and arguing with the investigator as to what was Soviet and what was anti-Soviet. For that matter, neither Kirinkin nor Sidorov was much disturbed by my refusal. They were probably thinking: "You've only just got into our hands. When you've been behind bars for a month or two, you'll sing a different tune."

Sidorov and I fell into a theoretical discussion as to how "Soviet people" would feel about my book if they were able to read it.

"Arrange a meeting for me with some workers," I said. "I don't know how they'll receive me at first, but they'll applaud when I've finished."

This upset Sidorov. "But you're slandering the Soviet regime when you say it won't survive until 1984! Instead of arranging a meeting for you, we're going to try you for libel."

"Then you'll have to wait until 1984. If the regime survives, you can try me for libel. If it doesn't survive, I'll be proven right."

I had the feeling, though, that neither Sidorov nor his superiors could wait that long.

"It's not that I want the Soviet Union to perish," I said to Sidorov. "But I do want to point out some potential dangers. After all, one must think of the future. In your opinion, how will things be in 1984?"

After reflecting a bit, he replied, "Things will be even better."

"I read your book," Kirinkin put in with a sneer, "and I didn't understand a bit of it."

"If you didn't understand it, why did you bring charges against me?"

Kirinkin was a simple man who (as he told me later) usually worked on murder cases and had got involved in this matter of my books quite by chance, just as it had been decided by chance to implicate me in the Sverdlovsk proceedings. The only aspect of my case that interested him (and, for that matter, Sidorov) was how much I had been paid for the books, and whether I would get my hands on the money. Kirinkin was plainly distressed that I had been able to make use of the foreign currency stores, which—sad to say— were not accessible to him. He kept hinting that I had written those things just for money. He would give me a meaningful look, expecting that I would try to justify myself; but I would always answer, "Yes, just for the money."

I had scarcely been put behind bars when several money orders arrived from abroad. The authorities froze them, but they couldn't confiscate them, because my signature was required before they could be accepted from foreign banks. The Foreign Trade Bank suggested to the Sverdlovsk Prosecutor's Office that the best solution would be for me to contribute these monies to the State. But I must give Kirinkin his due: knowing my attitude toward money, he didn't even pass on that suggestion to me, so that finally the monies were returned to those who had sent them.

I don't recall what route we took when returning from the USSR Prosecutor's Office to Butyrki. I remember only a general feeling of being in Moscow, and the freshness of the air after the rain. "Your Moscow is a beautiful city, Andrei Alekseyevich," said Kirinkin—no doubt by way of reminding me that I wouldn't be seeing the city again for a long time.

Amazingly enough, I had no regrets. Rather, I gazed about me like an indifferent tourist saturated with the sights he has seen. What I felt was very much in contrast to the eagerness with which I had looked at the Moscow streets through the window of a Black Maria five years before or the yearning with which I remembered the Moscow boulevards during my exile in Siberia.

The next day, they shoved me into a Black Maria and took me to the Kazan Station. I realized that I was being transferred to Sverdlovsk.

CHAPTER 11

The Sverdlovsk Prison:
On "Special Regimen"

On the two-day trip to Sverdlovsk I occupied a private compartment — or, to be more precise, a private cell in a Stolypin car.† Somewhere along the way a Mordovian woman—young, very fat, and with a gloomy expression on her face—was put into the cell next to mine. She had been convicted of setting fire to a warehouse; I thought she had probably been working there as a clerk and had torched the place in order to cover up a deficit in the books. I was mistaken.

"I did it because life was so hard," she said. "There was nothing to eat. The stores were empty. The pay was low, and you couldn't say a word to the bosses."

This was my first encounter with the traditional Russian "red rooster."‡ From time to time, fires due to "spontaneous combustion" break out—as a challenge to social injustice. It may well be that the fires that broke out in Moscow in 1977 were the work of such arsonists.

The *zek** who worked as bathhouse attendant at the Sverdlovsk Prison was quick to ask what I had heard from Moscow about a possible amnesty. As far back as 1965, the zeks were rejoicing at rumors about an amnesty on the centenary of Lenin's birth in April 1970. But their expectations came to nothing, except for a few curtailed sentences. And now, in late May, what was left to hope for?

"Well," said the bathhouse attendant venomously, "Brezhnev will push things so far that people will take to the ax. We need a new revolution! We need a new Lenin! We need another Party!"

---

†The special railroad car for transporting prisoners was nicknamed after Prince Peter Stolypin, Prime Minister and Minister of the Interior under Tsar Nicholas II.—TRANS.

‡A Russian appellation for arsonists of the Populist variety.—TRANS.

I often heard such things in labor camps or when being transported from one prison to another. The reason there is no systematic terrorism "from below" is that so far the opposition has been led by people who are opposed to terrorism on principle.

As in Butyrki, I was placed on special regimen, or *spets,* which meant that I was located in a block with cells holding from two to four persons (there were as many as sixty in the big cells) and intended for zeks who had in some way distinguished themselves. It was a sunny day, and the little window near the ceiling of the cell had no shield over it, so that the sun's rays danced on the yellow walls. The cell was five paces long and three paces wide. On the right there was a toilet seat, and in the corner behind it were two *vagonki,* or double-tiered metal bunks. In the center stood a little metal table and a metal stool, both of them firmly attached to the floor and the wall.

There was no one else in the cell. I sat down on the stool, filled a jug with water from the faucet, and stirred into it the remains of a lump of sugar. I felt the onset of a mood of dejection and hopelessness. Like boredom, the kind of oppression one feels in prison cannot be described. If you try to portray prison life, you clutch at this or that event, however insignificant. But life behind bars is in fact just one long non-event. Time drags on with unbearable slowness, though in your memory it shrinks into a pathetic little lump. My first feeling was of despair and may have been due to loneliness, to being in a strange city, and to the release of tension after my arrest and interrogation. My dejection worsened as the day wore on. That first evening I heard on the radio a song by Theodorakis, one the Greek poet had written in a German prison camp. It was a record that Gusel and I had often listened to together, and I could not hold back my tears.

The loudspeaker was located in the cell, and I could turn it off when I wanted to—a great boon. In other prisons it shouted from behind an iron grill and was turned off only at the discretion of the officials. It used to drive me almost out of my mind. The anguish of loneliness, painful as it may be, is easier to bear than the propaganda shoved into your ears like damp cotton wadding. Not even American commercials are so offensive.

On the other hand, I sometimes heard interesting things. I learned from the radio that the great composer Dmitri Shostakovich had written a march for the MVD* troops; and now they could escort zeks at gunpoint to the triumphant strains of his music. On another occasion I heard that the Canadian Prime Minister, Pierre Trudeau, had visited Norilsk and remarked that Canada did not have such a fine city beyond the Arctic Circle. I felt the urge to shout back at Trudeau through the iron grill: "Arrest a million Canadians; send them beyond the Arctic Circle; have them set up a barbed-wire fence around themselves, under the muzzles of machine guns; have them dig mines and build houses—and then you'll have as fine a city as Norilsk."

In order to keep busy, I mopped the floor of my cell, did my exercises, and paced back and forth. It was a great pleasure when they brought me books. Although the library was a poor one, I managed to scrounge some Russian classics.

Often, the librarian would offer me books that I would refuse. When I did, she would reply: "Once books have been written, you should read them." (To her, reading was a prisoner's duty.)

Every day of the week, except for Saturday and Sunday, they brought either *Pravda* or *Izvestiya* or the local paper, *Uralskiy rabochiy* (The Urals Worker).

I possessed a calendar on which I kept track of how many days I had spent in prison and how many more remained. Most zeks say that if you don't keep track of the days, your term goes by faster. But during all my years of confinement there was not one single day when I failed to remind myself of how much time lay between me and freedom.

On the fourth day, when the door of my cell opened, I came close to knocking a lieutenant colonel and captain off their feet with my teapot, since I was in the habit of thrusting it forward, at that time of day, to get it filled with boiling water. I could tell from their questions, which had a touch of saccharine in them, that they were security officers. I refused to talk about my case; but I did make a complaint about being alone in the cell. To this the lieutenant colonel replied: "It's just for the time being. You'll soon have somebody with you."

The next evening a tall, gloomy-looking young man was brought into the cell, and without a word of greeting he sat down in the corner. In time, we struck up a conversation: His name was Volodya. He had been chief supply clerk at a students' dormitory, and when the building was under repair, he had sold all the toilet bowls on the black market. Once we had established human contact with the aid of the toilet bowls and were engaged in lively chatter, Volodya said, "I don't know how you feel about it, but they put me in here to inform on you."

He had been called in by the lieutenant colonel, who was from the UVD,* and Captain Maslennikov, the prison security officer. They had asked him about his case, and had suggested that he become the cell-mate of a man who they hinted was a spy in the employ of the Americans. Naturally, being in the same cell with a spy would be interesting, although he didn't know how to behave with a spy—which explained his not saying a word when he came into the cell.

From time to time, Volodya would be called out of the cell, supposedly to meet with the investigator or his lawyer, but actually to meet with Maslennikov. I had the feeling that Volodya "squealed" on me to Maslennikov just as unconcernedly as he squealed on Maslennikov to me. Maslennikov gave him instructions as to what he should talk to me about, and how.

Volodya called himself an artist and claimed he had studied for several years at the Novosibirsk Art Institute. It may be that he was selected as a stool pigeon for my cell because, as an artist, he was just the right kind of informer to use on me, a lover of art. But it turned out that during the years when he was supposedly studying at the art institute, he had been in the armed forces, had done time in a labor camp for desertion, had driven stolen cars to Georgia, and had filched things from lockers at railroad stations.

If you can imagine two people quite alien to each other but doomed to spend months together in the confined space of a cell, you can understand how tense things became between us. We even got to the point of brawling.

After that I started taking boxing lessons from a new cell-mate named Zhenya. For the first two weeks after his arrival, the three of us were in the cell together; then for the next four months there were just Zhenya and I. He was older than I and of a quiet disposition. On the outside, he had worked as a mechanic and was taking a correspondence course at the Moscow Highway Institute. Also, he was a messenger and bodyguard for a certain Samokhin, who was engaged in smuggling gold from the Urals, where it was dug up, to Georgia, where it was buried again.

On one occasion, according to Zhenya's account, Samokhin met with a Georgian dealer at Zhenya's place in a communal apartment in Moscow. "While you two are billing and cooing," Zhenya said, "I'll go to the kitchen and fix an omelet." But when he returned with the steaming omelet, he found the Georgian lying on the floor with a broken skull.

"You wait here a minute, and I'll run out and call a doctor," Samokhin said. But he never saw Samokhin again, not to mention any doctor. He didn't know what to do with the corpse. The neighbors called the police; after that, everything happened as if in a fog: he came to in a room with a barred window and shouted, "Where am I?" "In prison," came the answer, accompanied by a laugh.

Such is the version he told to me. Actually, it may well be that both he and Samokhin killed the Georgian, or even that he himself did it and put the blame on Samokhin, who had fled the scene.

I don't know how the whole business ended. What I do know, however, is that he, too, was put in my cell as a stool pigeon. It was obvious that the authorities had talked with him beforehand and had told him what subjects to bring up with me. Among other things, he kept asking if I was Jewish; but perhaps that was because while he was in a labor camp before he was sent to Sverdlovsk, everyone had taken *him* to be Jewish. In time, he became quite friendly toward me. I don't know what he told the security officer, but he didn't give me away in one important respect—something I shall discuss later.

We got along well, playing chess without arguing, practicing boxing, and sharing food parcels. Although it was against the rules, he had brought along a "teach-yourself" book, and I began to study English. During my years of incarceration I took advantage of every opportunity to continue those lessons. When I was released I could read English fairly well, although I couldn't pronounce a single word correctly.

The main events in the prison schedule were reveille at 6:00 A.M., breakfast, lunch, dinner, exercise, and lights out at 10:00 P.M. The food that was provided us was disgusting. For dinner they might give us soup with rotten herring that I never ate. The bread was of a kind baked especially for convicts, and I merely gnawed at the crust. The gruel, which the zeks called "shrapnel," was made out of a kind of groats never found in the outside world, and had no vegetable oil in it. One serving of it scarcely covered the bottom of the bowl.

Semi-starvation as an educational measure is the basis for determining prison rations, and the fact that investigators and security officers can "fatten up" a prisoner when they so choose is a tool in their hands. Some of the food is pilfered by the administration and the commissary. Also, rations in a prison or camp depend on the conditions in that region. The Ural region of the Soviet Union is a famine area, with the lowest-quality food. I simply could not eat the local variety of sausage. It was a slimy, reddish stuff with a strong flavor of starch and hardly any taste of meat. When our warder saw the smoked sausage that Gusel had bought with foreign currency and sent to me in a parcel, he exclaimed in envy: "Oh, how I'd like to eat some of that sausage."

"Just get in the slammer with us, and you can eat some," Zhenya told him.

The reason I didn't starve was that Gusel sent money for the canteen, and every month mailed me the authorized five-kilogram parcel. I always looked forward to the package as if it were news from her. Correspondence was prohibited, so even the list of items of food drawn up in her own hand looked like a love letter. The regulations prohibit sending prisoners food parcels from Moscow, but the people in our local Moscow post office had good feelings toward me and accepted my parcels. Recently, an even more remarkable regulation was introduced: food for parcels can be bought only in the town or settlement where the prison is located—perhaps so that the warders will not be irritated by the sight of some good sausage. The authorities ascribe these restrictions to their concern for the zeks' relatives, a concern lest they spend too much and exhaust their budgets.

Twice a month, the women who clerked in the prison canteen made the rounds of the cells. From them you could buy sugar, butter, rolls, cheap candy, processed cheese, cigarettes, envelopes, and pencils—the total amount of your purchases being limited to five rubles. In all prisons the grocery items have been weighed in advance, and there's no way to check whether they are giving you 500 grams of butter or 400. Zhenya and I of course had no refrigerator, so once when he bought some cheese we crammed it into a jar. It gradually started to swell, forming something like a mushroom cap at the top of the jar. I was a bit dubious about that cap; but Zhenya sliced it off and ate it with gusto. The next day, another cap had formed, and he ate that one too. We were beginning to think that we had come into possession of a magic pot that would go on providing us with food indefinitely. But before long it started to give off such a strong smell that he had to throw it out.

The practice of keeping prisoners on a starvation diet angered me. On one occasion, I threw the contents of my bowl at the warder and cookhand through the chuck-hole, and the soup splattered all over the place. My position—how important I was in the eyes of the top officials—was still not clear, and all they did was reprimand me. So I decided to change my tactics. I waited (and I didn't have long to wait) until they gave us scarcely cooked gruel, and I put a bowl of it under my bed to use as material evidence. Then I sat down and wrote a complaint to the prison chief. If I had written that I was half-starved, that I had a bad stomach, and that prisoners should be given proper nourishment, I would have been told that a prison is not a health resort and that the thing to do is avoid being put in prison. But by this time I was rather experienced, and understood that in the Soviet Union a complaint can get results only if it is formulated as a denunciation. Without appealing to any humanitarian sentiments, I wrote that the regular practice of giving the prisoners rations below standard in quality and quantity led me to believe that the kitchen personnel were systematically stealing socialist property in the form of groats, vegetable oils, etc., and that I requested the punishment of the guilty parties.

The results exceeded my expectations. The first person to appear was a cook, a woman who was a free employee. She yelled at me, thinking she would get her way by such shouting. But I, finding that the enemy was panicking, remained calm and firm.

The next day an entire delegation in green uniforms, headed by a major, showed up and removed the gruel "for analysis." (The day before, I had managed to shove the gruel under the nose of my investigator several times. Each time he shied away in disgust, but it did make a certain impression on him.)

Finally, I was taken to see the commandant, Colonel Andryukhin. When he had previously visited our cell, each time he would find me just getting up from the toilet seat. After a while, he began to interpret that as a subtle challenge to the regime. I explained, however, that he made his rounds just when my bowels were beginning to function. He was one of those liberal wardens whose policy is "live and let live," and he wanted to avoid unnecessary complications. After greeting me as one would an old friend, he said that the matter would be looked into most thoroughly.

The next day we heard the rustling of a woman's clothes; someone peeked in through the judas-hole; then they shoved two bowls of soup in through the chuckhole. There were pieces of meat in the soup, and there was butterfat in the gruel.

We feasted in this way for a whole week; then everything reverted to normal. The analysis of the gruel had shown that it was the tastiest one could possibly enjoy.

Every day, if it wasn't raining, we would be taken out for exercise in a yard about three times the size of our cell, with concrete walls and a concrete floor, plus a barbed-wire mesh over our heads. Our warders were good-natured. Some of them were taking correspondence courses in law, and a few of them expressed a liking for me. But I was apprehensive about giving them any letters to mail. I trusted neither them nor my own cell-mates.

One could hear a kind of constant hum of voices in the prison. Many of the cell windows had no shield or blinds covering them, and the prisoners would shout back and forth at one another until those shouting most desperately would be dragged off to punishment cells. In one cell near ours, somebody with a deep, singsong voice, speaking in the accents of the underworld, was complaining that he had been accused of being a stool pigeon, and was threatening one of his cell-mates. Suddenly, his singsong speech was interrupted by a high, piercing screech: "Don't believe him, you guys! He's a fink—a stoolie!"

Across from our windows was a cell for prisoners sentenced to death. One of them, feeling no doubt that he had nothing to lose, began to shout at the top of his voice: "Long live Stalin! Long live Hitler! Long live Khrushchev!"

At least one of those three was bound to meet with the disapproval of the prison authorities. And sure enough, his shouting was soon choked off.

There were women in the cells on both sides of ours; and since the block had been built using the method of socialist competition, the walls were thin enough so that we could even talk through them. Zhenya got both himself and me involved in an "affair" with the cell to the right. But then I noticed through the window, when the girls from the cell to the left were being taken out for exercise, that they were prettier. So I immediately switched my orientation—much to the displeasure of our old girlfriends, who shouted through the window to the new ones: "Prostitutes! Masturbators!" (*Kovyryalka,* or "masturbator," was a prisoners' epithet for a lesbian.)

Whoever received a food parcel from home or bought some food at the canteen would throw pieces of bread into the yard, so there were always lots of pigeons around.

In the summer, we would take off the window frame, and the pigeons would fly in through the bars and peck away at the bread right on the sill. Zhenya caught several of them. We let them loose in the cell, and they would go under the bunks and find crumbs. Also, we provided water for them; so all in all, we had a kind of mini-zoo.

Two Lithuanians had just hijacked an airplane to a foreign destination, and the newspapers were carrying headlines reading "THE HIJACKERS SHOULD BE TRIED IN A SOVIET COURT." We cut out one of these headlines and hung it around the neck of one of the pigeons. He was the most timid of the lot, but now the others shied away from him in fright: such is the great power of the printed word. Then we let him go so that he could fly through the prison yard, frightening hijackers with weak nerves. But one day when we returned from exercise, we found the cell empty. Apparently the warders had seen him, chased him out, and closed the window.

In prison, it is usually a pleasant experience to meet up with a living being who does not resemble a human. In the Sverdlovsk Prison I sometimes encountered, on my way to the exercise yard, cats that hung around the kitchen; and in Kamyshlov I got to know a pair of horses used for hauling firewood. While I was in solitary, I filed a request that I be allowed to keep a cat in my cell. But the prison commandant replied that a directive from the Minister of Internal Affairs prohibited such things.

The investigator didn't summon me for interrogation for more than a month, until I had been softened up a bit. But one day someone knocked on the cell door, opened the chuckhole, and said in a cheerful voice: "Amalrik, without your things!"

The investigators' offices were at the far end of the prison. I was in front, with my hands behind my back, and the warder came along behind me. (Once, when my warder was a young woman, we even walked hand-in-hand, having a friendly chat as we went along.)

Kirinkin called me in five times over the course of the investigation. Each time, without declining to speak, I reiterated my refusal to give evidence. I did not respond to questions material to the case, and I did not sign any record of the interrogation. Kirinkin, therefore, so as not to give himself the trouble of calling me in, began in my absence to make out reports of interrogations that had never taken place, writing in my behalf: "I refuse to answer that question," or, "I refuse to sign." On one interrogation report he even entered a date on which, as it happens, I was being transported from one place of incarceration to another. But since he had never done me any harm, I did not use the fact of his negligence against him. When my home was searched, they confiscated Esenin-Volpin's "law handbook" titled *How to Behave During Interrogations;* Kirinkin told me several times, in exasperation, "Just think! He wrote a handbook, and I could have written it a thousand times better!"

While confined in prison, I worried a lot about Gusel. I was afraid she would get confused when being interrogated. That's exactly what happened—but with no bad consequences for her, thank God. When my investigation was over, I told both my lawyer and the investigator that before my arrest I had tried to explain to Gusel just how she should testify, but that I had then given up and said to her: "No matter, darling. You're going to get everything mixed up."

Kirinkin began by threatening me with Article 70. Then he said that I might even be charged under Article 64—"high treason"—which might very well mean the firing squad. I told him that so far as that went, I might be hit in the back of the head by a brick when being returned to my cell, which would put an end to everything. I also said that I realized they could modify the indictment so that it came under Article 70 and give me seven years, but I couldn't take seriously any talk about a death sentence. In general, I advised Kirinkin to be more cautious. Today, I said, they may be telling you to "pour it on"; but twenty years from now, investigators who are overzealous may well be barred from collecting their pensions.

I don't know whether Kirinkin took my advice seriously, but he did become more cautious. He told me he merely carried out orders, and that an experienced investigator did not needlessly impair relations with a person under investigation. On one occasion he told me he could reclassify my "offenses" under Article 70 rather than 190-1 only by written directive and not just orally, which meant he was still a bit apprehensive. Another time he remarked that in a bus he had heard talk among workers in comparison with which my book would prove to be nonincriminating. Yakir, he went on to say, had made a strong impression on him when he declared that since he did not consider my book either anti-Soviet or libelous, he would not give any testimony.

One day Kirinkin asked me if I knew the name "Ubozhko" and I replied truthfully that I had never heard it before. It seems that a copy of my letter to Anatoly Kuznetsov had been confiscated from Ubozhko in Sverdlovsk. He was arrested in late January, and interrogations had been completed by mid-

March. He had been sent to a hospital for psychiatric examination. It was just about that time that the decision was probably made to involve me in his case, so that I would not have to be tried in Moscow. Ubozhko was found to be mentally competent and spent another eight months in prison while they were looking into my case.

The first time I saw him was in October, when both of us were brought to the investigator's office to read the case file. Elbowing his guard to one side, he rushed up to me, shook my hand, and exclaimed: "Congratulations! We've won!"

Solzhenitsyn, who had refused to submit his work to the censors, had just won the Nobel Prize. And those who were in prison for having written and read underground books, could in truth say: "We've won!"

"Did you know Solzhenitsyn has gone abroad?" Kirinkin asked me. "How do you feel about that?"

It was plain to see that he had been instructed to talk about Solzhenitsyn. Such "ideological conversations" didn't come easily to Kirinkin. I didn't believe what he said. I decided they were just trying to sound me out, to test my attitude toward exile abroad. (Rumors about my expulsion from the country had been circulating even before my arrest; but the actual decision to eject me was not taken until late 1974.) On another occasion, Kirinkin asked about my articles for Novosti. Just in case it might come in handy, he and his colleagues had worked up a profile of me as a "double-dealer" who wrote one kind of thing for readers in the USSR and something quite different for readers abroad—as Daniel and Sinyavsky had been charged with doing. I replied that at Novosti an editor had made cuts in, or additions to, what I wrote without asking me; that question was not raised again. Finally, the notion of me as a "double-dealer" was abandoned in favor of another interpretation: that I was a rather stupid "half-scholar" who didn't really understand what he himself wrote.

Kirinkin tried several times to trap me. He asked why I hadn't circulated my manuscripts in samizdat rather than send them abroad. Was it because I held my compatriots in low esteem? Another time, puffing out his chest, he said, "Well then, go ahead and convince me that your views are right." But I recalled how Yakhimovich had "convinced" his investigator—until he ended up in a psychiatric hospital.

There is a surrealistic element in Soviet political trials, a mix of the comical and the sinister. It is perfectly clear to the defendant, the investigator, counsel for the defense, the prosecutor, and the judge that everything essential has been decided in advance; that a change can result only from recantation or betrayal but not from proving, or failing to prove, that this or that incident took place. Nonetheless, everyone tries to observe the prescribed procedures,

in a strange parody of a real investigation and trial. Thus, at my trial they
brought in a tape recorder to subject my voice to expert examination and so
ascertain whether I had in fact given an interview to the BBC, but I refused
to have my voice recorded. Also, the typewriters seized from me were subjected to expert examination, which, as it happens, was faulty, since they
compared the typewriters with each other but not with others of the same
make. The examination showed that my manuscripts had been typed on two
machines; yet they confiscated all four of my typewriters, and no subsequent
complaints were of any avail.

Toward the end of the investigation I asked Kirinkin just how they intended to prove my authorship. I had refused to give testimony, and my
interviewers had not been interrogated, although under Soviet law they should
have been charged as accomplices in the crime. Nor were the publishers of
my books questioned. The fact that my name was on the jacket was not
enough: it was necessary to prove that I had written the books. Kirinkin
hadn't even thought about these things. He became confused and said, "But
what will your friends think if you tell them you didn't write those books?"

On September 14, Kirinkin told me that the pretrial investigation had
been completed, and he showed me a new indictment. It had been necessary
to draft a new one, since he had previously forgotten to mention my open
letter to Kuznetsov. The document was replete with such expressions as
"preposterous situations," "wicked insinuations," "crackpot ideas," "vile
fabrications," "a malicious interview," and so on.

"What good is that?" I asked him. "Do you use the same kind of
language when you draw up charges against murderers? All that bathos and
gutter lingo make it look ridiculous."

Oddly enough, Kirinkin heeded what I had to say; the tone of the indictment proper, when he came to write it, was calmer and less judgmental.

As he was taking me to the door, he said that the interview with me had
been shown on American television and had been a success. It was plain that
he took pleasure in the celebrity of his "investigatee."

Kirinkin assured me that he couldn't locate either my wife or the lawyer,
Shveisky, she had retained; so he assigned an attorney from Sverdlovsk to my
case. Defense counsel enters a case only when the pretrial investigation has
been completed. He may (along with his client) read the dossier on the case,
file statements with the investigator and the prosecutor, participate in the
actual trial, file appeals, and take part in the appellate proceedings. In my
case there was really no practical role defense counsel could play. Even so, a
lawyer could provide me with moral support and contact with the outside
world. Also, I needed the kind of counsel who would assert at the trial that I
was innocent: this would be in line with the Democratic Movement's policy

of lawful resistance. A lawyer who was not known to me or my friends, even if he was not a KGB agent, would not take an independent position or serve as a link between my wife and me. Instead of giving me support, he would advise capitulation so the authorities would be more lenient with me. I therefore refused categorically the services of the Sverdlovsk attorney.

Finally, on September 30, Kirinkin introduced me to Vladimir Shveisky, who had flown in from Moscow. He was a man of about fifty, with a pleasant smile and curly hair, who spoke in a nasal voice. His appearance was plainly not Aryan. Later on, he told me that one day during the period of the "struggle against cosmopolitanism," when he took a seat in a streetcar next to an elderly Russian workingman, the latter said reproachfully, "With a nose like that, he still gets on from the front of the platform!"

Kirinkin was forever repeating that we both realized I should be tried under Article 70 and that it was only because of his very great humanity that I would get Article 190-1 and only three years. (There was no question of the court's giving me less.) The next year, when he threatened a Jewish "refusenik"* with Article 70, the latter replied that even Amalrik got only Article 190-1. Whereupon Kirinkin consoled him by saying, "Yes, but with Amalrik, things didn't stop there."

The Case File

Of the nine volumes constituting the case file, each of them running to four hundred or six hundred pages, the first three had to do with Ubozhko, and the last six with me.

Lev Ubozhko, two years older than I and by training a physicist, had worked as an engineer in Moscow while taking a correspondence course from the Sverdlovsk Law School, the same one from which our warders were taking courses. When he showed up for his exams, he brought some samizdat literature with him and handed it out both to acquaintances and to people he didn't know. Within a few days he was arrested.

Ubozhko's file consisted of the samizdat materials confiscated from him, plus the testimony of local citizens and depositions taken from girls that Ubozhko had made friends with while traveling around the country. Since each of the girls asked him to leave her something to remember him by, he would give one a copy of Sakharov's booklet, another Solzhenitsyn's "Letter to the Soviet Leaders," and still another a copy of Grigorenko's speech. He admitted having distributed the literature, confirmed the testimony given by the witnesses, and acknowledged that his views were anti-Soviet. But he would neither disown those views nor inform on anyone.

Three volumes were given over to my manuscripts, along with two reviews that concluded I was neither a historian nor a writer. The reader's report on my plays was as follows:

> . . . Amalrik weaves the so-called "Jewish question" into this play [*Is Uncle Jack a Conformist?*]. Being illiterate in all respects, he could think of nothing more intelligent to say even in this instance. All that matters for him is to give the reader a dirty, titillating

subtext—to throw fuel on the flames: on the one hand, to present the Ivanovs as idiots; and on the other, to go on and on about the Tsipelzons. It is hard to define all this unprecedented mockery of Russian history—of the Ivanovs and the Ivan Ivanoviches, who are symbols of Russia, in a way. However Amalrik may have masked his "Jewish question," you can spot him for what he is.

"I'm afraid the reviewer wasted his ammunition," I told Kirinkin. "I may or may not be a writer, but I'm not a Jew."

He spread his hands in a gesture of helplessness. The KGB had gone to great lengths to ferret out any Jewish ancestors that either Ubozhko or I might have had. In his case, they found one Jewish grandfather. Since they had made no such discovery among my own forebears, they insisted that even if I didn't have any Jewish blood, I was a Jew at heart.

The last three volumes of my file contained some clippings from Soviet and foreign newspapers, transcripts of Radio Liberty broadcasts about me, letters (my mail had been under surveillance since March), along with many orders and records of searches. In particular, there was an order to set up a special case file under Article 70 for some books seized during searches of my home. Ultimately it was decided to rescind this order owing to lack of proof that I had "circulated" them, and to burn the books. If they do actually burn books, rather than sending them to a special archive of the KGB, they don't do it in street bonfires, as in Nazi Germany. Probably there is a special remote place for this operation, in charge of some individual on a modest salary.

Most of the letters in the file were from foreigners who had read *Will the Soviet Union Survive Until 1984?* I remember one from a schoolgirl in California. She and her classmates had written a paper on my book, which all of them had liked very much. "But all that stuff you wrote in that book," she concluded, "is untrue, isn't it?" One man from Holland passed no judgment on my writings but warned me that I had got mixed up with a very dangerous character—namely, Karel van het Reve. He didn't say anything about Karel himself, but he reported that Karel's brother, in the course of a public debate, had written on the blackboard: "Long Live Capitalism!" In some Western countries, it would seem, writing such things is the same as writing obscene things publicly in Russia.

There were five letters from Soviet citizens whom I did not know, people who had heard about me on the radio and had been imprudent enough to write me between March and May. These letters were made the subject of "separate criminal cases." Attached to my "Open Letter to Anatoly Kuznetsov" was a report explaining that it had been opened only because the envelope had been accidentally scorched; but that when the workers at the International Post Office found out its contents, they forwarded it to the KGB.

At first I didn't understand what criterion the investigator was using in selecting witnesses. Then I realized he was simply calling in, often purely at random, anyone who had been noticed while I was followed before my arrest. Our neighbors testified that foreigners came to visit us and that we gave "what you might call" banquets for them. However, our friends provided little testimony: they had heard nothing, seen nothing, and read nothing. Set within the framework of my case file were three stories: one comic, one tragic, and one detective.

Among the enclosures to a letter from Major General Nikulkin of the Moscow UKGB* to Zhuravlev, Prosecutor of the Sverdlovsk Oblast, concerning "the transmittal of materials relative to the anti-Soviet activity of Amalrik" was an item assigned the number "3" and headed: "Statement by M. B. Shulman, and a letter from the U.S." In his statement to the KGB dated February 6, 1970, M. B. Shulman had written that he was an honest Soviet man and that with the permission of the authorities he had corresponded with his uncle, also named Shulman, in New York. Later, he had received a letter from his uncle, which at first upset him, then put him into a quandary, so that "I am obliged to forward you some excerpts from it"—excerpts that, as it happened, turned out to be the whole letter.

Uncle Shulman had written that all his life he had successfully propagandized the ideas of socialism and communism and the achievements of the Soviet Union, but that recently he had received a copy of a magazine with an article allegedly written by a Soviet citizen living in Moscow saying the USSR would not survive until 1984, that "the people would rise up against the Bolsheviks and the ComParty," and that he had spent a sleepless night, and his neighbors were all laughing at him. He was therefore asking Nephew Shulman if this was true. His letter, in the true Leninist style, ended with the question: "Is that villain still at large?"

Upon reflection, Nephew Shulman decided that this question should be referred to the KGB. I was amazed and saddened that a person like Uncle Shulman, who himself enjoyed complete freedom of expression, should feel it necessary to seal the mouth of a person whose views he disagreed with.

At first, Shulman was included among the witnesses to be called into court, but then he was taken off the list. Apparently it had occurred to the KGB that there was nothing he could really testify about.

After I left the Soviet Union, I learned something of the life story of Mikhail Shulman. He was born in 1906, the same year as my father and

Brezhnev. He served in the Cheka (the secret police), joined the Communist party, was arrested in 1937, and spent the years 1939–49 in penal camps in Kolyma, where he headed up an "underground Party organization." In 1950 he got a new sentence of eight years and was sent to Vorkuta. But in 1955 he was rehabilitated and allowed back into the Party, in which he had continued to believe during all his years of incarceration. I don't know what his views were at the time he received the letter from his uncle; but in 1974 he declared he had "broken with the Party, as though having awakened after a long and hideous nightmare," and he went to Israel.

The previous March, I had received a letter signed "Albert," which had been sent from Zlatoust in the Urals region. He had heard about me and wanted to get in touch. His next letter was confiscated by the postal authorities, and I didn't see it until I was going through the file. All it said was that in June he would be coming to Moscow and wanted to meet me.

That letter was made a part of the record in a separate criminal proceeding, and Albert was hunted down. He turned out to be "Boris Moiseyevich Bulyga, born in 1933, higher education, member of the CPSU,* no previous convictions, married, by profession an engineer." Bulyga had heard about me on the radio in March and had written me that he approved of what I was doing. On May 25, after hearing of my arrest, he went at 8:00 A.M. to the oblast administration of the KGB, but found no one there, owing to the earliness of the hour. Later, at the metallurgical plant where he worked, he went into the rolling mill and threw himself into a heat-treatment furnace where the temperature was 12,500 degrees centigrade. Two days later, two metal buttons—all that was left of Boris Bulyga—were retrieved from the furnace.

Almost everything in that order is false. First, in his letters to me, Bulyga said nothing about approving my actions: he merely wanted to meet me and have a talk. Second, it is very much to be doubted that he went to the KGB on his own, since a warrant for his interrogation had already been issued. Finally, it is simply nonsensical to say that there was no one at the KGB office at 8:00 A.M. There is always an officer on duty at such an office.

I am convinced that Bulyga did not voluntarily inform on me; that he was called in, just as other witnesses were called in at the same time; and that he was so frightened after he left that he committed suicide. I know of other cases where a person has committed suicide after interrogation by the KGB.

But there was no way in which Bulyga could have betrayed me, and I doubt whether he ever betrayed anybody. It is more likely that his suicide was due to the loneliness and depression one feels in a provincial Soviet town. In such places the KGB is virtually unrestrained, and a person feels especially defenseless. It is not hard to imagine the despair that would overwhelm a man lacking both self-confidence and support from others, if he is told, "We'll crush you! We'll destroy you! We have the power, and you won't get away from us. Your Amalrik is already in prison, and you'll be there tomorrow."

A barmaid by the name of Babushkina who worked at the Kazan Station in Moscow was interrogated on July 31. When Kirinkin asked her whether some person hadn't lived at her place during the second half of July, she replied unequivocally that during that time "none of the men spent the night there." I couldn't have passed a night with Babushkina in July, and in fact had never known of her existence. But one Gennadiy Sosnin testified that he had spent several days at her place.

According to the testimony of Police Officer Efimov, when he was on duty at the Kazan Station on July 27 he noticed a man "who was going around collecting empty bottles. Furthermore, another citizen I did not know came up to me and said that the man who had attracted my attention had anti-Soviet literature on him." It turned out that Gennadiy Sosnin, who had been in prison for several years in connection with a criminal case, had come to Moscow to "try to get a retrial." In the course of his attempts to do so, he spent the night at railroad stations or at the homes of chance acquaintances, supporting himself by collecting empty bottles. In early July, while resting in a park diagonally across from KGB headquarters on Dzerzhinsky Square, he noticed a suitcase under a park bench. He picked it up and took it to a secluded spot, where he opened it. Inside was a tightly rolled bundle of paper. But instead of money it proved to be a manuscript with the title *Will the Soviet Union Survive Until 1984?*

According to Kirinkin, Sosnin very much liked the ideas in the manuscript and wanted to pass it on to foreigners. But he didn't know how to go about that, so he decided to take it to its author, since my name and address were on it.

He came to our building three times, the last on July 26, but was told by some old lady that I wasn't at home. The next day he was detained at the station. And the day after that—oh, the amazing efficiency and vigilance of the head of the police detail at Kazan Station!—the manuscript, the police report, and Sosnin's explanations were sent to Sverdlovsk.

It is not difficult to figure out that Sosnin was under surveillance when the policeman detained him on the tip from the "citizen [he] did not know." When did the surveillance begin? From the time he first came to our place? But it's strange that the building was staked out—all the more so since on three occasions he did not find Gusel at home. From the time he first discovered the suitcase? But he had been carrying the manuscript with him for more than two weeks. And who had left the suitcase there? A distributor of samizdat? It makes absolutely no sense to put batches of pages in suitcases and then leave them here and there around the city, not knowing whose hands they will fall into. Was someone trying to get rid of the manuscript or pass it on to someone else? Such a person wouldn't choose the most crowded part of Moscow, right across from KGB headquarters. Then the suitcase must have been left there by a KGB agent? But what purpose did that serve? Finally, just who is Sosnin? And did he really discover the suitcase by accident?

I cannot give a firm answer to any of these questions. I do believe, however, that the whole thing was set up by the KGB, the idea being to begin with the "haphazard" distribution of a book and follow a chain of transmittals from one person to another. After all, it had not been shown that I had "distributed" my book. Kirinkin even reproached me for not having fed it into the samizdat network—then he would have had a case of "circulation." Sosnin and Babushkina, however, were very unlikely distributors of samizdat, so the operation was abandoned.

"Well, Andrei Alekseyevich, how do you like our town?" asked the deputy commandant of the prison.

It was October 2. That morning, he and another officer had come without warning and escorted me out of the prison gates. (Each was armed with a pistol, and they had warned me they would shoot if I tried to escape.) Now we were walking through a park. The leaves on the trees had turned yellow but none had yet fallen, and the air was limpid as it often is on days that are clear but not sunny. I had no idea why they were taking me to our destination on foot; perhaps they had decided this would serve as a kind of psychological softening up before the trial.

We didn't have far to go—only to the prosecutor's office, where they screened my TV interview with William Cole in front of a large audience. The women in the back rows oh'd and ah'd, Ubozhko applauded when I made my strongest points, and the prison commandant kept smiling broadly at me. I felt like a film star of sorts. The interview itself was much to my liking, but one thing troubled me: while answering questions, I rocked back and forth in my chair like a "wind-up" doll. Plainly, I was not used to sitting in front of a TV camera.

Bill Cole had managed to take part of the videotape of the first interview out of the country; but all of the sound track was confiscated, and a few days later it was played for me in prison. (This was called "presenting material evidence.") The audio-technician's wife, a young but exhausted-looking woman who was a police investigator, came in to listen and brought her husband two buns. Finally, after a considerable inner struggle, she offered me one of them.

Having looked through my case file, I signed a paper stating that I had read each of the nine volumes. And on October 6, after having viewed and listened to the videotapes, I did what prisoners call "signing the 201st"; i.e., I signed a paper stating that on the basis of Article 201 of the RSFSR Code of Criminal Procedure, I was familiar with all the materials in the file. When I saw Kirinkin for the last time, he showed me copies of his rulings in response to my lawyer's petition that I be recognized as an employed person, that my foreign royalties be unblocked, and that Ubozhko's case be severed from mine. The last of these requests was rejected indignantly; but the first two were granted, although the prosecutor kept calling me a "parasite," and the foreign currency was later confiscated from Gusel.

On October 29, my indictment was shoved through the chuckhole into my cell. But while I was still reading it, the turnkey shouted: "Amalrik, without your gear!" I was taken to see a man of short stature with a sallow face and glittering eyes. This was Kakitis, the investigator of especially important cases for the Riga Prosecutor's Office, who had served as investigator in Yakhimovich's case. The interrogation proceeded as follows:

"Have you ever been in Riga, and do you know anybody there?"

"I was there in 1965, but I don't know anybody there."

"Are you the author of *Will The Soviet Union Survive Until 1984?* And if so, to whom did you give it?"

I refused to answer that question on the ground that it had a direct bearing on my case, and I was not going to give any such testimony. The question was a trap they had set, so that later they could cite my answer as proof of my authorship of the book.

"Who sent the book *Will the Soviet Union Survive Until 1984?* to Riga?"

"I don't know."

Kakitis then played another trick: in the record of the interrogation, he made my answer read: "I don't know who sent my book." But I made him delete the word "my."

Then he cautiously asked what I thought of Kirinkin, who according to him was not an important investigator. (I later learned that the KGB was dissatisfied with the way Kirinkin had been handling the case.) I replied that Kirinkin was doing his best on the case.

He and Kakitis were of two very different breeds. Kirinkin was a bon vivant; I had noticed that when the clock hand was getting close to five, he would become nervous and squirm in his chair as though he didn't want to work one minute of overtime. But Kakitis was ready to drag out any interrogation and spend night after night scribbling away at reports: all he cared about was a well-drafted record of an interrogation.

Adopting the tone and manner of social chitchat, Kakitis went on to say that I should be given seven years instead of three, that after Stalin's death the people had got out of control, that the only true statement in my book was that the opposition had begun with rather innocent matters—from which it followed that people had to be put in prison, willy-nilly.

"But how many can you imprison?" I shouted, so loudly that the warder, who was eavesdropping on the other side of the door, began to fidget.

"Look here, Andrei Alekseyevich. You say you feel sorry for Soviet citizens. But you write 'works' and circulate them, and then we have to imprison the people who read them."

Then he asked me, quite unexpectedly, what I knew about the views of Maya Plisetskaya, Mstislav Rostropovich, Arkady Raikin, and several other people from the world of the arts. I replied that I was a humble mailman, so how could I know anything about the views of Rostropovich?

"Oh, no," he objected with a smile. "What with your book, you have come to be in a class with them, more or less."

On November 11, Shveisky, my lawyer, flew in from Moscow. I asked him if, after the trial, he could pass my statement to the court on to Gusel. (When I say "asked," I don't mean that I did so aloud: I wrote the question on a piece of paper which I then destroyed immediately.) Shveisky replied that he would have to think about it. After the trial, however, he categorically refused to do it. Naturally, that was a hard blow for me, since I had counted on getting my statements to the outside world via Shveisky.

The Trial

I was worried that they wouldn't give me a razor to shave. I could hear the teapot clattering in the corridor, and soon they began to serve out the miserable breakfast. Then, to my great relief, they brought me a razor and brush. Finally, the cell door was opened with a clang: on the day of a trial, even the warders could be taken for masters of ceremonies.

The oblast court was next door to the prison, but the paddy wagon took me to the outskirts of Sverdlovsk, to one of the raion courts, since they were afraid a trial held in the middle of town would draw a crowd.

On the way there Lev Ubozhko was lecturing the guards, and he went on with his talk after we had been ushered into the waiting room. The captain in command of the guards didn't know whether to argue with him or just keep quiet. The political instructor stuck his nose into the room, listened for a while, and then left in a state of fright. The conflict between Ubozhko and the system was one between Leninism as ideally interpreted and Leninism in practice. Brought up on the Soviet ideology, Ubozhko kept trying to make its imagined traits fit reality, which is why the authorities themselves called him a "psychopathic personality."

I can still remember four of our guards: two Kazakhs who never said anything, a Russian with the retarded look of an informer, and a sprightly Chechen who took part in the conversation. He said that if he were in the authorities' shoes, instead of locking up the dissidents, he would call a meeting with them and listen to their complaints and what they wanted. Ubozhko asked the guards, rather heatedly, whether in the event of new riots like those in Novocherkassk in 1961, they would fire at the people: "Surely you wouldn't shoot at your own mothers and brothers?" The Chechen, after hesitating, said that he wouldn't; but the others did not answer.

At this point a colonel came in. He was wearing gold-rimmed glasses.

Brezhnev wears glasses like that, and so do all officials down to a certain level. The colonel was at a low level for gold-rimmed glasses: one step lower, and they would have been "not in accordance with his rank."[7] He demanded that we hand over our statements so that the court could read them. Ubozhko gave him his notes: they were summaries and excerpts from Lenin that he hoped would help him in his defense. But I refused, not wanting them to know in advance what I intended to say. The colonel and the captain of the guards threatened to take my notes by force, but I said that in that case I wouldn't utter a word in court.

The trial began at 10:30. There were about fifty persons in the courtroom, all with the kind of faces that identified them as functionaries. Ubozhko and I sat down on a bench behind a low partition, with two soldiers on each side of us, and our lawyers in front of us. Facing them was Zinovy Zyryanov, a man of about fifty, who was assistant prosecutor of the oblast. Zyryanov had some kind of skin disease, and his face was all blotches and pimples.

The presiding judge, Aleksei Shalayev, was a man a bit older than the prosecutor, with a rather impressive appearance. He bore a faint resemblance to Jean Gabin, was polite, and conducted the trial in an easygoing manner. But like many people who have come to education fairly late in life, he spoke ungrammatically, and he read stumblingly.

The procedure was the usual one: announcement of the trial and of the composition of the court, voir dire, dismissal of witnesses from the courtroom, and identification of the defendants. When asked whether I wanted to challenge the composition of the court, I answered, "No." Ubozhko went on at length and none too intelligibly, saying that judgments must be rendered in accordance with one's conscience and that if the judge and assessors were conscientious, he had no objection to them. Finally, the judge read the indictment and asked us—Ubozhko first, and then me—if we pleaded guilty.

Ubozhko, knowing that I would not plead guilty, now stated that he, too, was pleading innocent, ascribing his partial admission of guilt during the pretrial investigation to the fact that the investigator had not taken down his words accurately and that he had signed the record without having given it due thought. In political cases, the chief aim of the pretrial investigation and the trial itself is to make the accused plead guilty and recant. If he does not plead guilty, his situation is bad. But if he first pleads guilty and then changes his plea, his situation is doubly bad. If Ubozhko had pleaded guilty and had ascribed everything to his "political immaturity," saying that he had fully matured under investigation in prison as a tomato ripens in the dark, he would have been sentenced to eighteen months. (And if I had done so, I would have got only one year.) But as a man of uncompromising honesty he wouldn't do so. At no time during the course of the trial, however, did he realize that his doom was sealed. Instead, he interpreted everything that was going on in a rather naïve manner. For instance, he told me that one of the people's assessors had looked at him sympathetically, and that was a sign of hope.

I read a statement saying that "no criminal court has the moral right to judge anyone for the views he has expressed. To oppose ideas with criminal punishment—whether those ideas be true or false—seems to me to constitute a crime in itself. . . . This court does not have the right to judge me. Therefore, I will not enter into any discussion of my ideas with the court; I will not give any testimony; and I will not answer questions put to me by the court. I do not plead guilty to the charge of having circulated 'false and slanderous fabrications,' but I shall not prove my innocence here, since the very principle of freedom of speech rules out any question of my guilt."

When I had finished and proffered my statement to the judge, he took it with the words: "For the record."

The judge had wanted to begin the questioning with me; but since I refused, he proposed that Ubozhko testify.

Ubozhko said that when he was a lecturer on international affairs, he had once attended a meeting between a group of lecturers and Shaposhnikova, secretary of the Moscow City Committee. In response to a question about Solzhenitsyn's *Cancer Ward*, she had said that it wasn't being published because it was too gloomy. Everyone applauded except Ubozhko, who decided to read the novel and only then pass judgment on it. So he made the acquaintance of someone named Victor, who first got the *Chronicle of Current Events* for him, then something by Sakharov, and finally the Solzhenitsyn book. When Solzhenitsyn was expelled from the writers' union, Victor asked Ubozhko if he would sign a letter in Solzhenitsyn's defense, and Ubozhko agreed. Arrangements were made for him to meet with a girl in a subway station, a girl whose name he didn't remember. She gave him the letter to sign and then asked if he had a typewriter. He had one at his place of work, and the girl herself typed my "Letter to Anatoly Kuznetsov" and gave Ubozhko a copy of it.

Taking with him the samizdat materials he had got through Victor, Ubozhko had come to Sverdlovsk, where he had read chapters of Solzhenitsyn's *The First Circle* to his acquaintances. "Solzhenitsyn really gives it to Stalin!" he added, carried away with admiration.

"In my opinion," the judge interrupted, "the way he gives it to him is stupid."

Ubozhko concluded his account by saying that he had passed on a copy of the *Chronicle* and of my letter to his old friend, Smirnov, so that the latter could read them if he wanted to.

I am giving only a general picture of his testimony. The main thing he talked about was his relations with his wife, something he came back to repeatedly. In my opinion, it was this battling with his wife that made Ubozhko into the staunch fighter we saw in the courtroom. He was born and grew up in the Urals, but went to college in Moscow. After graduation he wanted to stay in Moscow, so friends of his advised him to get married fictitiously. (In this situation, the man pays his fiancée a specified sum; they get married; and, being now his legal wife, she "registers" him as residing at her home. Of course, the "husband" doesn't actually live with her, but he has the legal right to live in the city.)

A "wife" was found for Ubozhko; he even really wanted to live with her, but it turned out that before the wedding she had had a lover, by whom she was pregnant. Ubozhko made haste to get a divorce; but the divorced "wife" maintained that he was the father of the child. Twelve paternity suits were brought, and at each trial the verdict was different. Meanwhile, the former wife demanded alimony and child support payments. (I would guess that when Ubozhko was sentenced, he at least felt consoled by the fact that his "ex-wife" was no better off than when she started—because you can't get much out of a zek.)

After Ubozhko's testimony, the court recessed. Outside, in the corridor, I spotted Gusel; we embraced and kissed before the guards could stop us. Earlier, when I had noticed that Gusel was not in the courtroom, Shveisky had reassured me, saying that they had been told only at the last minute where the trial would be held, and that while he had been driven there along with the prosecutor, Gusel and her friends had had to get there on their own.

Lena Stroyeva and her friend, who had come to Sverdlovsk with Gusel, were stopped by the police at the entrance. I asked the judge to do something about it, and the next day they were let in, although they weren't permitted to take any notes. As a witness, Gusel was not admitted to the courtroom until late in the day. She had a portable tape recorder with her, but the batteries turned out to be dead.

The first witness the second day was Ubozhko's friend Smirnov, whose denunciation had supposedly served as the basis for instituting the proceedings. He was melancholy and quiet, was lame in one leg, and had the look of an intelligent blue-collar worker. In response to questioning by the defense counsel, he said that he had previously worked at the same place as Ubozhko, that one bond between them was the fact that they both owned cars, that Ubozhko had taught him to play chess, that Ubozhko was a good-hearted but excitable man. When questioned by the prosecutor, he said that when he and Ubozhko met in January, the latter had given him some materials that he had looked through and then turned in to the organs.

At this point, Ubozhko, like a good-hearted but excitable man, shouted: "Don't get upset, Zhenya! I know the KGB searched your place and made you sign a predated statement!"

I had some questions and began.

AMALRIK (imitating the prosecutor): Did you read the materials you got from Ubozhko? Or did you just leaf through them?

JUDGE: Stand up! You must stand up when questioning a witness.

AMALRIK (standing up): But I've noticed that the prosecutor remains seated while questioning them.

JUDGE: That's his privilege.

AMALRIK (to Smirnov): Can you, then, state specifically that you read my letter?

SMIRNOV: No, I didn't read it—I just looked through it.

AMALRIK: You ,didn't read it, but you said that it "seemed inimical." Why?

SMIRNOV: There are things in it about labor camps.

AMALRIK: Well, *don't* we have labor camps? Aren't labor camps what's in store for Ubozhko and me? You said you turned the materials in to "the organs." Did you mean to the organs of the prosecutor's office? [Here I was setting a little trap for Smirnov: although our case was being handled by the prosecutor's office, his denunciation had been addressed to the KGB.]

JUDGE: You must ask only such questions as relate to you, personally.

AMALRIK: But you yourself acknowledged that our case was a joint one. Therefore, everything that affects Ubozhko affects me too.

SMIRNOV (not falling into the trap): To the organs of the KGB.

AMALRIK: Ubozhko called you an old friend, and you called him your friend. Then why didn't you have a talk with your friend and try to convince him he was wrong, rather than go straight to the KGB?

JUDGE (answering for Smirnov): That was his right, and he is standing by that opinion.

UBOZHKO (answering for Smirnov): They searched his home, and the KGB made him do it.

SMIRNOV (answering for himself): Ubozhko is a stubborn man. He wouldn't have listened to me.

I told Smirnov he had been wrong to act in the way that he did. At that point I wanted to describe just how badly moral concepts had been perverted in our country, to the point where one person can inform on another—even though he do so under coercion and not voluntarily—and testify against him in court, yet the two go on regarding themselves as friends. But Smirnov's life story was the mirror image of Bulyga's. Both were from provincial towns. Both were intensely curious about that struggle taking place somewhere outside their world yet directly affecting them. But no sooner had they touched the forbidden fruit than a heavy hand came down on them, and it seemed that there were only two ways out: death (for Bulyga) or betrayal (for Smirnov).

The psychiatrist Khodakov and the journalist Ustinov, to whom Ubozhko had read Solzhenitsyn, each behaved in a different way. Khodakov, rather corpulent and flabby with blond hair, tried to tone down the testimony he had given during the pretrial investigation. He said he had not really paid attention while Ubozhko was reading and that the latter had not given them the Solzhenitsyn material; rather, he and Ustinov had asked him for it. But Ustinov and his rat-faced wife were self-assured. Yes, Ubozhko had expressed subversive views; he had said he was a member of "Yakir's organization"; he had advised them to "get the cobwebs out of their brains"; etc.

"I was the first one to notice that the books were subversive," Ustinov said. "I looked at them only out of professional interest."

When Ubozhko's boss was questioned, he testified that on the job, instead of working, Ubozhko played chess and lectured on the international situation, and that he ordered his subordinates to repair his car. The schoolteacher Kuchina, a plump, bespectacled young woman of about thirty, testified that she had been "amazed by his strange elucidation of certain problems." In particular, she said, he had "made three untenable, anti-Soviet remarks." First, he had said that there should be well-educated people in the government. Second, he had praised Khrushchev. Third, he wanted to become a member of the Politburo. There was laughter in the courtroom, as Ubozhko tried to explain that what he had in mind was the necessity for regularly replacing officials so that the leadership would not become bureaucratic. I rose to question her.

"Tell me, Kuchina," I asked, "what do you find to be anti-Soviet in the statement that there should be well-educated people in the government? Surely you don't mean that our current leaders are not well-educated people? And what is anti-Soviet about Ubozhko's praise of Khrushchev? Did Khrushchev engage in anti-Soviet activities when he was first secretary of the CC* CPSU?"

Kuchina remained silent. I then asked her whether it wasn't perfectly natural for a Soviet man to want to become a member of the Politburo. After all, there was a time when its present members desired exactly the same thing. The soldier who does not wish to become a general is a bad soldier, so to speak. Conversely, it's a good soldier who carries in his knapsack the baton of a field marshal.[8]

The judge ordered a half-hour's recess without allowing Kuchina to answer my question.

Ubozhko was rather frolicsome in his behavior toward Kuchina. He greeted her with, "Hello there, dolly." And when she was leaving the courtroom after her remarkable testimony, he reached out from the defendants' bench and gave her a loving slap on the behind.

Only two witnesses were questioned with respect to me: Gusel and a customs employee named Stanishevsky.

JUDGE: What do you know about this case?

STANISHEVSKY (after thinking a long time): I don't know anything about it.

JUDGE: But don't you remember the circumstances under which the tape was seized from Cole, the American journalist?

STANISHEVSKY: The duties I perform at the customs office at Sheremetovo are those of political control. I stopped William Cole, a CBS correspondent accredited to Novosti, who was trying to take with him a few reels of tape. I asked him what was on the tapes, and he said: "Music." Since videotapes that are sixteen millimeters in length or longer can be taken out of the country only with the permission of the Ministry of Culture, I detained him and had the tapes analyzed. It turned out that what was on them was not music but an interview.

JUDGE: What kind of interview?

STANISHEVSKY (after long thought): I didn't see the visuals. I heard part of the sound track, but I don't remember it. I'm afraid I might mislead the court—it was so long ago. I do recall distinctly, though, that when we seized the tapes, the appropriate comrades reacted quickly.

PROSECUTOR: So that the tapes were seized only because they were sixteen millimeters?

STANISHEVSKY: Of course.

Neither Shveisky nor I asked any questions. But we could have asked why, if everything hinged on the fact of the sixteen-millimeter length, it wouldn't have been simpler to send Cole forthwith to the ministry for permission, without seizing the tapes.

It was now Gusel's turn to testify, and the judge solemnly told her that even though she was my wife, it was her civic duty to tell the truth about what she knew of the case at hand.

GUSEL (timidly): I know that my husband, Andrei Amalrik, was unlawfully arrested.

JUDGE (amiably): Unlawfully arrested by the investigative organs?

GUSEL: Yes.

JUDGE: What do you know about the publication abroad of your husband's books? Is he the author of *Will the Soviet Union Survive Until 1984?*

GUSEL (as per my instructions): I don't know anything about that.

JUDGE: But you *have* read your husband's books *Will the Soviet Union Survive Until 1984?*, *An Involuntary Journey to Siberia,* and others?

GUSEL (proudly): Of course I've read them! [Laughter in the courtroom.]

JUDGE: And what do you know about the television interview?

GUSEL: Nothing.

JUDGE: We'll remind you. Incidentally, your voice can be heard in that interview.

The judge then said that since I had refused to testify, the sound track of the interview would be played. It would not be screened, however, so as to avoid "leading people into temptation." We listened to a short section of the sound track—about psychiatric hospitals and the attitude of "Soviet persons" toward the U.S.—and the look on the faces of the people's assessors was one of horror and indignation.

JUDGE (switching off the tape recorder): I think that's enough. (To me): Is that your voice?

AMALRIK: I'm not going to testify.

JUDGE (to Gusel): Do you recognize your husband's voice?

GUSEL: I don't know. Maybe the tape was tampered with. [Indignation in the courtroom.]

The session the next day began with the prosecutor's speech. Recently, he said, we had celebrated the fifty-third anniversary of the Soviet regime. Since its very beginnings, its collapse had been predicted—at first in a few weeks, then in a few years. The prophecies had not been fulfilled, but that did not stop the "prophets." Amalrik's wife has said that he is the author of the books in question here, and he has not denied it. *Will the Soviet Union Survive Until 1984?* is a frivolous book. Amalrik writes that it was the result "not of investigations but of observations and reflections." (He should have said "fabrications.") And here is what was said about it by people who share his opinions: "A product of an immature mind."[9] The prediction of a thermonuclear war with China is nonsense; the seizure of power by the armed forces is nonsense; the choice of the year 1984 was a matter of pure invention. Obviously, this is slander. And how can a slanderer offer a sound judgment?

The prosecutor said that my books grew out of my resentment after having been exiled, that people should be grateful for repression as an educational measure, and that bitterness was regarded as ingratitude of an unnatural variety. He said very little about Ubozhko, but he asked that both of us be given three years. His speech was less harsh than I had expected.

Khardin, defense counsel for Ubozhko, emphasized his client's psychopathic personality. He said Ubozhko was attracted by the very idea of struggle, that he saw "little facts" but overlooked "the big truth," that he was curious but not subversive, that he didn't really have propagandistic aims, and that he should not be put in the same class with those who deliberately wrote and acted in a subversive manner. He suggested that Ubozhko be sentenced to the time he had already served.

Khardin had structured his plea in a way that was convincing in a professional sense. In my opinion, however, he should not have condemned, categorically, everything his client had said; nor should he have tried to protect him at someone else's expense.

In the first part of his speech, Shveisky completely endorsed the prosecutor's high opinion of Soviet achievements, saying that he found my beliefs strange and even repugnant. But without touching upon their substance, he asked whether they were really "slanderous and known to be false." Next, he analyzed the meaning and scope of Article 190-1 and argued that my books, being an expression of my opinions (even if those opinions were mistaken), were in no sense slanderous. He mentioned my expulsion from the university and my unjustified exile. Then he quoted from a decree of the 22nd Party Congress in which it was stated that the exposure of the "cult of personality" might incur certain costs and provoke a spirit of dejection. Having included me among those "costs," he exclaimed, "The rightness of our Soviet cause is something that should not be proved by a court but by the successes of communism and the force of our convictions." Finally, since nothing I had written was slanderous, he asked that the proceedings against me be dropped and that I be released from custody.

It was a good speech, considering the limited possibilities open to a Soviet defense counsel at a political trial. The rise of the Human Rights Movement was accompanied by the emergence of certain lawyers in Moscow who, in defending their clients, either denied some of the incidents cited by the prosecutor or gave them a different interpretation. The first bold speech of this kind was made by Boris Zolotukhin, at Ginzburg's trial in 1968. Zolotukhin was expelled from the Moscow Bar Association. And the authorities began to deprive other independent lawyers of their "clearance," i.e., their right to take part in political trials. That clearance—nowhere specified in the laws—is granted by the presidium of the bar association by agreement with (or more accurately, on orders from) the KGB.

Shveisky avoided passing judgment on my views and did not touch upon the matter of their circulation. Instead, he concentrated on the question of intent. He went off limits, however, when he asked for acquittal rather than a reduced sentence. When Shveisky returned to Moscow, proceedings to expel him from the Party were instituted by Kirilenko, a member of the Politburo. One charge was that he had not condemned my views in court "in a Partylike way." Some people said that the proceedings at our trial were transmitted to Moscow. I don't know whether that was true; but there was a lead-out cable in the courtroom.

Shveisky informed Gusel he could not take part in the appellate hearing. But then the proceedings against him were dropped. He was not expelled from the Party; he did participate in the appellate hearing; and he kept his "clearance." The authorities realized that some defendants may prefer to do without defense counsel rather than have one who is too dependent, and that this creates difficulties. For instance, people might say, "So-and-so was found guilty even though he didn't have a lawyer." The authorities are sensitive to this kind of thing. Also, sometimes what they want is pressure of a subtle kind—an informal "transmitter" from the court to the defendant, and vice versa. Thus, just before I made my final speech, Shveisky asked me whether I couldn't say—even though I didn't plead guilty— that the trial had made me see many things that I hadn't thought about before. I had no doubt he had been prompted to ask me that, so I replied, "That doesn't make sense: I'll get three years in any case." This, too, was said for "transmittal," since the "organs," although they may not believe you when you talk about your opinions, are quick to grasp practical arguments. Shveisky, who had managed to keep his balance somewhere on the razor's edge, was the lesser evil from the viewpoint of the authorities. And later on, he defended other stubborn and well-known dissidents, and likewise asked for their acquittal.

Ubozhko began his final plea with a quotation from Lenin about the danger of bureaucratic degeneration. Then he went on to discuss his troubles on the job, his lectures on the international situation, his marriage, the twelve paternity suits—and there he got bogged down for good. The defendant's final plea, in the course of which he usually asks for a reduced sentence or acquittal, is not subject to any time limit, but it is usually short. However, after more than an hour had gone by, Ubozhko was still talking about his wife. Of small stature, but muscular and solidly built like an athlete, with reddish hair around his premature bald spot, he seemed to feel himself on the rostrum again as a lecturer on international affairs, all the more so since there were Party "activists" in the courtroom. And he kept gesturing so vigorously that I removed the glass that had been put on top of the partition. From time to time, however, a guard would bring him some water to drink, since his throat kept going dry from his long speech.

At times it was interesting to listen to him, but at other times I began to resent his long-windedness. In the courtroom there were laughs, yawns, and occasional groans. The judge interrupted him several times, saying, "Ubozhko, get to the point!"

Ubozhko, however, continued to quote Lenin and tell about his fights with his wife and his troubles with the regime, remarking bitterly: "Anybody who thinks this doesn't concern him, will never understand it. The prosecutor, for instance, hands out sentences: three years for this man, three for that one. But he himself should be put in prison for at least three months."

"Ubozhko!" shouted the judge. "Stop insulting the prosecutor."

"I'm not insulting him," Ubozhko came back. Then, having somehow wrapped up the story about his wife, he went into a very detailed analysis of the indictment. After that, he digressed at length about drunkenness and the rising crime rate, until the people in the audience began to boo him, and someone shouted, "Is there life on Mars?"

"Ubozhko, that has no bearing on the case!" said the judge, rapping his gavel at both Ubozhko and the noisy people in the audience.

"The trouble is that people have no awareness!" Ubozhko exclaimed bitterly. I don't know whether he meant that the audience lacked awareness or that the entire nation lacked it, since the people had become disillusioned with Leninist ideology, and that the ones to blame for that disillusionment were the degenerate bureaucrats who refused to listen to Ubozhko in that courtroom. In any case, he concluded with a brief request that the court acquit him and make two special rulings: one restoring him to his job and the other declaring he was not the father of his wife's child. Then, greatly relieved, he drank a glass of water brought to him by a guard

Equally relieved, the judge announced a half-hour recess. I don't know whether he wanted to take a breather, or whether he figured that Shveisky would convince me, during that half-hour, to tone down my final plea.

In that plea I said that prosecuting people for their opinions was reminiscent of the medieval "witches' trials" and the Catholic Index of those times. The authorities realized that the collapse of any regime is preceded by its ideological capitulation; but they could compete with ideas only through criminal prosecution and psychiatric hospitals. Their fear of my ideas compelled them to put me on trial; but that very fear proved I was right. My books would not suffer from abusive epithets; and to imprison me for my views would not make them any less true. My country's chief task was to get rid of the heavy burden of its past, and that required criticism, not eulogies. I was a better patriot, I said, than those who prattle about their love for their country while what they really meant was their love for their own privileges. Neither the regime's witch-hunt nor this court could command the slightest respect from me, nor could they intimidate me. I realized that many people *were* afraid; but I still thought that ideological emancipation was an irreversible process. I had no requests to make of the court.

When I began reading my prepared text, I expected that the judge would cut me off after only a few words. But he never once interrupted me. When I finished there was a brief silence, and then he said, "The court will retire to chambers for deliberations, which will last about five hours."

The verdict recapitulated the indictment, and each of us was given three years. My sentence was to be served in an intensified regimen labor camp, and Ubozhko's under general regimen.† Also, the court handed down a special ruling—not about Ubozhko's wife, as he had requested, but about mine. The police were instructed to check whether Gusel was working and whether she was engaged in "anti-Soviet activity."

†There are four categories of labor-camp regimen: general, for most first offenders; intensified, for those who have committed a dangerous crime for the first time; strict, for one-time repeaters and those who have committed especially dangerous crimes against the State; and special, for recidivists. Amalrik was under special regimen in both Butyrki and Sverdlovsk prison.—TRANS.

The trial had been conducted more correctly than I had expected; but from a legal viewpoint, even within the framework of Soviet laws, it was seriously defective. Since I was charged under Article 190-1, the court should have examined three matters:

1. Whether what I had written and said was false and whether it was defamatory. The court took this point for granted. True, the prosecutor did analyze, in a way, *Will the Soviet Union Survive Until 1984?* He was concerned, however, not with whether the incidents cited therein were falsified but only whether they defamed the Soviet system. Any criticism of the system was taken to be synonymous with falsehood.

2. The question of malice: whether I had erred in innocence or whether I had known that what I wrote was libelous—this, of course, after its falsehood had been proven. My counsel's speech was entirely devoted to this question, but neither the prosecutor nor the court touched upon it.

3. The matter of "circulation." The court took that point for granted too, since my books had been published abroad. The case file, however, did not contain any evidence that I had passed those books on to anyone. Indeed, the manuscripts of *Involuntary Journey to Siberia*, the "Letter to Kuznetsov," or *Will the Soviet Union Survive Until 1984?* could have been stolen from me and published without my knowledge, in which case I could not have been responsible for their circulation. Likewise, it was never established whether I actually gave an interview to James Clarity or whether he quoted my words accurately. The article on art was never published anywhere, and the copy of it found at my home was not necessarily intended for circulation. The only thing that could be regarded as an established fact was the interview with William Cole. But it was "circulated" in the U.S. and Western Europe, not in the USSR, so that it came rather more under the jurisdiction of the American and European courts.

When I emerged from the courtroom, Gusel threw me some flowers, which the captain of the guards snatched away. Then he stamped on them, plainly venting the rage that had been building up in him for two days. Gusel picked up the flowers, dried them, and kept them until they suffered the fate of all dried tokens of remembrance and crumbled into dust. My last sight of Ubozhko came when we were shoved into the Black Maria.

C H A P T E R   1 4

The Place from Which
No One Returns

Being sentenced resembles being arrested again. The next day, Shveisky said he would file an appeal with the RSFSR Supreme Court. (I myself had decided not to appeal the verdict since I had not recognized the court.) When I asked him whether he would give the text of my final plea to Gusel, he categorically refused. Only one chance remained: a meeting with Gusel. While I was talking with Shveisky, my final plea was literally stuck in my teeth. Early that morning I had recopied the plea in small letters, rolled it up tight, wrapped it in cellophane, and tied it with a thread. It was now in capsule form. I hid it in my mouth all the time, so as to learn to speak normally with it. Then I again recopied the plea on a regular sheet of paper which I hid in my pants, hoping that when I was frisked before the visit with Gusel they would find that piece of paper and look no further.

It was impossible for me to recopy my plea without being noticed by Zhenya, and he could have betrayed me when I was taken to see Shveisky or he could have betrayed me when I was called out again. Two warders frisked me, found the paper in my pants, and, with expressions of satisfaction on their faces, took it into the next room. Then I was led to the visitors' room, where I saw Gusel. Zhenya had not betrayed me.

They seated us on either side of a long table and warned us we were not to kiss or touch each other. There was a solid metal partition under the table; and at each end of it sat a female warder, listening to us and watching us. But at least we could see each other and talk. Such conversations always begin confusedly: you want to say something important, but what comes out of your mouth is trivial.

It seemed to me that we had lots of time left, since visits can last up to two hours. But scarcely twenty minutes had passed when one of the female warders said, "Your time is up!"

We argued, but it was plainly useless: they were already pulling us in opposite directions. At just that moment, leaning over the table, with the warders right on top of us, we embraced and kissed. While I was kissing Gusel, I tried to push my little cellophane capsule through her teeth with my tongue, something I had had in mind throughout our visit. But she didn't understand me; there was only love and tenderness at parting in that kiss. The capsule fell to the table, but Gusel caught it and quickly put it in her mouth.

Both of the warders shouted, "She's swallowed something!"

"Darling!" I said. "Swallow it and vomit later." I had no doubt that they could extract my message from her mouth, but it was hardly likely that they would cut her stomach open.

She told the warders in a calm tone of voice that she hadn't swallowed anything; it was just that in her excitement she had drooled a bit.

I spent months memorizing my final plea, thinking that if they managed to get it away from Gusel or if it dissolved in her stomach, I could dictate it to her later on, during a visit at the labor camp. Later she told me that her throat was so dry from excitement that at first she simply couldn't swallow it, but that she finally managed, half-choking, to get it down. Just at that moment a doctor showed up; and Gusel, really afraid they would do a cesarean section on her, began to reiterate her story about drooling. But the doctor, after listening to her in some puzzlement and with an ironical smile on his face, said that medical science was powerless in this case, and left. Gusel was released some two hours later.

Gusel was afraid my final plea wouldn't stay long where it was, so she dashed to the nearest restaurant where, to the astonishment of the people at the next table, she mixed vodka with port, added some pepper, and dashed off two glasses of the mixture. When she began to feel sick, she walked unsteadily to the toilet. "The first time, nothing came out. But I strained and vomited once again, and what a welcome sight I saw! There in the washbowl was the little packet, undamaged. It had been so well wrapped that only one word dissolved."

She also told me that when her plane had arrived at Sverdlovsk, someone said over the PA system: "Comrades, who is going to the conference of power engineers?" Whereupon several men from her plane, both young and middle-aged but all with heavy briefcases, rushed up to him. The next day, when Gusel entered the courtroom, she noticed that all the "power engineers" were already there, mixed in with local gebists. So we baptized that trial "the power engineers' conference."

Three days later I was transferred to another cell, after I had been carefully frisked, and all my notes had been confiscated. "What are you doing time for?" asked the senior warder. "For politics? Oh, that's a complicated thing—almost like frisking."

I spent several days in the cell alone; but afterward they put another prisoner in with me, an eighteen-year-old moron sentenced for rape, the back of whose head was completely flat. His excuse was the same as that offered by rapists with more brains than he had: "She wanted it." I spent my days reading, did exercises for a long time every morning, and even continued to practice boxing, using my pillow as a punching bag as per the criminals' maxim: "Beat up on your own people so others will be afraid of you."

On December 1, I was informed that my case had been sent to the Supreme Court for an appellate hearing; the next day, early in the morning, I was taken out of my cell for a "transport." In prison, all transfers come unexpectedly, but this one was completely out of the ordinary. My sentence had not yet entered into legal force, and so they couldn't transfer me to a labor camp. Were they going to take me to Moscow? Hour after hour went by, as I sat there in the transit cell on a worn bench or paced back and forth, admiring the walls—walls filled in with concrete and splashed over with dirty pink paint. (In my dreams of prison, I always see that color.) I had looked at the clock in the corridor when I was being brought there: it was midnight.

The duty warder, after some indecision, escorted me along a seemingly endless corridor.

"Where am I being taken?" I asked.

"The engineer of the train knows where," he replied with a smile, and opened the door of a railroad car.

I went through the door and stopped on the threshold: the large compartment was full of women. Obviously, an order had been issued that I be kept isolated. But there were no unoccupied cells. And the duty warder must have been guided by the Russian proverb, "A chicken isn't a bird, and a woman isn't a person."

The women had been crowding around the door leading to the men's cell. But when I was brought in, the tide began gradually to ebb, so that finally most of them were surrounding me. They were being transported to Novosibirsk, to a labor camp. But where was I going?

When we had traveled for about four hours, the door was opened with a clang, and a guard said: "Out!"

The train had stopped at a small station in the Urals scarcely illuminated by a lantern swaying in the wind. It was terribly cold, and the snow crunched under the boots of the guards. The dogs showed their teeth. Six of us, including one girl, were ordered to line up in the snow, and then we were led to the empty platform. The sign on the station building read: "Kamyshlov."

It was a small town. Gusel told me later that it had a pretty church and the bread baked there was tasty; but of course I didn't see the church, and the bread I got was loathsome.

The prison was nearby. After having been frisked with great thoroughness, I was taken to the office of the commandant, a black-haired captain of about forty who was wearing felt boots. With him were his deputies for political work and security. They greeted me cautiously but not hostilely, and asked me in general terms about my case. We had a brief argument, with no mutual insults, about whether the Soviet regime was good; and then the commandant said that in any case, the cell they had prepared for me was good.

Once again I would be alone in my cell. This is forbidden by law. But I realized that I was being put in solitary as punishment for my final plea at the trial.

The first evening was one of misery and depression. It's always that way; then the routine smooths things out. For people whose inner resources are limited, solitary confinement—even for a short period of time—can cause mental disturbances. I suffered less, but there were times in camp, where it was rarely possible to be alone, when I yearned for a quiet cell. Yet solitary confinement *is* hard to bear.

Unfortunately, I couldn't get books for my studies, not even a textbook for studying English. Nor could I get good books in general: the library was worse than the one in Sverdlovsk. In order to keep my mind active, I would memorize one page every day. I continued my morning exercises and used my pillow as a punching bag.

My isolation was not complete. Three times a day, food arrived; once the woman who brought it whispered: "When you get out of here, write about how they feed us in this place."

Twice a day the duty officer would come to my cell. Once a day I was taken out for exercise—still alone. Despite the extreme cold, I tried to keep walking around for a whole hour, although the warders would attempt to cut it short so they wouldn't freeze up in the watchtowers. (Once I didn't take outside exercise for several days, and I noticed that I began to feel worse.) Each week I was taken to the bathhouse—not a bad one.

Prisoners are supposed to mop their own cells. But when I returned to my cell from outside exercise, I would find everything washed, and even the books and papers neatly arranged. The women in the next cell mopped the floor of the corridor and my cell at the same time. I must say to their credit that they stole nothing from me except for a bar of soap that Gusel had sent me. And that was a deed easily forgiven, considering that what we were issued was a disgusting, black, crumbly mess that only faintly resembled soap.

It wasn't long before I found a note that had been left for me, asking who I was and what I was doing time for. This was the beginning of a correspondence between me and one of my neighbors, whose name was Lida. After some time, I saw her—for just a moment before the warder slammed the chuckhole right in her face. Lida turned out to be a petite, somewhat plump blonde. I found out later she was twenty-six; she had been a teacher, then had become director of a commissary; and several months later was sentenced to four years for embezzlement. My letters to her were rather abstract, like those Voltaire wrote to Catherine the Great, but hers became more and more passionate. She wrote that she yearned to give herself to me, that she would remain faithful to me all the time I was in prison, and she reproached me for being cold toward her.

From time to time I would see the doctor, a very kindhearted man. After finishing medical school he had taken a degree in history; but when offered the post of *zampolit*,* he refused. "I'm a doctor," he would say with a smile, "and I observe strict neutrality."

At Kamyshlov nobody tried to humiliate me. To the contrary, if the commandant, Captain Rubel, could do something for me without violating his instructions, he would do it.

Once a month the prison was inspected by the raion prosecutor, a one-eyed man. Then there was the time when we were visited by a UVD inspector, who had the look of an ulcer patient and who got upset because I had four notebooks in my cell.

"He shouldn't have more than one," the inspector insisted. And then he asked if I wanted anything.

"All I want," I said, "is for you to get out of my cell."

On one occasion when I was taken to the commandant's office to make my routine complaint about the cold water they gave us to make tea, he announced to me joyfully: "My wife and I saw a film of yours on TV last night. It was one that we liked very much, and then in the credits we saw that the director was Amalrik."

"That's my uncle," I said. The commandant was deeply disappointed to learn that the director of such a wonderful cartoon was not an inmate in his prison.

Captain Rubel's pride in his prison was enhanced by a *Pravda* article on December 17 about one of his inmates—namely, myself. Of course I can't really say that the entire article, which was called "The Poverty of Anti-Communism," was devoted to me. It led off with words about the "agents of the imperialist intelligence networks," the "venerable professors of disinformation," the "mercenary hacks of the bourgeois press," and the "transoceanic obscurantists." But this was followed by praise for those people who were opposing such dark forces: Benjamin Spock, Dick Gregory, Norman Mailer, Paul Goodman, Angela Davis, Ralph Abernathy, and Senators William Fulbright and Margaret Smith. The article concluded with the words: "The Soviet people are stepping up their political vigilance . . . and this is something that should be borne in mind by the organizers of anti-Soviet subversive activities, and by those who carry them out."

The purpose of the article was to "prescribe" the correct attitude to be taken toward Solzhenitsyn's Nobel prize, my conviction, and the impending arrest of Vladimir Bukovsky. The author, "a certain" Aleksandrov (this is said to be the pseudonym of Mikhail Suslov, the chief ideologist), had the following to say about me:

> Take, for instance, a certain A. Amalrik. . . . Almost every day, Amalrik haunted the threshold of foreign correspondents, to whom he purveyed dirty rumors and gossip, which were subsequently thrown together as "reliable reports." Using those same rumors and bits of gossip, anti-Soviet Western publishers put together two whole books, one of which is now being shoved down the throats of American readers at a price of $6.95. It is precisely those dollars that chiefly attracted Amalrik. . . . That petty slanderer and foreign-currency speculator has been sentenced by a Soviet court to three years of incarceration.

The Soviet press has several carefully graduated epithets for its enemies. "A certain . . ." is the most disdainful; "the not-entirely-unknown . . ." is for persons who are of higher rank but have not merited genuine celebrity; then finally comes "the well-known . . ."; I was awarded that honor only seven years later, when *Pravda* called me "the well-known scandalmonger, Amalrik."

At the camp library I got the issue of *Pravda* containing "The Poverty of Anti-Communism" and gladly showed it to some zeks, who commented reasonably, "What do they mean by 'poverty,' when you latched onto a whole lot of dollars?" And one foreign-currency speculator—a real one, and not a "slanderer and foreign-currency speculator"—said, "Well, they sure won't last until 1984 if they can't come up with better arguments than that!"

At the time, *Pravda* was full of articles about "the heroic Angela Davis." Miss Davis, a member of the American Communist party, had bought a gun for a black youth who had subsequently shot a judge and several other persons; for this she had been arrested. All of the murderers, rapists, and holdup men I met were furious that a possible accomplice in a murder should be extolled as a heroine. And when Miss Davis was acquitted, there was groaning throughout the camp. From what the Soviet papers were printing about events abroad, one could tell what was causing them anxiety at home. The trial of

Miss Davis was chosen as a kind of counterweight to the political trials in the Soviet Union—and to mine in particular. And Angela Davis did not let her defenders down; when she was asked to support the liberal Communists arrested in Czechoslovakia, she replied that a socialist state had the right to punish its enemies.

From the example of Miss Davis, I understood that ideology can kill the most human part of a human being—the capacity for empathy, sympathy, and compassion. I read that while in prison she had given an interview in which she talked about the "inhuman conditions" of her incarceration. I asked Captain Rubel why she, under those "inhuman conditions," was allowed to meet with a television crew, whereas, under "human conditions," I was not even allowed a visit from my wife. His reply was: "Because they have capitalism, and we have socialism."

In late February, however, they did allow a visit from Gusel, after the appellate decision of the Supreme Court had been handed down. They permitted a two-hour visit; and although the young chief of the security section sat next to us, he did not interfere with our conversation.

When the judgment entered into legal force, my status changed from that of a defendant to that of a convict; and I mentally prepared myself for transfer to a labor camp. I wrote my first letter—one out of the three letters per month that a prisoner is permitted to send—to Gusel, who had already flown to Moscow:

> I regard myself as an investigator and explorer who is going off for three years to study the life of wild beasts in the wilderness, or perhaps the customs of the Papuans in New Guinea. Although an explorer realizes that he will undergo deprivations, troubles, and even danger, his interest in science and his passion for research outweigh all that.

On the night of March 2, I was taken by escort guards to the transport for Novosibirsk. I had lost my privileged status. For the first time, I found myself just one of a group of zeks: creatures in dirty gray quilted jackets with indistinguishable faces, likewise gray, who were sitting or lying down in the compartment of the railroad car. I had thought at first that I was being taken to the Kamyshlov camp, but when the time came for us to leave, the commandant just gave me a strange look and said nothing. Equally strange was the expression on the face of the old top sergeant who looked at me through the bars of the compartment. In his hands was a bundle of papers—my case file.

"An anti-Soviet, eh? With that stretch—and you're going to Kolyma!"

The fatal word: So they weren't going to leave me in the Urals. And they weren't going to take me to the Altai, to western Siberia, to the Trans-Baikal, or even to Sakhalin. I conjured up the boundless, icy wastes of Kolyma; the winds blowing from the Arctic Ocean; the Kolyma Road, built on human bones; the gold mines: the most remote and most horrible part of the Gulag Archipelago of the thirties and forties. And I remembered the most famous labor-camp song:

> *A curse be on you, Kolyma—*
> *the place that's called "a marvelous planet."*
> *There, a man goes crazy, willy-nilly,*
> *and nobody ever comes back.*

"Yes, an anti-Soviet!" I said, even feeling some pride in the fact that they had decided to send me to such a place.

"Well, come on out," said the top sergeant, opening the barred door. And he led us through the passageway. "You'll be more comfortable here." And with a smile he opened the door of the next-to-last cell, where there were three of us for three sleeping shelves. So it was that I rode in comfort to Novosibirsk.

On other occasions, too, I met up with escort commanders who weren't vicious people. But in comparison with 1965, the escort guards had become tougher and less disciplined, especially the young lieutenants who had recently been graduated from the MVD's officers' training schools. There was no control from above and no resistance from below. A crude and unstable young man could be complete lord and master of two hundred people for some days—they became vicious rather quickly. And the same thing happened with the enlisted men, especially if their officer set the example. On the run from Sverdlovsk to Kamyshlov, a husky private shoved me so hard that I flew from one end of the railroad car to the other. Another time a lieutenant with whom I got into an argument began to shout: "Beria was right to shoot you anti-Soviets!" Yet as a political I was given more consideration than the others. And that same Beria-admirer would kick zeks into the compartment with his booted feet.

"Get a move on, you fucking bastards!" shouted an attractive woman in a military uniform as she herded along a bunch of us who had just been unloaded from a Black Maria and were straggling through a corridor of the Novosibirsk Prison.

Through underground passageways with dim bulbs and damp walls, we were taken to our cells. In each there were several shaky bunk beds, but there was no space for us—not even on the floor. We had to put a rotting mattress under the bunk bed, like a miner working in an old stope.

Unexpectedly, space was found for me on the bunk of a teenager who had something of the Kalmyk in his features, and a good-hearted smile. When he reached eighteen, he was transferred from a labor colony for juvenile offenders to a regular labor camp. Some youngsters managed, before reaching their late teens, to put in time in a colony for offenders less than fourteen years old. For those who were sent directly to a camp for adults, there was still some hope of getting off the merry-go-round. But for those who went through "the teens," there was no hope.

"So you're in stir because of politics? Did you get three?" asked a man of about fifty. He was what is called in camp slang a "profiler,"† and had been on special regimen in the Arctic and just about everywhere. "Well, you won't get out all that quickly. You're not the first of your kind I've seen. They give people like you three years for a primer, and when you get near the end of it, they give you a new term."

"No!" cut in the good-hearted teenager. "You'll get out. You'll get out when your term is up."

According to law, prisoners are not supposed to be in transit for more than two weeks, but they can be and are in fact kept longer. In order to get out of that place as soon as possible, I decided to file a complaint about the bad conditions, figuring the prison authorities would say: "Let's get that pettifogger on his way right now!" Some other zeks had the same idea, and those who couldn't write asked fellow inmates to do it for them; so that when the chief warder made his rounds we had a whole pile of complaints to give him. Of course he may well have thrown all of them into the nearest wastebasket. But by now the discontent and rebellious mood among those of us in the cell was in need of an outlet; so I suggested that until we got an answer to our complaint, we should refuse to return our bowls after eating.

Scarcely had we fortified ourselves with watery borscht and rotten cabbage when the "gruel ladler" stuck his fat mug into the chuckhole and, as usual, shouted, "Give me your bowls."

To which my teenage friend replied, "Come and get 'em, you bastard!"

The guard on duty soon showed up, followed by the chief warder. They tried both suasion and threats, but the excited zeks kept on making a rumpus and shouting, "Get 'em yourself! Send us away from this place! Suck my cock!" And the most reckless ones banged their bowls against the wall. The "Great Bowl Mutiny" had begun.

†Someone putting on an act.—TRANS.

But the headiness of the struggle was short-lived. Within a half-hour the door was opened with a clang, and the top sergeant commanded: "Out!" Behind him stood several supervisors and a detachment of soldiers. The zeks went on making a rumpus, and those farthest from the door kept banging away with their bowls. But the soldiers, to use the military phrase, "reformed for the attack," and our ranks wavered. One zek broke away from the rest of us and went out of the cell, then the others straggled along after him. The teenager and I were the last to go out, leaving a pile of dirty bowls behind us. But the zeks who wanted to show they were loyal to the authorities came out with their bowls in their hands.

At this point, the sheep were separated from the goats. Most of the mutineers were put into nearby cells, but a few, including me, were taken down into the basement and placed in a cell on death row. It had a metal cot and table, both fastened to the wall and the floor; and the chuckhole was so designed that you couldn't see the guard. The tiny window under the ceiling gave onto a cement-lined refuse pit. No daylight reached the cell, and the bulb hardly illuminated it. Somewhere in the plumbing a blockage occurred, and foul-smelling sewage began to overflow from the gurgling toilet bowl. After a few days I started to get dizzy and feel nauseated. Things kept getting worse: I began to vomit, the cell seemed to sway before my eyes, and I could hardly make it to the cot. I heard my cell-mates pounding on the door and calling for a doctor. But a supervisor standing outside answered: "We didn't invite you here to get sick." The last thing I remember was a sergeant calling out my name for transport.

It was a very small room, but white and well-lit. I was lying on a bed and couldn't move either my hands or my feet. I couldn't recall where I was, what had happened to me, or who I was. It wasn't until the next day that I remembered my first name. Then, two or three days later, I remembered my last name. I had a recollection of railroad cars and of someone taking me someplace, but it was all very foggy. And then something distinct surfaced in my consciousness: a knapsack. I had had a knapsack with all my belongings in it; and in a kind of unreal way, the memory of that knapsack served as a link to the reality of my past experience.

I looked around and saw a man dressed in either white or gray, sitting on a bed against the opposite wall. He was staring at me. I didn't know, then, that a half-hour before he had removed a corpse from that cot.

"Where is my knapsack?" I asked, moving my tongue with difficulty.

"Well, so you've come to!" he said, in a tone expressing both surprise and pleasure. "And we thought you were going to die."

They shaved me so that I could be "shown to the general," as they say. Then I could see the bespectacled face of someone leaning over me; but it was not a general's face. He seemed to be wearing my glasses, and I asked: "Why did you steal my glasses?"

That was the last conscious impression I had that first day. I lay on my cot in that room for a week. The first thing I fully realized was that I was in a hospital; next, that I was in the camp hospital; and later on, that I was in the ward for terminal cases—where they are kept before being sent to the morgue.

When the top sergeant had come into my cell on death row and called out my name, I couldn't get up. They had put a jacket on me, and grabbing me by my arms—which, like my legs, were doubled up in pain—they had dragged me through the corridor. The captain of the guards refused to accept me when he saw that I was unconscious and in a state of paralysis, since he was afraid that I would die during the trip. Then they took me to the prison hospital, where I spent the night, constantly mumbling, crying out, and making delirious strange movements with my one unparalyzed hand. The next day I was transferred to the camp hospital. There they made a spinal puncture, which yielded only pus, and diagnosed my case as one of purulent meningoencephalitis. They injected me with antibiotics—I got so many injections that my behind looked like a punchboard, and for a long time I could neither lie nor sit on it. Two days later they made another spinal tap. This time, when they shoved the needle in, I began to swear obscenely, and the doctor told the orderlies, "He's going to live." The doctors, incidentally, were of the opinion that if I did miraculously survive, I would always be mentally defective. And later on they dubbed me "the man who returned from the other world."

I was unconscious for a whole week. For two weeks after I could hardly walk; and for several months my right leg was partially paralyzed. But gradually I regained my memory and (I hope) a sound mind. At first I was afflicted with insomnia and quasi-delirium. While still in the ward for terminal cases, I heard (or thought I heard), from the radio in the next ward, the endlessly repeated phrases: "Comrade Stalin said . . ." "Comrade Khrushchev said . . ." They were making ready for the 24th Party Congress; and while they may very well have mentioned Stalin on the radio, they certainly wouldn't have mentioned Khrushchev.

I realized I could have died. But when a person is critically ill and is approaching that fateful bourne, he becomes indifferent toward death; and I felt no anxiety about it. Yet on one occasion, when I was twenty-six, the sudden realization that I would die sometime—not right away, but eventually—threw me into such a fright that my hand grew cold; I went up to a girlfriend and took her hand in my cold hand so as to feel the touch of something alive.

Gradually I began trying to walk, holding onto the back of one bed, then another. Finally, I risked a trip to the toilet. There was no regular bathroom in the hospital—just a small room with a pail in it for patients who were enfeebled by serious illness. When they had filled it, one of the orderlies would take it outside.

There was no sewage system, only a latrine outside with a kind of shed built over it. It was not very pleasant for the patients to go there in the extreme cold of winter or through the mud in the spring, and they often quarreled with the orderlies as to whether they still had the right to use the pail.

But the bathhouse proved to be the worst experience of all. It was located at the other side of the camp. I would make my way there through a snow-storm, trudging along in deep ruts and led by other patients. In the smoke and steam of the bathhouse, among a crowd of irritated zeks, I would try to lift a tub of water, but I could never manage, since the tub was almost heavier than I was at the time. (I weighed only slightly more than 100 pounds.) The bathhouse was nearly as much of an ordeal as the latrine.

I began to read a little, although at first the printed lines were only a blur. And when I went outside, I would do my setting-up exercises. Once a tubercular patient from the next wing of the hospital, seeing me waving my arms as I stood on the steps, shouted, "Hey, you! Don't frighten us zeks with your muscles." I had to give up my boxing practice, however.

There were lots of thugs in the hospital, and they were always trying to scrounge. Once, when I gave one of them an orange, he told me he had a good friend to whom I should also give one. To which I replied, "He's *your* friend, so *you* give him the orange." I had a run-in with two others: holding onto the back of the bed so as not to collapse from weakness, we traded punches to the stomach. Both swore they would do me in someday. The thugs were continually talking other patients out of pills for various kinds of ill-nesses and then gulping down about twenty of them at once so as to get high.

One night a young thug was brought to the hospital in serious condition. As the loser in a card game, he had had nothing to pay up with, so he had squealed on his fellow players to the security division, and they did time in the punishment cell. Later, when the opportunity presented itself, the card players put some poison in his tea. He was groaning and unconscious upon arrival at the hospital. When they tried to give him an enema to flush the poison out of his intestines, he began to yell: "Guard! Guard!" Apparently, in his delirium, he thought the gamblers were raping him, this being the usual way of settling debts of honor in a labor camp.

"Seems as if your friend is calling you," said some of the bedridden zeks to the guard on duty, who was just standing there watching the proceed-ings with a stupid smile on his face. Other zeks were in a less playful mood. "That little shit!" they said. "Now he'll keep us awake all night." And the doctor in charge of the ward, as he came up to me, remarked, "Material for your future memoirs."

That young thug spent several more days in our ward. He regained consciousness, but he didn't converse with anyone. As I passed his bed, I would notice a look of hatred in his eyes. (I won't say bestial hatred, because at forty I have decided that the most dangerous beast is man.) Not long after, he was transferred to the cell on death row that I had been in—"the place from which no one returns."

Nothing was quite so frightening as the cancer patients. One, a mere skeleton with bluish skin stretched over him, would begin to scream as soon as the morphine wore off. While I was still in the ward he was written off and released from incarceration owing to his serious illness. The authorities write off only terminal cases, to make the MVD's mortality statistics look better. In this case, the man had less than a month to live.

The patient in the bed next to mine said he was a "colonel's son." During my years of incarceration, especially when in transit, I had seen a good many "sons" of colonels, prosecutors, generals, admirals, *obkom**
secretaries, and other highly placed persons. And whenever some tramp found it impossible to pass himself off as a "colonel's son," he would say that on the outside he himself had been a major. But Kolya Ustinov, judging from everything about him, was not from the streets. Of his fifty years, he had spent more than half behind bars (usually for theft), yet he had retained a remarkably cheerful disposition. "Sometimes on the outside, I would really miss the camp life," he told me. "I wanted to get back there and talk the camp lingo again."

Space is lacking to recount his many adventures, half of which he made up. This regrettable defect in his character made him akin to General Ivolgin, who told Prince Myshkin that he had buried his own leg in the Vaganskovsky Cemetery, with an inscription on the headstone that read: "Rest in peace, dear ashes, until that Glorious Morning."†

Every day, Ustinov had one or two epileptic seizures. A seizure can be brought on by a piercing shout, a sharp rapping sound, a shot—not to mention the fact that one person's seizure can provoke the same thing in another person. In the Stalin era, someone who didn't want the bother of dealing with epileptic prisoners individually thought up the idea of putting all of them into one camp. Ustinov had been in that epileptics' camp and still had horrible memories of it.

One day he experienced an especially violent seizure, and several people

†Actually, General Ivolgin complained to Prince Myshkin that it was Lebedev who had told the general about his own leg by way of mocking at the general's reliable account of how he had been a page with Napoleon, and who had advised him to leave Moscow. (Note for those who have not read Dostoyevsky's *The Idiot*.)

threw themselves on him and forced him down onto a bed. But an hour later he had another seizure and then another. He had seven in all, by which time he was completely devoid of strength. "Do you know why I had those seizures?" he asked me the next day. "It was because of you. In the morning they called me into the security chief's office. There was one man there from the UVD and another from the KGB in civilian clothes, and they all questioned me about you."

Ustinov had said in the ward that even though he had known me for only two weeks, he trusted me better than many people he had known for years. But the KGB trusted *him;* and so they proposed to an epileptic that he keep tabs on a paralytic. They told him, in effect, that even though he had spent a quarter-century behind bars for various petty crimes, he was one of theirs— a Soviet man—whereas I was a dangerous ideological subversive who wanted, unfairly, to get off with only three years.

There were bull sessions every evening. Usually they would begin with a debate as to whether the window should be opened. I alone maintained that it should be, so as to air out the ward. But the majority view was that fresh air was bad for one's health. Sometimes these arguments would be shifted to a higher, theoretical plane. For example: Is science necessary? The view that it is necessary (again, maintained by me and no one else) was easily disposed of and destroyed by the arguments of all the others. They held that the man in the street gains nothing from science; that scientists are clever frauds who fool the common people and live off the fat of the land. "But," I tried to object, "medicine helps you. Doctors cure you."

"What do you mean, cure? They cripple us. Any old peasant woman can cure you better than a professor, and she takes less money for it. That's why they did away with those women."

I remember a violent quarrel between two former POWs as to whether they had been well- or ill-treated when they came back from German POW camps. They had gone through pretty much the same kind of experience, but one of them tried to prove that everything had been good, while the other maintained that everything had been bad. Of course, different people can carry away different impressions even from the same camp. There are those who, on the outside, say that in camp they lived better than they have since lived on the outside. And there are those who, in camp, say that life is intolerable, whereas on the outside they got everything out of life.

"What do you mean, everything?" a skeptic asked on one occasion. "What did you get out of life?"

"Well," retorted the man who had been talking, "for one thing, me and the boys used to get a case of vodka and tank up so much that you could've fucked us doggy-fashion."

Naturally, the next subject to come up after vodka was women. Those prisoners who didn't have wives spent their leisure time in the hospital writing letters to women they didn't know but whose addresses they had got somewhere. Since the kind of male brutality that attracts some women could not be conveyed in a letter and since it was forbidden to send snapshots through the mail (for that matter, snapshots would no doubt have frightened off the lady at the receiving end), the men relied chiefly on womanly pity. The most impatient of them began to hint, even as early as the second letter, that there was almost nothing to chomp on in the camp. When one of these fellows asked my epileptic friend for a stamped envelope, Ustinov replied that not every female correspondent was worth five kopecks. But to Ustinov's great shame, when the lady answered the letter she promised to send a food parcel. That parcel was eagerly awaited by a lot of us, and those who had only recently made fun of the letter writer now tried to get in good with him. There was much speculation as to the contents of the parcel: sugar, butter, suet, sausages, sides of meat, cigarettes—and the most discriminating gourmands even talked about fruit. Finally, the parcel arrived and was opened, in a most ceremonious way, by the guard on duty in the guardhouse. It contained a baked potato.

Overwhelmed with ridicule by his disappointed friends, the letter writer, in a rage, threw the potato away. Later, however, he regretted what he had done: in camp, there are worse things to munch on than a homegrown potato with salt.

By late April I was taking short walks and looking in at the windows of the camp barracks. I was horrified at the thought that I had to spend two more years under such conditions.

"Hey, buddy!" shouted a tubercular patient across the barbed wire fence that separated him from me. "Are you Amalrik? Your wife has shown up!"

Then Ustinov came on the run and told me, "They saw a woman, who from all indications is your wife, standing on the embankment and waving a handkerchief!"

As soon as I was able to write, I had sent Gusel three letters, but when I received no answer, I figured they hadn't reached her because of the censorship. I went up to the second floor and looked out the window, but there was no one on the embankment. Next, I walked to the guardhouse, but nobody knew anything. Finally, a barber who had come to shave me told me that my wife had arrived. But we were not granted the visit. The pretext was that since I was sick, a visit from my wife might upset me too much, and that would have a bad effect on my health. By way of feeble compensation, they allowed Gusel to leave for me the kind of food parcel that is forbidden by law—with chocolate and caviar. But they removed the foreign labels from these items out of fear that they might be coded instructions sent to me by intelligence agencies.

Although I could walk, read a little, and even write, my condition was not good: I was still running a fever. I was given a Group Two disability classification, and the doctor said there could be no question of my being sent to Kolyma.

In early May I was discharged from the prison hospital and sent to a nearby camp. The doctor had predicted that I would suffer from headaches for the rest of my life. It is hard for me to tell, now, whether my health came back to me gradually or quickly. Even after my release from prison, there were days when I could not read or write a single line. Whether from prolonged reading or from staying out in the cold, I had the sensation of a heavy hand gripping the back of my head.

Nikolai Buyukli, the hospital's chief of internal medicine, and Zinaida Dontsova, my attending physician, were well inclined toward me and did what they could. (A few years later, I was told they had said that they had obtained medication for me from the Kremlin Hospital, since the authorities didn't want me to die in a camp.) But the doctors were also "processed." Dontsova was usually friendly, but when she noticed me reading an article about Buddhism, she asked with pursed lips, "Why are you so interested in Zionism?" One day I was taken to the chief physician, who asked me how I felt, whether I was satisfied with the treatment I was getting, and whether I didn't want to express my gratitude to the doctors in writing. I was in fact grateful toward the doctors, but instead of feeling the natural human impulse to express that gratitude, I suspected a trap. And I replied that I would be glad to put it in writing, but not until the eve of my departure.

On April 29, a guard told me to get ready to leave. When I had dressed and was standing in the corridor, wearing my padded blue jacket and holding my knapsack, Dr. Buyukli caught sight of me and asked in amazement where I was going.

"*Where*? But you yourself discharged me!"

"I know nothing about it," he replied. "You should stay on here for at least another week." And he went off to see the chief physician to clear things up.

A half-hour later he returned, looking guilty, and said that I had been discharged by Dr. Dontsova (the enemy of Buddhism and Zionism) just before she went on vacation. Of course Buyukli, as chief of internal medicine, could have kept me there. But ultimately the decision was not that of the doctors; it was made by someone in the oblast MVD or UKGB, people the doctors dared not argue with. Left to themselves, the doctors would not have done a bad turn to someone dependent upon them. But they were in no position to oppose a bad turn done by someone upon whom they themselves depended.

CHAPTER 15

Prisoners on the Move

At the Novosibirsk Prison, I told the officer on duty that I was being transferred to the prison hospital.

"Who needs you there?" he sneered. And I was taken to a cell identical with the one where I had begun the "Great Bowl Mutiny" two months before. There were five double bunks for forty men. To the left of the door, I noticed an empty space between the wall and a bunk and put my mattress there. I slept in that cavelike space fifteen nights. Although the floor was disgustingly dirty, it was wooden, and the bulb that burned twenty-four hours a day didn't glare directly into my eyes. After my stay in the hospital, I found the cell to my liking, despite the onerous conditions. It did not have that atmosphere of sickness and death, that specifically hospital atmosphere that has always oppressed me (even outside of prison), an atmosphere that itself can make a person sick.

One of my cell-mates was a surgeon from the Crimea. He took my pulse and my temperature, which was still rather high; and even that much medical attention had a calming effect. He had only recently been sucked into the Gulag, and was astounded by everything he saw. In particular, he was amazed that they had seen fit to discharge me from the hospital and send me off on a trip of more than five thousand miles.

Every day a nurse peeped in through the chuckhole, handed out anti-flu medication to those who wanted it, and put me down for a visit from the prison doctor. I sent in several written requests for the same thing, but never once was the doctor summoned to see me. The only time I saw her was just before the transport. She was sitting in the dressing room in the bathhouse, checking to see whether every prisoner's groin was shaved.

"I know about your illness," she told me in an irritated tone of voice, "but you didn't die on us."

"And if I die in transit?"

"That's a problem you'll have to take up with the doctors along the way."

No sooner had I come back to the cell when someone said to me, "You've run your mouth more than enough! Now sit it out!"

But I had some spirited defenders in the cell. One of them had been a miner and then a *raikom* instructor, but since he drank too much, he became a miner again. He said that conditions in the Ukrainian camps were much worse than in Siberia. The greatest hardship was hunger. No kind of meat was allowed the prisoners, even in food parcels; in one camp a piece of rotten lard was nailed to the wall with a sign in big letters reading, "Shame on pork eaters!"

"Why? Was the camp commandant a Jew or a Moslem? Is that why he prohibited pork?"

"He was a swine," replied the miner.

I was very interested in attitudes toward the regime both as an institution based on a definite political philosophy and as the power exercised by a certain group of men. The convicts' attitude was almost unanimously negative, and the younger people were more antigovernment than the older generation. To what extent the community of zeks is representative of Soviet society as a whole is a controversial question. Those who rely on crime as a way of life have a negative attitude toward any regime; but in the camps, they are in a minority. The majority want to return to a normal life, and the ideas they live by coincide with the views of a considerable part of the lower strata of society. Camp life, which exposes the mechanisms of government, has merely given them a final polishing and loosened their tongues. "This mass . . . ," wrote Julius Margolin, "represents 90 percent of Russia's population. One could, in a single day, release all these millions and replace them with others, with equal justification."[10]

It is widely believed that the less educated a person is, the more freedom of speech the authorities grant him. A student who was serving his second term for armed robbery told me that what most astounded him upon his return to prison was the change in the zeks' attitude toward the regime. Earlier, he said, he had never heard so many anti-Soviet remarks. When I compared my experience of five years before with my current one, I agreed with him. One example of this concerns a film about the civil war that was shown in the camps. At one point, a character in the film cries out with great feeling, "Do you know that in our town the Whites shot ten thousand Communists?" Whereupon half the audience would shout: "That's not enough!" The authorities, much upset by this, found a Solomonic solution to the problem: in 1972 an order for the execution of several prisoners for anti-Soviet activity was read aloud in the camps. Nothing was said as to the article under which they were charged, but the officers explained that they had been shot because they "ran their mouths too much." After that, the zeks quieted down for a while.

I do not, however, mean to say that the general attitude of the people toward the regime (as distinguished from the individuals in power) is negative. The attitude of many people could be called one of passive acceptance. I do not even mean that "love of the people" for the regime that propaganda drums into one's ears is purely fictive. If you are being raped daily, you will either hate the rapist or come to love him. And the "love of the people" is of that kind, since hating demands a greater effort. When I hear someone say that the Soviet people can simply shed the past sixty years and go back to the values of pre-revolutionary Russia or that they can adopt Western values, I am skeptical. If we want to compare the experience of the Soviet people with that of a man who has been incarcerated, we can say that the zek will of course agree that he himself lived better when he was on the outside than he did later behind bars and that a person who lived on the outside while he himself was doing hard labor in a camp could get more out of life than himself. But he will not agree that his life behind bars was in vain and that he got nothing out of it. He feels that he learned something significant through suffering. And when the zek, with a feeling of superiority vis-à-vis the person who has never been in prison, remarks, "He has not gone through what I went through," he is saying something that might well be echoed by the people as a whole, who will never dismiss the half-century since the Revolution as a waste of time. If we use the terms of the Hegelian triad, then the "thesis" of the Revolution was "February" (the attempt to Europeanize Russia) and the "antithesis" was "October" (the reaction of Russian Asianism against Europeanism, of the "people of the steppe" against the "city dwellers"). But the big question is: Will there be a "synthesis" of our Revolution? And if so, of what kind?

I also met up with some Stalinists. In my cell there was a quiet fellow who, when he began to talk about Stalin and his great wisdom, would gesticulate with enthusiasm. It was usually (but not always and not only) such illiterate and downtrodden little fellows who turned out to be Stalinists. For them, Stalin was a kind of universal Robin Hood who took the side of the humiliated and the oppressed, who destroyed their evil superiors—secretaries of *raikoms* and *obkoms*, plant directors, marshals and generals, professors and academicians, writers and artists. He was continually destroying them, but he didn't destroy enough of them, so that once again they became a burden on the poor working stiff. As for the fact that Stalin sweated the working stiff more than anyone else, it was not forgotten, but it seemed of secondary importance. Why shouldn't one suffer in the name of a good cause?

I had scarcely time to look around the cell at Novosibirsk when I was approached by a young man named Igor. He asked if the name "Ubozhko" meant anything to me. He had been in the Omsk Prison with Ubozhko, and the latter, as he put it, propagandized him for a week. Igor behaved as if the three of us belonged to the same underground organization. Ubozhko, he said, had failed to provide him with a certain secret address in Moscow, and I was supposed to give it to him.

I was put on my guard. That evening his friend Oleg said to me quietly, "Don't trust Igor. They called him into the security chief's office, and he agreed to inform on you, figuring they'd shorten his term."

Two days later, Igor was transferred to another cell, but Oleg remained along with me. He kept repeating that he sympathized with my views and could smuggle letters to the outside and make other necessary contacts. Gradually I gathered that both he and Igor were playing the same game. And the device employed was a classic one: by betraying Igor, Oleg would win my trust. For that matter, they had been well chosen for their roles: there was something nervous and repulsive about Igor; while Oleg, a husky athlete, was even-tempered in an attractive way. (Both, incidentally, were doing time for rape.)

Later on I would occasionally meet people who had been fellow inmates of Ubozhko's, and I found out what I had been expecting to hear. In Omsk they had instituted new proceedings against him under the same article, but this time they had deemed it expedient to find him mentally incompetent and have him confined in a prison psychiatric hospital.

In Novosibirsk I first encountered that system of extortion that was widely practiced during transport, and to a lesser extent in the camps. A bunch of thugs and near-thugs would get themselves assigned to the same cell. (The makeup of the group might change, but they all knew one another, like Masons.) They would take over the best bunks and then begin to extort food and other things from the other prisoners. The opening gambit was to ask another zek to "give" them something or "trade" something with them. Many victims preferred to buy them off. But if a man didn't yield right away, he would be threatened and then perhaps beaten up.

Sometimes, during a prisoner count, a victim would report the robbery to the chief warder, and the thugs would have to give the loot back. (They always did so very unwillingly, of course, while saying something like, "You gave it to me yourself, you shit!") Then the victim would be transferred to another cell, where the same thing usually happened again.

The rationale for this kind of extortion is the "thieves' ideology." Like all revolutionary ideologies of our century, it is based on Nietzsche and Marx, although its followers may not even have heard of their names. It proclaims, on the one hand, the right of the strong to disregard the interests of the weak, of the active person to disregard the interests of the passive individual; and on the other hand, it proclaims social equality. Later, I had a debate with one such ideologue, who had told an approving audience of teenagers: "A manager's son gets everything, while a working stiff's son gets nothing. Does the working stiff's son have the right to steal? Of course he does!"

That was different from the "thieves' philosophy" that I had heard about from my father or read about in Shalamov's stories, just as the thugs I had come across differed from those my father and Shalamov had talked about. The gist of that philosophy was that the thieves' world was entirely separate from the ordinary one, that they enjoyed an exemption from all human laws and morality and constituted a kind of mystical order. I gather, however, that such ideas have become obsolete.

It is the young thugs—or *tsapany,* as they call themselves—who leave one feeling the most demoralized. One often has the impression that their only feelings are those of animals. I am convinced that there is such a thing as an innate penchant for crime: the need always to be fleecing someone else is instinctive. I recall one time when I was sitting on the "bed boards" with a *tsapan* and noticed that he kept shoving me toward the edge. He wasn't doing it because he needed room but merely out of habit. So I stiffened and gave *him* a shove.

Yet there are criminals with the rudiments of noble traits (howbeit somewhat distorted), so desperately in need of protesting against injustice that crime is the only way they can find to express that protest. Once when I was drafting an appeal for a pardon for another prisoner, I wrote that the man in question had been driven to crime by "a misunderstood sense of his own dignity." When I read it to him, he looked at me dumfounded. "*What?* What did you say? That's just the way I felt, but I didn't know how to say it!"

The thugs were strengthened by their willingness to take risks, willingness lacking in those who have something to lose. Also, they operated in groups, whereas the other prisoners acted individually. But sometimes the latter managed to join forces, and then the thugs would retreat.

For my part, during my first days behind bars I made a resolution never to offend anyone and never to bow down to anyone. I decided that if anyone tried to extort something from me, I would refuse to hand it over, even if I got beaten up. (It is humiliating to give in.) And no one bothered me. One day, however, a toothless young criminal who had been eyeing my ball-point pen said to me, "That's a fine pen you have there. Naturally, you're going to give it to me?"

We stood there trying to stare each other down, until I finally broke the tension by saying: "I'm a writer, and I need that pen the way you need your switchblade."

Some eighteen months after I first landed in camp, I was again on the move as part of a transport of prisoners. I was carrying a big knapsack and was wearing a Norwegian ski suit and a fur cap, things I had managed to keep intact while in transit prisons in the Urals and Siberia.

In Khabarovsk a young thug said to me, "You're a nervy guy—I can see that!" From the criminal's viewpoint, this was the highest praise. As they say, "Nerve is an extra dose of luck." Of course, if I had come to blows with anyone, I would have had a hard time of it, what with my lack of skill, my dislike for fighting, the glasses on my nearsighted eyes, and the fact that I was constantly exhausted, since I had not yet recovered from the meningitis. The attitude that others take toward you, however, is not determined by your strength but by the way you carry yourself, by your self-confidence or lack of it. Also, the fact that I had been put behind bars for politics played a big role. Back in the thirties and forties, to be a political meant that in the eyes of the thugs you were a fascist and were first on their list of people to be fleeced. But the current tendency was to respect the "refusers."

It was in Novosibirsk that I first became acquainted with the relationship between the "refusers" and the *aktiv*.* "Refusers" is the name adopted by those prisoners who are unwilling to cooperate with the prison officials and who seek instead to live by their own rules. The *aktiv,* on the other hand, are those who collaborate with the prison administration. In the camps, with the help of the officials, the *aktiv* have the upper hand. But during transports of prisoners, the refusers try to make up for this—all the more so since there is a deliberate policy of transferring people from camp to camp, so that the camp groups will be broken up. As for the *aktiv,* most of those transported are former "chemists."

Even in the Khrushchev era, during a time when there was expansion in the construction of chemical plants, the number of prisoners was rapidly growing and there was a need for manpower on such projects. So prisoners with terms of no more than three years (and sometimes more) who were not disabled and had not violated prison regulations were sent, when they had completed one-third of their term, to construction sites under a police guard. In official lingo this was called "conditional release to construction sites of the national economy," but in the vernacular it was called "chemistry." And beginning in 1971, first offenders with short terms (but not those charged under certain articles, of course) were sent directly from the courtroom to a construction site. While this was a quasi-release from incarceration, if the prisoner violated the regulations or if he didn't meet with the approval of his superiors, he would be sent to a labor camp, and the time he had served in "chemistry" would not be counted. In 1972, on the occasion of the fiftieth anniversary of the USSR, the routine dispatch of prisoners "to chemistry" was solemnly represented as an amnesty. Apparently, they had decided to cut down on the number of "chemists."

Our cell was full of such returned chemists from the *aktiv*. Then one day the door clanged open and in came several refusers with the air of a master entering his own home. There was a quick determination of who was who, and then those who only a few minutes before had been lying on their bunks looking important had crawled under them and were afraid to speak up from there.†

In the refusers' eyes, I was a kind of brother, and one of them wanted to express his fellow feeling for me the best way he knew how—by socking somebody in the kisser. "I really have it in for the Commies," he told me. "I'm a little short on brains, but I know what to do."

I was an inmate in many cells, and they struck me as a convenient model for the study of human society—a rather primitive model, perhaps, but accurate enough and very accessible to inspection. The inmates had their own laws, their own code of ethics, their own leaders, their own exploiters and exploited, and their own "silent majority." The cell leader was not elected by a democratic process of voting but instead assumed his position spontaneously, as it were. Nor should it be thought that he was necessarily the physically strongest zek or the one readiest to take risks. The primary qualification was that he express most fully the ideology of the majority of his cellmates. Since I was the same kind of outsider inside the cell as I was outside of prison, no one took me to be "one of us."

Being called out for a transport is almost as welcome as being released. The cell where the prisoners being sent to Irkutsk were being assembled was still almost empty. One man was sitting at the table; in the corner, on the floor, was a young fellow with remarkably clean-cut features. I said something to him by way of greeting, but he didn't answer: he was silent and motionless. Only once did he move—to get up for a drink of water: it seemed to me that he walked with some difficulty. Then, with much shouting and furor, some young thugs came dashing in. For them there was nothing mysterious about the boy; he was a "Mashka," or passive homosexual.

In my previous cell I had taken particular notice of another young man

---

†To be forced to "crawl under the bunk" is a great humiliation for a prisoner in a Soviet labor camp.—TRANS.

who was at once impudent and fearful, with the spiteful look of someone downtrodden. Once I saw him washing some thugs' shirts and socks in the washbowl and realized that he was a Mashka, the most despised breed in the camp hierarchy.

In the camps, the epithet "pederast" is applied only to passive homosexuals, who are also called *pidery,* "goats." Active homosexuals would be insulted if they were called pederasts. The thugs are very proud of their "scores"; when I was in the hospital, one of them, toward whom I felt only loathing, bragged in the ward that he had worked over one "goat" so well that there was a kilogram of shit on his penis when he pulled it out.

The passive homosexuals do not comprise only, or even mainly, those zeks who have that proclivity. They tend rather to be people of weak character who are easily scared and may have lost at cards. Usually, the debauching of a prisoner follows upon his violation, in some way, of the underworld code— often by way of a frame-up. There is a special slang word meaning "to turn (someone) into a passive homosexual": *opidarisit'*. And once a person has acquired such a reputation, he can never shake it off; it will follow him from one camp to another. Some subsequently make their new condition into a source of income, prostituting themselves for butter, sugar, cigarettes, or a bowl of soup.

In debauching a fellow prisoner, the older zeks tend to use persuasion rather than force, often buying the favors of boys; and sometimes stable couples are formed. But the younger thugs simply use threats: "Take your choice, you shit! It's either a knife or my prick that'll go into your ass!"

The young thugs who had rushed into the cell, shouting like schoolboys out for recess, wanted to take advantage of the boy sitting in the corner. They even argued as to how to fuck him—in the ass or in the mouth. He was forced to crawl up to an upper bunk. Some of them followed him; and soon one could hear heavy breathing and threats: "Let up with your teeth, you bastard, or things will be rough for you!"

Both while resisting and while yielding, the boy remained silent. It is painful for me to recall that incident, all the more so since I might have prevented it. But an experienced zek later told me that there is really no way to help these people, and that the boy would end by either resigning himself to his situation or sticking a knife into someone.

Yet I would not say that those young thugs were especially vicious. It is just that young people more easily accept the norms of behavior in their milieu. One young man quite simply aroused feelings of sympathy in me. He was doing time for having murdered his stepfather, who had been tormenting his mother. He showed a good sense of humor when talking about the reformatory, and there was nothing of the thug in his psychology. One night, very

late, he woke me up: "Andryukha, teach me how to become an anti-Soviet!"
"Why do you want to do that?"
"So I can kill the Communists," he replied with a good-natured smile.

I was taken with a contingent of zeks from Moldavia to Sakhalin. Traveling
with a bunch of young thugs for two days was sheer hell. They were always
bugging the escort guards, who in revenge didn't give us anything to drink.
In transit they provide you with black bread and so-called *gamsa*—slithery,
salted, almost-inedible sprats—so that it is very hard to do without water.

As they lay on the narrow shelves that served as beds in the Stolypin car,
the young thugs sang sadly:

> *Forgive me, Mamma, for what I've done:*
> *Forgive me for not listening to you.*
> *I thought prison was only a joke:*
> *But that joke has been the ruin of me.*

"Uncover, and put your hands behind your backs!" the duty officer at
the Irkutsk Prison greeted us. "Do you have any complaints about the escort
guards?"

The crowd of zeks kept a sullen silence. Then came the roll call: last
name, place of birth, age, article under which convicted, sentence. As the
prisoners' names were called out, they were taken off to "boxes." Finally I
was the only one left.

"So you're from Moscow?" a black-haired, middle-aged lieutenant said
to me. "I am too, but I'm a real Muscovite. I defended Moscow against the
Germans."

"I imagine I would have defended Moscow too." I replied, "if I were
the same age as you."

Instead of putting me in a box, the lieutenant took me to his spacious
office. It turned out that he had heard about me on the Voice of America and
Radio Liberty, and he wanted to talk to me. His own views were a strange,
yet not unusual mix of Stalinist leanings (this is often a species of nostalgia
for one's lost youth) and dislike for the neo-Stalinist bureaucracy. Something
that is not direct opposition but rather an awareness that we Russians are not
living the way we should—a state of mind opposite to the public's mood of
ten years ago—is spreading ever more widely, although the opinions as to
what changes are needed are many and vague.

I was placed in a solitary cell, so damp and cold that I slept without
removing my cap or boots. For exercise, I was taken out into a damp, gloomy

yard. I spent ten days in that cell. The worst part of it was that I had nothing to read: they didn't even give me the local newspaper. I was terribly hungry, and more in need of food now that my body was on the mend. I kept daydreaming of how, after my release, I would go to good Moscow restaurants. It was a kind of gastronomic masturbation.

In Irkutsk I had yet another run-in with prison medicine. I didn't have the expected headaches, but I felt a burning sensation in my groin. At first I thought I was simply itching because of being dirty. When I took a close look, however, I saw some little insects jumping around in my pubic hairs like monkeys in a jungle. They were crab lice that I had picked up in the bathhouse.

The next morning I entered my name on the chief warder's sick list, so I could get some sulfur ointment. Then, when the doctor made her rounds without looking in on me, I began to pound on the cell door. A short, red-haired woman of uncertain age with the face of a polecat, who was wearing a doctor's white coat, came to the chuckhole and told me in an irritated tone that I had not put myself down for sick call. She added that she had no time and was not going to talk with me. But I held out for my rights, and the guard went to find the chief warder. Ten minutes passed while the doctor and I stood there, on each side of the chuckhole, saying nothing. Finally, the chief warder arrived and confirmed the fact that I had entered my name on the sick list.

"What's your trouble?" the doctor asked.

"Crab lice."

"We'll give you some ointment." With that, she slammed down the cover of the chuckhole.

An hour later, a zek serving as orderly brought me a vial of ointment. The guard stood there and watched me put it on, just to make sure that I didn't swallow it, which would have been one way of avoiding serving out the rest of my term.

"This isn't Moscow," the guard said, obviously proud of Irkutsk. "You can get things worse than crabs here. You won't get coddled."

The trip from Irkutsk to Khabarovsk was the worst one yet: four days in a crowded compartment. I managed, though, to get a bottom shelf for myself. In the same compartment was a workingman with a tattoo on his arm that read: "DEATH TO TRAITORS!" He kept complaining that even on the outside, a working stiff like him had to sleep leaning up against a doorpost, whereas white-collar types, even in prison, could sprawl out as if they were on a sofa. Finally, I told him, "Okay. You're a working stiff, so work, already! Me, I'm a white-collar type, so I'll lie down and rest.'' That argument struck him as irrefutable, and he shut up.

The next night I was robbed. In the morning, I noticed that an old thief was going through his knapsack, and that put me on my guard: plainly, he was trying to show me that he didn't have any of my things. I dragged my knapsack out from under the shelf. It had slimmed down remarkably. The young thugs who had been put on the train while I was sleeping had cleaned it out. What was left of my sugar cubes had been consumed by them during the night. I did get my notebooks and envelopes back, and my soap dish and soap were returned to me by the fellow I had played chess with the evening before.

I later gathered that during the night my pens and socks had been traded for tea to the escort guards (without whose connivance the theft could not have been committed). These guards sometimes deliberately put thugs in the same compartment with newly committed prisoners who have knapsacks. The new arrivals are ruthlessly robbed, and some of the loot goes to the escort guards. When prisoners in the compartment would ask me, "Why did they put a political like you with us criminals?" I would reply, "They put me in with you so I would have as hard a time as possible.''

I was telling an older criminal that the theft could not have taken place without his blessing, and he responded by giving me a shabby rabbit skin, saying it would come in handy in Kolyma. I accepted it indifferently, as a kind of symbolic compensation for my stolen pens, but it turned out to be priceless. Thanks to the waistband that I made out of that rabbit skin, I did not get radiculitis in the far-below-zero cold.

In the courtyard of the Khabarovsk Prison, as we were dragging ourselves along in a miserable column, I glanced through the barred window of the basement, and it was like taking a look at one of the last circles in Dante's Inferno. A glaring bare bulb illuminated a room as huge as a railroad station, with a black ceiling, a rough cement floor, and iron beds. Half-naked zeks lay curled up on the table, on the floor, and (by twos) on the iron springs of the beds. I asked myself in horror: Are we, too, going to be put in that place? And as it turned out, we were. I spent three days there, with the iron bedsprings stabbing my body. They never issued us any spoons, so we gulped down our soup like dogs. There were no books or newspapers, and even the radio was turned down to a hoarse whisper.

I went to Magadan in a plane. (The practice of transporting prisoners there in ships was discontinued when the other camps in Kolyma, except those for local inhabitants, were closed down.) As the normal passengers eyed us curiously, we four zeks were taken to the rear compartment. The kind of meal that is usually served on a plane was a great event for a zek.

Because of the bad weather, we first had to land at Irkutsk. En route to Irkutsk, we flew over the Okhotskoye Sea (still icebound, although it was early June), then over Kolyma and Yakutia. It was already getting dark, but there was no sign of a human dwelling or any lights—just treeless swamps, as though we were flying over a lunar terrain.

In Yakutsk we spent the night in a cell at the airport police station, where I first saw some bums of the type called *bichi*—the word comes from the English "beach." There are plenty of dissolute drunks all over Mother Russia. But in the port cities (where the word was first used), and in the north, vagrancy is associated with the seasonal nature of work—in fisheries, in gold mines, and on geological surveys—where labor is needed only in the summertime.

At the Kolyma gold mines, there is the following gimmick: In the summer, no vodka is available. But as soon as cold weather sets in and mining comes to a stop, vodka makes its appearance. The workers proceed to get dead drunk, so there are legal grounds for discharging the majority of them for absenteeism. Many miners, having thus hired out from season to season, start drinking when winter comes and hit the road, subsisting on odd jobs and having no permanent home. At any airport, bus station, or post office you can see bums smelling of booze and filth. In the cold season some of them spend the night in the city sewers. They are called "tankmen" because when one of them climbs up to the surface and throws back a manhole cover, he looks like a soldier crawling out of a tank. In combatting the *bichi,* the authorities periodically round them up and jail them for vagrancy. But when they get out, there is no place for them. Moreover, there are so many of them that they can't all be put in jail. (According to official but unpublished estimates, there are about a million such bums.)

At Magadan I went to see Captain Pinemasov, the nervous, flaxen-haired security chief, who was fond of political discussions. He had served in Kolyma since the middle 1940s.

"So you've been slandering our motherland," he said to me, "and meantime you're eating Russian lard."

Alas! I thought. The last lard I ate was when I was in transit; now I would have to be satisfied with the gruel they serve in prison.

The captain's remark was a typical example of the Soviet ideologues' habit of thinking in terms of the belly. When they heap reproaches on "cosmopolites," "anti-Soviets," "Zionists," or even "abstractionists," they first of all reproach them with having eaten Russian lard—though I doubt whether a Zionist would eat lard.

At one point I was summoned by the prison commandant, Lieutenant Colonel Podolsky, a solidly built man with gold-rimmed glasses who, as I discovered, was strong-willed. He told me that my wife had filed a request for my release on account of my sickness and that he and his colleagues had to draw up a report. He asked me if I wanted to file a request, and I said no.

Although Gusel submitted a good many requests for my release after that, I was never again questioned. On this occasion, however, they kept me at Magadan for a month. I suspect there was some vacillation as regards my future. Podolsky told me he had been warned that Amalrik was coming his way, and he'd have trouble with me. He added that he had imagined me as something quite different from what I was.

"It's not very likely that you'll achieve much," he said to me. "The regime is stable. Also, what matters to the majority of people is not ideas, not freedom of speech, but goods and services. And the standard of living is rising."

"What does the majority amount to?" I replied. "In baking, you use a lot of flour and just a little yeast; but it's the yeast that makes the bread rise. Moreover, it isn't starving people who carry out revolutions—it's well-fed people who haven't eaten for a day or two."

His response was: "I advise you not to say anything like that in the camp."

The widespread view that the majority is not concerned about freedom of speech but cares only about goods and services strikes me as wrong. True, most people do care about their comforts, but not only their comforts. The need to speak out, to unburden one's soul, is deeply rooted. And things left unsaid gradually unsettle even the most prosperous person.

Soon I was transferred to a common cell with no shields on the windows, so that I could see the daylight. One of my cell-mates had been chief of electrical services at an Arctic airfield. When some ditches were being dug, he had padded the reports on the amount of earth-moving work, and had been convicted of "embezzling socialist property." Now he was waiting for the decision from the appellate court. Like most novices, he was hoping that his sentence would be reduced. Like most people who are imprisoned unexpectedly and for something that is commonly practiced, he still couldn't understand what had happened to him.

"I just can't figure it," he would say to me. "Not long ago I read in the paper that three people had distributed anti-Soviet leaflets and they got only three years apiece. Me, I was trying to serve the State. I took a trip to get some cable and reimbursed myself a little for my expenses—and they gave me six years."

When I told him what I was doing time for, he said in a changed tone of voice: "Well then, when you get out, write about my case. People in the West should find out what kind of sentences they give us."

I am now complying with his request. And if not everyone in the West learns about the fate of Victor Ivashchenko, at least those who read these *Notes* will.

After being in solitary, you feel an especially great need to talk with others, and the investigators take this into account. During my stay in that common cell I quarreled a lot with Ivashchenko. I shouted so loudly that once a puffy-faced female warder looked in at the chuckhole and barked, "Hey, you! Stop making speeches!" (I didn't know whether she was referring to what I had been saying or to my loud voice.)

Gusel's petitions for my release having proved fruitless, on a sunny morning in June I was called out for transport. In the Black Maria there was room to sit down, but not enough room to turn around. We traveled the last 185 miles northward along the unpaved Kolyma Road to the settlement of Talaya. And during that trip, the aftereffects of my meningitis made themselves felt: I vomited all the way, and by the end of the day I was unconscious. The man sitting next to me, who had been most attentive up to that point, took advantage of my unconsciousness to steal my sugar. I consoled myself with the thought that I was traveling under such conditions for the last time, since I was supposed to serve out the rest of my term at Talaya. If anyone had told me that I would be making that trip seven more times, my guts would have turned inside out seven times.

Corrective-Labor Colony 261/3: Singing and Dancing

It was already growing dark when the Black Maria pulled up at the guard-house. I saw a two-story, whitewashed barracks, a fence with barbed wire strung along the top, the gate of the camp, and a short soldier with a flat face.

My name, sentence, and the article under which I had been convicted were entered in the log by the work-assigner, who looked like some kind of castrato. As he made his entry, he said to the duty officer in a high-pitched, lilting voice, "This guy got into trouble by scribbling stuff he shouldn't have."

Among those zeks who were close to camp officials (a kind of camp "establishment") the rumor persisted, just as it did in the Moscow establishment, that I was a KGB agent. I was the only one sent to Kolyma from Moscow with a short term and a case no one understood. Even earlier, while I was en route, I had gathered from snatches of conversation among various officers that they thought I might well be a special envoy of the KGB disguised as a prisoner and that it was my mission to check on conditions in the camps and the state of morale among zeks and camp officials. It was the old Russian story: "An inspector general is on his way here."[11]

As I came out of the guardhouse, I could see, beyond the board fence, a moor with a sparse growth of trees—a kind of green backdrop for the sad stage setting of the camp. I was horrified at the thought that I would be spending two years here.

No sooner had we been shown around the barracks than I was called back to the guard shack. I figured that perhaps the commandant wanted to talk with me. But the man who had summoned me was the duty guard, Master Sergeant Kochnev.

"Pick that up!" he commanded, pointing to some bread crumbs in the hallway, crumbs from the bread that had been issued to us en route to the camp. Naturally, I didn't pick them up. But I realized that I couldn't count on any indulgence here. "When you were on the outside, you could write your little books. But here, we're going to bring you back to your senses in a hurry."

I was already dropping off to sleep, lying on the dirty bed boards of the half-empty barracks, when someone asked me, "Do you have some kind of hammer I could nail up my nameplate with?"

I was surprised by my neighbor's polite tone of voice and his well-bred appearance. He explained he had not once been reported for a violation of discipline since he started serving his term. An order had been issued for prisoners to nail up a nameplate on their bed boards, and he wanted to do it immediately.

"How long are you in for?" I asked my educated neighbor.

"Fifteen years," he answered proudly. It turned out that he was doing time for having raped his three young daughters. I dropped off to sleep with the thought that I would be spending my time in good company.

Like any Soviet labor camp, ours (which, by the way, was not officially called a "camp" but "Corrective-Labor Colony 261/3") was divided into two zones: the living zone and the working zone. (Zeks almost never say "camp" or "colony," but rather "zone."*) The living zone took up no more than one hectare and comprised three wooden two-story barracks, a one-story school, a cafeteria (which was also a club), the canteen, a dispensary, a toilet, and an administrative building where the camp officials "received" the zeks. To these was added, while I was in the camp, a stone bathhouse.

The toilet was a little shanty erected over a latrine. The latrine was heaped with frozen excrement, with frozen urine as a kind of frosting. It wasn't pleasant to sit in when the temperature was below freezing. Once when another zek and I were squatting there, I asked my young neighbor, "Listen, I don't mean to be critical or anything like that, but why are you pissing right on the floor instead of through the hole?"

He looked at me in amazement. "Does it make any difference?" he asked.

In the area between the barracks and the service buildings the zeks played soccer or volleyball, until soccer was prohibited. The living zone was surrounded by wooden fences with electrically charged barbed wire running between them. Between the fences there were police dogs and sentries, but there were no sentry towers. A single tree grew in the zone.

The zeks were split up into five companies of from 120 to 160 men. Each occupied one floor of a barracks, which was divided into two sections separated by wooden or metal bunks and the lockers between them. The zeks stuck pictures cut out from magazines on the walls and the lockers. From time to time Captain Garafutdinov, the officer in charge of political indoctrination, would make the rounds of the barracks. As he tore down the pictures, he would say, "Learn to love monotony!"

Sometimes the campaign against the pinups would slack off, but then the prohibition against keeping things under mattresses would be enforced. One camp song even included the following verse:

> We're squaring things away like in the Navy—
> from under mattresses, onto the floor.
> Take to your heels, zeks! Montik's searching us,
> And Shmyglo's coming on the run to help!

Montik and Shmyglo were duty guards for the barracks. "Montik" was an actual last name, but "Shmyglo" was a nickname, though it could have been the other way around.

Garafutdinov greeted us newcomers with a little speech, saying that those men who worked well would get privileges, but that those who worked badly or shirked work altogether would be punished. Then he read out a list of job assignments. But as a Group Two disabled person, I was left to myself. I spent my time lying on my bunk reading a copy of *Crime and Punishment* I had found in the camp library, strolling around the dusty plot of ground in front of the cafeteria, or listening to the screeching sounds of pop music, sounds wrung from electric guitars by a bunch of hooligans. In general, I "lived it up," as the Americans say.

One of the first persons to pay me a visit in the barracks after hearing about me was the camp blacksmith, Kutsky, a young man with a thin face and an intent gaze. While in the army he had organized a group for the study of Marxism; and one of the members, who was either an anti-Marxist or too much of a Marxist, had informed on the others. When Kutsky heard about it, he pulled out a knife and stuck it into a table in front of the culprit, telling him, "That's what's in store for you, you shit!" For "the business of the knife" he was given six years as a hooligan.

In camp he wrote an opus called "Paper Socialism," the aim of which was to expose Soviet "nonsocialism" once and for all. While still a child, when he read that the Bolsheviks were rallying for a May Day celebration and saying, "There's going to be a festival on our block too!" he thought what they had in mind was the time when the Soviet regime would be overthrown. It was only later that he realized they had that very same regime in mind when they said "festival."

I refused to read his treatise, since his Left-Communist ideas had already begun to annoy me. After talking with doctrinaire left-wingers—for all their decency, and their ofttimes subtle critique of the Soviet system—one is always left with the impression that they carry the truth in their pockets like some kind of collapsible yardstick and that at any moment they are going to display that yardstick and measure everything you say.

Shortly thereafter, I met up with another "leftie." Or maybe a right-wing reactionary. Who knows? In any case, one day when I was taking a walk I was approached by a dark-haired fellow with a smile on his rather feline face. He was a workingman named Petya Vasilyev, whose father had served under Chapayev.[12] Petya was doing time for murder and was well known for the many complaints he had filed with the authorities. He never stooped so low as to submit them to some oblast prosecutor, but sent them directly to Brezhnev. He protested at the least provocation. Petya once saw a poster in camp that said: "YOU ARE GUILTY TOWARD YOUR OWN PEOPLE." It was the kind of thing that the other prisoners totally ignored. But Petya promptly wrote to Brezhnev: "Of what am I guilty toward my own people? I didn't raise prices; I didn't lower wages; I didn't crush people with tanks. So what am I guilty of?"

On another occasion Master Sergeant Shmykov pulled out Petya's footcloths from under his mattress and threw them away. Petya immediately sent off a complaint to the Presidium of the Supreme Soviet that began with long quotations from Marx, Lenin, and Brezhnev, followed by a mention of Chapayev. Petya went on to say that whereas he used to think the Fascists were his chief enemies, he now regarded the Chekists as their successors. Also, that the "bloody sword" of Sergeant Shmykov (that "bloody sword" always figured in his complaints) was hanging over his head. Only then did he get to the matter of his footcloths.

Petya usually concluded his letters of complaint with the words: "For the time being, I am writing only to you; but if necessary, I can address myself to the Embassy of West Germany." And when, in 1971, realpolitik and détente were put into effect, he said to me bitterly, "Coming from anybody else, that low-down trick wouldn't have surprised me. But I never expected it from Willy Brandt."

Petya subscribed to a tremendous number of journals, from which he extracted the Marx and Lenin quotations he used in his complaints. But then he changed his tactics. The historical and sociological journals often quoted the opinions of American professors on the Soviet Union—with the aim of unmasking such scholars. Thus the phrase "in the opinion of the progressive economist Galbraith" or "in the opinion of the reactionary historian Pipes" would be followed by a brief quotation. Petya would put the quotation in one of his complaints, replacing the preceding phrase with the words "in my opinion." He would say to me, "Those people in the Presidium will rack their brains trying to figure out how come I'm so smart, and I never went past the eighth grade."

But the views of J. K. Galbraith or even of Richard Pipes on the Soviet Union struck Petya as too moderate. So he chose a third tactic: he would copy out the opinions of Soviet professors on the U.S. and present them as his own opinions on the USSR.

I don't know what channels Petya's complaints went through—whether they reached the Supreme Soviet or whether Sergeant Shmykov used them to wipe his rear end. But I do know that the only response to them was Petya's getting sent to the ShIZO†—especially after he started using the quotations from the Soviet professors.

I soon got to know Lesha Ivanchenko, our "culture organizer." He was my age, short and stocky, with shifty eyes, and wore a neat blue T-shirt. Lesha said he had been a truck driver who hauled oats to the same camp where he would later be incarcerated. At a filling station he met a fifteen-year-old girl, who asked him to give her a ride. On the road they put away a bottle of vodka, after which everything happened (in Lesha's words) "by mutual consent." Fatigued by the long drive, the vodka, and lovemaking, Lesha and his victim (or girlfriend) parked the truck along the side of the road and went to sleep, the girl not even having managed to put her pants back on. Meantime, her mother had set out in search of her. Coming upon the parked truck, she yanked open the door, and the first thing she saw was the naked rear end of her own daughter. "What woke me up was somebody pulling on my hair," Lesha told me. "Then I saw some woman standing there, who was in a rage. 'What happened between you and my daughter?' she asked me. I should have said that I gave her a ride, and her pants came down because the road was so bumpy. But instead I told her straight out: 'You'd better ask your daughter about that!'"

Those words were Lesha's undoing: he was arrested, and the girl testified. According to the language of the decision, "she was smeared with an abundance of vomit and excrement; she cried, sang, and said she wanted to become a movie actress."

"You're an idiot," the police chief said to Lesha. "You should have fucked her and tossed her into the ditch, and you wouldn't have had any more trouble. But now you're going to get three years."

"So there I was, sitting in the courtroom," Lesha continued, "and thinking: Am I really going to get three years? What had I really done? After all, she put out. No, they just can't give me three years. And then the judge

---

†Punishment cell where one can be confined for a period of up to fifteen days.

read the sentence: a tenner! You could have knocked me over with a feather.'' It was stated in the judgment that he had raped not just any girl but an ''active Pioneer,'' which made his crime even more heinous.

Lesha wanted to become a teacher (I don't know what his experience with the Pioneer had to do with this), and he subscribed to the journal *Family and School.* In the evenings, sitting in the library, he would read *Eugene Onegin,* learning it by heart as he went along. By the time he had served half his term, he had got up to the second chapter.

Often, after dining on gruel made from the oats that Lesha had left on the road for someone else to deliver to the camp, I would play checkers with him. After pouring me a glass of tea, he would recite Pushkin's immortal lines:

> *Thirst demands yet more goblets*
> *To wash down the hot fat of the cutlets . . .*

Since he had no hopes of becoming a teacher, Lesha was consumed with a desire to work for me at Akulovo. ''We'll dam up the streams near the house,'' he said. ''Then we'll raise ducks and sell 'em.''

''But won't the ducks' quacking bother me when I'm writing?''

''But we're going to sell 'em! And who's ever been bothered by the jingling of money?''

The library where Lesha worked occupied two rooms. Books were kept in the smaller room and issued there. The larger room contained bound newspapers and magazine racks. One rack was labeled ''The Political Knowledge Corner.'' On it were several thick brochures and a photograph of Brezhnev. Another rack was called ''The Legal Knowledge Corner.'' *The Corrective Labor Code* that had been carelessly put on display there was stolen the next day. (It is almost impossible to get copies of the code, since the investigators and camp officials don't want the zeks to know about their rights and the limits to the punishment that can be meted out to them.) A third rack bore the identification ''Our Glorious Soviet Armed Forces'' and held photographs from the magazine *Ogonyok.* Finally, the fourth rack was titled ''Our Active Readers.'' There one found, inscribed in oil paint, the names of zeks, many of whom had since been released, and some of whom had already been rearrested, convicted, and sentenced again.

Hardly any of this propaganda achieved its aim, since almost no one used the reading room. And those few zeks who did try to use it were carefully screened by Lesha to make sure they didn't tear the newspapers and didn't steal anything. The display was chiefly intended to impress officials.

In each company's section of the barracks was a kind of miniature reading room called "the Lenin Room," with photographs of Politburo members and a shelf containing some battered books. This was supposed to be a place where prisoners could find cultural relaxation, where they could do some reading or write letters. But as a rule, the key was kept by the senior barracks orderly, who (like Lesha) didn't issue it to everyone. Along with the slogans, the chief propaganda weapons were the wall newspapers. They were usually published just before the great Communist holidays, May 1 and November 7. They carried items with headings like "A FESTIVAL OF THE SOVIET PEOPLE," "OUR SHOCK WORKERS," and "WHO IS MAKING IT HARD FOR US TO LIVE?" Often all three of them would be the work of one and the same "activist." While I was still at the camp, they began putting up photographs of "heinous malefactors." Also on display were oil paintings, done in cartoon technique, of typical criminals: murderers, rapists, hooligans, holdup men, and embezzlers.

The culture organizer's duties also included getting zeks to sign up for newspapers and journals twice a year. Just as on the outside, one could not subscribe to any Western periodicals except Communist ones. Later, even these were banned. Still later, the authorities prohibited Yugoslav periodicals; and finally, Eastern European ones. By the time my term was up, you could subscribe only to Soviet periodicals—and not even to all of them. But on the average, prisoners take out more subscriptions than do people on the outside: reading is a compensation for unfreedom. The journal *Man and the Law* had more than a hundred subscribers (out of about seven hundred). *Izvestiya* had fifty, and *Pravda* had one. Many zeks subscribed to local newspapers. The majority preferred magazines with illustrations.

The zeks' favorite reading material was articles about crimes and trials. I remember how one gloomy old fellow, sitting on the bunk next to mine, read in *Ogonyok* (moving his lips as he did so) about Dmitri Mikheyev, a graduate student at Moscow University, who had tried to flee to the West disguised as a Swiss tourist. Halfway through the article, he stopped reading and said to me, "They'll probably give him three years, the way they did you. I can see why they keep calling him 'Dima' in such a friendly way. But with people like me they don't waste much time talking: you get six years, and off you go—the bastards!"

Actually, Mikheyev got eight years. By now he has served out his time, and I gather he is somewhere in the West. As for the old fellow who was reading the article, I very much fear he is again doing time in Kolyma.

The library subscribed to only three or four newspapers. No books were ever purchased for it; instead, they were obtained in a rather unusual manner. The prisoners were entitled to order books through the mail; and once or twice a month a van would bring them from a bookstore. But the prisoners had no place to keep the books, and for that matter they were not allowed to have more than five at any one time; so most of the zeks simply gave their books to the library. On the other hand, some of the "active readers" tore up the books they had borrowed from the library and used them to wipe their rear ends, since there was no toilet paper in the barracks. The result of all this was a kind of balance, with the number of books neither rising nor falling.

In the library we played checkers and talked. I didn't know at the time that a listening device had been installed there to record my statements.

In early 1972, there was a furious spurt of activity in this smoothly functioning "cultural work." The good Captain Garafutdinov had apparently not been zealous enough in propagating the love of monotony and was replaced by a Captain Ovechkin. Upon his arrival, Ovechkin was promptly nicknamed "The Jerk"—a rare honor for an officer in the security forces, where no one is especially distinguished for his intelligence.

In the course of making preparations for his arrival, Lesha got nervous about how he was going to show off his wares. I advised him to draw up a graph showing the "rise in the number of active readers" as evidence of how much work was being done in the library.

"But there hasn't been any such rise," he said in tragic tones, "and I haven't kept any records."

"So much the better," I said. "Just give me a piece of paper."

In a few minutes I had drawn a graph with a curve that climbed gradually upward—sometimes fluctuating, of course—until, in anticipation of the new *zampolit*'s arrival, it suddenly shot straight up. When he saw how easy it was to achieve a growth in readership, and that he was in control of everything, Lesha took heart and decided he would be able to hang onto his job as culture organizer.

The new *zampolit* first familiarized himself with the personnel dossiers and then took a look around the compound. The kinds of slogans that had got Petya Vasilyev so upset were displayed everywhere: slogans about a prisoner's guilt toward his motherland, about honest work, and about conscientiously meeting the demands of the regime. Among them was one that read: "THE MOST DIFFICULT VICTORY IS THE VICTORY OVER ONESELF." A former culture organizer had taken that quotation from Blaise Pascal and posted it on a wall with the permission of the camp officials. Unfortunately, another Pascal—a Jew from Odessa who had been convicted of speculating in gold—was an inmate of our camp. When Captain Ovechkin saw the familiar name, he was furious. "Who put up all those kike sayings?" he demanded of the frightened Lesha. "Take them all down! Then pick out ten or twelve wise sayings from Lenin; and when I've approved them, I'll have an artist letter some new slogans."

When I went to the library that evening, I saw that Lesha had in front of him, instead of the usual *Eugene Onegin,* a huge pile of tomes by Lenin. He was going through the last one. "I've looked through forty volumes," he said in desperation, "and haven't yet found one intelligent idea."

"Who needs Lenin now?" I said. "Do you have any Brezhnev?"

As it happened, right within reach was a little book by Brezhnev called *A Course in Leninism.* Hardly had we opened it when we came upon one brilliant idea after another, so many we couldn't copy them all out. We even abridged them, so as not to tire the minds of Ovechkin and the poor zeks.

"There you are, Lesha!" I said. "When the going is tough, always look to the works of Leonid Ilich Brezhnev for inspiration."

I am inclined to believe that he did not know the library was bugged, although later I had the feeling that he was guiding our conversations toward certain preselected topics. As a member of the SKK* and the SVP* he was of course connected with the camp security office. The penal camp system is a miniature version of the Soviet system as a whole: the body social actively helps the authorities to oppress the members of that body and keep track of them. There is a kind of "elected" council of prisoners that comprises several sections: health, culture, supervision of commissary service, etc. Membership in any of those sections confers certain benefits. Thus, a man in the health section can get into the bathhouse without waiting in line, a member of the section for supervision of the commissary service can receive an extra helping of gruel, etc. But the main section is the SVP, a kind of intramural police department. Wearing red armbands, these prisoners periodically patrol the camp. (When one of them had his arm cut off, the other zeks said with malicious satisfaction: "The arm he lost was the one he used to wear the armband on!")

Those who became members of these "social" organizations were officially called the *aktiv* and, less formally, "finks." The number of finks began to rise steadily when the zeks found out that becoming a member of one of the trusties' organizations was the only way to get out of camp early. But whereas during my first months in camp, a prisoner could still get sprung by serving in the health or cultural section, guidelines were soon laid down: the only way to get out ahead of time was through the SVP. Also, it was not enough just to strut around wearing a red armband once a month; you had to write a report on other zeks.

Those prisoners who had an ideology of "activism," people who on the outside had held some position or other, often flaunted their armbands. But the others said, in effect, "What can I do? I'd rather not have joined up. But then what?"

It was especially the long-termers who looked hardest for a way to be freed earlier, although it was not considered ethical to capitulate right away.

As one zek said of another, "It's not because he writes for the wall newspaper that I despise him, but because he agreed right off to become a fink."

It is hard for me to judge to what extent membership in the "social" organizations "reformed" criminals, or whether the SVP did much to hold in check the hooligans in the camp. But in general the effect of "activism" was destructive. Nothing cripples people morally quite so much as the realization that their own well-being can be gained only through the misfortunes of others, that the shortest route to freedom is one that prolongs the term of a fellow inmate.

As I said earlier, the *aktiv* was opposed by the "refusers." The latter included the young thugs and some of the "muzhiks."* They had their own ideology behind them and were led by people who had been rejected by society. Some of these people could be trusted. But I distrusted all of the "activists," even though I had friends among them as well as among those in the group at the other extreme. As for the majority of the "muzhiks," they stayed in the middle and tried not to offend either of the other groups.

A less important but more attractive part of "social work" was the amateur entertainment. Most of the musicians were from among the refusers. Concerts were given two or three times a year. First on the program was the inevitable chorus. Then someone would read poetry, someone else would dance, and yet another performer would play the accordion. But the culmination of every concert was a performance by Bronislav Zhuk, a hunchbacked zek of seventy who was nicknamed "Lady-Bird." He was in prison for having molested children at the kindergarten where he was a supply clerk. When I was at the camp, he was completing his fifteen-year term, so that he didn't have to look for a quick way out, and took part in the concerts strictly for the esthetic pleasure they afforded. No sooner would he come on stage than the audience would start shouting: "Lady-Bird! Faggot! To the attic with him!" (The "attic" was used for homosexual assignations, and "to the attic" was considered an insulting expression.) Quite unperturbed by this, Zhuk would go into his number. First he would read from Sholokhov's *Virgin Soil Upturned,* and then he would do magic tricks.

It is hard to say which made the greater impression. His reading from Sholokhov would constantly be interrupted by comments that were very offensive to him as a reader and by remarks from the officers in the first row: "You people who are making all that noise—do you want to go to the hole?" And when the actor-reader uttered the word "kolkhoz," dozens of voices would ring out: "My prick in your nose!" All this, mixed in with Sholokhov's dreary text, was more absurd than the zaniest of Ionesco's plays.

Nor were his magic tricks any less successful. While the audience hooted, Zhuk would show them a newspaper, then begin to tear it up. At this point there would be shouts of: "You bastard! You tore up a photo of Brezhnev!" Unperturbed, Zhuk would tear the paper completely to pieces, squeeze it into a wad, and then—as the audience sat stock-still—display a completely whole newspaper. For a few seconds there would be absolute silence (zeks can be very childlike and inclined to believe in miracles). Then someone would shout in a piercing voice, "You tore up the 'Komsomolka,' and now you're showing us the 'Magadanka.'† You've played a dirty trick on honest zeks!" And once again the audience would be in an uproar.

But Zhuk's chief enemy, Mikhail Chernov, never lowered himself so much as to shout at him. Chernov, who was about the same age as Zhuk, had been convicted of a similar offense: debauching his own daughters. Their mutual enmity, however, had nothing to do with whether it was better to debauch one's own children or those of other parents. Rather it had grown out of the fact that they were the only two people in the camp who had seen Lenin in person, and they disagreed as to which of the two encounters was the more important. One of them had spotted Lenin in a corridor of the Kremlin, and the other during a mass meeting in Red Square. The former maintained that it was more important to have observed Lenin in an unofficial setting and hence to have been in close touch with his thoughts and feelings. The latter would object that it was much more important to have seen the great leader when he was addressing the broad masses and was hence directing the course of history.

In the realm of "the spirit," one can distinguish four more camp institutions: the radio, the movies, the school, and the political courses. In each section of the barracks there was a loudspeaker, dubbed a "scuttlebutt box"‡ by the zeks. That epithet well expressed the zeks' attitude toward the "scuttlebutt" that came out of it. It emitted a flow of propaganda excrement from Moscow and Magadan, occasionally interrupted by a camp official's voice announcing "Lights out," summoning prisoners to the guard shack, or announcing a working Sunday. The zeks never really listened to the political broadcasts, although some of them needed that noisy verbiage in order to fill up the vacuum in their heads.

The movies were shown once or twice a week, in the cafeteria. Mostly they were on revolutionary or military-patriotic themes and were repeated two or three times a month. Zeks who had been in prison for as long as five years might have seen some of those movies twenty times. I stopped going to the films about the middle of my term, but the majority of zeks lived from movie to movie. Twice they showed indoctrination films made by the MVD; and it

---

†The "Komsomolka": *Komsomolskaya pravda.* The "Magadanka": *Magadanskaya pravda,* a local newspaper.—TRANS.

‡*Yashchik-parashnik,* from *parasha:* "latrine pail."—TRANS.

was even more painful to watch exhausted zeks on the screen than to see them in real life.

There was a ten-year school in the same barracks building with the library. An eighth-grade education was compulsory for all prisoners younger than fifty, and those who wanted it could get a tenth-grade education. Classes were held after working hours, on a crash schedule. There was no instruction in foreign languages, since it was feared that a zek who learned a foreign tongue might flee the country.

Political indoctrination is an inescapable element of Soviet life. At first the political classes were held once a week; then, beginning in the middle of 1972, they were held every day except Sunday. For a half-hour, and sometimes for a full hour, an officer or teacher would mumble sentences copied from *Pravda,* thus depriving the zeks of what little free time they had. The classes were held in the living areas of the barracks. In the summer, the zeks who tried to avoid going to them were herded into the barracks, but in the winter there was no place to go *but* the barracks. As a rule, nobody listened to the droning of the lecturer, as the propagandists themselves realized. They said, however, if at each lecture only one-thousandth of what we say gets into your heads, you'll still be getting something. The zeks laughed at the lectures, the working Sundays, and the slogans. But they came to regard them as indispensable, like icons in a church; of itself, the repetitiveness of the ritual made one feel that it was necessary.

Later, in Magadan, I knew a con man whose specialty it was to pose as a doctor, make friends with women supposedly with a view to matrimony, and then extort money from them. On his jacket lapel he wore a *poplavok,* a badge of higher education; he even carried a fake diploma in his pocket. But he often gave off a stink so bad that one could hardly get near him. It turned out that he had shit in his underpants—something hardly compatible with the lofty title of Soviet physician. When he noticed how skillfully I wiped my behind with soft paper (we were all taken out to the toilet at the same time), he went into raptures. He thanked me profusely for this scientific instruction, declaring that from now on, no woman would leave him.

Some of the zeks went in for self-education in such subjects as foreign languages and philosophy. As a rule, nothing came of it, owing to lack of time, the difficult conditions, and an inadequate background.

There were several poets in our camp. One of them, a man of about fifty, was a genuine romantic, and as such, he had planned to commit suicide. He had decided he would use a hunting rifle for the purpose, and would combine his suicide with a twenty-four-shot "salute to the nation," so that the death of a poet would not go unnoticed. With his tenth shot, however, he wounded somebody and was arrested.

Along with the poets, there were authors of learned treatises like the aforementioned "Paper Socialism," or of things with titles such as "A Discussion of the Importance of the Pancreas." Then we had a fiction writer, one Yunchenkov, who had turned out a novel about life in an industrial plant. He was a bus driver, rather intelligent and reserved, who was doing time for a brawl in a bus. I don't know what prompted him to start writing, but when he asked me how much he would get for his novel when it was published, I said that he would make much more as a bus driver.

His novel was written in the same style as the reportage in the wall newspapers and showed that he was totally lacking in talent, although certainly not in persistence. If he had gone on writing, Yunchenkov might well have become one of those mediocre writers that are so familiar on the Soviet literary scene. But he came under suspicion because of his contacts with me, and his manuscript was confiscated and sent to two kindred organizations in Magadan—the KGB and the Writers' Union.

Once when he was sitting in the drying room, writing away amid felt boots and shoes set out to dry, another zek came up to him and asked, "Tell me, buddy, what is it that you're writing? Can I have a look?"

Flattered, Yunchenkov handed him the first chapters of his novel. When the other zek had read the first two pages, he burst into a rage: "So you're praising the Commies!"

With that, he hit Yunchenkov over the head with his manuscript, and the pages scattered in all directions. The author, equally enraged, seized his reader around the chest. But they both calmed down when Yunchenkov explained that the only reason he had praised the Communists in the beginning was so that he could give them hell at the end.

After that, the author and his reader often drank tea together, and they would invite me to join them. The reader kept asking us whether he smelled of shit, and we would reply: "No, not really."

Then one evening he took a tumble, head over heels, from the second floor, and broke his arm. "He's making as if he was crazy," the other zeks said, "so he can get into the hospital." But he had only two months left to serve (of a five-year sentence), and I seriously doubt that he would deliberately have crippled himself. It was a clear case of mental illness.

I came across quite a few psychotics in camp. Of course, a certain number of prisoners did try to fake mental illness (as a rule, they couldn't keep it up for long), and others were on a kind of wavering borderline, so that it was hard to judge. Along with the zek who imagined that he smelled of shit, there was one in our company who really did stink of it. Every morning, when he awoke, he would find himself lying in his own excrement. (This affliction had begun after he had been beaten at a police station following his arrest.)

One psychotic was a *bich* named Nikolai Pavlovich who was doing time for vagrancy. He was not a member of any of the "social organizations," but whenever an official showed up, he eagerly put on a red armband and just as eagerly "reported." His term was one year, and the closer he came to the end of that year, the gloomier he became. He was the first person I met who didn't want to get out of prison. (In his case, it was because he had no place to go.)

The mentally ill prisoners, who were confined together with the mentally healthy ones for years on end, did not arouse the latter's sympathy. To the contrary, they provoked hostility and the suspicion that they were "faking" in order to be exempted from work or to get sprung before their term was up.

About six weeks before his arrival, I heard that a psychiatrist was coming to see us—not, of course, to treat the psychos among us, but to examine me. I was really scared. I figured that the officials had decided, after all, to shove me into a psychiatric hospital, where I would be deprived of the most minimal means of defending myself, and where I could be confined indefinitely under the pretext that I was ill. (My recent case of meningitis gave them good grounds for that.)

The psychiatrist turned out to be an elderly bearded Jew with the appearance of a real scientist. The examination was not so much psychiatric as neuropathological, which was a relief. The doctor had heard about me from colleagues in Novosibirsk and was astounded that I had survived and was in good condition.

"And now," he said to the camp paramedic, "I want to be left alone with the patient to ask him some intimate questions." As soon as the paramedic had left, he pulled a letter from his pocket and handed it to me. He had received it from a friend of Esenin-Volpin. She had written to tell him that I was in Talaya and to ask whether he couldn't examine me, since he had connections with the MVD administration. When he was leaving, he warned me: "You mustn't drink anymore, because the least little bit of alcohol might cause a relapse." Later, when I was released from the camp, he was the first person I had a drink with.

I was transferred to the barracks of Three Company, where most of the prisoners were short-termers. There I came under the protection of the senior barracks orderly, whose name was Obraztsov. He had been given the death penalty for an especially heinous murder, but the sentence was commuted to fifteen years. Later, that term was reduced on appeal to ten years, of which he was now serving the last one. At first, he struck me as repulsive. However, he treated me well. He got me a lower bunk, found a place where I could do my work, and gave me an electric hot plate. Since kindness warms the heart, my first impression of him was somewhat effaced. He used to say the Soviet regime was like a certain kind of zek: if he can't drink a bottle of vodka on his own, he would rather pour out the rest than share it with someone else.

His nickname was "The Kike." I don't know if he was in fact a Jew, since Russians tend to apply the epithet "kike" to everyone who is a bit clever.

When I was still in the other barracks, I had obtained a textbook for learning English, and I used to copy out words on little cards, memorizing them. But it was hard to concentrate amid shouts of "Suck my cock!" "You shit!" and "Shut the hell up!" A half-day was the most I could work, since one aftereffect of the meningitis was that I tired quickly. So I tried to extend my strolls around the camp until the cold season came on. In the evenings I would read Paul Samuelson, John Steinbeck, Kurt Vonnegut, and Kosterin's *Kolyma Tales*. I nailed up a bookshelf above my bunk and put a shabby rug on the floor, and on my locker I set some flowers that I had picked by reaching through the barbed-wire fence. But I wasn't allowed to enjoy this luxury for long, since the rug, flowers, and bookshelf were particularly exasperating to the officials.

A zek is exhausted by the daily struggle arising from his "Give me what's due me" and the official's "Do what you've been ordered to do." It is more reasonable to avoid many of these conflicts, but not all of them. If the zek yields first on one point, and then on another, the line between "trifles" and "important things" begins to blur. If the zek's willpower begins to weaken in his conflicts with the prison officials, it will be all the easier for the investigator to break him. And finally, what does anyone have that is more important than his self-respect? To those officers who addressed me as *ty*, I responded by calling them *ty;* and they promptly switched to *vy*.† In order to avoid conflicts, whenever I heard a key being turned in the lock of my cell, I would get up quickly so that I could greet my guest standing and would not have to rise to my feet in his presence. But when anyone ordered me to stand up, I would refuse—especially if the person giving the order accompanied it with the kind of gesture used toward a dog.

Relations between me and the majority of camp officers soured rather quickly. After one exchange of insults, Captain Shevchenko, the DPNK,* dragged me off to the punishment cell, shouting: "This is the way people like you should be dealt with!" In the cell, he and Shmykov tore off my clothes and banged my head against the wall, which of course was not pleasant for one who had recently had meningitis. I spent the night lying on a cement bag and was released the next morning by Captain Garafutdinov.

Shortly after, I had a squabble with Captain Zhmak, the security offi-

---

†As similarly in many other European languages, *ty*—the second person singular pronoun in Russian—is used as the so-called familiar form of address, and the second person plural form, *vy*, is the formal or "polite" term used with someone who is not an intimate. And, again as in other languages, to address a non-intimate as *ty*—as did the officers Amalrik refers to above—is insulting, insofar as it implies that the person thus addressed is an inferior; it is much like, in English, calling an adult man "boy."—TRANS.

cer—who in camp lingo is called the *kum*†—because the letters I wrote were disappearing. "We don't have time to mess with your illiterate letters!" he shouted at me. Although always stiffly erect in his bearing, he had about him an air of concealing some wound to his pride.

To one degree or another, one could sense this wounded vanity in almost all the officers. Frequently, the officers who elect to serve in the MVD have a secret need to compensate for their inferiority complexes by exerting authority over others. The isolation of camp life—one that is both social and geographic, since the camps are usually located in remote areas—and the nature of the work intensify that feeling. The conditions also intensify the urge to wreak vengeance on the zeks, especially those who do not feel themselves to be inferior to the officers. The guards' attitude toward the zeks was a bit simpler: the former were not especially self-important in their behavior, and hence were less vulnerable. Yet the constant conflicts with the zeks exhausted them morally, and many of them quit, saying they couldn't do that kind of work for long without going crazy. Some of them, on the other hand, actually liked their work.

Serving in the security section along with Zhmak was a young, slightly built lieutenant. One night he got it into his head that the Chinese had attacked Magadan and rushed to the guard shack to report this event. Salasyuk, another DPNK, a naïve chap, phoned Magadan to find out how the battle was going and to get instructions. He was thoroughly cursed out for this, and the lieutenant was sent off to a health resort for treatment, after which he returned to his duties.

Captain Salasyuk, whose nicknames were "The Pea" and "The Blue Horse," was the most harmless of the officers, and a laughingstock. His great weakness was a fondness for making long speeches over the radio. "Reveille," "Lights out," and other commands were issued over the camp radio, the "scuttlebutt box," and when Salasyuk was on duty, each would be accompanied by a long speech.

Still another DPNK, Captain Tsimarny, had formerly been chief of the security section. He owed his nickname, "Canaris," after the German intelligence chief, to his success in spying. But later he got into trouble: When Tsimarny learned that Shaidurov, first secretary of the *obkom,* was due to inspect Talaya, he had sentries posted all around the settlement to protect Shaidurov against any possible attempt on his life. But this didn't win Tsimarny any points with the big shot, because when Shaidurov saw submachine guns aimed at him from every hill and knoll, he became thoroughly frightened.

Tsimarny was one of the few military men who seemed at home serving

---

†In ordinary usage, this word means "godfather."—TRANS.

in a prison camp. Other officers felt disdain for their work, and consoled themselves with the thought that somebody had to do it. But Tsimarny would have crawled up his own mother's anus to check whether she was concealing "articles forbidden by law."

Captain Zolotarev, deputy chief for security and discipline, was a big man, but as fragile as Pavel Litvinov. He had a somewhat swollen face and a habit of scrutinizing people closely, and was very self-confident. Being not at all stupid, he figured that he deserved a better lot, and he expended no little effort in trying to unseat the camp commandant, Colonel Nichikov. But it was not the Jew Zolotarev who was named to replace Nichikov, but the Ukrainian Major Butenko. And as a result of this power struggle "between the *khokhol*† and the kike," Zolotarev was transferred to another camp—without a promotion.

†A pejorative epithet for "Ukrainian."—TRANS.

C H A P T E R   1 7

Corrective-Labor Colony
261/3:
Weeping and Groaning

I was entitled to two three-day visits a year, and immediately upon arriving in camp, I put in a request—one that Zolotarev approved by scrawling on it: "Granted." I had to get on a waiting list for the visitors' room. Finally, the visit was scheduled for October.

Gusel flew in from Moscow, but for a time our meeting was disallowed, so that I spent two days nervously pacing the compound. It turned out that a microphone was being put in the visitors' room. (It was installed in such a way that during visits the camp radio had to be turned off, and Captain Salasyuk was deprived of the pleasure of making speeches.)

Finally, I was frisked, given a change of clothes (since I might have sewn something into the clothes I had on), and sent into a narrow hallway. I had only gone a few steps when I saw Gusel—weeping. She had suffered the humiliation of a frisking by "the censor," Tsygankova, who went through her clothes, her hair, and her bag. This wizened little woman, who read the zeks' letters and frisked their wives, reminded me of a rat sniffing the air and wriggling her forefeet. Actually, she wasn't old, but loneliness and hatred of others made her look that way.

Fortunately, before long Gusel was smiling. We spread out a red tablecloth that she had brought so that we could dine by candlelight, as it were. The scene was exactly as if we were in a room at a poor hotel. Or rather, it would have been, except for the bars on the windows and the voices in the next room, barking orders.

I don't know how Gusel managed to bring so much food. But I was so tense, and so unaccustomed to eating regular food, that I began to have sharp pains in my stomach. The next day I had to call a doctor, who gave me an injection; for the rest of the time Gusel was there, I simply could not eat.

It was at this same time that the real hostilities between me and the camp officials began. After I had been sent back into the compound, they kept Gusel in the visitors' room. A woman doctor by the name of Tsarko, who had come back from vacation during Gusel's visit to me, was summoned to assist the censor. The two of them wanted to search Gusel (the doctor even came in wearing rubber gloves for a gynecological examination), but she refused; so the three of them sat there for five hours. Finally, the prosecutor ordered her release, and to my great relief she and I managed, that evening, to exchange a few words through the transom in the guard shack.

I found this degrading treatment of Gusel harder to bear than if it had happened to me. Besides, I was shocked at the idea of a doctor's frisking someone. (I wasn't yet entirely cured of idealism.) Gusel, however, managed to take with her a letter from me, which she passed on to Karel van het Reve.

In the course of our visit, she said she wanted to give me a pair of undershorts with money in them. But I didn't take them: I knew that when I was searched, they would find the money right away. They confiscated the money from Gusel when they found it, although there was no law against her having money anywhere she wanted to keep it.

This incident struck me as a good peg to use in "settling accounts" for her detention by the censor, so I drafted a complaint to the oblast prosecutor's office. Along with the confiscation of the money, I listed the beating I had been given in the punishment cell, the disappearance of my letters, the bad food, and the fact of Gusel's detention. I made sure not to drop my letter in the complaints box at the guard shack.

I sent off my complaint in November, and in early February the prosecutor summoned me. The first thing I did upon entering his office was to put in front of him a piece of indigestible bread with some string baked in it, exclaiming, "Here's the way they feed us!" The prosecutor looked even more disgusted than Kirinkin had when he tasted the gruel, and backpedaled.

It turned out that copies of my letter had made their way throughout the broad expanses of our motherland. Shmykov and Shevchenko unanimously claimed that I had almost killed them when I was put in the punishment cell. Also, they said I had been granted extra visiting hours, which was true, and that I had gotten my parcels ahead of schedule, which was also true. But they couldn't trump my ace, the confiscation of the money; so it was transferred to my account. Later I learned that Zhmak, Shevchenko, and Salasyuk—about whom I had not complained but who received all the blame—had been given reprimands.

As far back as the time of Gusel's visit, I had begun to feel pain in my ears. Now pus was oozing out of them, and I could scarcely hear. Inflammation of the middle ear is common in the Far North, and several men in the camp had gone deaf. The hot summer was over by the end of July, and in November the temperature would sometimes drop to sixty degrees below zero. On such days you could hardly see farther than an arm's length ahead of you. But even on ordinary days (i.e., when it was a mere twenty degrees below zero), I would feel a sharp pain in my ears the moment I stepped outside. My government-issue cap didn't keep me warm, so I made myself a pair of earmuffs out of an old pair of woolen socks. "You look like a radioman," the zeks would say to me. And the stool pigeons suspected that I was listening to the Voice of America through my earmuffs.

I no longer went to see the camp doctor after she had tried to frisk Gusel. For that matter, she couldn't have helped me anyway. After twenty-five years of service in camps, the summit of her achievement was to lance zeks' boils. So at the dispensary I asked the nurse, a fat, apathetic woman, to give me a vial of boric acid. I put that in my ears, but it didn't help. I drafted a request for a specialist to examine me, and I wrote Gusel, asking her to see what she could do in Moscow. The result of her efforts was a telegram from camp chief Butenko saying that a doctor had examined me and I was in good condition.

Actually [I wrote to Gusel later] Major Bessonov, chief of the medical service of the Magadan UVD, did come here on February 3, and he did examine me. He may be a fine chief of service, but he's a surgeon, and my ears are neither better nor worse as a result of his examination. He began with the nervous system: very shattered nerves, with residual effects of meningitis. Next, the stomach: acute gastritis. Blood pressure: high. Weight: 117 pounds, as compared to 152 at the time of my arrest. Heart: defective mitral valve. Temperature: high—an aftereffect of meningitis. Ears: inflammation of middle ear. Conclusion: general condition good.

It seemed to me that he had come not so much in order to treat me as to: (1) show that my condition was good; and (2) send me to the hospital. After the examination was over I asked him why, if my condition was good, he was insisting that I be sent to the hospital.

He has prescribed injections, but I'm apprehensive about them. Incidentally, something unpleasant happened just before he arrived. You remember the woman doctor who came to frisk you during our visit? She's Captain Raisa Tsarko, chief of the camp dispensary. On February 1, people at the dispensary were talking about me in my absence, and someone said that I looked exhausted. Whereupon Tsarko said, "Why talk about Amalrik? He's no concern of mine. I don't care whether he's sick or well." And she added, "He shouldn't be fed at the Soviet table, because he's not one of us." Naturally, her remarks were promptly passed on to me. I was amazed that a doctor should have talked like that about her patient, and the next day I asked her if it was true that she had said such things. She repeated the same things right to my face, and then shouted, "Why does the Voice of America talk about you and not about me?" (I gathered from what she said that the Voice of America had broadcast something about my illness.)

At the time, B. P. Vorontsov, senior deputy prosecutor of the Magadan Oblast for inspection of places of confinement, happened to be at our camp, and I told him what Tsarko had said. He said he would take steps to see that a doctor would examine me; Major Bessonov, Tsarko's immediate superior, showed up shortly thereafter. The two of them threatened the prisoner with whom Tsarko had talked about me that they would send him to a psychiatric hospital. And Tsarko told the other prisoner who had been present during the conversation she would give him pills that would make him mentally incompetent. Bessonov did not speak to me so bluntly, but his hints were so transparent that my trust in him was hardly increased. A few days later, when I went to the dispensary to get some cotton for my ears, the nurse told me that Bessonov had prescribed an injection. She was wondering whether, in view of my condition, it was not wrong to give me such strong medication. At this point, Tsarko shouted from the next room, "Keep your mouth shut and inject him!"

Naturally, I left right away. I'm not going to take any injections, and I'm not even going to speak to Tsarko. I won't go to the hospital voluntarily for anything in the world. It's not just that I'm apprehensive about the trip along the rough road—I'm even more fearful of such "doctors," under whose complete control I would be.

I sent one copy of the letter through the censor (it was confiscated), another via Obraztsov (it never reached Gusel), and a third through a young zek named Volodya (which did reach her). I knew, of course, that the letter would be confiscated; but I wanted to put a little pressure on the camp officials, so they would get a doctor for me. I realized that Tsarko, offended that I had not gone to her and frightened by the arrival of the prosecutor, had been unable to restrain herself. And I was even glad that she had made those remarks about me, since I now had a chance to catch her out. Yet when I observed the corporate solidarity of the camp doctors and heard the hints about a psychiatric hospital, I was actually frightened. Moreover, I figured that for a person with meningitis to travel 700 kilometers in extreme cold in a Black Maria would be fatal. So I decided (in the phrase of Mao Zedong) to "rely on my own forces," although those forces were negligible. They were negligible because, in addition to other illnesses, I was afflicted with avitaminosis: my whole body was covered with boils, and saliva was running out of my mouth.

In April Gusel and I managed, despite everything, to arrange for a specialist from Magadan to examine my ears. But by that time my hearing was almost back to normal. While in the camp he examined other patients whose cases may well have been worse than mine. But they had behaved more humbly than I and hence would not have been seen by a specialist if I had not kicked up a fuss.

Toward the end of my stay at the camp, the staff of the dispensary consisted of two doctors—one a surgeon, the other a public health doctor—a dentist, a paramedic, nurses, and an attendant. This staff took care of seven hundred zeks. From the standpoint of an American town, this ratio might well seem enviable, but only if one fails to realize that the main job of the medical personnel was not to treat patients but to keep them in more or less able-bodied condition and to ferret out malingerers. A patient would come in and groan: "Ooh, Citizen Captain! My head hurts!" To which Tsarko would riposte: "And doesn't your ass hurt?" And by virtue of these miracle-making words, the patient would suddenly get better, especially if he was given some aspirin tablets or vitamin pills that had long since outlived their shelf life.

But even if Tsarko had been replaced by a skillful and humane doctor, his possibilities would have been limited. He could not feed half-starved patients, because hunger was used as an "educational measure." He could not provide warmth for people suffering from the cold, because even when the temperature was far below zero, the only clothing allowed a prisoner was a cotton jacket, pants, and a quilted jacket. He could not exempt sick men from work, because there was a quota. He could not give his patients the kind of medical care they needed, because equipment and medication were lacking. Finally, the chief of the dispensary was not the only chief: the apportionment of food was mostly determined by the security section, which had an interest in fattening up its healthy informers and not "violators" with stomach ulcers.

Tsarko was not a bad person; she was an average woman who had accepted the system. During her years of service, the humanity in her had been deformed; she used to say she could no longer regard zeks as human beings. Her attitude was rather that of a veterinarian. She did help some people; and it is also possible she would have treated me decently if I had accepted the frisking of Gusel. Her personal life was unhappy; her husband, a former zek, was a drunk, and her son became a hooligan.

Similarly, Major Bessonov was not a bad chief of the UVD's medical service. After his appointment, there was an improvement in the supply of medicine. A dentist and another doctor were added to the staff, and he brought in a psychiatrist who sent several real mental cases to the hospital. On the other hand, Bessonov would never hesitate to send a mentally healthy person to a psychiatric hospital, or leave a patient untreated, if it was in his own interest or requested by the KGB.

It should not be thought that putting people in psychiatric hospitals is a prerogative of the KGB alone; for officials of any kind, this is a way of settling accounts with people or getting an undesirable witness out of the way. Thus, at the Nuclear Physics Institute in Dubno, inadequate safety measures resulted in a number of workers being exposed to radiation. When they complained, they were plunked into a psychiatric hospital. In Magadan a local surgeon quarreled both with his wife and with the chief of the oblast health department. The latter asked the surgeon's wife to file a statement that her husband was mentally incompetent, and the surgeon was put away in a mental institution for several months.

Despite my victories over the security section and the medical unit (or, more likely, because of them), Zolotarev began to harass me at every opportunity. In a camp, the scale of values is reduced as the barbed-wire enclosure tightens around you. As I wrote to Gusel, "You tell me in your letters, darling, that I shouldn't wear out my nerves on trifles. But I'm now living in a world of trifles and among people who have made a profession of trifles."

The senseless prohibitions were the most humiliating. When, in prison, they took away my scarf, I could see some point to it: they figured that I might use it to hang myself, whereas I would steer clear of using a government-issue sheet. But why the ban on using an electric razor in camp? Or why, in prison, the prohibition against using a clothes brush? In what way is a clean-shaven, neat zek any more dangerous than a dirty one?

For my part, I kept looking for things to complain about. In my letters to the authorities, just as in Petya Vasilyev's complaints, I saw something comical. But writing complaints is about the only legal means of resistance available to a zek, and the sooner your will to resist weakens, the sooner your personality will begin to disintegrate. "If all the other zeks were like you," an officer in Magadan said to me in great irritation, "nobody would work in the camp." That was one of the greatest compliments I have ever received.

Both in camp and while in transit I met officers and soldiers who expressed sympathy for me when they were sure no one was listening. Likewise, among the zeks I rarely encountered any hostility toward me as an "anti-Soviet"; I can say the same about social contacts outside of prison. Notions as to the isolation of the dissidents are hardly accurate. Often, dissidents isolate themselves from people who are attracted to their ideas: among intellectuals, the "guilt-toward-the-people" complex has been replaced by a "guilt-of-the-people" complex.

In spite of my quarrel with Tsarko, I sometimes took advantage of one of the good things the dispensary had to offer: the bathtub. Rytov, the dispensary attendant, was doing time for embezzlement. So great was his affability that sometimes after I had bathed he would invite me to his room to drink a beaker of the dispensary's alcohol and chat about "the country and the world."†† A job in the dispensary, with a private room to boot, was one of the juiciest plums a prisoner could get; and I constantly wondered whether Rytov had not invited me on orders from the security section, rather than out of kindheartedness. Such, it turned out, was the case. The subject of informers in the Soviet Union is inexhaustible, the number is infinite, and the evil they do is immeasurable. Along with other kinds of evil, they destroy trust among people.

I would say that informers can be grouped in three general categories. First is the kind of person who becomes a stool pigeon out of weakness, under a threat or in the hope of getting something absolutely necessary to him. He feels guilty toward his victim and often has a good deal of sympathy for him. He tries to do something kind to compensate for having informed, and does not report everything. Lesha Ivanchenko was this kind of informer.

Then there is the indifferent type, like Rytov. He turns stoolie strictly in his own interest and is indifferent to the fate of his victim. He will not do his victim an act of kindness; on the other hand, he will not harm him unless ordered to do so.

Third, there is the informer who goes about his job with a kind of recklessness. He has no qualms about provoking his victim or making up all kinds of stories about him, and he is bitterly disappointed if his denunciations do not bring immediate results. We had a trio of such informers—Fedoseyev, Moiseyenkov, and Skvortsov—who were even assigned bunks near to mine. The three of them became very close friends: they "buddied up," as camp slang has it.

As a workingman, Moiseyenkov played only a minor role in their machinations. Fedoseyev was more imposing in appearance. He had worked as a mechanical engineer, and was in stir for stabbing his girlfriend. Skvortsov had once been a military pilot, and he called the MVD officers, with the greatest contempt, "the trade-union army." His decline began rather dramatically. One day he told his wife and a woman friend of hers: "I'd like to fly off to some place where I wouldn't see hide nor hair of you two whores." Whereupon his wife wrote a denunciation to the KGB saying he wanted to fly

†The Russian title of a book by Andrei Sakharov, published in the West under the title of *My Country and the World.*—Trans.

to a foreign country, and he was grounded. After that, he went downhill rapidly, aided by vodka. Having been given a lesson by his wife, he maintained connections with the KGB from that time on. Later, he turned up at one of the mines in Kolyma. A murder was committed there, and when the murderer was caught and handcuffed, he was turned over to Skvortsov, who had orders to take him to the police station. On the way to the station he killed the murderer. He was convicted, but was given only three years, since the murderer he killed was a former zek, while Skvortsov was a former officer and a friend of "the organs." He was one of those who love to propose the strictest measures—who figure that the more people you have shot by firing squads, the more order you will have in the world—yet scream bloody murder if the shoe pinches *them*.

After a year of going hungry, I found a means of subsistence: drafting appeals for other prisoners. My prestige was so great that for each appeal I received a kilo of butter and a half-kilo of sugar, the equivalent of what a successful lawyer would be paid. It is hard to say whether those appeals produced any practical results; while I was in the camp, no one's sentence was reduced on the basis of an appeal. But their therapeutic effect was far more important. In the first place, the embittered zeks found an attentive listener. (Sad to say, in our harsh world the mere opportunity to have someone listen to you is worth a kilo of butter.) In the second place, while the appeal was making its way up from one level to another, the zek could live on hope.

So I got better acquainted with the other inmates and studied many court verdicts. They dealt, for the most part, with five kinds of crime: murder, rape, "hooliganism," armed robbery, and embezzlement.

The murderers impressed me as the most pleasant and self-possessed of the criminals—an impression that was to some extent illusory. As a rule, they were not thugs, but ordinary citizens who had killed in a state of high excitement. Often they were amazed by what they had done, though sometimes they were quite indifferent. At least half were men who had killed their wives or lovers. As people with no political convictions, murderers readily agreed to become stool pigeons. They dislike the professional criminals, and so they join the *aktiv*.

One murderer doing time in our camp was a fat old man of about sixty—a former top sergeant whom the young thugs had nicknamed "ass-belly." He had been living with his fifty-year-old wife in a northern settlement where the ratio of men to women was four to one. She worked as a cook and had taken up with a male cook of twenty. "What's this?" her husband asked her. "Aren't you about fucked out after fifty years?" "No, I've just begun to enjoy it," she replied, and that sealed her fate. Later, he was so remorseful about having killed his wife that he tried to throw himself out of a window.

There were, of course, wives who survived. One meek-looking young man had taken an ax to his wife because she "didn't love" him. She lived, however, and testified at his trial, where he was given twelve years. "You're an idiot," some of the luckier murderers told him. "If you'd done her in, you'd be doing two years less." (The usual sentence for wife-murder is ten years.) In the court decision, it was stated that he had dealt his wife twelve blows, and he thought he had been given one year for each blow. "During the investigation I said I had hit her eight times," he complained, "and I said the same thing at my trial. But the bastards gave me twelve years. After something like that, how can you believe in human decency?"

"Yes, it is hard to believe in it," I replied, going on with my job of drafting an appeal for him. Seeing how humanely I viewed his misfortunes, he too made a very human gesture. He reached out toward me and said, "Finally I've found somebody I can have a heart-to-heart talk with. When I took my ax to that bitch, I didn't hit her twelve times—I hit her thirty times."

He worked in the mess hall; and it wasn't butter and sugar that I got for writing his appeal, but onions—which saved me from avitaminosis.

Some of the murderers had no notion of why they had committed their crime. They would just say, "The Devil made me do it."

"But don't you feel at least a little bit sorry that you did it?" I would ask.

Then, after some hesitation, as if my interlocutor were looking into his own soul, would come the reply: "No, I can't say as I really feel sorry."

The most frequent requests for appeals came from the rapists—the "safe-crackers" who had broken into "the shaggy safe." Or, as they themselves joked: "Article 117 is political." "Why political?" "Because I fucked a Komsomol girl." Some of the rapes, especially the gang rapes, were accompanied by extreme cruelty. Thus, by way of degrading their victim still further, the rapists would jam a bottle into her vagina. Then there was the type that might be called the "persistent rapist." One such was a former druzhinnik who, as a friend of the police, had got only "chemistry" for rape. But scarcely had he arrived at the "chemistry" site when he committed another rape, and was again put behind bars.

Yet for all this, I had the impression that in about half of the cases, no criminal rape had occurred. Sometimes the "rapist" and the "victim" had simply failed to understand each other. For each kind of crime there is not only a definite type of criminal but a definite type of victim. Certain types of women are most prone to being raped, and some even provoke it. But very often the "victim" arouses the "rapist," either because he has refused to marry her or because she wants to justify herself in the eyes of her parents or husband. Since a complaint by the "victim" suffices for instituting criminal proceedings or even for a conviction, the possibilities for blackmail are great.

The most distressing cases are the "hooligans" (called *baklany* in camp slang), most of whom are young. For purposes of convenience, investigators often classify as "hooliganism" such crimes as wife-beating. But real hooliganism is a crime devoid of any rational motive such as greed, vengeance, or pleasure. And a real hooligan can almost always be recognized by his vicious, vapid look: he hates everyone. In some cases, however, one can discern behind the hooliganism a distorted form of social protest, a kind of challenge to the system.

The number of people serving sentences for armed robbery is immeasurably greater than those doing time for theft. There has been a sharp increase in crimes involving violence rather than skill or professionalism. The stickup men are mostly young, and mostly regular criminals; i.e., people with an "ideology" or code. Some of them are vicious types who have lost almost all of their humanity; others are not so bad. They were friendly, but almost none asked me to draw up an appeal: they had known what they were doing and what sentences they would get.

The *aktiv* included about half of the rapists, a few hooligans, and almost no robbers. On the other hand, every single embezzler joined the *aktiv*. On the outside they had been Communists, and communism, as one engineer explained to me, means: "Say what you will, equality is something that never will exist and never can exist. So grab the best spot you can." And once a person has grabbed a good spot, he wants to exploit it. Such a person was the camp supply chief, a powerfully built man who was serving a sentence for graft. He wanted to maintain good relations with everybody—with the refusers, the muzhiks, the finks (to which group he himself belonged), and with me, a "political." Every time I met him, he would ask me, "Well, are you going to turn fink?"

"No, not really," I would reply.

"You're wrong, you know. You should turn fink. The Russians love fools."†

Arguments frequently arose as to how many prisoners there were in the USSR. Since the statistics are secret, people would cite fantastic figures, ranging from three hundred thousand to 30 million. In the Magadan Oblast, which has a population of four hundred thousand, there is one general-regimen camp, one intensified-regimen camp, three strict-regimen camps, one special-regimen camp, one settlement/colony, one colony for alcoholics, one camp hospital, two remand prisons, and about twenty preventive-detention cells. Women, minors, and persons sentenced to death are sent to the "mainland." At the most conservative estimate, the total number of prisoners is

†The word I have here translated as "fink"—*pridurok*—has the same root as *durak,* meaning "fool."—TRANS.

about six thousand, or 1.5 percent of the oblast's population. For Sverdlovsk Oblast I was able to make indirect estimates, and I came up with a figure between 1 and 1.5 percent. If these figures are extrapolated for the entire Soviet Union, one reaches a total of about 3 million prisoners, not counting the "chemists," people sent into exile, those banned from certain cities, or ex-prisoners under administrative surveillance and living under restrictions.

Many people agree that the corrective labor camps do not correct anybody; the number of repeat offenses is much higher than the number of first offenses. Whether punishment should be harsh or mild is a complex question; but in any case it should not destroy the human personality, as the camps do, but rather restore it. In order to reform, a person must have a feeling of guilt; but the majority in the camps feel that they were unjustly convicted. This opinion is held by 77.5 percent of the rapists, 69.7 percent of the murderers, 68.9 percent of the hooligans, and 68.3 percent of those convicted of armed robbery. Those doing time for white-collar crime agree that they were justly convicted. Nor is this difficult to understand: all are members of the SVP who have joined up so that they can be released before their term is up. Those convicted of crimes against the State or resisting the authorities likewise hold a unanimous opinion: that they were convicted unjustly.[13]

If such are the feelings of the majority of the prisoners, do these people offer any resistance to the corrective-labor system? Strong antagonism exists between the zeks and the camp officials, just as in the USSR generally between the people and the regime. But "they" represent a purposeful and largely effective system, whereas "we" represent a disorganized mass. For the most part, complaints and appeals do not get results, though they do serve to restrain the camp officials. Nonetheless, only a few prisoners in the camps file complaints or appeals; some prisoners do not know how to write, others are reluctant to complicate their relations with officials, and collective complaints are forbidden. Another— and much less common—form of resistance is the hunger strike. There were no hunger strikes in the camp where I was confined, but I am familiar with some such incidents in prison. Occasionally, the officials would make small concessions so that the zek would call off his strike; but more frequently he would prove unable to keep it up. Refusals to work were also rare. For a first offense of this kind, the prisoner would get fifteen days in the punishment cell, and for the second offense, six months in the camp prison.

More typical, especially for the common criminals, were other forms of protest: insulting officers, damaging property, arson, and maiming. There were several cases of beatings administered to zeks who collaborated with the officials—especially the gang bosses, since the question of wages was involved. During my stay in the camp, there was even one murder. When a few men beat up on a gang boss at our camp, they got sentences ranging from four to six years. The gang boss in question had been a cheerful fellow, but when I met up with him in prison, after his release from the hospital, he was a different man. They had damaged his kidneys, and he had to spend a half-hour on the latrine pail before he could urinate. He got a transfer to another camp in order to avoid being killed.

Vodka played a role in many protests, and not a day went by but what some drunks were sent to the punishment cell. The hungry prisoners quickly got stupefied on vodka, and since getting one's hands on some of it was a matter of prestige, the younger zeks wanted to show everyone that they were drunk. On several occasions some of the refusers asked me to drink with them. I didn't decline, but I never drank more than a half-glass. It was also common practice to sniff acetone that had been stolen from the paint shop. One day a zek who had sniffed too much of it collapsed in the snow and nearly froze.

In camp, vodka and narcotics represented the same kind of escapism as they did on the outside. But there was a more literal kind: escape from the camp "without prior permission" as a way of avoiding further punishment. Two attempts at escape were made while I was there. In one case, the prisoner got as far as Magadan (he had gone there to see whether his wife was cheating on him), where he was caught the next day. Two years were added to the twelve he was serving for rape. In the second instance, the zek was caught the same day, not far from the camp. But his term was actually reduced, since it turned out that he was a minor who had been put in an adult camp by mistake. (After these two attempts, the number of guards was increased.)

Group action would have been the most effective form of resistance, but while I was in the camp this was tried only once. It was decided to take the zeks of our company to the woodworking shop, some two and a half miles away, in a closed trailer. On the very first day, the trailer slipped its coupling and began to roll down a hill. Fortunately, it stopped just at the edge of a ravine, so there were no injuries. But the next day the prisoners on the shift refused to ride in the trailer and wouldn't even leave the barracks. As Gogol wrote, however, "the police captain's visor was itself enough to put down the rebellion." Zolotarev showed up and, after a little talk that began with jokes and reassurances and ended with threats, he forced the zeks to line up and get into the trailer.

For a zek, the art of living consists of being able to adapt himself to the rules and to get around them. This applied in particular to two problems that Schiller wrote about: hunger and love.

When I first arrived at the camp, the rules regarding meals were still liberal: you could take your bowl back to your barracks after a meal, and when the zeks went to the mess hall, they went in a crowd and took seats wherever they wanted. Then orders came down that the zeks had to form up by companies, that each was to have his own permanent place at a mess hall table.

Morning, noon, and night we got soup—thin and sometimes disgusting. In addition, for breakfast we were given a brownish mixture with fifteen grams of sugar in it; for lunch, gruel with no vegetable oil; and for dinner, those who had fulfilled the work norm got a ladleful of pureed peas with oil. (I hesitate to say just what kind of oil it was—machine oil, most likely.) Posted above the urn was a table showing ration norms (they averaged out to three-quarters of the minimum daily requirement of calories) and a poster that read:

AT LUNCHTIME, DON'T TAKE TOO MUCH BREAD—JUST TASTE IT.
BREAD IS A VALUABLE THING, SO DON'T WASTE IT!

Sometimes the bread ration was handed out to each zek individually; at other times the bread was left on the tables. There were days when only the crust was edible, so that the rest was "wasted." On occasion, we would get white bread for a whole week. There was a silver fox farm not far from the camp, and herring that was found unfit for use there was sent to the camp and issued to the zeks twice a week. If you picked up one of those herrings, it would fall to pieces. A cauldron of soup for twelve men would have a few little pieces of meat in it—always less than twelve. Everyone, including myself, would rush to the table so as to be the first to ladle out some soup for himself. After a while I realized that this was a dangerous thing to do, and I behaved more worthily: I would take the ladle and distribute soup to everyone, leaving myself for last. But I always kept a piece of meat for myself.

Although many of the prisoners suffered from avitaminosis, ulcers, gastritis, and malnutrition, the camp was, on the whole, not famine-ridden. (New arrivals from the "mainland" were amazed that bread was put out on the table.) There were two explanations for this state of affairs. First, the Magadan Oblast itself was, by Soviet standards, well supplied with foodstuffs, and this fact had its effect on the camp. Second, in addition to the "visible" distribution of food—via the mess hall, the canteen (where you could buy six rubles' worth of food a month), and food parcels (eleven pounds every six months after you had served half your term)—there was an "invisible" distribution system. It worked as follows. In the camp there was a furniture workshop, a shoe shop, and a garage where cars and trucks were repaired. If an officer or a free worker wanted the zeks to make him an armchair, let's say, he would have to smuggle them butter, sugar, condensed milk, vodka, or money—the last would of course be spent on food or vodka. Any truck driver whose vehicle was being repaired in the camp garage knew that if he didn't bring the mechanics some vodka, his truck, although seemingly O.K. when he drove out of the compound, would break down within two miles. It was the responsibility of the inspector for the security section to watch for violations of this kind. But when his own car broke down, and a zek's wife sent him spare parts from Moscow, he invited the zek to his office—it was New Year's Eve—and treated him to vodka and sausages.

Money was also passed to zeks by their wives and mothers during visits, since not all of the prisoners were frisked as thoroughly as I was. The money was used to buy food smuggled into the camp by free workers—truck drivers, craftsmen, and stokers who worked alongside the prisoners—and unguarded zeks who were permitted to leave the compound during the day. Naturally, this smuggling was not done altruistically. Thus, of the food that Gusel had left for me after her visit, I got only half from Obraztsov. During my last months in camp I bought sugar, condensed milk, and canned meat from a storekeeper who had previously obtained them from the mess hall manager. These foods originally came from a truck driver who would bring more of them into the camp than were required under the norm, so that the mess hall manager, also a zek, could sell them to "his" people. But some food was simply stolen from the "poor" zeks and sold to the "rich" ones. Such goodies were available only to those who had connections and sources of income. Yet everyone in the camp gained from this constant influx of foods: since a "rich" zek would not consume his ration in the mess hall, a "poor" one could get extra portions of soup, bread, and gruel. As in the outside world, corruption tended to humanize the Soviet system.

The real evil was thefts from the mess hall, and the culprits included not only the mess hall manager and his cronies but camp officials. The chief of the commissary service would sell some of the food to line his own pocket. When a mess hall manager went too far, he would be removed from his job. But a few months later he would get it back again, replacing someone who had been practicing the same graft. One manager had set up a harem consisting of boys to whom he gave food; at night he would party with them near the mess hall.

Such was the solution found for the second Schillerian problem—that of love. I have no idea how many homosexuals there were in the camp. I did observe, however, different attitudes on the part of the active homosexuals. The older ones would say, in effect: "What can a man do? Human nature is imperfect." But the younger ones, conforming to the spirit of the times, would flaunt their homosexuality. Homosexual relations are punishable in the USSR; and while I was in the camp, several prisoners were convicted and

sentenced to three or four years. The security section had a list of the passive
homosexuals, and from time to time the most obvious of them would be sent
to other camps—where they were immediately identified. But the threat of a
new sentence didn't seem to deter anyone from practicing homosexuality.

There were also the masturbators. Some of them would crawl up to the
roof of the barracks, unbutton their pants, and try to spy out, in the settlement
located some distance from the camp, a woman who might serve as an object
of their love. Others took their pleasure while looking at photographs of
women. No copies of *Playboy* reached the camp, so they had to settle for
photos of gymnasts and milkmaids in the magazine *Ogonyok*. Also, there
were lots of zeks who were fond of "catching a performance"; i.e., of getting
a peek at some concealed part of a woman's body. Many of them hung around
the dispensary or the school, where women were employed, to admire a
derrière or legs. The school had a special outdoor toilet for women; and the
most daring of those who were fond of catching a performance would crawl
down into the latrine so as to have a good view. One day the camp supply
chief, having noticed a young thug down there, ordered a carpenter to close
up the latrine opening. The worshipper of female beauty was dragged out of
the latrine a few hours later, unconscious and smeared with excrement; and
in that state he was thrown into the punishment cell.

Any conversation that started up among the zeks, even on such subjects
as space flights or the Egyptian pyramids, would come around, gradually but
inevitably, to fornication.

One often heard the opinion that "all women are whores," and I was
unpleasantly surprised to hear how some zeks talked about the women with
whom they had lived before their arrest and with whom they intended to live
after being released. For many zeks, however, a mother, a wife, or a sister
was a gleam of light seen through the surrounding darkness. I had the impression that happy marriages were not destroyed by the camp experience: the
wives waited for their husbands and helped them. Sometimes, these fortunate
men could not restrain themselves from telling anecdotes to show what good
wives they had. But as the old Novgorod song has it:

> *The prudent man boasts about his old father,*
> *The fool about his young wife.*

In the winter and spring there were several mini-epidemics of dysentery,
owing to the polluted water in the camp. Major Bessonov showed up; the zeks
were lined up in front of the mess hall; and he commanded: "All sick men
fall out!" Not a single man stirred. But the next day, almost a hundred were
in their bunks with a high fever. The medical staff did blood work-ups and

gave us injections, which in my case caused the skin to peel off my head. But I did not come down with dysentery. In general, however, these measures didn't help much, since our drinking water was still being taken from the same well. A quarantine was declared for an indefinite period; and this made me apprehensive that my next visit from Gusel, scheduled for May 12 (my birthday), would be canceled. Bessonov gave permission for Gusel to visit on May 13—a bad omen.

This time Gusel's pens and pencils had been taken away from her, so that we had to use lipstick and eyebrow pencil to write with. Not only was she prohibited from going to the nearby settlement, but we were locked in our room. When we had to use the toilet, we pounded on the door. The orderly would notify the DPNK, and he would open the door for us. They didn't want Gusel in the kitchen, so they put a hot plate and small refrigerator in our room. In this way we spent three days—days that were both happy and unhappy.

Gusel left the camp without being detained, and on May 17, I got a telegram that read: "HAVE REACHED THE AIRPORT SAFE AND SOUND STOP LOVING KISSES." This put my mind at rest. But hardly had I read the telegram when the orderly rushed in to tell me I was wanted at the dispensary immediately.

With a note of triumph, Tsarko informed me that Gusel had been taken off the plane at Magadan and sent to the hospital, owing to the dysentery quarantine in Talaya. Also, I was to be hospitalized for some analyses.

My rage knew no bounds. Now I realized why Bessonov had authorized the visit. Nixon and Kissinger were due to arrive in Moscow on May 22, and the KGB had removed the dissidents and Jewish activists. Many of them were put under preventive detention; confinement in a hospital provided a good pretext for a thorough search. But Nixon and Kissinger voiced no dissatisfaction with what had happened. Apparently they felt that the arrests were a natural side effect of détente and had been made for the sake of their security.

After cursing out Tsarko, saying I was not about to submit to any diagnostic procedures (something she didn't insist upon), I wrote to friends in Moscow about Gusel's detention. A few days later I received a letter from Gusel telling me how frightened she had been when, just as the plane was about to land, she was seized by a woman in a white coat and a man in civilian clothes. Fortunately, she was not carrying any of my letters. At the Magadan hospital they of course found no symptoms of dysentery. But they kept her there for two weeks because of an "ulcerated colon." In Moscow, no traces of that mythical ulcer could be found. But later, after those experiences, Gusel did in fact get an ulcer.

Hardly had I learned of Gusel's confinement in the hospital when there was a new development: "Gavrilych" had been frisked and sent to the punishment cell. Yury Gavrilovich Shabalin, an old zek with the face of a young man, was serving his second ten-year term for homicide and armed robbery. I often played chess with him, and we talked freely with each other. He behaved with equanimity and never interfered in anything, but he was respected by the other regular criminals.

I began to realize what role had been played by Obraztsov, who six months before had been transferred to the settlement colony. We had agreed that through the intermediary of a nonprisoner who worked as a stoker, Obraztsov would get the food from Gusel to Gavrilych in the woodworking shop, and Gavrilych would then smuggle it into the compound. And now Gavrilych had been picked up, supposedly by chance, at the guard shack. (Naturally, they didn't want to expose Obraztsov.)

Ten days later, Gavrilych was released from the punishment cell. He told me that Zolotarev and Zhmak were in the guard shack when he was picked up. When they found, concealed in one of his boots, a package of sugar and some newspaper clippings of a performance of my plays in London, they pounced upon the reviews, although none of them could read English. The theater was called The 84 Club. Having deciphered that name, Zolotarev asked Gavrilych, "Did you let eighty-four people into the club?"

"What you should have answered," I told Gavrilych, "was: 'I was the eighty-fifth to join.'"

Subsequently, KGB Major Eliseyev told me that Gavrilych had been an MVD officer assigned to the camp, but that he had taken up with a gypsy woman, and gone over to the thugs. I don't know how much of that is worthy of credence, but I do know that it was said in order to cast aspersions on Gavrilych.

Despite the brilliance with which the operation to catch us smuggling was conducted, its results were pretty much zero. I didn't pass on anything to anyone nor did I take anything from anyone. And Gavrilych apparently didn't report anything. Then Obraztsov decided to "brazen it out." He called me up from the guard shack and told me he had some things he wanted to give me. While the barracks orderly listened, eagerly trying to catch every word, I replied that I would neither see him nor take anything from him. Without a moment's delay, I reported to Zolotarev that Obraztsov had appropriated my things and was attempting to get me involved in illegal operations. And Gavrilych told him the same. This may well have been the first time that Zolotarev was not overjoyed by denunciations.

That summer there was a new visitor, a short lieutenant colonel with an intelligent face. Not long after his arrival he came to our barracks. His first words to me were: "I hope you'll forgive me, Andrei Alekseyevich, for not having recognized you sooner." This opener was enough to alert anyone who is used to hearing: "Get a move on, you cocksucking bastard!" The lieutenant colonel, who turned out to be the UVD's deputy chief for political education, wanted to hear my opinion of détente, which was just then getting under way. And I must say my opinion was rather favorable, even though détente had already cost Gusel two weeks of freedom.

The next official who came to see me was an instructor from the UVD's political section—a captain who was polite to the point of being mealy-mouthed. He wanted to know how I was feeling, what I thought about this and that, and what my life on the outside had been like.

Finally, I was invited to see Ovechkin, the *zampolit,* and Sholokhov, the prosecutor; and we had a social conversation. This was hard for Ovechkin to manage, but not for Sholokhov. He told me about his acquaintanceship with the wife of Oleg Troyanovsky, later the Soviet ambassador to the United Nations; and I, not to be outdone, told him of my acquaintanceship with the widow of Maxim Litvinov, the former People's Commissar of Foreign Affairs. When we, like a couple of name-droppers, had exchanged this information, Ovechkin apparently felt that the decisive moment had arrived, and he asked me if I would write a letter to *Izvestiya* renouncing *Will the Soviet Survive Until 1984?* I replied that I didn't want to, and that ended the conversation.

(Later, when making the rounds of the prison, Sholokhov noticed my copy of Engels's *Anti-Dühring;* with his fondness for polite conversation, he asked me how I liked it. The book contains a lot of quotations from the German Socialist Dühring; and when you first read them, you think nothing could be stupider. Then you read the rebuttal by the German Socialist Engels, and you have to admit that there *are* things even stupider.)

In those three conversations with the different officials, I detected a hint that things were changing for the better; and this seemed to be confirmed when Victor Krasin was released that spring. But a few days later I learned from the Voice of America that Petr Yakir had been arrested.

(The use of radio receivers was forbidden in the camp, but transistor sets found their way in from the outside, just as vodka did, and I was able to listen to the Voice of America for almost a month until they confiscated my set. Of all the Western broadcasting stations, the Voice of America was the only one that reached Kolyma. All the free workers in Talaya listened to it, and when it was reported that I was there and mention was made of Colonel Nichikov, the commotion was incredible. In the settlement colony everyone stopped felling timber and crowded around the radio. "Now the whole world knows about Talaya," they said with pride. Later, when Gusel was in Talaya, a women came up to her and said, "Please tell the Voice of America right away that I've been fired!")

Today, considering Ovechkin's proposal that I renounce my book in conjunction with Yakir's arrest, I am inclined to believe that the authorities needed a kind of "downgrading of bourgeois influence" within the USSR as a counterpoise to rapprochement with the West. They may actually have given serious thought, just as they had a year before, to releasing me in exchange for my recantation. That would have made a good impression in the West, would have helped grease the wheels of détente, as it were. But then the authorities saw that détente was going full speed ahead anyway and that it was time to give thought to the domestic aspect of détente. Yakir's arrest was the first signal of what détente would mean at home.

In August, I was brought before a medical board. The examiners, including a psychiatrist, ruled that I was fit to work and changed my disability classification from Group Two to Group Three. But the way things turned out, I didn't have to go to work that soon.

CHAPTER 18

I See Kolyma

"To the guardhouse on the double! With your things."

A penal camp is not a prison, where "with your things" may mean merely a transfer to another cell. I was going to be taken away. But to where? And why? To another camp where the regimen was harsher? To undergo investigation for a new term? To be released? To testify at someone's trial?

The camp officials, hoping to see no more of me, played their last dirty trick: they withheld a parcel from Gusel that had arrived just before I was sent off—to go jolting along the Kolyma Road.

Magadan: an empty cell. I have a set of dominoes. To my right, I place enough of them to equal the months I have already served, and to my left those indicating the months yet ahead of me. My head droops over the table, and I doze off, dreaming. Then someone is shaking me, and I wake up with a cry: "Where am I?"

Somebody laughs, and then answers: "You're in prison."

After "sanitary treatment," I was taken to a common cell. A lively and obviously friendly zek jumped up from his bunk and greeted me. "Amalrik? We've heard about you!"

This was Yuzek Damansky. He and his accomplice, Liu Fu-u (a curious coincidence, since the skirmishes between Soviet and Chinese troops on Damansky Island were still fresh in everyone's memory), were both dentists from the Ukraine. Taking with them a suitcase full of instruments and a small supply of gold, they had flown to Magadan. Because of the harsh climate there, almost everyone is toothless. You must wait at least a year to get into a dental clinic, and sometimes it all comes to naught, anyway. So when Damansky and Liu Fu-u set up a practice there, charging sixty rubles for each tooth made from their gold, they were welcomed as benefactors of mankind.

After a month, however, they were arrested on a charge of "trading in gold by means of inserting dentures" and were given three years each. They would have received longer sentences if they hadn't bribed the judge through their lawyer.

I waited ten days for my interrogation—the usual procedure employed by investigators to fray the nerves of their victims, although a strong-willed person can use that time to ready himself for the encounter. On August 31, I was taken downstairs, hands manacled behind my back, to a small office where there was only a desk, a chair for the investigator, and a stool for the prisoner. A short man in civilian clothes with a face that was impassive and yet rather affable asked me to sit down. This was Captain Boris Denisov, Senior Investigator of the Magadan UKGB. Copies of the Criminal Code and the Code of Criminal Procedure lay on the desk—an indication, as it were, that my rights would be observed. Captain Denisov even gestured toward the books, as if to say I could make use of them if I wished. On the other hand—and here force of habit came into play—when he warned me against giving false testimony or refusing to testify, he said that the penalty in both cases was a sentence of up to seven years, although I knew that for refusing to testify it was six months of compulsory labor.

Denisov asked me how I felt and how I liked the weather in Magadan. Then he questioned my knowledge of Yakir's "anti-Soviet activity." I replied that I first wanted to know in connection with what case, and in what capacity, I had been called in. Denisov said I had been summoned as a witness in the case of Petr Yakir, indicted under Article 70 of the RSFSR Criminal Code.

There is a difference between the way a case is handled by an investigator who is personally in charge of it and the way it is conducted by an investigator assigned to do the job for a colleague in another city. In the first instance the investigator usually has strong feelings about the case, since often his career depends upon it. But in the second instance, it is just "somebody else's case." So it was that Denisov began his inquiry without any great show of feeling, running down the list of questions that had been sent him from Moscow. I replied that I knew Yakir, that I had neither heard nor seen any anti-Soviet statements uttered or written by him, and that I knew nothing of any anti-Soviet activity or ties with anti-Soviet organizations on his part. I said I had seen various people at his home, but I didn't remember their names.

"And you didn't meet any foreigners at his home? Didn't you introduce them to him?"

"I didn't introduce any foreigners to him, and I don't recall having met any at his home."

"That's no good, Andrei Alekseyevich," sighed Denisov. "You keep saying 'I don't know,' 'I didn't hear,' 'I never saw,' and 'I never met.' I'm afraid you'll be ashamed of that later. After all, our hands aren't exactly empty."

"I realize they're not empty. Probably you have something in that black briefcase. But I have nothing to be ashamed of, because I'm telling the truth."

At that point, Denisov reached into his leatherette briefcase and took out an excerpt from Yakir's depositions, which he read to me. There were many rhetorical phrases to the effect that *Will the Soviet Union Survive Until 1984?* was an "anti-Soviet, libelous, subversive book," etc. As for the matters of fact dealt with in the deposition, they boiled down to the following. I had introduced Yakir to the CBS correspondent William Cole, and had set up an interview with him; I had given Yakir the manuscript of *Will the Soviet Union Survive Until 1984?* in October or November 1969 in Zinaida Grigorenko's apartment; in March 1970, I had written a laudatory review of my own book and given it to Yakir to sign, after which I had sent it abroad.

Along with the foregoing, Denisov read personal comments that Yakir had made about me, all unflattering—e.g., in addition to my other virtues, I was a drunk and virtually a rapist. It was plain that Denisov was reading me these comments so that I in turn would spare no pejoratives in describing Yakir's character.

I had thought that Yakir's arrest would be a kind of catharsis for him, but it turned out to be just the opposite: it destroyed the last defenses of his personality. I could hardly sleep that night, so unexpected was the blow. And yet in a way it was not entirely unexpected. From the very beginning, something in Denisov's behavior had suggested to me what might happen; that perhaps behind the persona of the Yakir I knew was another Yakir who was a stranger to me. And so I remained outwardly calm while listening to Denisov. When he was through, I told him the whole thing was false. What annoyed me most was Yakir's claim that I myself had written the laudatory report on my book. When Denisov showed me a typewritten copy, I said I couldn't judge whether that was the letter that Yakir had in mind, but that I had written no letters for him to sign. As for the manuscript of *Will the Soviet Union Survive Until 1984?* I said I did not give it to him. For that matter, in October and November of 1969 I was at my house in the country.

"But what about the CBS interview? And the meetings with foreign journalists?"

I replied that Yakir himself had testified that the CBS and *New York Times* correspondents had asked him whether I wasn't a KGB agent and said that, obviously, they wouldn't arrange for an interview through such an agent. As for the meetings with foreign journalists, I said I could neither confirm nor deny Yakir's testimony, because I simply could not remember. Some journalists had been at my home, and I had visited many of them; it was quite possible that he had happened to come to my place on some such occasion or that I had run across him at someone else's place.

"If you don't remember anything, maybe we should put in the report that your memory has been impaired by the meningitis."

"No. Why should you do that? I don't remember right now; but later, you know, it'll suddenly come back to me. If you put in the report that I have lost my memory, God knows what they might pin on me."

Actually, I *had* introduced Yakir to the CBS correspondent; I had suggested that he interview us; and at about the same time I had given the manuscript of *Will the Soviet Union Survive Until 1984?* to Yakir, since he had started complaining that "everybody was talking about it" but he didn't have a copy. But one doesn't say these things to a KGB investigator.

At the second interrogation I said that Yakir's depositions could be explained by the fact that he, who had already spent a good many years in prison, had been badly shaken by his arrest, that in his eagerness to please the investigator he had slandered both himself and others. I also requested an entry in the interrogation record to the effect that I had not seen Yakir's depositions but had merely heard what was read to me from a typewritten copy. Denisov was amazed, and sighed as if his feelings had been hurt. But he did make the entry, and after that I was left in peace. I was even transferred to another cell, which obviously was not bugged, because the KGB had lost interest in what I had to say.

Not long afterward my new cell-mates and I were joined by a hunchback of about forty. While working as a bookkeeper in the State trade network, he shut his eyes to a padded voucher for breakage in the hauling of empty bottles. The truck driver and the dispatcher reported the "breakage" as recycled bottles and split the take with the bookkeeper. The hunchback got about 2,000 rubles—and seven years in a penal camp. At Talaya his only consolation was meeting up with a former neighbor, the film projectionist Kovalev—the same Kovalev who had previously installed a microphone in the library so that Zolotarev could listen to my conversations. One night the hunchback went to see Kovalev in the projection booth and found him eating some tarts. Uncomfortable about eating in the presence of his guest, Kovalev offered the hunchback one of the tarts. As soon as he had bitten into it, however, he realized that only his own wife could have baked it, since it tasted exactly like those she had baked for him all their married life. He then understood that she was Kovalev's mistress and had been sending tarts to the camp not for her husband, whom she didn't like, but for her lover.

The next morning a guard found Kovalev in the projection booth with a knife between his shoulder blades. The booth was sealed off, and an investigation was begun. Many of the hunchback's friends, seeing how grief-stricken he was, tried to console him for the loss of his friend: "Don't take it so hard—they'll find out who killed your buddy."

Another one who took the murder very hard was my old friend Ivanchenko. Finally he could no longer control himself and spoke to the hunchback: "I understand your feelings, but please try to understand mine too. I procured a pair of shoes to wear when I get out of here, and I hid them in the projection booth so they wouldn't find them during a search. You didn't happen to notice them there before your friend was killed, did you?"

"I understand your feelings very well," replied the hunchback. "I myself left two cans of condensed milk there."

Having confided their feelings to each other, the two parted, realizing that there was nothing to be done.

But eventually, the hunchback got so sick of hearing condolences that he confessed to the murder. The projection booth was unsealed; Ivanchenko walked out of the camp to freedom in a new pair of shoes, and two years were added to the hunchback's sentence. Such is the structure of our judicial system: for broken bottles belonging to the State, you get seven years; for the life of a zek, two years.

On September 11, I was taken to Moscow under special armed guard. For the first—and perhaps the last—time in my life, I had a compartment of a plane all to myself, leaving out of account three armed guards and a KGB courier. The officer in command of the guards, an old MVD captain, had apparently never flown in an airplane, and he was so nervous that he upset his tray of food.

On that trip, I realized what it meant to be a VIP. If I expressed a desire to go to the toilet, the guards would push aside the line of passengers in the forward compartment and then stand outside the door of the toilet like a guard of honor. And when I was taken off the plane at Domodedovo Airport, I found myself in a lounge identified by a sign reading: "FOR DEPUTIES OF THE USSR SUPREME SOVIET."

I was the only passenger in the Black Maria. It was so tightly sealed that there were no chinks through which I could see the streets of Moscow. Yet I *felt* that I was in Moscow; and I realized all the more painfully what it means to be incarcerated 8,000 miles from home.

"Do you know where you are?" asked the guard on duty.

"In Lefortovo."

"I myself don't know where we are," said the frightened captain of the guards. "And we didn't tell him anything."

But it wasn't hard to figure out. The guard on duty was wearing a KGB uniform, and Lefortovo is their remand (or "investigative") prison, the Lubyanka Remand Prison having been closed in the middle sixties.

My cell was large and well-lighted. The window had been painted over in white, but it had no shield over it. There was a toilet, a washstand, a wooden table, two stools, and two bunks. The only trouble was that I was all alone. Lieutenant Colonel Stepanov, the deputy commandant, a big man with a rather nasal voice, said that this was now forbidden, and that I would be given a cell-mate. He loved to chat and even gave me his versions of some paradoxes of the ancient Greek Sophists.

"Get me somebody at least halfway intelligent, please."

"What a way to talk!" he replied.

Two days later I was transferred to another cell just like the first one. My cell-mate was a short, wiry young man who was now serving his second term for illegal dealings in gold. The KGB had begun to handle "economic cases"—gold, diamonds, foreign currency—under Khrushchev, when the era of massive repressions was coming to an end and employment had to be found for the huge machine of terrorism. In general, the gold and currency speculators were not bad people: they usually had a sense of humor and were not hard to get along with. (One of the jokes my cell-mate told me went as follows: What is the highest point in Moscow? Lefortovo—from there you can see Kolyma.) But hardly any of them could understand that there were other values in the world besides money.

I had heard a lot about Lefortovo. In the late thirties, it was the place where they tortured those prisoners they hadn't managed to break in the Lubyanka. Lefortovo, which incorporates the highest achievements in prison architecture of the early twentieth century, is built in the form of a K, with empty bays between floors. A kind of traffic cop is stationed at the point where the wings of the building intersect; and he uses signal flags to direct the traffic. The warders snap their fingers to warn that a zek is coming. Two upper floors and two wings of the prison have been preserved. There were about 200 inmates and a lot of warders, so that order was assured. In addition to free workers, convicts from Butyrki Prison were used for housekeeping duties. If they chanced to be present when a zek was being escorted through a corridor by a warder, they would turn and face the wall. I never touched a doorknob while I was there: all the doors were opened and closed by warders.

After reveille, I was served black bread and issued toilet paper—worth its weight in gold, and rationed accordingly. (Complaints of diarrhea were of no avail.) At the same time those prisoners whose eyeglasses had been taken from them for the night got them back. (Apparently a prisoner had once tried to slit his wrists with glass from his lenses.) During the day, a guard would peer in at the judas-hole every five minutes. They fed us better than in other prisons, but I remained a bit hungry. At the canteen you could not buy more than a pound of butter per month without special authorization from the investigator; the same authorization was required for more than two pounds of sugar sent in by parcel. I couldn't eat the black bread because of my gastritis, and without bread I was vulnerable to constant hunger pangs. But they wouldn't give me white bread since, as one doctor put it, "half the human race has gastritis." (Fortunately, half the human race is not in prison.) So I decided to pester the medical personnel. I put myself down for sick call—at first once a week, then twice a week, and finally every day. The two woman doctors, one old and one young and both of them squeamish, looked at me with undisguised hatred. They did a work-up on my gastric juices and said they were normal.

"How can they be normal when I have stomach pains?"

"Are you trying to say that we switched the sample?"

"Of course you switched it," I said without blinking an eye.

And my pressure tactics succeeded. One morning a piece of white bread was shoved in through the chuckhole. I put it on a shelf, intending to eat it when I had my tea; and in the meantime, I would feast my eyes upon it, as visible evidence of a triumph. But before breakfast time arrived, an excited sergeant rushed into my cell shouting, "Where is the bread?" And he snatched it up. It seems that the security people, in checking the food items authorized by the dispensary, remembered that I had "taken the wrong line" while being interrogated and hence was not entitled to white bread. Nonetheless, I was issued two sheets, whereas in Magadan I got only one, and in other prisons none at all. But the chief respect in which Lefortovo differed from other prisons was its library, made up of confiscated books.

On the eighth day I saw the investigators Tuliyev and Aleksandrovsky. In some ways Tuliyev reminded me of Kirinkin, although he was even younger. Had Yakir complained about his financial situation, and was his apartment clean? Tuliyev had to rewrite the record of the interrogation, because I refused to sign the draft stating that Yakir's apartment was dirty. I didn't want to engage in mutual mudslinging or mutual apartmentslinging.

After the questioning, I told Tuliyev that until I was granted a visit from my wife, I would give no more testimony. His response was that everything would be done according to law. After three weeks of waiting I filed a complaint with the USSR Prosecutor General. "You know the law," Stepanov said to me. "But in this specific situation its application is not feasible."

Some forty days after my first interrogation, I was led out of my cell and, as the warders snapped their fingers, taken first through several corridors of the prison and then through an iron door into the right wing of the investigative annex. I ended up in the office of an investigator named Anatoly Istomin. I told him I would not answer any questions until I was granted a visit from my wife.

"And if we grant the visit, will you give meaningful testimony? Or will you give us the same kind of frivolous answers as before?"

"That remains to be seen," I said, in exactly the same tone he had used with me.

At this point Gennady Kislykh, who was heading up the team of investigators on the Yakir case, and Lieutenant Colonel Povarenkov came into the office.

Povarenkov immediately adopted a condescending tone with me, using the familiar pronoun, *ty*. "One thing that bothers us about you, Amalrik, is that you're always sending in complaints."

"So far as I know," I said, "you and I didn't go to the same school, and we didn't serve time in the same penal camp. So you have no business calling me *ty*."

Povarenkov instantly underwent a transformation. Like Gogol's character Chichikov, he sidled up to me with a smile and held out a piece of paper. "Your demand has been satisfied. Here is an order from the general who is the chief of the KGB's Tenth Administration." The document did, in fact, authorize a visit from Gusel.

"Are you the general?" I asked sternly, although I could plainly see that he was a lieutenant colonel.

"Oh, no! I'm Lieutenant Colonel Povarenkov, temporarily serving as prison commandant."

"Well," said Kislykh, "now we can begin your testimomy."

"Not yet. I asked for a visit, not an order authorizing a visit."

"But we gave you the slippers that your wife brought!" Povarenkov shouted.

They had indeed given me the slippers, but I wanted to see Gusel herself. I realized that no one could cancel the order from the chief of the Tenth Administration; but in this specific case its application might prove to be "unfeasible." At any rate, they would first see what kind of testimony I would give.

After some ten minutes of wrangling, Istomin began to read out, and then enter into the record, those questions that I refused to answer. I explained I was refusing to testify since they were not granting me a visit, "in the interests of the investigation" (to use Stepanov's phrase).

Major Kislykh then ordered that I be returned to my cell. But before an hour had passed, they brought me back to the same office. Kislykh was standing to the left of the door, Prosecutor Ilyukhin was by the window, and behind a little table on the right sat a bearded, heavily built man in a sweater. At first I took him to be a prosecutor, although I was amazed that a prosecutor should be wearing a sweater. But the moment I was brought in, he stood up and bowed—that is, he bowed to the extent that his big belly would allow him to—and it was clear that he was not a prosecutor. Then I looked at the man closely and saw that he was Yakir.

I said that I would not take part in any confrontation until I had been granted a visit from my wife.

"Don't forget where you are," Kislykh warned me.

"It's too bad," put in Ilyukhin, "that we're no longer living in a time when other methods could be used on you."

"And what do *you* have to say on that subject?" Kislykh asked Yakir, who had felt the full force of those methods thirty years before.

"Andrei knows the laws," Yakir said, after some hesitation. "If he requested a visit from his wife, it means he's entitled to it." Then, turning to me, he added, "You must understand my position. They're threatening me with the death penalty!"

"Nobody's threatening you with the death penalty," Kislykh said with a sneer. Then he began reading the questions.

Expressing himself less categorically than he had in his previous testimony, Yakir confirmed that I had given him the manuscript of *Will the Soviet Union Survive Until 1984?* and that I had set up the television interview. He did not say he had signed the letter I had written without first having read it. Rather, he claimed that it corresponded to "his opinions at that time" and that therefore he had signed it. This was a mitigating circumstance, and it plainly infuriated both Kislykh and Ilyukhin. With respect to the interview, Yakir said that he and I had been to see an "NBC" correspondent.

"Do you mean CBS?" Kislykh cut in.

"A leading question!" I objected.

"That's just like you, Andrei Alekseyevich!" Kislykh and Ilyukhin exclaimed in unison.

But that was my only comment. Every time I was asked whether I could confirm Yakir's testimony, I said I refused to answer. Meantime, as the questions and answers were repeated like a refrain, Ilyukhin was talking on the telephone; and from his remarks I gathered that Krasin had been arrested again.

By way of summing up the results of the confrontation, Ilyukhin said, "Yakir is faced with a seven-year sentence, and because of that he's behaving sensibly. You have three years, so you're being brazen." Then, in his capacity as "supervisory prosecutor"† for the KGB, he added, "If you have any requests or complaints, get in touch with me right away."

I replied I had lost all faith in him as a prosecutor, since he had not authorized the visit from my wife, and, moreover, he had threatened me with "the old methods."

I was then dismissed, while Yakir was left behind—no doubt so that

---

†Under Soviet law, the prosecutor (actually, procurator) is empowered to review cases "by way of supervision."—TRANS.

they could reprimand him. Although I had been "brazen" (to use Ilyukhin's adjective), I had been haunted by fear throughout the session. Ilyukhin had struck me as the most loathsome of all the officials of our various "organs" that I had ever seen. I don't know why—it was just an instinctive feeling. Nor was my dispirited state due solely to Yakir's slavishness toward the investigators: I think it was also the result of a premonition, not fully realized at the time, that a heavy blow was in store for me.

Two days later, Stepanov announced to me: "You have been granted a visit on Thursday, for one half-hour. No violation of the law is involved, since the law specifies *'up to'* two hours."

"Wonderful!" I said. "God forbid they should grant me *more* than two hours. There are enough violations of the law as it is."

The following evening, someone shouted through the chuckhole: "Amalrik! With your things."

The Black Maria; the Krasnopresenskaya Transit Prison; the familiar hole in the wall at the Kazan Station; the railroad car with the barred windows, coupled and waiting on the snowed-over tracks; the guard dogs; the stony faces of the armed guards ("left, right, left, right . . .")—and ahead of me, Kolyma, which can be seen from Lefortovo. I was about to travel clear across Russia in a prison-type railroad car for the third time. Gusel told me later that she had put on her best dress for the visit, only to hear an indifferent voice tell her, at the prison gate: "Your husband is gone."

During routine searches in prison I would sometimes have a little fun: I would pretend to be nervous, and the warder would rummage around with mounting excitement, expecting to find some booty. But joking was out of the question when I was going off on a transport. When I heard the shout, "On the double!" I would haphazardly shove back into my knapsack the things that a guard had already thrown out of it and gone over, only to be roughly frisked again by the armed guards who were taking over as escorts.

Before the transport set out from Sverdlovsk, the officer on duty wanted to deprive me of my English can opener, claiming that it was a sharp instrument, although it was plain to see that he wanted it for himself. I objected loudly that can openers were permitted and said that if he wanted to confiscate it he would have to make a record of the confiscation. Finally, much miffed, he tossed the can opener back to me, exclaiming, "You're a worthless prick of a revolutionary! You're always moving around the country, just to stir up the people." (In Boston, Mstislav Rostropovich said to me, "You're always moving around the country—to Washington, to Boston, to San Francisco . . ." To which I replied, "But you see, I have to stir up the people!") It was this incident that gave me the idea of calling my book *Notes of a Revolutionary*.

In Novosibirsk, we had scarcely stretched out on the floor to sleep when a huge rat, accompanied by her little baby rats, came out of a hole and made for us. Meantime, bedbugs were attacking us from the rear.

"Those bedbugs aren't ours," said the chief warder. "You brought them with you."

"And the rats? I suppose we brought them along too?"

"No, the rats are ours," the warder replied proudly. And indeed, the bedbugs could hardly stand comparison with the rats.

My memory, unfortunately, is such that I can't forget anything. Right now, in my mind's eye, I can see a whole gallery of individuals that I met during transports—as if I had just come off a transport myself. One of these was a runty zek who looked every inch the workingman but who said that if, at the age of twenty, he had "known what I know now," he would have been a professor at thirty. Then there was the young thug who explained to another that if somebody is being murdered, he shouldn't interfere, because the man is probably being killed for good reason.

One of the more interesting was a man who "could have been a professor" but plainly was not. This robust young man with a red beard, wearing glasses and a knitted ski cap, was a biologist: Dr. Mashkov, from Leningrad. He was in stir for having murdered the director of his laboratory. He and another scientist had cut the cadaver up into little pieces, but then had second thoughts about concealing the crime. Mashkov got the death penalty, but it was commuted to fifteen years. Sitting at a pockmarked table, he explained his anti-Darwinistic theories to me. In the long run (he said) the survivor is not the one who adapts best to the environment but the one who adapts least to it. When the environment changes, the former perishes; but the latter, although he has a hard time of it, adapts to the new environment. From that point of view he and I had a good chance of surviving in the camps. One favorable sign was the fact that we were sitting there at the table chatting, after having eaten our gruel. In an overcrowded cell, it's not everyone who eats "in the presidium," meaning at the table.

One of the young thugs confided his secret ambition to me: when he got out, he was going to rob an ice cream vendor's stand; he had already cased one in his hometown. (One should, after all, have a goal in life.) A theatrical producer from Leningrad, tall and sad-faced, wanted somebody to read a story that he had written in camp. The mistress of a young zek, thinking that the producer was badly in need of a woman, asked her friend, the camp's female doctor, to accommodate him. With his permission, he was tied down to a table, and she got on top of him. Then, when he was about to have an orgasm, she rolled off and said: "The next performance will be a week from now." (The producer had been sentenced to twelve years for taking part in a gang rape.)

A handsome and intelligent-looking young man took over leadership among the thugs as soon as he arrived among us. He told me: "I hate the underworld, but I want to be somebody you have to reckon with. You must be like them."

After listening to our talk about politics, one goon commented: "I don't envy you. The less a man knows, the better he lives."

Prisoners in a transport are always hungry. While still in Irkutsk, I reached an agreement with some young toughs (keeping in mind what I had learned from our "Great Bowl Mutiny" in Novosibirsk) that we would refuse the gruel served out for supper and would demand thicker gruel. When mealtime came, my accomplices crowded around the chuckhole and started shouting, "We won't take it! Eat it yourself! We're on hunger strike!" The rest of those in the cell, seeing that there was a whole group of us, were afraid to take their own gruel. Paying no attention to the howling youngsters, the guard dragged me out of the rear ranks and took me to the deputy warden. With the warden was a young woman, the deputy prosecutor for juvenile offenders' cases. I suggested that the two of them come along and try the gruel themselves. The three of us set out for my cell, taking an indirect route; on the way, the warden pointed to a cook's helper who was shoving bowls in through a chuckhole. "See?" he said. "They're all taking it without complaining."

"Then I suggest that the Citizen Prosecutor try some herself," said I.

"There aren't any spoons," the warden objected in some distress.

"Yes, there are," I replied, taking one out of my pocket.

"What a bad one you are!" the warden exclaimed, much put out. But the prosecutor didn't accept my offer.

When we got to my cell, there was a big cauldron of gruel standing near it. And what gruel! It fairly glistened with fat and emitted the appetizing smell of cracklings. A spoon was ready at hand, and the prosecutor sampled the contents of the cauldron. "Excellent gruel," she pronounced.

And indeed, that evening everyone in our cell was given edible gruel, although the next day the old watery stuff was back.

In the transit cell a Georgian with a dried-up-looking face was about to take a piss. He opened the lid of the latrine pail and immediately slammed it shut with an expression of great distaste.

"What's the matter?" I asked. "Doesn't Russian shit smell good?"

The young thugs laughed with approval, as if to say, "Our Russian shit hasn't let us down: it hits the 'beasts' right in the nose."

In general, the Georgians, Armenians, Ingushes, Kazakhs, Uzbeks, Lithuanians, and other non-Russians I met up with impressed me as more self-possessed, more polite, and more kindly disposed toward others than the Russians; there were fewer stool pigeons among them. One reason for this, I suspect, is that each of them regards himself as a representative of his people and doesn't want to give that people a bad name, whereas the Russians feel they represent the Soviet Union as a whole and hence have nothing to lose. It is true that, being a people of the steppes, we are hospitable. But are we tolerant? Are we good? If one wants to compare the character of nations as manifested in their revolutions, we must compare ourselves not with the English or French but with the Chinese. We regard the Chinese as a cruel people, yet that comparison is not favorable to us. We Russians shot not only our emperor but his whole family. The Chinese emperor (who had collaborated with the Japanese) was only made to serve a few years in a Communist prison, after which he was released, given a job working in a botanical garden, and even elected to the All-China Congress of People's Representatives. Can one imagine Nicholas II being chosen for the Supreme Soviet? Deng Tsao-ping, a "right-wing communist" who lost his post during the purges of the Cultural Revolution, and who was branded an "enemy of the people," became the leader of his country a few years later. Can one imagine Bukharin's return to leadership in the forties?

During the four-day trip to Khabarovsk—I was being taken there along with some tubercular prisoners, eating and drinking out of the same mugs with them—I consoled myself with the thought that this was the last leg of my journey. But in the plane, things were better: I had friendly chats with the stewardess, the steward, and the young armed guards.

"What do you expect?" the captain of the guards asked me. "You can't get along without authorities."

"Then they should be replaced from time to time," I said, recalling Ubozhko's comments. "The terms of office should be limited."

"If you limit their terms, they won't acquire experience," he objected.

"Shave off that pirate's beard!" ordered Lieutenant Colonel Podolsky, as I was brought into the intake office of the Magadan Prison wearing the beard I had grown during the two months' trip from Moscow. A young guard with cold, moist hands searched me from head to toe, peered into my anus, and went over each page of every book I had with me. Then he said spitefully, "You read books in English, while I have to spend my time frisking people!"

It serves you right, I thought. But despite this unfriendly welcome, after the exhausting trip from Moscow I was almost as glad to be back at Magadan as if I were home.

All the zeks were looking forward to being amnestied in December, on the Fiftieth Anniversary of the founding of the USSR. Those with terms of no more than three years should be amnestied, I thought; or at least their sentences should be reduced. In fact a guard at Lefortovo had told me, "It's not just regular criminals that we're going to amnesty." I began to feel that I couldn't stick out the rest of my term without an amnesty. And an amnesty *was* proclaimed. However, not only were all of the politicals excluded, but even the petty thieves came off badly. Out of seven hundred prisoners at Talaya, two were completely amnestied, and twenty were sent "to chemistry." Moreover, the process of amnestying took five months.

The camp officials greeted me with rejoicing: I had to spend three days in the hole. In the prison I had argued with some warders because they tried to make two new prisoners, both young soldiers, sleep on the cement floor with no mattress. I got a mattress for the two of them and the hole for myself.

It was almost fifty degrees below zero, and in the concrete punishment cell with the broken window I couldn't lie down for long, even at night. I did sitting-up exercises to keep as warm as I could; or else I would sit hugging the heating pipe, which ran about three inches above the floor. They had taken my clothing away and issued me a threadbare jacket, pants, and some wretched boots. I was issued soup every other day and a piece of bread with salt and a mug of hot water every day. In order to keep myself occupied, I composed poetry in my head.

Finally, I was released—before reveille on a bitterly cold January morning. As I came into the compound, lit up by searchlights, and rounded the corner of the barracks, this was the sight that greeted my eyes: on a metal arch, a sign reading "SPORTS ARENA." Below it, a poster reading: "COMPETE FOR THE RECORD IN LABOR AND SPORTS." And behind all that, a gallows. It turned out that the sports arena was the idea of Captain Ovechkin. He decided to build it so that the young prisoners, instead of goofing off and raising hell, could play on the swings. The hellraisers, however, swung so hard, striking their heels against the walls of the school, that the swings had to be taken down. All that was left was a gigantic crossbeam with ends of rope dangling from it.

CHAPTER 19

Corrective-Labor Colony 261/3: Works and Days

I, too, soon had a chance to compete for the record in labor. I refused to work in the paint shop—there, painters with grayish skins and an unhealthy luster in their eyes put coats of acetone-base paint on furniture—and I was assigned a job as janitor in the furniture shop. As I wrote to Gusel: "Considering that in Siberia I used to clean out stinking manure, whereas now I clean up shavings smelling of the forest, I can say that I have not spent these years in vain, and that my new position marks a step forward."

Reveille was at 6:00 A.M., with the national anthem roaring in our ears, and at 8:00 the march off to work began. In the bitter cold and the mist, we lined up by fives at the gate to the work zone. The First Detachment worked in the automobile repair shops and at the diesel electric power station, the Second in the furniture shop, the Third in the woodworking shop, the Fourth on camp construction projects, and the Fifth in the prison service department and the footwear shop. The manufacture of furniture was the main kind of production. I followed the entire process, from the drying of the wood to assembly, and concluded that if such furniture lasted a year, one should be grateful to God.

A penal camp is a microcosm of the Socialist society. It guarantees all those social and economic rights of which the Soviet authorities are so proud, and toward which Socialists strive: the right to paid labor, food, clothing, housing, and free medical care. I do not believe that the camp system is founded on economic needs. The economic rationale is really more of a rationalization of unconscious impulses. It is something like the "rational explanation" that the Cambodian Socialists found for the senseless and horrible deed of driving all city-dwellers into the countryside, claiming that it was impossible to feed them in the city.

It is hard for me to judge to what extent, if any, the camps show a profit. I have heard of some that did, but ours operated on a subsidy. Almost all of the prisoners worked, since the officials did everything in their power to eliminate absenteeism, but often there was no work to do. In the woodworking shop, for example, many of the prisoners grossed only two or three rubles a month. The wear and tear on equipment was severe, because the zeks were not exactly careful in handling the machine tools. Worn-out equipment was not replaced, and the accident rate was high. As usual in the USSR, savings were effected at the expense of the infrastructure (if indeed such a learned term can be applied to barracks and latrines) and of wages. On paper, we worked an eight-hour day and got the same rate of pay as workers on the outside, although without any extras. Actually, however, we worked more and were paid less. Moreover, 50 percent of our pay went for the maintenance of the camp, and 50 percent for food, clothing, bunks, heating, illumination, water, canteen items, subscriptions to newspapers and magazines, books, and savings. "Deprivation of canteen privileges" was the officers' favorite expression. It wasn't enough that you earned the money; you also had to have a record of no violations before you could spend it at the canteen. My gross monthly wages were ninety-six rubles, and my take-home pay was nine rubles. On a job requiring more skill, a man could lay aside twenty or thirty rubles a month. The prisoners' attitude toward work was ambivalent: on the one hand, they hated it and felt that going to the hospital was a blessing. On the other hand, they were eager to work, since it enabled them to pass the time more quickly, and to have some money when they were released.

The superintendent of my shop, Popov, was a zek who occupied a kind of middle position between the camp officials and the prisoners. After two weeks of hauling crates of wood shavings, I told Popov that I wasn't going to do it anymore, because I had a weak heart. The next day I was given the job of janitor for the Bureau of Engineering Design (KTB), the production section, the commandant's office, and the stairways. I had to mop the floor of the KTB; in the other offices, I only swept the floor. This took two hours, and the rest of the time I sat in the KTB office reading books. Once when I was wiping the desks, the chairman of the SKK looked in on me. "Why are you working so hard?" he asked. "Take a leaf from my book. When they're watching, I act busy. But when it comes to real work, why strain yourself?"

I followed his advice to the letter. And if anyone pointed out to me that a floor had not been properly mopped or swept, I quoted Marx to the effect that slave labor is unproductive, a viewpoint to which I clung through thick and thin.

In the KTB worked Lomov, a pathologist convicted of graft (as an expert for the MVD he would find either that a girl who had been raped was still a virgin or that a girl who was still a virgin had been raped). Lomov was famous because of an incident in the settlement of Bilibino, beyond the Arctic Circle. It seems that a miner had flown in from the Ukraine, and at the airport he asked a bum where he could rent an apartment.

"Housing is hard to come by," said the bum. "But I see you're not a bad sort of guy, so I'll let you in on something. My brother just died, and I don't need our house anymore, so I'm willing to sell it."

They looked the house over. It was a fine one, although it had almost no furniture, since the bum had sold all but a single table for drinking money. On that table lay "his brother's" cadaver.

"Just give me a deposit of three hundred," said the bum. "Then, since the house is on runners, you can just hook up a tractor to it and haul it away."

A short time later, Lomov looked out of the window of his office in the hospital and saw, to his amazement, that his house had been hooked up to a tractor and was being hauled away. He raised a hue and cry; things didn't quiet down until the investigation led to the bum. When they found him, he and his bottle buddies could hardly stand on their feet.

The KTB shop superintendent, Lieutenant of Engineering Gaivoronsky, was colorless and weak-willed, but could get worked up if pressured from above. The director of the operation, Senior Lieutenant Korpushevich, a self-confident man of massive build, never gave me any trouble. In contrast to him, Lieutenant Ragozin, the chief engineer, a pink-cheeked young man, seemed out of his element. He had only recently been commissioned, and on one occasion, he tried to make like an officer with me, pointing out that I had not mopped the stairs. I shouted back at him, even mentioning his pink cheeks. Engineer Rogov, a young man with a considerable belly, was someone I had already met; he had once brought some chocolate into the camp for me. But I soon realized he had done it on instructions from the KGB, in order to worm his way into my confidence.

In their relations with prisoners, engineers and doctors who have only recently come into the MVD system often lose the style that is natural to them and adopt that of their colleagues. But with respect to officers, they are unable to place themselves on a sufficiently independent footing.

I was assigned to Barracks #2, which housed a good many Chukchis, Yakuts, Evenks, Koryaks, and Eskimos who on the outside were hunters and breeders of reindeer. There was something childlike about them, including a quickness to take offense. The Russians' attitude toward them was one of hostility and mockery. The Chukchis are literally perishing from alcoholism, and they get intoxicated from two or three drinks. As they say: "One drink— good. Two drinks—very good. Three drinks—gotta fight. Four drinks— gotta fuck."

One joke has it that the peoples of the Soviet Union were arguing as to which of them Lenin belonged. The Russians said he was a Russian, the Chuvashes said he was a Chuvash (his father was a Chuvash), the Kalmyks said he was a Kalmyk (his grandmother was a Kalmyk), the Germans said he was a German, the Jews said he was a Jew (his mother was from the Blank family), and a Chukchi, after listening to all this, said: "Is all wrong. Lenin, he Chukchi."

"*What?* Why do you say that?"

"Because Lenin, he very smart."

Most of the men in our company were long-termers. Papiashvili, a Georgian with a black mustache and bulging eyes, was distinguished by his rare stupidity and rare persistence, having stayed for several years in the fourth grade. He had been sentenced to twelve years and fined 150,000 rubles for illegally trading in gold. His fine was the biggest in the camp. The monthly deduction from his pay was three to five rubles, and it would take him several thousand years to pay his debt to the government.

Polyannikov, who had murdered his wife, had by contrast a lively mind. He used to start bull sessions by saying that the USSR would last forever, to which I would reply that not even the solar system was going to last forever.

A few people had warned me to be more careful. Immediately after I had been taken off to Moscow, many of the zeks in the camp had been questioned about me. Ivanchenko had not managed to hang on to his job as "culture organizer" and was looking for an opportunity to talk to me. As soon as I was taken away, he was questioned by a KGB investigator; and now there were rumors that a new case was in the making, that Zolotarev had said, "We're not done with Amalrik." This was unwelcome news, but I had hopes that they were merely trying to blackmail me so as to get my testimony against Yakir and Krasin. As I read various articles about détente with the West, I naïvely believed that the authorities no longer needed another political trial, and I marked off the days on the calendar. There were fewer and fewer of them left to serve, but time drags at the beginning and end of one's term.

On February 15, the melancholy face of the staff orderly loomed up in the doorway of my cell. Fixing his gaze on me, he announced: "They're calling for you. One of those people has showed up." "One of those people" turned out to be Captain Solovev, a KGB investigator. Solovev was a dapper, mustachioed gentleman, slow of movement and too slow of wit to be a good investigator. When he judged that we had wasted enough time talking about the weather and my health, he let it be known that I had been summoned as a witness in the case of Yury Shikhanovich. I didn't know Shikhanovich, but I had heard that he was a gifted mathematician. I said as much, and that was the end of my testimony.

A month later, Solovev questioned me about Krasin and Irina Belogorod-skaya. When he asked me what had been the subject of conversation when Belogorodskaya came to see Gusel and me, I replied that she was wearing a pretty dress with daisies on it, and that we had talked about that dress. I figured that when she read the file on her case in prison, she would be pleased to learn that her dress had produced such an indelible impression. When it came to drawing up the record of the interrogation, I insisted that I should write it in my own hand. It was the first time Solovev had come up against such a demand, and he was perplexed. Finally we agreed that he should record the questions and I the answers. Poor Solovev! He got a reprimand from Moscow, since it turned out that the entire record should have been in one and the same hand, either the investigator's or the witness's.

On the last day of March I was again taken to Magadan. At the prison I came in for a jolt: I was locked up not with convicts but with people still under investigation. One of them was a low-level raion functionary. All he could talk about was the privileges enjoyed by the workers of the *raikom*, saying they even had tangerines to eat, while the people on his level had a little less—nothing. At the same time he was indignant about one working-man who had said that in America you could live better by collecting empty bottles than you could in the USSR by sweating from morning till night, and he concluded with satisfaction: "He later disappeared without a trace."

Another of my cell-mates was a cabdriver, and his stories were less complicated. While taking a few nips in a park, he saw a bum crawling on top of a woman. But no sooner had he got on her than his cap fell off. So he crawled off her, picked it up, put it on, and then got back on her. But then his cap fell off again, and the whole business recommenced. At this point the cabbie could no longer contain himself. He said to the bum: "Listen, buddy! Either fuck her doggy-fashion, or tie your cap on so it won't fall off."

While this kind of idiotic talk was going on, I kept pacing back and forth from one corner of the cell to another, wondering whether I was really going to get a new sentence.

After two weeks of waiting, I was taken to see my old acquaintance, Prosecutor Vorontsov. My heart pounded as he leafed through some papers on his desk. Finally he said, "You filed a request for an interview with a KGB official, did you not? I hereby inform you that you were brought here to the remand prison in connection with that request."

Back in January, while I was in the punishment cell at Magadan Prison, I kept wondering what I should do to get back at them for putting me in the hole; and before I was sent off to Talaya I filed a request for an interview with a KGB official. I figured I would already have been shipped out before my request reached the KGB and that they would reprimand the prison officials.

Then, if later on they asked me what I wanted, I would tell them they should have asked me sooner.

That was the answer I gave to Captain Solovev the next day. In the state of euphoria that had come over me, I never questioned why they had brought me to Magadan and called me in to see the prosecutor, or why Solovev hadn't asked me about my request when he visited the camp. As for Solovev, he was even more affable than usual. He asked me how long it would be before I got on a plane to Moscow and wished me a happy landing. A month later I remembered those words vividly.

As a result of the KGB's "shuttle diplomacy," I again found myself in the camp—just in time for a "Lenin Sunday." This was one of the inventions of the Brezhnev regime. Once a year, on Lenin's birthday, everyone in the country put in a day's work for nothing (in principle "voluntarily"), in accordance with the Great Leader's dying wish. Cursing Old Baldy on their way, almost all of the zeks and free workers went out to work that day. Of our company, only three men refused. The first, a young tough, said the Lenin Sunday could go to hell. The second, a murderer, said that he had the greatest respect for Vladimir Ilich Lenin and Leonid Ilich Brezhnev and he would have been overjoyed to take part in the proceedings, except that he didn't feel well. For that matter, he added, it was altogether possible that his illness would recur on that same Sunday the following year. The third was myself; I simply said that since it was not a working day, I was not obliged to work.

What concerned me much more than Lenin's birthday was the fact that the frame of my glasses was broken. Fortunately, a colleague in the KTB, Lepeshkin, who had been a student at a machinists' school, was able to repair it rather professionally. But no sooner was the job done than I was again ordered to make ready for a transfer.

"Forgive me," I said to Lepeshkin. "I didn't even manage to give you a packet of tea."

"You mustn't say that," he replied. "I didn't do it for tea—I did it out of friendship." Those words, too, I would remember vividly.

So once again I found myself in the same old cell in Magadan Prison, this time with amnestied "chemists." I simply couldn't figure out my status. Was I a witness? Or was I under investigation? I didn't rule out the possibility that, despite my worthless testimony, I might be called to testify at Yakir's trial.

As things turned out, I was questioned in connection with Krasin's case. My interrogator was Lieutenant Colonel Leonid Tarasov, chief of the investigative section of the Magadan UKGB. He was a very short man, with the skillful investigator's gift of grasping things quickly; and, unlike Solovev, he took down my testimony accurately.

Krasin had testified that I had attended his "Wednesdays," that he had given me books to read, that he and I had gone together to the demonstration in Pushkin Square, and that on the way there he had made a phone call to a foreign correspondent. I told Tarasov that I had been at Krasin's home only rarely and that I didn't remember the particular days; that Krasin's talk about "Wednesdays" and other meetings was a childish attempt to build up his self-importance; that he didn't give me anything to read, or vice versa; that I had absolutely no recollection of whether I had gone with him to Pushkin Square, and even less did I recall whether he had phoned someone on the way.

It was plain that Krasin was taking the same position as Yakir. Indeed, I was expecting to hear that he had said I had collaborated with Litvinov on *The Trial of the Four,* but apparently that matter had not come up in his interrogation. On the other hand, he did testify that he had obtained a tape recorder and cassettes from abroad, via Gusel.

The "testimony" of Yakir and Krasin was a terrible blow to the Movement. It was especially hard on their families and friends. But even people who were not close to them told me later that for a good six months they were virtually paralyzed. Not only did both Yakir and Krasin repent; they gave evidence about associates and called upon others to repent. In prison, confrontations were set up between Krasin and other prisoners, and he urged Irina Belogorodskaya to give testimony. He also asked the KGB to set up a meeting with me so that he could persuade me to recant. There is no doubt that Yakir's and Krasin's repentance encouraged the authorities to demand the same thing of other prisoners, threatening them with extensions of their terms.

Each behaved somewhat differently from the other, however, in his recantation, in letters, in court, and in issuing statements after the trial. Yakir, as though realizing that he had nothing to lose, spoke straight out. But Krasin, dropping curtsies and hedging, attributed his actions to a well-defined philosophy. He set forth that philosophy in a letter sent from prison to the members of the Democratic Movement. That communication, however, did not go through secret channels, nor was it swallowed by his wife during a visit: it was delivered by a KGB officer. Krasin wrote that the Movement had collapsed (read: Krasin and Yakir have been arrested) and that all that could be done now was to record its history for posterity. Since the KGB had magnanimously assumed the role of historian, all Movement members should tell the KGB whatever they knew. Finally, since everyone would have laid down his arms voluntarily, the KGB wouldn't punish anyone.

The disorder created by Yakir and Krasin lasted for about a year and a half—until early 1974. Now that the authorities had begun to expel dissidents from the country, some members of the opposition (not to mention KGB officials) believed that the Movement was over and done with. Great was the rejoicing of those who had said the Movement was a tempest in a teacup and that the thing to do was to mind one's own business and patiently wait for mercy. Everyone from the drunken workingman who knew he should fear the authorities, and not vice versa, to the sober academic who feared both the authorities and the drunken workingman expected executions and torture, thereby urging on the authorities. They had to imprison some people so as to reassure others. ("Don't be ashamed of being cowards! It's the bold ones that we punish.")

It somehow turned out that Yakir, the jovial drunkard, was held less accountable than Krasin, who was more crafty and pretentious. When he came out of prison, Yakir said, "I'm a fink!"—although at the same time he naïvely wondered why everyone avoided him. Krasin, though, tried for a much longer time to prove he had been right, or to find loopholes. It wasn't until he was abroad that he published a letter of self-condemnation and reported that the KGB had given him money for the trip. On the other hand, Krasin was picked up at a time when Yakir had already decided on his line of behavior, and he followed Yakir's example. The fall of the one hastened—and justified in his own eyes—the fall of the other. After having been in prison for more than a year, each of them was sentenced to three years, which was commuted to a brief period of internal exile, near Moscow.

It has been reported that Yakir was provided with vodka in his cell, that some kind of narcotic was given to him and Krasin, and that they were tortured. In my opinion, none of this is true: they didn't give them anything, and they didn't torture them. As a rule (and not as an exception), physical torture is used when it is necessary to rush through cases in a short time by getting real or false confessions. Thus physical torture was used by the Nazis, and during the Great Terror in the USSR, when millions were put through the meat grinder by investigators. But when a case involving two men is being handled by a team of twenty investigators; when the investigation may last, not one week and not a month but more than a year; and when there are no "secrets" to be discovered, why squeeze a man's balls—as was done in that same Lefortovo Prison in 1938? The realization that you are faced with a sentence of fifteen years, or even seven years; that you will be separated, perhaps forever, from everything that is dear to you—that in itself is torture, especially for a man who is no longer young. And that torture is kept up from one day to the next, from one month to the next. The investigators test your weak points: they are not soldiers probing a minefield, and they can afford to make mistakes. The brainwashing technique is simple but effective. I have already told how they took me from camp to prison and back again, swinging me back and forth between hope and despair, thus weakening my willpower. The very experience of being in a penal camp is a kind of torture. Hunger, cold, and isolation are enough to destroy a person, although cases of physical beatings during investigations, while prisoners are being transported, and in the camps, are not unknown.

I think that the determining factor in the behavior of both Yakir and Krasin was the long terms they had served in Stalin's penal camps. Both had been sent there when they were young (Yakir at the age of fourteen), at a time when there was no hope. And the camp experience had built into them an unconscious imperative: to survive at any cost. Also, that same experience had imbued them with a deep fear—a realization that a human life is worth nothing, that they might be annihilated at any moment. The camp complex asserted itself as soon as they were locked up in Lefortovo. What had struck me, a greenhorn, as the source of their strength was in fact the cause of their weakness.

I am even more struck today by the fact that until their arrest, they had found the courage to oppose an inhumane system. Not many former zeks protested when the regime veered back toward Stalinism. But it is doubtful whether all of them, if they had found themselves in the position of Yakir and Krasin, would have behaved as those two did. After all, some of those who were imprisoned under Stalin reacted with dignity when they were again arrested in the sixties and seventies.

"You can see how Yakir and Krasin testified," Tarasov said to me. "They were thinking of themselves. And yet you're afraid to say anything."

"I'm thinking of the future," I replied, not yet having learned that Krasin had called upon other dissidents to send informer's reports to the KGB for the sake of posterity. "I'm thinking that in the future, people will read all these records of interrogations and will judge us."

This put Tarasov on edge. "But who will those people be?" he demanded. He wanted to prove that those future readers would be just such tried and true comrades as himself. I must admit that bastards like him really believe in their own future.

After my third interrogation, Tarasov and I parted company (not for good, alas!), and I began thinking about my trip home. I wasn't sure whether it was necessary for Gusel to meet me in Talaya. I heard they would set some trap for me if I were alone, so I decided she should come. In the telegram that I sent to her via Podolsky, I said that I had one week left to serve, and it looked as if they were not going to start new proceedings against me.

I asked one of my cell-mates, a mechanic, what kind of car I should buy when I got out, but I didn't purchase one until five years later, in Cambridge, Massachusetts. It was very big, like our grand piano, and when I had to drive through the crowded streets of Cambridge, I had cramps in my innards. But the hardest thing was getting rid of it—something I had to do because I could never find space enough to park it and had to keep driving around, feeling hopeless and depressed. While still in the Magadan Prison, I knew nothing of all these problems; but even then I was planning to travel through America in a car, which was why I bought it when I did.†

On May 17, four days before my term was up, when we were walking in the exercise yard and talking about cars as usual, I was set upon without warning and put in a Black Maria. I saw that we were pulling up in front of the government-type building that housed the prosecutor's office. But when I was taken into an office where a man in a prosecutor's uniform sat behind a desk, I understood everything without anyone's having to say a word.

---

†In August 1978, Gusel and I did drive through America, from the East Coast to the West Coast. In Indiana we had a collision with a truck. By the grace of God we weren't killed; we had to buy a new car that same day.

THE RETURN
(1973–76)

I Yield to Conquer

Oleg Botvinik, a prosecutor from the investigative section of the Magadan Oblast Prosecutor's Office, was a short, elderly man who did not so much resemble a Soviet prosecutor as a magistrate from the days of Alexander II. He informed me that criminal proceedings had been initiated against me on a charge of "disseminating information defaming the Soviet system in places of incarceration"; i.e., Article 190-1 once again. Through a window of his first-floor office I could see a street flooded with spring sunlight, and behind me I could hear the wheezing of two policemen. (They were on hand in case I should attack Botvinik.)

I thought of Gusel: of how she had been waiting; of her passing youth; of her hopes that we would be reunited in a few days. Then, images from the past three years crossed my mind in a depressing sequence: the prisons, the camps, the friskings, the transports, the zeks, the officers, the bowls of gruel, the crates full of wood shavings, the bunks, the plank beds, the concrete walls, the dim bulbs. And I would have to go through all that again. In impotent rage I told Botvinik that the charges were false and that I was still being persecuted for my book. Therefore I would give no testimony.

"You are wrong," he said. "You are faced with charges, and you'd do better to defend yourself."

I talked loudly and excitedly, and Botvinik, his voice softer and softer, told me I would be called again after two or three hours. He hoped that I would calm down.

The moment I returned to my cell I drafted a statement to Botvinik: "Every citizen has the right to express his views. . . . Since my fate has been decided beforehand, in protest against this frame-up I refuse to take part in the investigative process, and beginning today I shall refuse to take food." I also wrote a statement saying I was renouncing my Soviet citizenship, but then I decided that such an extreme step was premature.

The worst of it was that I was not prepared for a new arrest. In 1970 I had known what I was in for. But why hadn't I prepared myself this time? There had certainly been warnings. Probably because the thought of a new sentence was unbearable. So I clung, mentally, to indications of hope, since there had been quite a few of them too.

I spent most of the time in my cell lying with my face to the wall. Gusel had recently written me that everything was ready for my return, except that she had not wound up the grandfather clock. That was my job; and now, I vividly remembered that clock. I hid this letter among other papers, so agonizing was any mention of my trip home. I now understood how a heavy blow could destroy a man. My thoughts were concentrated on *how to get out*. If, at that moment, Vladimir Kolomiychenko (who will soon make his appearance in this sad story) had entered my cell and said, "Sign this repudiation of everything you have written, and you will be a free man," it is possible that for the sake of breathing the air of the sea and the hills instead of the prison, and of looking upon my wife instead of the vagrant who was my cell-mate, I would have signed. And yet I do not believe I would have.

Lying on my bunk, I began to work out a plan of defense. Was I right to refuse to testify, when the charges against me were based on false testimony? The uncompromising position I had taken was no doubt the most honorable one, but might it prove fatal? After my illness, would I survive three more years of prison and camp? And why would it necessarily be only three years? If it had been that easy for them to extend my sentence for things that I had not in fact said, they could extend it for a further three years. Those three years that I had marked off on the calendar, one day after another, were a fiction: I might well be given something like a life sentence. On the other hand, the idea of recanting or pleading guilty was unbearable for me. What kind of person would remain after such a total surrender?

In camp, I had read *The Sakura Bough* by V. Ovchinnikov, who for several years had been a *Pravda* correspondent in Japan.† It was an interesting book, and I remembered in particular what Ovchinnikov had related about the man who invented judo. He had noticed that when there was a snowfall, the boughs of the pine trees kept bending under the weight of the snow until it slid off, and then they straightened up. And he formulated the basic principle of judo as follows: yield in order to conquer. I decided to follow that principle. I would pretend that I was almost repenting, and I might even go so far as to repent fully. But I would not do two things that the authorities wanted me to do: plead guilty, and write a letter to a newspaper repudiating my books. Of

†In 1977 he wrote about me in an article, "How Sensations Are Made."

course, it was not going to be easy to slip between Scylla and Charybdis, especially since the authorities were not simpletons to whom one could promise anything. That they were in fact skillful investigators had already been demonstrated in the way they had processed me for the second trial. It was plain that what they wanted from me was not promises but documents. And yet those who believe that the bad element in human nature will always prevail are almost as naïve as those who believe that the good element will always prevail. And it was on that fact that I placed my hopes.

I don't want to give the impression that I had accurately calculated everything during the first days of my hunger strike. My moves were rather the result of an instinctive urge to *do* something and not just wait passively. Thus I wrote to Brezhnev that "the proceedings instituted against me are based on a painful misunderstanding: I am prepared to answer for my own views, but not for the fabrications of others, or for fabrications that are alien to me." That letter served no practical purpose for me. But for the KGB it served as a signal that I was weakening, and hence that they should increase the pressure. In a dispirited state, I failed to realize that the tactic I had chosen did not permit getting ahead of the game; I should have waited to see what they would offer. Also, my letter had in it something of that naïve Russian faith that the people at the top would treat me less harshly than the agents on the spot.

When Podolsky was making his rounds of the prison, I told him I wanted to see Botvinik. But I continued my hunger strike until I was summoned for questioning on May 22.

The day before, I had fainted in the bathhouse, so I was afraid I wouldn't hold up during the questioning. But I was able to give the investigator a statement in which I said that "without changing my opinion of the case, I am now willing to testify with a view to establishing the truth, and I am calling off my hunger strike." My first mistake was to declare a hunger strike when I was not psychologically ready for it. My second was to cancel it after five days.

Between May 22 and June 4, I underwent four interrogations and four confrontations with witnesses. The charges were based only on the testimony of prisoners—of witnesses both voluntary and coerced—and all such testimony concluded in August 1972, when KGB Lieutenant Colonel Tarasov arrived to ask questions about me. The investigator had no letters, articles, or statements of mine in his possession: in camp, I had been afraid to write. But what had I said? Naturally, over a period of eighteen months, it's hard not to talk to *somebody*. But none of those toward whom I had been outspoken was among the witnesses except Ivanchenko, and even with him I had usually been facetious.

The first "source" for the witnesses' testimony was a transcript of my

CBS interview. (It was appended to my case file, and I very much enjoyed reading it.) The investigator had used it as a basis for instructing the witnesses, figuring that if I had said this or that to the CBS correspondent, I might well have repeated the same things in camp. The second "source" was the zeks' own imaginations, stimulated by their eagerness to please the officials. They testified that I was always turning off the radio, which was true, and then added that I called the broadcasts "Communist vomit," which was false. They frequently ascribed to me opinions that were really their own, or that were widespread in the camp (in the camps, everybody is always cursing the regime), and sometimes they did this sincerely. After all, who but an *"antisovetchik"** would say such things? I was reported, also, to have expressed dissatisfaction that the USSR was sending aid to underdeveloped countries. This, again, was a view held by most Russians: since we ourselves are living poorly, why help those "black-assed people"? Likewise, I was reported to have said: "Khrushchev traveled abroad, and Brezhnev will travel till he comes to a bad end." This was another commonly held view, the idea being that it's better to stay at home. Those zeks who hated me thought up things on their own. Others merely testified that they didn't understand what I was saying, but they had the general impression that I was slandering the regime.

The investigator's summary of the testimony, although more carefully worded, also played fast and loose with the facts. For instance, Obraztsov had allegedly heard me say, "Lots of Jews want to leave the USSR so they can start businesses." In the investigator's rephrasing, this came out as: "The USSR is a spiritual prison for the Jews." Actually, of course, the USSR is a spiritual prison for all its peoples. But the authorities have had to reckon with the Jews. Gusel once told me, during a visit, "It's too bad you aren't a Jew. If you were, they'd be making a big fuss over you."

Some witnesses testified that since I had drafted appeals for them, it meant I didn't believe that Soviet verdicts and sentences were just. Others said that since I refused to draft appeals for them, it meant I didn't believe that just treatment could be obtained in the Soviet Union. This thesis and antithesis were synthesized as follows in the judgment: "In his talks with convicts, Amalrik, fully aware that he was uttering a falsehood, said that there was no socialist legality in our country. . . ."

The indictment boiled down to the following: I had said that the Soviet system was a dictatorship; that it was not socialism but state capitalism; that democratic freedoms were lacking, especially freedom of speech; that the populace was almost poverty-stricken; that a system based on violence would not last long; that I had called the socialist countries "Soviet colonies" and had said that the union republics did not enjoy equal rights. Also, that I had expressed contempt for heroes of the war and said I was sorry that the USSR had not been defeated; that I approved the territorial claims of China; that I had scoffed at the Soviet press and radio; that I had said Soviet youth were not capable of feats of valor and that the Communist party did not have the support of the people; that I had insulted its leaders—in particular, Leonid Ilich Brezhnev. Ivanchenko maintained that while looking at a photo of Brezhnev and Nixon I remarked, "What a disagreeable person!"

Before my trial, Podolsky tried to console me by telling me that recently a man who had murdered four people was not given the maximum sentence. I replied, "You make a comparison between killing four people and calling Brezhnev a disagreeable person. But in the first case, when one ordinary man is killed, another is born who can take his place. Our Leonid Ilich, though, is unique—one of a kind." At the trial, the prosecutor and defense counsel argued as to which person I had in mind, Brezhnev or Nixon; and the court agreed with the prosecutor. By that time, however, I might have been convicted and sentenced for insulting Nixon, a founding father of détente. And if anybody asked me today which one I had in mind, I would say, "Both!"

I denied all the utterances ascribed to me. In a confrontation with Obraztsov, who had been released, I declared he was an informer. In addition, he had a personal interest in seeing that I was not released, since he had obtained a jacket from me by fraudulent means and was afraid I would sue him. He replied, with great dignity, that he had given me food for the jacket, that no one had instructed him how to testify, and that "Amalrik is a man with little soul and a feeble intellect."

Fedoseyev, another informer, glued together some bits of tape from conversations he had bugged and added that I hadn't trusted him and never talked with him. I said that Fedoseyev disliked me because I told him he had stabbed his mistress to death because he was impotent, but that "the knife was still erect." Botvinik entered my remark on the record, but only after some hesitation.

Botvinik conducted the interrogation calmly and politely, but he did the job he had been ordered to do. He tried to give me the impression that I would not serve more time in camp, and he even encouraged me to petition for a release from custody before the trial. I did, and he promptly rejected it. He suggested several times that I plead guilty to at least some of the charges; e.g., to having said that there was no freedom of speech in the USSR. The sentence, "He slanderously maintained that there is no freedom of speech in the USSR," was included in the judgment handed down against Ubozhko and in the new judgment against me. I replied that I wasn't pleading guilty to anything: there is freedom of speech, period.

"When you said that the fabrications in the record did not correspond to your views, just what views did you have in mind?'' Botvinik asked me at my last interrogation, implying that a great deal hinged on my answer.

"I had in mind the fact that the October Revolution was a natural phase of Russian history and that the Soviet system could not have lasted for fifty-five years without having the support of a considerable part of the people."

The investigator's final gesture was to confiscate a photograph of Gusel. Apparently the portrait of Mao in the background was evidence of my intention to give China half of Siberia. (The photograph was returned to me a year later.)

I was taken to the same office where I had first read my case file. Supposedly, the case had its beginnings in a report from Lepeshkin, who had repaired my glasses "out of friendship." It was taken down "from the words" of Lepeshkin by Zolotarev on March 20, the day KGB Captain Solovev came to Talaya. On April 21, Major Butenko, the camp commandant, took the report to Vinokurov, the oblast prosecutor; and on April 23, Guryayev, chief of the investigative section of the prosecutor's office, instituted criminal proceedings. Twenty-nine witnesses were questioned, and eighteen of them, all prisoners, testified that they had heard "anti-Soviet utterances" from me. It was easy to discern the pattern of the pressures used on them. At his first interrogation, Lomov, realizing he had to say something unfavorable about me, testified that I ate very sloppily and spilled crumbs. This was entered into the record, but it was not enough. So two weeks later they got him to testify that I had said: "Israel is fighting a just war." Ivanchenko was questioned three times. He began by saying I had called Brezhnev "a capable leader." At this point there was a hiatus, and then things went the way they were supposed to.

I sent a telegram to Gusel on May 25: "DARLING DON'T GO ANYWHERE STOP WAIT FOR A LETTER FROM ME AND HOPE FOR THE BEST STOP LOVE ANDREI" It was the first news she had had after my latest arrest. On June 6, I sent another telegram via Botvinik asking her to hire a lawyer immediately; but there was no reply. On June 28, I received the indictment, and right after it came a letter, but not from Gusel. It was signed "Liberman," a name that meant nothing to me, and had no return address. What it turned out to be was a poison-pen letter about my wife, so foul a blow that for several days afterward I couldn't even eat the diet the prosecutor had arranged for me. It is not the practice to deliver letters to persons under investigation. This one, however, was not only given to me but it bore an index number as official letters do. I realized that the KGB wanted to sow discord between my wife and me so that I would be deprived not only of a lawyer but of contact with the outside world in general. As for the Jewish name, they had no doubt figured that it would stir up in me a hostility toward Jews.

I told Podolsky (who had been awaiting my reaction with interest) that I was flatly refusing the services of a local lawyer and handed him the text of a telegram to be sent to Gusel: "DARLING I WAS HANDED MY INDICTMENT YESTERDAY AND NEED A LAWYER URGENTLY STOP WIRE ME IMMEDIATELY UPON RECEIPT OF THIS TELEGRAM STOP LOVE ANDREI"

As it later transpired, Gusel had sent me several telegrams in June, but none of them was delivered to me. I had been invited to lecture at Harvard University, and she had hoped that the authorities, instead of sending me back to camp, would let me leave the country. But the people at the OVIR* told her: "What? Are the Americans so short of professors of their own that they have to invite a dropout to give lectures?"

My former lawyer, Shveisky, had agreed to take my case, but he had not received clearance.† Apraksin, president of the Moscow College of Counselors, on whom the decision depended, advised Gusel to retain a lawyer from Magadan. And he added: "If you succeed in retaining Shveisky, you will have my congratulations. But I'm afraid your efforts will be fruitless." Meantime, the oblast court was demanding that Gusel get a lawyer immediately, and notified me that the hearing was scheduled for July 10.

After Gusel's request that she be allowed to retain Shveisky had been turned down by the RSFSR Ministry of Justice, she appealed to the International Commission of Jurists for help. She sent along a copy of the letter to some foreign correspondents, and the next day it was broadcast by the Voice of America.

On that same day I was in the punishment cell, where one is not supposed to get letters or telegrams. I had been sent there because of the unsatisfactory sanitary condition of my regular cell. Calling me an "old employee," Podolsky had demanded that I keep things neat. Each time I promised to "keep account" of the black marks against me, citing Lenin's statement that "socialism is accountability." Finally, that phrase of Lenin's—along with the total socialist disorder in the cell—had proven too much for his patience.

Saturday morning he came into the punishment cell with a smile on his face. "Congratulations," he said, and handed me a telegram. It read: "DON'T WORRY DARLING STOP SHVEISKY IS TAKING THE CASE AND HAS SENT A TELEGRAM TO THE COURT STOP WAIT FOR HIM AND HOPE FOR THE BEST STOP LOVE GUSEL"

---

†In accordance with an unpublished directive, a Soviet lawyer must be cleared by the "College of Counselors" (bar association) before he can act as defense counsel in a political case.—TRANS.

"Now give that telegram back to me," said Podolsky. "It'll be given to you officially on Monday." And then he announced that he had granted me amnesty: I could return to my regular cell.

When Shveisky read the witnesses' testimony and my own, he sighed dejectedly. The picture was totally different from three years before. He would ask me whether this person or that might possibly have testified truthfully, but I told him everything was a lie. Our conversation was likewise not free from falsehoods, since it was intended primarily for the microphone in the wall. Shveisky thought the policy of détente was a wise one, and I agreed with him. Even the "speeches" I made in my own cell were ideologically restrained. Of course, the KGB people realize that no one really changes his convictions as a result of threats. But they believe that a prison term can make a person recant his convictions, and from no other vantage point does the regime look so stable as it does from a prison cell.

The trial was delayed, and then finally set for July 13—a bad omen. Once again I took the road to Talaya. But when I got there, I was, much to my surprise, put up in a two-room apartment. I made myself comfortable in the bedroom, while an officer stayed on guard in the next room—as did a soldier with a carbine in the kitchen, and another under the window. However, my behavior in court the first day showed I was not deserving of such luxurious quarters; so I was taken to the concrete cell where I had been twice before. Soon Sergeant Kochnev showed up and greeted me with, "Attaboy! Hang in there!" When I had first come to the camp, two years before, I had had a run-in with him. But now he was bringing me a pot of tea to which he had contributed some of his own leaves. I shall always be grateful to him for that.

The trial was held in the "clubhouse" that served the settlement of Talaya, and on my way there I passed through the village for the first and last time. It was hot; and the dusty, treeless streets and dreary-looking barracks reminded me of dozens of such communities in Russia. I had always wondered how people could live there year after year.

At the entrance to the clubhouse, a gebist with a movie camera aimed at me backpedaled as I moved ahead. Once again, I felt like a film star. Later, when a witness complained that the camera was bothering him, the judge told him, "You're not the one they're filming."

The courtroom was overflowing. Gusel, in tears, was not allowed to come near me. After a short time she was removed from the room under the pretext that she would have to testify later as to whether she had sent the famous jacket to Obraztsov. I asked that Zolotarev be called as a witness, thereby depriving him of the pleasure of hearing the trial. Captain Ovechkin, who had been questioned during the pretrial investigation, was not called to testify, and Shveisky told me "they" had asked him not to insist on calling him. A year before, acting on instructions from the KGB, Ovechkin had proposed that I repudiate my books; now they were afraid that he would get confused under questioning.

The judge, Rybachuk, looked like a sycophantic petty bureaucrat. He was reserved when the trial began; but the further it proceeded, the cruder he became. When the witness Gryaznev testified that I had turned off the radio while Brezhnev was speaking and that he (Gryaznev) had threatened to sock me in the jaw, I replied that I didn't recall his saying that. "It's too bad he didn't sock you in the jaw," said the judge. "Then you *would* have remembered it!"

At this, even Shveisky waved his hands in a gesture of helplessness.

"And so," the judge asked Gryaznev with an encouraging smile, "you turned the radio back on and listened to Comrade Brezhnev's speech?"

"What did I need with that?" said Gryaznev, provoking laughter in the courtroom. "I thought there'd be some singing. When I heard that tub-thumping, I just walked out of the barracks."

I began my testimony by saying that the views of any person change over the course of time; that the indictment was based on a misunderstanding; that the investigator had tried to make me out to be somebody different from who I was, by attributing to me things I had never said; and that I was especially upset by the allegation that I had said I was sorry the USSR had won the war against Germany. From that point on I repeated the arguments I had used during the investigation, as to the motives of the witnesses.

When two company commanders, Captain Bogachev and Captain Kozhevnikov, were called as witnesses, both said they had heard nothing, but that my "behavior gave no indication of any reform." The next witness, the dispensary attendant Rytov, hemmed, hawed, and sweated, but then testified that I had praised the feminists, calling their movement "serious"; that I had said that in the U.S., blacks could join the police force; that the Jews had transformed Palestine into a blossoming orchard; that juvenile crime was growing in the USSR; and that schools should not depend upon the State.

"Who can confirm those utterances?" Shveisky asked.

"Nobody. The talks were between the two of us."

"Then why were you questioned at all?" I asked. "How did they learn about our conversations?"

Rytov was silent. Then I asked him if he had been promised "chemistry" for testifying. He replied he had testified not for "chemistry" but out of a love for the truth; but that he had been sent off to "chemistry" anyway, since all witnesses got some kind of benefits or other.

The others had an even harder time of it. It was one thing to give testimony when alone with an investigator, but quite another to repeat it before an audience—especially in front of the person whom you are sending to prison with your testimony.

"What testimony can you give us?" the judge asked one such witness.

"Nothing."

"Do you confirm the testimony you gave during the investigation?"

"I do." And then silence.

Four of them had to have their testimony read to them. One, when asked why he had not responded to a question, said: "They didn't tell me how to answer that one." Another said that from the beginning, the KGB had suggested his answers. Each of them was, I think one may fairly say, drawn and quartered—by Shveisky, who was obviously enjoying himself, and in particular by me. During the recess, Shveisky told me that "they" had asked him not to bear down too hard on the witnesses. But I was already too worked up, and I couldn't stop. As for Obraztsov, I pinned him to the wall, making him admit that on certain points he was lying to the court—something the judge took quite calmly.

The last to be questioned were Lomov, Lepeshkin, and Ivanchenko. When Lomov entered the courtroom, he first bowed to the judge and the prosecutor, then said, "Hello, Andrei," and shook my hand. He said he had heard nothing "anti-Soviet" from me and that when someone asked me about Israel, I replied that that country had existed several thousand years ago.

"You complained that you were compelled to write reports on other prisoners," I said to Lepeshkin, after he testified. "Did anyone force you to write a report on me?"

The judge ordered my question stricken from the record. He did the same with other questions of mine. And whenever he was slow about doing it, some of the spectators would shout: "A leading question!" Whereupon he would promptly cut me off.

Ivanchenko had told me that if I were brought to trial, he would repudiate the testimony he had given during the investigation. But now, when the prosecutor asked him whether he had heard me make anti-Soviet remarks, he unhesitatingly answered: "Yes."

He continued: "Amalrik said that when the warders were frisking him and found a photograph of a general, they almost saluted; but later they took it away from him anyway. I asked him, 'What kind of general is that? Is he maybe an antisovetchik?' And he said: 'Sort of.' 'But what did he do?' 'Well,' Amalrik said, 'when everybody else was praising Khrushchev, he said he was no damned good. And when the others started saying he was no damned good, the general praised him.'" (Laughter in the courtroom.)

Somehow or other, they did get something out of Ivanchenko. When

Shveisky and the prosecutor began arguing about whether I had Brezhnev or Nixon in mind when I used the words "a disagreeable personality," the prosecutor asked Ivanchenko, "Did you hear Amalrik say anything else about Leonid Ilich Brezhnev?"

"Yes, I did," replied Ivanchenko. "He said that when things got really bad, I should always turn to the works of Leonid Ilich Brezhnev."

"Ah!" exclaimed the prosecutor, leaping to his feet. "So he said that in mockery!"

I later remarked how strange it was that a government prosecutor should lack confidence in the force of Leonid Ilich Brezhnev's ideas and not believe that one could take them seriously.

The judge, in a kind of comedian's patter, kept asking each witness: "How did you get along with Amalrik? Were you on good terms with him?" And all of them, even those I had insulted right there in the courtroom, replied that we were on good terms, meaning that they were testifying not out of personal hostility (my favorite theme) but out of a love for the truth.

The third day of the trial began with the questioning of Zolotarev. And when the same question was put to him, he answered, "Why should we have been on good terms? Our relations were those between a prisoner and a deputy commandant for security and discipline."

"Well, then, that means they were good," the judge said. Then he asked me if I wanted to question the witness. (Zolotarev was the only witness called by the defense.)

"Don't you recall," I asked him, "that I requested to be called for verification if there were any reports of alleged anti-Soviet conversations?" (Throughout the trial, I kept bringing up the point that if I had in fact said something prejudicial, I would have been warned by the camp officials during my first term.)

"I don't remember," Zolotarev said, although I had indeed had such a conversation with him.

"And is it your opinion that I had enough influence in camp for a man to be killed on orders from me?"

After looking at me in amazement, Zolotarev replied, "No, of course you didn't have that kind of influence."

On every hand, people were whispering to him that he should have said I could order a man killed. Some of the witnesses, in response to Shveisky's question as to why they, as honest Soviet citizens, had not immediately opposed my subversive utterances, had replied, "Because in camp you can go to sleep and never wake up. Amalrik was in solid with the young thugs, and if he gave the word, you could be killed."

Both the trial transcript and the verdict itself contained testimony the witnesses had given during the pretrial investigation rather than what they said during the trial. Moreover, in some cases what was entered in the record was the opposite of what was said. Thus the witness Brygin testified: "I never heard any anti-Soviet utterances from him." But this was entered as "I heard." And Ivanchenko said he had not heard the phrase "a spiritual prison for Jews" from me, but in the record he is quoted as having heard it from me. The court in Sverdlovsk could not hold a candle to the one in Magadan in its disregard for the truth. (I have no idea of the reason for this: whether it was because the case was different, the judge different, and the oblast different; or whether in three years the situation had changed that much for the worse.) The prosecutor's summation was crude, and he even used the lingo of thugs. He called my testimony "a verbal balancing act" and asked for a sentence of three years in a strict-regimen labor camp. Shveisky began his plea in the same way as at my first trial: by agreeing with the prosecution—in this case, as to the high moral and political standards of Soviet prisoners, who had rallied as one man in defense of the system. But then he went on to say that nonetheless their testimony was self-contradictory, unconfirmed, and motivated by personal animosity, and that I had categorically denied the statements attributed to me. Therefore, he asked for a verdict of not guilty.

In my final plea, I told the court I was nearly overcome by a feeling of hopelessness when I realized that everything I said was simply ignored; that if I was to be judged by what I said, then what I said should be taken seriously. But the case had been decided in advance; the witnesses had been coached, and the trial was an empty formality. The prosecution had persistently tried to prove that I entertained anti-Soviet convictions and that I should for that reason be incarcerated. If such a view prevailed, it would mean that there was no place for me in Soviet society. I was innocent. The conclusions I would draw from this trial would depend upon whether the verdict was just. I asked to be exonerated.

On the first day of the trial, the spectators had been hostile toward me, but their mood gradually changed. They evinced no particular approval for the prosecutor's summation; and afterward, many of them expressed their sympathy to Gusel. On the second day, since she could find no toilet in the clubhouse, Gusel had gone to the adjoining house and knocked. To her horror and amazement, the door was opened by Raisa Tsarko. But Tsarko seemed glad to see her. She asked her in and suggested that she take a rest, have a bite to eat, and freshen up. And she told her: "Your husband is bearing up very well. He certainly doesn't lack for words!"

Later, one officer told me that my trial had reversed his attitude toward the regime and that he no longer felt himself to be a believing "Soviet man." This kind of thing is well understood by the authorities, who see to it that even the best-prepared political trials are not open to the public. "Soviet man" possesses, in regard to politics, something like the human body's innate feeling for space. Just as instinct keeps a person away from the edge of an abyss, so instinct (and not reason) keeps "Soviet man" at a distance from words and deeds that have a political coloration. And the fact that this is a matter of instinct, and not of reason, has two consequences. On the one hand, "Soviet man" exaggerates what is forbidden to him; on the other, he is amazed by the harshness with which the system reacts to any "violation." He stays as far away as possible from the edge of the abyss. But when someone falls into it, he gasps: "Is it really that deep?"

On the evening of July 15, after those few hours of consultation that decorum requires, the court announced that I had been found guilty and sentenced to three years of strict regimen.

CHAPTER 21

The Magadan Remand Prison: Singing and Weeping

If one employs the enemy's methods to defend oneself, has one been partially defeated by him? The authorities used deceit against me, and I used deceit to oppose them. They were demagogic; and I, as if in mockery, turned their own demagogy against them. I was guarded by soldiers carrying carbines. But if I had been given a carbine, would I have been able to resist the temptation to mow down the judge, the prosecutor, and the gebists sitting modestly among the other spectators? In 1970 I had refused to yield and had been sentenced to three years. In 1973 I had compromised and had again received three years. Of course, the authorities had not made me repent or plead guilty. But they had seen that I was wavering and maneuvering, and had concluded they needed to put on more pressure.

Why hadn't I been outspoken in court? Why had I given testimony that was disagreeable for them but that nonetheless made me a participant in their game? Why had I rummaged around for prudent phrases? Why had I taken their hints—and myself hinted—that some kind of agreement was possible? But it's useless to keep throwing punches after the fight is over. And besides: the three-year sentence was not definitive, but a means of pressure: the appellate hearing was still in the future.

I was granted a twenty-minute visit from Gusel—in the same room where we had spent eight happy-unhappy days. This time, however, we were under the close watch of the captain of the guard, who kept hissing like a snake. We embraced and wept. Still in tears, Gusel said I should put something on paper that would gain me my release. I said that I would petition for a pardon, but that I would not repudiate my books.

Four days later she came to the prison again, and I was sure of myself. I had decided to come out alive without having betrayed anyone, including myself. I would pretend that (1) I was a sick man who had given up the struggle; (2) I was willing to reevaluate my books in a way that was suitable for the sake of appearances, but to do this only after I had been released; (3) I was strong-willed enough not to yield, so that a mutually acceptable solution would have to be found.

I told Gusel I would declare a hunger strike at the same time that I filed my appeal. She tried to dissuade me. But regardless of what effect a hunger strike might have on the authorities, it was essential to me by way of rehabilitation for my first, failed strike.

In my appeal to the RSFSR Supreme Court I wrote, "Since I consider that my trial was a frame-up and that the court's judgment was unjust, I shall refuse to take nourishment as of July 20, and shall continue to refuse it until a just decision is handed down."

On July 23, I sent to the Presidium of the USSR Supreme Soviet a petition asking that I be deprived of my citizenship as a person "inwardly far removed" from the Soviet system. I also petitioned that "my new sentence be replaced by expulsion from the Soviet Union. I request this in view of my poor state of health; also, in view of the fact that expulsion from one's own country is a punishment no less severe than incarceration."

The hunger pangs, which were strong the first day, gradually diminished. After one week, if I sat down or stood up, I felt dizzy; but my general condition was better than during my first hunger strike. During that first week I even did some exercises and went out for a walk every day. I was tormented by the cold, and I remember how glad I was when they started giving us heat in late September; yet I never once caught cold.

My hunger strike was not a dry one: in the morning I would drink a half-jug of cold water; and I took some hot water in the evening. On August 1, by which time I was very weak, they began forced feeding. A special solution of powdered milk and semolina (sometimes with a base of bouillon) was fed into my stomach via a tube. The tube can be introduced through your mouth (there is a special device for unclenching your teeth), through your nose, or through your anus. I resisted until the warders tied me down and the doctor's assistant put the tube up my anus. (This is a painful method of forced feeding, and the diarrhea that follows is even more painful.) When they are force-feeding a person through the mouth, they insert a tube in the same way as they do a probe for gastric juices, and then they pour in the liquid through a funnel. Although artificial feeding replaces to some extent the calories lost by one's organism, it does not provide the necessary vitamins and minerals. Also, a lot depends on who is doing it, and how it is done. Thus unrefined pearl barley may be used in the liquid mixture, or the latter may be too hot; in either case, deterioration of the stomach sets in promptly. It was my good luck that the female paramedic was kindly inclined toward me. She told me about the zek who, saying he had been unjustly convicted of a murder, stayed on hunger strike for seven years. During that time his stomach was almost entirely removed, and all his teeth fell out.

They fed me once a day, except for Saturdays and Sundays. I had the impression that the kind-hearted paramedic was giving me more of the liquid mixture than she was supposed to. But when another zek declared a hunger strike, the ration was divided between the two of us. He, however, didn't hold out for more than a week. At first, I didn't feel hungry; but then, an hour or two before each feeding, I felt gnawing pains in my stomach. On Saturdays and Sundays that sensation went away, but I felt dizzy.

The purpose of forced feeding is not just to preserve the zek's life but to compel him to give up his hunger strike. The feedings are withheld from time to time; then, when the patient's mouth begins to smell of acetone, they are resumed. In this way a person's will is worn down.

I don't know whether I lost much weight, because I was never on the scales. My blood pressure did not fall below 60/110; and when I was angry, it jumped to 80/160. My pulse rate dropped from 80 to 38. I did not feel acute pain, but I was generally weak. I tried to remain supine as much as possible and often indulged in gastronomic dreams; e.g., how, once in camp, I would make myself some pancakes out of flour and kissel. I also gave some thought as to what I would do if the sentence was not revoked. I decided I would refuse to work and would decline official rations, but would eat what I could get on my own.

My weakened condition did not prevent me from reading a lot—especially Marx, whose books I could obtain from the prison library. I wanted to know if he was responsible for my being in prison. If I had read Marx in Paris instead of in Magadan, I would have got other things from him. But under the circumstances I was astounded by his antihumanism. For Marx, there was no such thing as an individual in his own right—an individual was only a part of the system. As Walt Whitman observed, people follow those who have the greatest contempt for them. And yet any human being wants to be an individual. It is touching to see how the aged Brezhnev, now that he is able to raise himself a half-inch above his colleagues, has vigorously set about awarding himself decorations and titles.

Marx was a keen critic of society and a brilliant journalist. But he was amazingly one-sided, and he made his observations the basis of an all-embracing philosophy. The gebists were not happy about what I was reading. "You may not understand Marx correctly," they said. Yet it was thanks to them that I understand Marx really well. His philosophy is a rationale for the world view held, not by the mythical proletariat, but by the ordinary man of all classes of society. Many observers have noted how accurately Marxism ("the philosophy of the belly") reflects the views of the common man. In the West, almost all Marxists (whether identified by their label or by their way of thinking) will tell you that material conditions determine everything. In ninety-nine cases out of a hundred, they are right. But the one case in which they are wrong creates a historical explosion, producing events that determine the development of history.

According to the regulations, a man on hunger strike is supposed to be kept in solitary. But in my case, since they wanted to observe me and provide materials for the microphone, they always put one, two, or three persons in the same cell with me. And so, from the very outset of my second term, I met a whole rogues' gallery of zeks. There was, for instance, the black-mustachioed chap who came into the cell with a loud "Heil, Hitler!" He was the son of a Czech Communist whom Stalin had had shot, and as a fatherless young man he became a thug. He said he had worked as assistant manager of a department store and had made a good living.

"If you were making a good living, why did you rob people?"

"I made a good living *because* I robbed people."

Another cell-mate was a pickpocket who was "playing crazy." He was due for a psychiatric examination and kept asking the rest of us for advice on the tactics he should use. Should he tell the psychiatrists he was the Emperor Ivan VI, who had died in the prison-fortress of Peter and Paul more than two centuries ago? Or should he propose to them a new source of energy: ordinary shit, which, collected in huge reservoirs, would begin to ferment and give off the gas necessary to heat the buildings of Magadan?

A young holdup man who had heard about me on the Voice of America and was proud of being my cell-mate expressed great admiration for what I had done and in the next breath said he was trying to get a job with the KGB.

"Why do you want to work for the KGB?" I asked him.

"Why? Because they wear civilian clothes and carry briefcases."

An old man whose face was mottled with the blue veins of a drunkard always called me "Andryushenka"—something I hadn't been called for a very long time. But he was a former hangman or, to use the language of officialdom, a "bailiff." In the 1940s, in that same Magadan Prison, he had executed zeks. Now he was doing time in his old stamping grounds as a vagrant.

A huge number of bums, all of them filthy, with swollen faces, surfaced (quite literally: from the sewers through which they crawled to get into liquor warehouses); all they could talk about was the vodka they had drunk. One, a former partisan, seeing that I was studying an English-language textbook, said to another, "He's wasting his time studying. With all they've got against him, he'll never get out of here."

A man with a full belly is always irritating to a hungry man, and once, when quarreling with that particular bum, I threatened him: "If you say another word, I'll throw your bread in the latrine pail!"

He immediately said something, and into the latrine pail went his bread. In order to quiet him down, a cook's helper shoved him a bowl of soup through the chuckhole. I took the soup, poured it on his head, and hit him with the bowl. At this, he splashed his tea on me, thereby depriving himself of his last source of nourishment. Then he pounded on the cell door, demanding that I be taken to the security office.

"Well, I hear you've been fighting with the vagrants," Pinemasov reprimanded me. Then he asked whether I would prefer being in the same cell with murderers.

The "murderer" they sent me turned out to be a meek little fellow who had once rushed at somebody with a two-by-four shouting "I'll kill you!" And for that shout he got eight years.

For another run-in, this time with a couple of warders, I was called on the carpet by Podolsky. He had just returned from vacation to find himself faced with both my hunger strike and my complaint that the warders had dragged me by the hair from the third floor to the basement. As usual, he devised a Solomonic solution: I was to have my head shaved so that in the future nobody could drag me around by the hair.

First Lieutenant Abramov, the doctor who refused to certify that I was bruised after my tussle with the warders, was neither a bad man nor a good one. In his dealings with me he was unpretentious, and towards his superiors he was servile. My hunger strike gave him the idea of writing an article on the subject. He asked me whether I dreamed of food and requested that I write down my dreams—for the sake of science.

At one point I did start to write them down, but I didn't give my notes to the doctor. A person has "prison dreams" both before going to prison and after getting out. A few months before my arrest I dreamed that I was trying to escape from a sealed room: I struggled with some celluloid molds, and broke out into the street. In a recurrent dream I am walking through an endless series of splendid big rooms with a feeling of mounting danger, and I can't find my way out of that series of rooms. A cat is walking in front of me, and at first I'm sure that with its animal instinct it will lead me out. The cat seems very friendly. Suddenly I realize that it is a treacherous creature, that it wants to lead me to that place "from which no one returns." I turn around and open a side door. Instead of a big room, there is a locker, as in a barracks. I open another side door, and go out into the street.

In Sverdlovsk I had a bad nightmare: I was being chased, and at any moment they were going to catch me and put me in prison. My heart pounding, I woke up: silence, and sunlight playing over the yellow prison walls.

Everything was so simple, it turned out. In Magadan Prison I also awoke from a nightmare with a feeling of relief: I had dreamed I was in the camp at Talaya. And in camp I dreamed that Gusel had decided to leave me and take up with some German. The dream was so real that I promptly sat down to write her.

Food never figured prominently in my dreams during the hunger strike. In one I was walking with my father along Tversky Boulevard and eating grapes. We went down into a cave, and my father told me not to go straight ahead but to turn. There was a lock without a key and a vaulted ceiling. I saw a big saucepan with a skull in it and realized that people were killed there. Then I was riding in a van: I saw a procession of cars, and soldiers on the street. I was on the bank of a river, and an artist I knew tried to embrace me, but I made as if I wanted to push her into the water. Then I saw that on the opposite bank of the river, cows were turning into reindeer. Next I was in an elevator that couldn't go up. The canteen clerk brought sugar in dark blue packets; there were heaps of them in crates in the yard. I was eating black bread with butter, but I had to force myself to do it. I was eating cheese with great pleasure. I saw the room in Moscow that I lived in as a child, and a quarrel with my father: I felt that I hated everything old.

After my release I often dreamed that I was back in camp or prison. Sometimes my prison cell was at the same time the office of the head of the Magadan UKGB, and I wondered how he, who put me in prison, was now going to look me in the eye. (Only in dreams does one ask such stupid questions.) Even now, in the course of writing this book, I dream of prison and camp; and I wake up with cramps in my legs, as I did when I was in Lefortovo.

I was expecting some probing by the KGB pending the appellate decision, but six weeks went by without anything happening. I realized that they were waiting for the end of my hunger strike. Then one day toward the end of August, the doctor—the friend of science and obviously not an enemy of the "organs"—began to say something about Israel, and about my wife. But he slipped up and said he was only a doctor and his concerns lay elsewhere. It seemed to me that the KGB had not made a very successful choice of emissary or intelligence agent.

Two weeks later I was summoned to the first floor, where I found Leonid Tarasov waiting for me, along with a man in civilian clothes whom I didn't know. This was Major Valentin Eliseyev. He had previously worked in the Party apparatus, doing "ideological work," and his voice was somehow imperious: I never heard him say a single word in a natural, human way.

He began by telling me that the people who knew me could be counted on the fingers of one hand—and he even spread out his fingers as he said it. I replied that at least seven hundred people knew me, having in mind my fellow inmates at the camp. Actually, my books had been published, the TV interview with me had been aired, and even the Soviet newspapers had printed articles about me, so that opening gambit didn't strike me as particularly clever. But gradually everything began to become clear. Tarasov said he had been instructed to talk to me about my renunciation of citizenship. In my petition I had said that I did not consider all my views to be correct; Tarasov wanted to know which particular views I meant. I listed a few points, and both of them began wriggling in their chairs. Tarasov, though, took down everything carefully.

Then came the proposal to the hostage that he pay ransom. "You should put all that in a letter to a newspaper. The court would certainly take it into account."

"That's a good idea; but it doesn't seem quite fitting, somehow, to do it from prison. Besides, people might think I had written the letter under pressure. No, I'll do it when I get out."

We quarreled a bit. I said that while my body was being confined in prison, my books were circulating all over the world, and *that* is what they should be combatting. Both were straining in their eagerness to do battle; I, for my part, indicated I wasn't opposed to repudiating some of my "false" ideas. But I said I tired easily because of my hunger strike, and I wanted to go back to my cell.

"If you wish to see us, notify the warden, and we'll come right away."

Naturally, I didn't send for them. But ten days later I had a meeting with *two* Tarasovs: Leonid, the lieutenant colonel, and Boris, a full colonel. The latter was a heavily built, towheaded man with an air of confident well-being. Before joining the KGB, he had been a security guard in the Kolyma camps. He had risen rapidly since 1968, when he rendered "brotherly aid" to the Czechoslovaks. He possessed the keenest mind for police work of anyone I encountered.

But as I have already mentioned, the gebists are naïve in a way: not so much a "naïveté of evil" as a "naïveté of the belly." They are convinced that humans are governed only by self-interest or fear. In theory, they admit the existence of spiritual motives; but since they themselves don't possess them, they can't grasp them intuitively in others. I realized that in order to reach agreement with them and, ultimately, to deceive them (or, as one of them said later, to lead them around by the nose), the main thing was to pretend to be worse than I was: that would be our area of understanding.

I later asked Eliseyev if he had read Shakespeare: "You no doubt remember what Hamlet said to Guildenstern: 'You would play upon me; you would seem to know my stops. . . . 'Sblood, do you think I am easier to be played on than a pipe? Call me what instrument you will, though you can fret me, yet you cannot play upon me.' Can't you play the flute?''

"No, I can't," Eliseyev replied honestly, although the "organs" are supposed not only to know everything but to be able to do everything. For that matter, playing the flute struck him as frivolous. (Playing on people was another matter.)

In my interview with the Tarasovs, the colonel did the talking, and at first he said nothing about any deal whereby I would repent and they would release me. He kept to ideological considerations, and I readily agreed that in those matters we both took idealistic positions. Then, having talked enough about such things, Colonel Tarasov asked, "If, now, we are to come down to brass tacks, I ask you: What guarantee do we have if you are released that you will in fact write a letter to a newspaper repudiating your books?"

"And what guarantee do I have that if I wrote such a letter now, you would release me? The difference between us is that even when I'm out of prison I'll still be in your power, whereas all you have to do is walk out of this office and I'll never see you again."

That argument, so understandable to a bureaucrat, may or may not have had an effect on him; but the next morning, to my surprise, my handsome red ski suit was given back to me and I was put not into a Black Maria but into a Volga.

"Vladimir Fyodorovich Kolomiychenko, chief of the administration," said one of the Tarasovs the moment we entered the office of that dignitary. The man who rose and came a few steps to meet us was in civilian clothes. He was short, with slicked-down hair, and his way of looking at you was not exactly distrustful but rather as if he were peering at you from ambush. In the lapel of his jacket I noticed the badge of a deputy to the Oblast Soviet. He headed up the oblast council's committee to oversee observance of "socialist legality"; that is, he "oversaw" himself. He was a nervous man, and on this occasion he was especially nervous: it was plain to see he had no experience in talking to zeks. I found it most interesting to gaze upon the man who had organized my second term.

I don't remember the details of our conversation. Toward the end I expressed the hope that it had been recorded on tape so that it would not be lost to history. I realized that Kolomiychenko, who would have to take the responsibility for the report to Moscow, had wanted to have a look at me.

He proposed that I write a letter to a newspaper condemning my books and my activities as a whole and partially acknowledging my guilt. As a *quid pro quo*, the RSFSR Supreme Court, taking into account my illness and my repentance, would quash the judgment and I could return to Moscow. I insisted that I could make such a declaration only after I had been released.

I was again asked to let them know immediately if I wanted to meet with them, but I intended to let them make the next move. Three weeks went by before I again found myself in that office.

"I was beginning to think I wouldn't be seeing you again," I told Kolomiychenko. "Let's decide on something. Prison is like cold water: at first you're afraid to jump in, but later you get used to it, and it doesn't seem cold anymore." (I didn't add that if you spend too much time in cold water it can be fatal.)

With that, we got started on yet one more of those talks in which they repeat the same thing over and over again in the hope that your willpower will weaken and you will give up. It was important, however, to reach the point where the pressure peaks. If you get over that hump, they will begin to make concessions—provided, of course, that they are really interested in achieving a result. And in my case they needed a positive result. The chief of the UKGB would not have been talking with me if Moscow had not intervened. Still, I figured I would not be able to obtain my release, or even a reduction in my sentence, unconditionally. As Kolomiychenko said, in a happy slip of the tongue, it was essential that "the sheep eat their fill, and the wolves remain whole."[14] But what concession from me would they regard as the essential minimum?

"All right," Kolomiychenko finally said. "You don't want to make a public disavowal of your pernicious books until after your release. But as a first step, you could petition for pardon, and in that petition you could pass judgment on your books."

"Ah, but a pardon implies repentance, and I don't acknowledge my 'guilt.'"

"All right," he agreed. "Then don't say that you acknowledge your guilt, and we will agree on the following: (1) without acknowledging my guilt, I will petition the Presidium of the USSR Supreme Soviet for release because of my poor health; (2) without repudiating my books, I will mention that I do not now agree with everything in *Will the Soviet Union Survive Until 1984?*; (3) I will then be released, either on parole or by means of a pardon; (4) after my release, we will consider the matter of 'disowning my past views.'"

The negotiations had been going on for two hours; toward the end I was exhausted. Even for a healthy man, the endless discussion would have been trying, but I had been on hunger strike for three months, and forced feeding had been discontinued for the week preceding this meeting. So I said that I wouldn't write the petition then and there: I would rest in my cell and then write it that evening or the next morning. Leonid Tarasov promptly volunteered to come to the prison and pick it up.

In my petition I was cautious in the way I described the blackmail of my second arrest. I wrote:

> It seems to me that my second conviction was the result of an attitude toward me as a person regarded as hostile to the Soviet system whose words and actions were therefore . . . subjected to an *a priori* interpretation. From the very outset, certain passages in my books were misunderstood. In particular, the title of one book does not express a desire to see the collapse of the Soviet system before 1984: that year was chosen merely as a literary allegory. . . . The last thing I would want to see happen is that my own country should undergo violent shocks.

Tarasov made a few slight criticisms, which I accepted. But when he suggested I add a sentence saying I regretted that my books had been utilized by forces inimical to the USSR, I said that the only things I would regret or not regret were my own actions and that I would not pass judgment on the actions of others.

While I was making a copy, Tarasov was reading a book intently. I was curious what books were read by lieutenant colonels in the KGB. *"Songs of the Komsomol,"* he replied, proudly showing me the volume. "The songs of my youth."

Later, when Gusel read my petition in a hotel room in Magadan, she wept. As for me, I can't say that I wrote it with a light heart, or that rereading it gave me any pleasure. And yet, disregarding its evasive style and the circumstances under which it was written, I still agree with the gist of it today.

I did not acknowledge my "guilt" in either the first or the second case brought against me. I did not recognize the State's right to put me on trial for my views, be they right or wrong. I did not repudiate my books and articles. And I did not express regret that they had been written and published. I said that I found certain passages in *Will the Soviet Union Survive Until 1984?* to be incorrect, and I did in fact find them to be so. (I enumerated them in the preface to a new edition of the book in the West.) I retracted my definition of Russia as "a country without faith, traditions, or culture," and I would have retracted that phrase without any defense of "traditions and culture" by the KGB. I wrote that I was not "an enemy of the Soviet system" but really its friend. In 1976, when I was already in the West, I wrote:

> When Lenin came out with his slogan "All power to the Soviets!" he was talking about the power of multi-party soviets and not

the power of one party. So that when I speak out for restoration of
the genuine role of the soviets, I am speaking as an authentic Soviet
man. And Mr. Brezhnev, who heads up the Party that has usurped
the role of the soviets, is a typical antisovetchik.[15]

As far back as 1968, I had told Pavel Litvinov that I thought it was
politically wise to retain the adjective "Soviet," since the people were accustomed to it and that restoring the real power of the soviets was the simplest
path to democratic parliamentarianism. Also, I thought the Communist party
could be retained in a multiparty Soviet society, so I suggested that the slogan
for the Kronstadt rebellion of 1920, "For the soviets without the Communists!" be replaced by: "For the soviets, including the Communists!"

Once again I was left to myself. Sometimes it seemed to me that I had
conceded too much; at other times, that I had not made enough concessions
for my petition to be granted. It was always possible that Moscow had changed
its mind and now felt that my release would be inadvisable. I had a telegram
from Shveisky saying that the appellate hearing had been set for November
13—another bad omen. But on the 14th, I was summoned to see Podolsky,
and I realized that the news was good.

"A telegram has come in from your lawyer," he said, watching me
expectantly.

I said nothing. Then he smiled, and added: "Congratulations! Your term
in camp has been commuted to exile."

This was of course a violation of my agreement with the KGB, since
exile is by no means the equivalent of release. But on the other hand, I for
my part had no intention of writing a recantation.

One day in prison counts for three days of exile, and I had been in prison
for almost six months, so that almost half my term of exile was already over.

"My hunger strike is over," I announced as I entered the dispensary. I
asked for a spoon and ate the liquid mixture that had been prepared for me: I
don't even remember what it tasted like. I had been on hunger strike for 117
days and had been force-fed on 70 of those days.

The next day Kolomiychenko congratulated me on "having gone from
the worst to the less bad." Then he told me my place of exile was to be
Magadan. Leonid Tarasov was especially happy about the new development.
As he led me along the corridor, he whispered, "Andrei Alekseyevich, hang
in with us, and you won't come to a bad end. You'll always have money and
good suits to wear."

Gusel told me later that at an opportune moment during the appellate hearing, she was approached not by a friend but by Vladimir Sidorov, who had arrested me in Akulovo. In conspiratorial tones, Sidorov said to her, "Gusel Kavylevna, if you stick with us you'll both have it good. But you won't have it good if you're with *them*." And he glanced toward Andrei Sakharov.

I realized that the KGB wanted to set up confidential relations of a special kind. Kolomiychenko even suggested to me that after my release, when I was summoned to a KGB office, I should tell my wife that I was going to work, or something of the sort. I replied that the KGB was not a mistress of mine, so I had no intention of concealing the fact from Gusel.

I also realized that my sentence had been commuted to exile so as more easily to bring me around, and that I was faced with the difficult task of reversing my willingness to recant, yet not so much as to get sent back to prison. (As I learned later, the KGB was even more interested in getting me to join their side than in making me repudiate my books.)

I had to stay in prison until the certified copy of the court's decision arrived. I filled out a slip to get some money from my account to buy some eggs. But the regulations of Magadan Prison prohibit giving salt to an inmate, and what are eggs without salt? The gebists, eager to please me, demanded that Podolsky issue an authorization for the salt. But he was a stickler for the rules. He said that if he did issue the authorization, he would have to put me in solitary so the contagion wouldn't spread to the other prisoners.

"That adds up to exchanging a cell-mate for salt," I said.

My cell-mate was a young murderer who annoyed me with his listlessness. Still, I did have a live creature in the cell with me—something like a cat. And I understood the spiritual torments of Podolsky, who was afraid of the KGB yet wanted to remain loyal to his anti-salt regulation. I remembered how he had brought Gusel's telegram to me when I was in the punishment cell, and so I didn't pressure him: eating unsalted eggs for a few days wouldn't be a tragedy.

On November 22, I received a telegram: "AM TAKING FLIGHT 67 ON THE NIGHT OF THE 22ND STOP EVERYTHING FINE STOP WE WILL SOON BE TOGETHER STOP LOVE GUSEL"

That same day, Boris Tarasov told me that the certified copy of the decision had arrived and that I would be released the next morning.

But the next day lunchtime came and went; then they brought us supper—and as each hour passed, I became more and more nervous.

"Amalrik! With your things!" Finally—and for the last time.

"Andrei Alekseyevich," Tarasov said to me in a half-reproachful tone, "I really had to sweat to get you released. Red tape everywhere, and you couldn't make sense out of anything."

I wonder how hard he had to sweat when he put me in prison, and to whom he complained of red tape on that occasion.

Meantime, I myself got involved in red tape: I had to obtain a document certifying my release, I had to collect my money and belongings and sign for them, I had to fill out forms—and I lost sight of Tarasov. Yet I had been told that I was free.

Podolsky accompanied me as I left the prison, like a polite host escorting a departing guest.

As I shook his hand, I asked, "Are you glad to be getting rid of me?"

"Of course," he answered sincerely.

Freedom! It was pitch dark, and there was not a single light in the fields around the prison. I had no idea of where the city was. From outside, the prison walls looked even more uninviting. A freezing-cold wind was blowing, and I scrunched up, trying to keep warm. There was nobody around, except for the driver of the black Volga parked at the prison gate, who looked at me with total indifference. But then the corpulent figure of Tarasov made its appearance, and he offered me a seat in the Volga.

"I again congratulate you," said Kolomiychenko, standing in the middle of his office. A room had been reserved for me at the Magadan Hotel. Within an hour a bus would go to the airport and I could ride it to meet my wife.

"Would you perhaps like to buy a bottle of champagne to celebrate her arrival?" he asked.

I did want to. But I had no idea where either the liquor store or the hotel was located.

"Do you have an available operative?" Kolomiychenko asked one of his colleagues. And an "operative" promptly made his appearance, wearing a red scarf. (Is that their uniform?) He came to attention respectfully.

"This is Andrei Alekseyevich Amalrik," said Kolomiychenko. "Have you perhaps heard something?"

The operative had heard everything. First he took me to the hotel, where my room seemed luxurious after my prison cell. Next he drove me to a liquor store, where in my enthusiasm I bought not only champagne but cognac. Finally, he brought me back to the hotel, and then to the bus. I was so excited I didn't even notice that I was still wearing a jacket with a prisoner's badge on it. Everything seemed foggy to me. For two weeks after that, I was afraid to go out unless Gusel went with me, and I would lose my way in the streets of the town.

Naturally, the plane was late. After ordering a taxi, I paced impatiently in the wretched lounge. But at last the flight's arrival was announced. Then the first passengers were coming off the plane, and finally, Gusel. Amazed that I was already there, she threw herself into my arms.

CHAPTER 2 2

The Capital of
the Kolyma Territory

The mist thickened over the sea,
the wind and the waves howled together;
ahead of us loomed Magadan,
capital of Kolyma.

These lines are from that same camp song about that accursed territory "from which no one returns." In the 1940s, "Magadan" sounded like "Auschwitz" or "Dachau." Almost all the inhabitants of the town were prisoners and guards. At construction sites bulldozers often turn up human bones: several million persons found their eternal rest in the frozen ground of Kolyma.

This is something people talk about calmly. Everyone seems to know about the past of Kolyma, and yet it has been forgotten: for the average Soviet citizen Magadan is a symbol not of horror but of privileges. Kolyma and Chukotka are regions where gold and other rare metals are mined. In order to attract and keep manpower, a "zonal coefficient" is applied to the wage scale in these regions, as elsewhere in the Soviet Far North. In Kolyma, the coefficient is 170 per cent, plus six bonuses of 10 per cent each for every six months of work. In Chukotka, it is 200 per cent, plus ten bonuses. Thus for the same amount of work that in Moscow would earn 100 rubles, a worker in Kolyma gets 230 rubles, and one in Chukotka gets 300 rubles. No wonder there is a constant influx of manpower in Kolyma—more than is needed, in fact. The local officials are lobbying to have Kolmya declared a closed region, as it was before. In an area surrounded by seas that ice over, the climate is unusually harsh. The figure for per capita housing is the lowest in the country, and there is a constant threat of unemployment. Except for teachers' colleges, there are no institutions of higher education; and the pensions for old people are no higher than anywhere else in the country. All this makes for a rapid turnover in population, nowhere so noticeable as in the old cemetery: not a single grave has been left intact nor is there any indication of concern for the upkeep of the graves. Old people who go back to "the mainland" die very quickly because of the radical change in climate.

The region has only slightly less area than all of Western Europe; but the population is four hundred thousand, of whom one hundred thousand live in Magadan. The city is built on a tongue of land projecting into the Sea of Okhotsk, and hence is exposed to all the winds. The main avenue, Lenin Street, was constructed by Japanese POWs, and is an example of Stalinist classicism; the other streets are in the style of Khrushchevian functionalism. Lining the Kolyma Road and the sides of both bays are the dwellings forming the outskirts of the town, where most of the inhabitants live: barracks from the Stalin era or huts of the dugout type, with earth packed in between the double walls of wood for purposes of warmth. Such dwellings are also abundant in the central part of the town, along with the inevitable latrine pits.

From the ends of the lanes leading off from the main street, one can see pretty, rather low hills. The view of the sea, iced over or with leaden-colored waves and white ships in the distance, is also handsome. The low hills are covered with stunted trees; once a year, for a week, the north wind permeates the town with the scent of pine.

"I don't see a woman!" This exclamation came from a guest of ours—a straightforward fellow with a fat, good-natured face—when he looked at a self-portrait that Gusel had done. She told me it was the best proof of her fidelity: in three and a half years she had gradually lost all her femininity.

Our first guests turned out to be correspondents from *Pravda* and the All-Union Radio Network. The radio correspondent had been on the flight with Gusel. The *Pravda* reporter, a connoisseur of paintings, stayed in the hotel room next to ours. He was not a bad sort—a man who liked his bottle and could never figure out what kind of person I was. The radio journalist made fun of him in a cautious way.

We sent to see the psychoneurologist who had once examined me in Talaya. (I shall give him the name of "Mark," because it has never become clear what kind of role he played.) He was basically capable, but inclined to be indecisive and to complicate everything: he wasted his talent on details. Mark had spent several years in the penal camps of the Stalin era and was still traumatized from that experience. Recently, he had written a dissertation on alcoholism in the Northeast; but since all the data were secret, he had to get a clearance from the KGB before he could defend his dissertation. Gradually, I began to get the impression that he wanted to trade me for that clearance. If he was a KGB informer—and perhaps he had been since his days in camp—it was out of fear of the powers that be. But he tried to influence me in the way the KGB wanted, and I saw he was using cunning on me.

I told him of my talks with the KGB, just as I had mentioned them to two other people in Magadan. (I didn't want to have any secrets in common with the KGB.) Since I regarded him as a weak-willed, unhappy man, I hoped to have a heart-to-heart talk with him; but nothing came of it. It was difficult to tell him that I suspected him; but after that our conversation became even more senseless. He denied everything, and I wasn't really sure I was right. You don't kill your wife just because you're jealous; but if you have feelings of jealousy, you can understand a man who murders his wife. Thus I could comprehend a man who wrote denunciations of somebody he hated; but informing when there is no such motive is something that has always puzzled me. I could explain it, but I couldn't understand it in my heart.

Mark tried to convince me that he was not a stoolie. But when we parted company, he said, "If the KGB wants to, they can even find out what you shit"—and I realized he was working for them. When Kolomiychenko told me that Moscow had queried him as to whether Mark's wife should be allowed to leave the country, I passed the word on to Mark, and the KGB found out that I had.

When describing my talks with the KGB people, I always gave Kolomiychenko a clean bill of health and derided Boris Tarasov and Eliseyev: each time we gathered, Kolomiychenko would greet me with a smile even broader than the time before, while Tarasov and Eliseyev were increasingly grumpy.

A month after my release from prison I checked in at the local police station and was handed a document stating that "Amalrik . . . is restricted in his freedom of movement and not authorized to reside anywhere outside the city of Magadan. He is under the supervision of the UVD, Magadan Oblast, and must register once a month with the commandant of the special settlement."†

This kind of certificate was commonly issued in the Stalin era. By now, however, I was the only person to have such a document: the oblast was no longer a region having special settlements, and there was no commandant's office for the latter. So I reported to the UVD office for registration.

In Mother Russia somebody is always asking you for your papers, but not everybody could understand my ill-printed certificate. When I went to take a driver's training course, the oculist told me my document was a forgery. I replied that if I knew how to forge papers I would have made myself something better than a deportee's certificate.

---

†"Special settlements" are areas set aside for deported people ("settlers"). In the Stalin era there were a great many such "special settlements" for "kulaks," national minorities regarded as "unreliable," etc.—TRANS.

I had more run-ins with doctors than with the KGB. At first no one wanted to examine me, since I didn't have a residence permit for Magadan. When I did receive a residence permit, it turned out that our district doctor, a woman, had been on the staff at the penal camp. Talking with her sent my blood pressure up so high that I decided I was endangering my life.

The maritime climate was hard on me. I could work only during the first half of the day, and some days I could neither read nor write. It's quite possible that if I had been sent back to camp, I would not have survived. I lost three teeth, and periodontosis set in; but thanks to the KGB (once again) I was able to get treatment. Gusel's hair started to fall out, but I shaved her head twice, and some of her hair was saved. (In those regions we came across women who were almost bald.) Gusel was sick much of the time and spent a month in the hospital. Not only did I have to bring her food every day, but I had to buy medicine or order it from Moscow, since there wasn't any in the hospital. Among the doctors were some fine people and good specialists, but they were so dispirited by the low pay and difficult working conditions that it was hard for them to give the right kind of attention to their patients.

The day I was released, Kolomiychenko said he would pass the word to the first secretary of the oblast committee about getting us an apartment, for which people in Magadan sometimes wait for decades. Obtaining an apartment for an exiled person was a generous gesture on Kolomiychenko's part, because it wasn't easy even for the KGB.

After about three months, I got the apartment, which was of course the KGB's biggest "carrot." With the ingratitude that is typical of me, I didn't justify their expectations. Later, I even made fun of "their" apartment. But they weren't left holding an empty sack; when I left, the apartment was returned to them.

There was a hill about half a mile from our place: we could ski there in the winter and climb to the top in the summer. Magadan is less well supplied with the necessities of life than Moscow, but more so than Sverdlovsk. The beer in Magadan is especially good. In the spring and summer, Georgians sell vegetables in the marketplace. In March a kilogram of tomatoes cost twenty rubles—one eighth of an average month's salary—and in July it cost five.

We tried to lead a bourgeois way of life. We bought furniture and even silverware with which to entertain our informer-guests. Sometimes, though, we felt downhearted and could well have said what Pushkin did when he was in exile:

> And you, wine, friend of autumn's frosts,
> flood my breast with easeful drunkenness—
> with brief forgetfulness of bitter woes . . .

Sometimes, especially during the first months, the joy I felt at having been released and reunited with Gusel went hand in hand with a strange feeling of depression and indifference, something I suspect is familiar to many people who have been in prison. "You're a strong-willed person," Colonel Tarasov once told me. "You'll overcome it."

As soon as it was known that I was to serve a term in exile, the KGB people asked me where I would like to work—in the library, the theater, or some institute. Magadan had a good library, where I often did research later on, but I was put off by the fact that the librarians were women: I would have been a kind of rooster among hens. All the performers at the Magadan theater had been zeks: Vadim Kozin had sung, and Leonid Varpakhovsky had directed. But when the theater "got out of stir," it went downhill: the most talented people had left, grown old, or died. The theater was desperately in need of a play dealing with life in Magadan so they could take it on the road and perform it in Moscow. They even hinted to me that perhaps I could write a play for them. But all the positions in the theater were filled, so that notion also fell by the way.

There were four institutes, the most prestigious of which was the USSR Academy of Science's Multi-disciplinary Scientific Research Institute. The laboratory of comprehensive economic problems was headed by an intelligent Jew with an Armenian name, Eduard Akhnazarov, and I asked for an assignment under him. The KGB got me my job at the laboratory through the *obkom*, and I was made a senior lab technician. Since a college degree is usually required for that position (the lowest one for a college-educated person), the KGB had, in a sense, conferred upon me the diploma for the lack of which they used to reproach me. When Akhnazarov found out that Mark had advised me to make such a request, he cursed him out roundly. I was told, later on, how much fright my impending arrival had caused him. He was expecting a powerfully built, bearded muzhik like Pugachev to show up and shout from the threshold: "Down with the Soviet regime!" And then what would he do? Tie me up? Call the KGB? Or plug up his ears?

Before long, however, we became friends. And yet, like King Midas, at whose touch everything turned to gold, I left my mark on everyone who became too friendly with me. After my departure, the laboratory, having been exposed to such dread contagion, was closed down, and most of the staff were transferred to other institutes.

Akhnazarov, with his lively mind and his sad eyes, seemed out of place among the people of Magadan, who gave one the impression that they were made of cast iron. I suspect that Akhnazarov would have liked to live somewhere else, but lacked the nerve to make the move. He was one of the better-known local characters because, although he earned about 1,000 rubles a month, he never had any money, went about in down-at-the-heels boots and an overcoat bought for him by the laboratory staff (who had got up a pool for the purpose), and was in debt to the tune of several thousand rubles. He never saved any money; to the contrary, he bought two bottles of champagne every day (although he himself couldn't drink) plus Lord knows what else for his wife's relatives, who lived off him and filled his small apartment with their elephantine bodies and their braying voices. "It's as if Russia herself had come to live at my place," he would sigh.

Often, he quite simply lost money. (There are no credit cards in the USSR, so that one has to carry cash all the time.) I advised Akhnazarov to get a piece of string, thread banknotes on it like dried mushrooms, and then fasten it to his pocket, so that if he dropped the money he would drag it after him.

"But wouldn't people laugh at me?" he asked worriedly.

"You don't really know the Russian people," I replied. "They'd say: 'We've seen many a skinflint in our day, but this is the first time we've seen a man with money on a leash. He's quite somebody—not a man to be trifled with.' "

A mining engineer by training, Akhnazarov took up economics, and then became involved in sociology and anthropology. He wanted to elaborate, within the framework of Marxism, a theory explaining the development of human society on the basis of the contradictions between mental and physical labor. In response to this proposal, the chief of the *obkom*'s science section said: "In the Magadan Oblast we don't do science!"

Akhnazarov's deputy was a kind-hearted, intelligent woman named Batayeva. But for all her intelligence, she was a dogmatic Marxist. And in her case I could clearly observe how, whether out of fear or out of caution, a person can draw a "magic circle" around himself—a circle beyond which his mind will not reach.

The laboratory staff included two capable scientists, Yadrshnikov and Kilin, who, like Lomonosov, had trekked in from the depths of Siberia wearing little more on their feet than shoes. Yadrshnikov I remember chiefly as a man who was afraid of everything. He was even afraid to defend his dissertation for the degree of Candidate of Science.

"Just what are you frightened about?" Akhnazarov asked him. "What do you risk in defending a dissertation?"

"A man never knows from what direction danger may come," replied Yadrshnikov. Then, putting his cap on his head, he left, putting a stop to the disagreeable conversation.

Another staff member, Krasnopolsky, was his exact opposite. Big and with a big voice, he was eager to defend his dissertation as soon as possible.

That he was a climber by nature could be plainly seen at every step of his way. One day someone brought to the lab a test for determining character, and all of us took it. The ratings came out as follows: the majority got "gentle intellectual"; I got "a teacher of limited scope" (actually, I am fond of teaching); and Krasnopolsky got "scumbag." He managed a slight laugh at this (the test was in fact a joke), but then said he wanted to take the test a second time and answer the questions seriously. He did; again it came out "scumbag."

Just before Easter, somebody put postcards in all the mailboxes. They read: "Dear Brother: Greetings to you on Easter Sunday."

"We have to turn these over to the KGB immediately!" exclaimed "Dear Brother" Krasnopolsky, who was much upset.

I had the habit of beginning some of my remarks (partly in imitation of Dostoyevsky's Foma Opiskin)[16] with the words: "I know the people . . ." At this, *Partorg* Kilin would throw me a glance of amazement. Then I would go on: ". . . and the people know me," causing Kilin's eyes to virtually jump out of their sockets. Being a young man from a peasant family, he was rather naïve; yet he was skillful at finding his way through the bureaucratic labyrinth of science. As for his lack of culture, he made up for it with a most unusual capacity for work. He represented one of the two extremes found in any scientific laboratory—the person who does half the work of the entire staff. At the other extreme is the person who does nothing at all.

The work at the laboratory involved economic forecasting, problems of balancing the economy and of the optimal distribution of industrial complexes in the oblast. Such a problem as whether to mine minerals in the area where the best deposits were found or to locate the mine in the area with the most highly developed infrastructure may seem simple, but for the Magadan Oblast it was a tough one. The research carried on at the lab involved classified information (if not directly, then indirectly), and Akhnazarov had a terrible time before he finally assigned me to work on the problem of "interests." I read one book by a certain Soviet economist—300 pages of pseudoscientific garbage without the slightest glimmer of a real idea—and realized that if I read another one like that I'd go out of my mind. After that I spent my time in the lab reading Marx (for my overall development) and collections of articles in systems analysis. I got so interested in the latter that in Moscow I began to study mathematical logic.

But I could read books at home or in the library, and I didn't see any sense in going to the institute every day. I went there only to pick up my check or to talk on the phone with Karel van het Reve, who called me once or twice a month from Amsterdam. Our conversations were quite innocent, but they got everybody all worked up, and the KGB demanded that I put an end to them. I replied that Reve was calling me, not I him; and of course they had no desire to cut off telephone service to the institute.

As a matter of fact, I was trying to maintain good relations with every-body so as not to get the reputation of being standoffish. The less I worked, the harder I tried to compensate for that lack by active participation in all kinds of picnics, etc., and by going to the parties thrown at staff members' homes, and sometimes even in the laboratory.

From time to time Colonel Tarasov would ask how people were treating me at the lab, and I would answer "Fine!"—to his evident dissatisfaction.

"But," he said to me once, "there is talk at the institute that you are somehow connected with us. For one thing, you got an apartment. Don't they think you're our agent?"

"If they do, that's perfect," I replied. "In this society, a KGB agent is rated almost as high as a top executive. You get more respect."

Once I took part in a joint excursion for the purpose of sorting rotten onions. Several times every year, scientists, engineers, blue-collar workers, white-collar workers, and sometimes even KGB agents are sent out in teams to harvest or sort potatoes and other gifts of nature. This is done because the socialist system cannot otherwise cope with the harvesting and storing of vegetables. (More than one Russian who has emigrated to the West, when he sees the piles of vegetables at a greengrocer's on one side of the street and, on the other, a demonstration by underprivileged homosexuals, mutters to himself: "They've been pampered with too much good food! They ought to be sent out to sort rotten potatoes for a month or two!") Five clerks at the vegetable storehouse supervised the work of ten scientists; and we were warned we would be searched to make sure we hadn't stolen any onions.

I had already been frisked enough when I was in camp. So the next time I was ordered to join a potato-sorting expedition, I replied that my soul would go with the others but my body would remain home.

"Really now, Andrei Alekseyevich," Akhnazarov said to me with a smile. "I'm the head of a laboratory and a member of the ruling Party, and you're a half-scholar living in exile. Yet look how much more self-confident you are than I am."

One of the VIPs in Magadan was Nikolai Shilo, director of our institute, the only member of the USSR Academy of Sciences in the Soviet Far East. When Kosygin came to Magadan in 1974, it was said that he wanted to take Shilo back to Moscow as an adviser. "That's hardly likely," Kolomiychenko told me when I asked him about it. "It wouldn't make sense for him to go to Moscow, where he'd just get lost among the other academicians."

Shilo was a scientist of the new breed. In the Stalin era he had been a major in the MVD, although he never did duty in the penal camps. Later, he took a degree in geology. Since he was Number One in Kolyma, he was offended by the fact that whenever I met him I failed to recognize him. But unfortunately, I have a poor memory for faces, and his looks were so unprepossessing that he would have got lost not only among other academicians but among a bunch of bums in a beer joint. As a great Kolyma patriot, he wrote an article in which he said that he felt better in Magadan than in Paris, where the air was polluted by exhaust fumes from automobiles. After then, whenever he asked me how I felt, I would reply, "Better than in Paris."

I don't know how good a geologist Shilo was, but his advice to Kosygin boiled down to the following: since the price of gold on the world market was rising, the Soviet Union should sell as much of it as possible. Gold is Kolyma's secret. The cost of the gold mined and processed by the government's concentrating mills is so high that it would almost be better to buy it rather than sell it to Switzerland. The marketing of Soviet gold is a covert form of dumping: the cost of mining is covered at the expense of other parts of the economy, including the sector that, if not out-and-out private, is semi-private. The Kolyma prospectors buy equipment and as a rule are allocated areas that are either not very promising or already worked over by the government. They must deliver the gold they mine at a fixed price of no more than one ruble per gram; whereas the cost at the concentrating mills, when I was in Kolyma, ran as high as fourteen rubles, and the government was selling it at a price of twenty rubles in 1974.

It was interesting for us to meet Vadim Kozin, who in the 1930s had been the most famous pop singer in Russia. In the late forties he had been arrested on a charge of homosexuality and sent to Kolyma, where he was one of the ornaments of the "court theater" maintained by Nikishov, the chief of Dalstroi. The authorities felt, however, that it was awkward for such a famous person to do time for "his rear end," so they gave him a second term for "talking." Today, he is living out his days in a small apartment, surrounded by countless paintings of cats. (He himself rather resembles an owl.) Some time after we had met him, he told us that when he had heard of my intention to pay him a visit, he had promptly phoned the "organs" and asked whether that would be okay. To which the "organs" had replied that it would.

There was yet another acquaintance we struck up that in my opinion could not have been made without consultation with the "organs." That person was Anna Nutetegrene, former President of Chukotka and former Vice-President of the USSR. One can still find brochures from those days, written by local toadies. Thus one journalist wrote that while riding in the subway at a time when the Supreme Soviet was in session, he noticed that the Muscovites were reading, "with special attention," Anna Nutetegrene's speeches in their newspapers. According to the Magadan legend, she had lost her position after demanding Chukotka's secession from the USSR. Actually, her wrongdoing consisted in the fact that she had (1) married a Jew, which of course displeased the regime, and (2) divorced him, which went against the rules for the Party elite. Not knowing what to do with her, they named her secretary of the *raikom* closest to Magadan. In the Soviet North, a *raikom* secretary is supreme lord of his domain. But she felt as if she were in exile, and there was something of the rebel in her behavior. One could see from her case how much the Soviet system squeezes a human being. I am not convinced that upward mobility is adequate compensation for the impossibility of moving ever so slightly to one side.

We also got to know some artists, headed by Lydia Timasheva, a fat woman of about fifty who ruled them like a veteran top sergeant. In the past she had been a ballerina, at present she was an art critic, and she was a past, present, and future KGB agent, something that all the artists warned us about.

She was organizing an exhibit, and I told Kolomiychenko that it wouldn't be a bad idea to invite Gusel to show some of her work there.

"Well," said the best local patron of the arts, "what's the hitch?" Then, to Tarasov: "Boris Vasilyevich, have a chat with Timasheva."

The artists were to be interviewed on local television, and Timasheva handed out prepared texts, cleared by the censor, to all of them. Gusel was supposed to say she was glad they had exhibited her *Still Life with Rhododendrons*, but she refused to read a text written by somebody else, saying she couldn't pronounce the word "rhododendron" in front of a microphone.

"Then what do you intend to say?" Timasheva asked nervously.

"I'll say that I like the hills of Kolyma."

"That should be all right."

So it was that the people of Magadan saw Gusel on their TV screens.

"It's Amalrik! Amalrik!" It was the kind of shouting heard when a wild beast breaks out of its cage.

I had gone to the office of the oblast court, and the secretary had recognized me. I had decided to visit the court on the pretext that I wanted to read my case file—which, of course, I wasn't allowed to do. My real reason, though, was simply to have a look at the people who had convicted me. Judge Rybachuk hid behind a thick tome. Time was, he had expressed regret that I hadn't been given a smack in the jaw; now he was afraid that *he* was going to get one. Prosecutor Guryayev was noticeably nervous. As for Investigator Botvinik, when I asked him why he had got involved in such a dirty business, he replied he was just doing his duty.

The witnesses, too, had followed orders. In March 1974, I saw Lesha Ivanchenko coming toward me on Lenin Street, and he recognized me.

"I suppose you won't shake hands with me now, Andrei Alekseyevich," he said.

"I most likely won't."

He asked what he could do, and I told him he could write an account of what really happened.

He then told me he had petitioned for a pardon and that after he had testified at my trial, his four remaining years had been commuted to a suspended sentence, and he had just been released.

We went to my place together and, sitting at my desk, he wrote the following letter:

Dear Andrei Alekseyevich:

After hesitating for a long time, I have decided to write the truth about the circumstances under which I testified against you. When I was questioned by Botvinik, prosecutor of the investigative section of the Magadan Oblast Prosecutor's Office, on April 26, 1973, he was guided by the testimony that I had given to the KGB investigator. A transcript of that testimony was lying on his desk, half-covered with a sheet of paper. When I began to argue with him and testify differently, I was taken to the KGB investigator . . . and he persuaded me to repeat my previous, inaccurate testimony.

When he had finished, Lesha sat there, pen still in hand, thinking the whole thing over. I could see the beads of sweat forming on his forehead. Then, with a sigh, he signed the letter.

"Oof! That's really a load off my chest," he said. Then, after thinking a bit more, he added: "You know, Andrei Alekseyevich, I don't have much money, but I did earn a little something during six years in camp. If I gave it to you, could I have this letter back?"

I had never really felt a deadly anger toward Ivanchenko, but Obraztsov was another matter. I had decided to settle accounts with him: not to kill him, as the old zek Gavrilych had suggested, but at any rate to hit him where it would hurt him most—in his wallet. I had filed a claim that he had stolen my jacket. When the trial was held, Obraztsov said that now he was sorry he hadn't murdered me. As for the jacket, he denied categorically that he had ever got it.

The court ordered Obraztsov to pay me seventy-eight rubles and fifty-two kopecks in satisfaction of my claim. Choking with rage, he managed to say, "If only it had been a good jacket. But it was too small for me."

Afterward, Judge Churikov said to me, "I hear you're planning to write a book on Soviet legal procedure. Go ahead. But don't let the same thing happen to you that happened to Solzhenitsyn. The Swiss gave him permission to live there, but 'without the right to engage in political activity.'"

This phrase was repeated at all public meetings, as if to say: "In our country, Solzhenitsyn engaged in 'political activity,' and he stirred up trouble. The Swiss, though, have put him in such a bind he's afraid to open his mouth."

C H A P T E R   2 3

Saint Olga
and the Jew

I don't know about the Swiss and Solzhenitsyn, but the KGB was putting me in a bind: I was out of prison, they had got me an apartment, and now the time had come to repudiate my "wrong ideas." I told them that as an exile I was not yet at liberty, so that my reservations still held good.

In January 1974, Andrei Pustyakov, a "specialist in dissidents," arrived from Moscow. Our talks were arranged with considerable pomp and ceremony; if anyone phoned while they were in progress, Kolomiychenko would say: "Call back later. We're in conference."

Having studied the gebists' lingo and procedures rather thoroughly, I never cited the Universal Declaration of Human Rights in my talks with them. Instead, I would take my arguments from a source that was more authoritative for them.

"Andrei Alekseyevich," Colonel Tarasov said to me, "certain difficulties have come up in connection with your apartment."

To which I replied, looking the colonel straight in the eye: "Comrade Stalin taught that there were no strongholds that the Bolsheviks could not capture. You must learn how to overcome difficulties."

Kolomiychenko brushed nitpicking objections aside with a wave of the hand, saying, "But those things are mere trifles, Andrei Alekseyevitch!"

"Ah," I came back. "But Comrade Stalin used to say you should never neglect little things, because great things are built up from little ones."

My ability to fall on my knees before the fountainhead of Stalinist wisdom was something I had come by easily, since Gusel had brought me a cookbook published while the Great Leader was still alive. It began with Stalin's pronouncement: "We are beginning to live better, we are beginning to live more happily." And in every succeeding section of the book, whether it dealt with wines or soups, there was some quotation from Stalin, whether relevant or totally irrelevant. I leafed through that book before each and every talk with the KGB people.

When they countered my quotations from Stalin with the example of Lenin, I hinted that Lenin was a Jew. (I had long ago realized that the best response to the idiotic arguments of officials was even more idiotic arguments.) After much wrangling as to whether Lenin's grandmother was Jewish, I said, in exasperation, "Even supposing his grandmother wasn't Jewish, I see hanging on the wall there a portrait of Dzerzhinski, and *he* certainly was Jewish!" Actually, of course, Dzerzhinski was from the petty Polish nobility; but any name that didn't end in "ov" or "ko" had such a magical effect on Kolomiychenko, Tarasov, and Pustyakov that they promptly fell silent.

Kolomiychenko argued that now was the time to "rebuke those well-wishers" of mine in the West who had tried to use me as a puppet and that the first one I should rebuke was Karel van het Reve, because "it's plain to see where the money for his Herzen Foundation is coming from."

"That's not a bad idea," I said. "But just think for a minute. Today you and I can get together like this for a talk, and we're on easy terms with each other. But how would you like it if I later described you as idiotic and rather ugly?"

Kolomiychenko responded with a wry look that plainly showed he wouldn't like it, and I remarked that I was equally unwilling to say uncomplimentary things about van het Reve.

Our talks had finally begun to gain momentum. Pustyakov proposed that instead of sending a letter to a newspaper, I write an exposition of my views for some "high authorities" in Moscow. So that I could better cope with that task, he gave me a copy of *Will the Soviet Union Survive Until 1984?* with a great many notations indicating just what, in the KGB's opinion, I should repudiate and how I should repudiate it. I also asked for copies of *Involuntary Journey to Siberia* and my *Articles and Letters*. Tarasov opined that in *Journey* I gave too much space to trifles, and I replied that he knew better than anyone else how important trifles are in the life of a zek.

In addition, I asked for a typewriter. Tarasov promised me one, but he dragged his heels, apprehensive that I might write anti-Soviet works on a typewriter furnished by the KGB. So I had written a letter—neutrally addressed to the USSR Supreme Soviet—on a typewriter provided by an artist I knew.

It was not that I simply caved in to pressure. I was one of many seduced by the charm of détente. I felt that although Nixon and Kissinger were cynics, they were at the same time firm and farsighted statesmen who would compel the USSR to pay a price for détente. I believed that rapprochement with the West would necessitate gradual changes within our country and that this would open up possibilities for a dialogue with the regime. In ten pages, expressing myself cautiously, I repeated the ideas I had first set forth in 1967 in a letter to *Izvestiya* and had again formulated in my book in 1969.

I said that I regarded "any public 'act of repentance' as not only demeaning but useless. I can serve the interests of my country in a worthier manner." My purpose in writing *Will the Soviet Union Survive Until 1984?* was "to call attention to the dangers threatening our country; however, my eagerness that my appeal be heeded had prompted me to present things in their most dramatic form." I went on to say that the following problems still struck me as urgent: (1) China and stability in the Far East; (2) Germany and Eastern Europe—the problem of the "rear area"; (3) the U.S. and competition for influence in the Third World; (4) the economy; (5) the ossification of the methods of government; (6) the class of "specialists" and information exchange; (7) nationalism; (8) the disillusionment of young people; (9) the ideological vacuum.

> In any stable society the problem of ideology is usually kept in the background, only to come to the forefront in critical situations, when it turns out that even the most splendid rituals cannot replace a vital ideology. Right now, one gets the impression that Soviet ideology . . . is in a state of almost complete stagnation. Apparently, the current technological revolution is leading (and will lead) to changes in the world such that the problem of ideology squarely confronts every social system, including those of both the USSR and the U.S.

The problem is certainly confronting them, but Lord only knows how it can be solved. I wrote that neither Marxism, nor Russian nationalism, nor Western liberalism was the answer.

I wrote that the Soviet system was facing the same kind of economic crisis that the capitalist system had experienced in the 1930s, but that "socialist society does not have its own Keynes. Czechoslovakia might perhaps have become the model for a new socialist economy—a kind of proving ground—. . . but that did not come to pass." It was conceivable, I added, that rapprochement with the West "might lead to the erosion of Soviet society, which because it is such a closed one has not developed its own ideological immunity, and that this would mean a loss of control over the development of that society. . . . But the world is changing too swiftly for us to afford such a luxury as isolationism. The only important thing, really, is that this process of social modernization should flow from the traditions of our country and our system. The further the process of détente proceeds, the more attention will be paid by the governments and public opinion of the West not only to our foreign policy but to what is happening within the USSR." (Six years later, it became plain how correct my assessment had been.)

I concluded by saying that I wanted to promote rapprochement with the West. Kolomiychenko offered a few criticisms. I had capitalized the words "Democratic Movement," whereas I should have used lower-case letters. I had been mistaken about nationalism; relations among the peoples of the Soviet Union were good. I had called Marxism "old-fashioned"; but one should not and could not, all that simply, give up one ideology for another. The tone of my memorandum was too pedagogical.

So I made a few changes, using the soft pedal here and there. As for the tone, I told Kolomiychenko that whereas he was apparently used to writing reports to his superiors, I was accustomed to teaching my wife, so that naturally our styles were different.

He sent the memo off to Moscow. A month later it was returned with the comment that I should be sentenced to a new term for it.

A few months before my attempt at a dialogue with the regime, another one had been made—one that was similar in its attitude toward ideology but opposite in that it counseled salvation through isolationism—and had likewise got a mute No as an answer. I refer to Solzhenitsyn's "Letter to the Soviet Leaders," which was published abroad in the spring of 1974, about the same time that I was writing my own "letter to the leaders."

After I had gone abroad, whenever I was asked about my attitude toward Solzhenitsyn, I would reply that I had a high opinion of him as an individual, since he had staunchly opposed an inhuman system, that I esteemed him as a writer, but that I did not agree with him as an ideologue. This schema is a bit forced, since Solzhenitsyn's opposition to the regime is indivisible from his books, just as his books are part and parcel of his ideology. And yet it is generally accurate, since Solzhenitsyn was first a fighter, then a writer, and only later an ideologue.

Quite by accident, I was one of the first to read *One Day in the Life of Ivan Denisovich*—about six months before it was published—and I have a distinct recollection of the single-spaced typewritten text on both sides of each sheet of paper. I could see that the author was talented; but his novella struck me as just another of those neo-populist tales that abounded in the literary magazines, except of course that the subject of life in prison camps was not suitable for such publications. But I was mistaken in thinking that Solzhenitsyn was a populist writer. When I read his novels, I realized how much more scope he had. And yet, in everything he has written, one finds the indelible imprint of provincialism. He thought that:

> . . . *with his provincial language, he would bring*
> *all the fantastic, unimaginable*

movement of human life into
a state of harmony and clarity.[17]

In some ways, he reminds me of Zverev. Solzhenitsyn possesses not only talent but culture, a great capacity for work, and a tremendous strength of will. Yet, like Zverev, he lacks a critical attitude toward himself: his creativity plainly prevails over his selectivity.

With the publication of *Ivan Denisovich,* Solzhenitsyn became famous overnight. But it was with the "nonpublication" of his big novels that he began really to acquire tremendous significance. *Ivan Denisovich* had come as a shock, but it was still within the framework of current policy. Now, however, this writer who had been "for" was "against"—the most honorable position for a writer.

For a long time I thought that the authorities could have tamed Solzhenitsyn, bargaining for cuts in *Cancer Ward* and publishing some of the chapters from *The First Circle,* in return for which he would have made some concessions. But I was wrong; a clash was inevitable. The authorities might have postponed it by using kid gloves, but they could not have prevented it. Indeed, even during his honeymoon with the authorities, Solzhenitsyn had ready at hand his secret weapon: *The Gulag Archipelago.*

With the appearance of *The Archipelago,* the world paid heed for the first time to a member of that generation that, so it seemed, would pass away unnoted. And among the Soviet authorities, something was shattered. I was expecting pensioners to publish statements saying that in the past they had suffered, but that now everything was splendid—so why give the enemy these distressing pages to leaf through? But the newspapers were full of hysterics. And when Colonel Tarasov talked to me about *The Archipelago,* his hands trembled.

I read every volume straight through, I reread them, and I shall reread them. But I myself had been in prison, and not many people will read them in the same spirit as I did.

Solzhenitsyn's failure to be selective is evident in those passages where he tries to write about historical matters at the same high emotional pitch he maintains in writing about personal experiences. Hence he strikes notes that are not really false, but slightly off. Moreover, he makes no attempt to understand the other side. With him, evil remains unexplained: it is merely condemned and thus remains insurmountable.

I was really upset by Solzhenitsyn's remark that the occupation of Czechoslovakia had gone unprotested because he, Shostakovich, and other famous people had remained silent. But what of the Red Square demonstration on August 25? Did it fail to qualify as a protest because the demonstrators were such unknowns as Dremlyug and Babitsky instead of the world-famous

Solzhenitsyn and Shostakovich? And what if, at the time of the incursion into Hungary in 1956, a protest had come, not from Shostakovich (which in any case is unthinkable) but from an unknown schoolteacher from Ryazan named Solzhenitsyn? Would that protest have had no moral force? Would it simply not have taken place? The "hierarchy of protests" is all too reminiscent of the kind of thinking typical of Mother Russia: if people didn't differ in rank, how would you know whom to serve first at the table?

Solzhenitsyn's fame gave him new strength for the struggle. True, he didn't march in demonstrations, he didn't sign petitions, and he didn't speak out in defense of anyone (except Zhores Medvedev). But he didn't have to do those things: his books were enough. That a writer should become a symbol of resistance was something traditional for Russia; it offered hope after the moral decline of the "Soviet writers." When Solzhenitsyn was charged with being a political leader, he replied, "What? A writer and a leader of the political opposition?" He was a leader of the *moral* opposition, which is why everyone saw in him what that person himself believed. The defenders of human rights regarded him as a defender of human rights; the writers, an enemy of censorship; the religious believers, a fighter for religion; the neo-Slavophiles, a representative of the "Russian spirit"; the Georgians and Armenians, a defender of national minorities; the gradualists, a gradualist ready to use suasion on the authorities; and the radicals, a radical who rejected compromise. So long as he expressed his views through his novels, he was everything to everybody. All those against the regime could say, with equal justice: he is one of us. Even ideologically, Solzhenitsyn belonged to everybody. He began, in his youth, with orthodox Marxism. He went through all the phases of ideology—revisionism, liberalism, populism, etc.—and finally ended up on the right wing of Slavophilism. And he shows the effects of that journey: he is covered all over with ideological scars and bruises.

But when he moved from the position of an artist to that of an ideologue, he could not for long continue to satisfy everybody. And since his prestige was great and no one wanted to break with him, he began to lop off his supporters. It was then that the crest he had been riding began to sink, though not right away. I was put off when he said that the Democratic Movement was "shrill" and was demanding "merely freedom." For Solzhenitsyn, freedom is a temporary condition needed to build a society that is ideal without freedom. For me freedom is the highest goal of life. I exist so long as I am free, so long as I have the right to choose.

Solzhenitsyn's "Letter to the Soviet Leaders" reminded me, above all, of Lenin's *The State and Revolution*—the same way of excluding all doubts or questions concerning whatever the author himself believes; the same way of substituting parts for the whole in describing one's ideal; the same disdain for the question of how that ideal can be attained. Solzhenitsyn writes that he is ready to withdraw his proposals if someone comes forward, "not with witty criticism but . . . a better way out." This is the Russian "all or nothing": let's get rid of "all-explaining" Marxism and embrace "all-explaining" Russian Orthodoxy. Yet among the things he has to say, one is more likely to agree with his witty criticisms. Indeed, it is hard not to agree with them. That reliance on steady economic growth will lead us into a dead end is something that many have come to realize. There is much charm in Solzhenitsyn's romantic conservatism: I myself have nostalgic memories of a Moscow with streetcars and clean air. I certainly agree as to the dangers of gigantism, and I repeat after Solzhenitsyn and Schumacher: "Small is beautiful." But, given the existing competition in the world, it is hardly possible to stop technological growth.

I have tried to keep tabs on Solzhenitsyn's travels, and I am in full agreement with what he has said about the lack of political purposefulness in the West. But I believe he is addressing himself not so much to the West as to fellow inmates of the 1940s. It matters much that, after a quarter-century, the voice of that generation be heard. But the world, after all, did not stand still while Rip van Winkle was sleeping. And it can hardly be said that that world is a black-and-white one, that communism is the only source of evil, or that the best way to combat dictatorship is to gauge which is preferable, right-wing or left-wing dictatorship. Authoritarianism is always more bearable than totalitarianism, and the degree of freedom in Franco's Spain was much greater than it is in Brezhnev's Russia. But are we entitled, on those grounds, to tell the Spaniards they shouldn't be in too much of a hurry to achieve democracy? We keep telling everybody that "we have it worse," without the faintest realization that they may reply, "If our problems mean nothing to you, why do you insist that *we* understand *you*?" Indeed, some Ugandan might well say, "What are you complaining about? They put you in prison for a few years, where you had food and drink, and then threw you out of the country. But in Uganda they smash your skull with a hammer or throw you to the crocodiles."

"As you know better than I do, the industrial importance of the Soviet Northeast is constantly growing," I wrote in 1974, to Shaidurov, the first secretary of the Magadan *Obkom*. The KGB people, after having returned my "exposition of my views" to me with a warning about a new term, had by no means let me off the hook. I still had one year of exile to serve. And so, in accordance with my tactic of putting on the brakes, I proposed, by way of compromise, that I write a series of articles about the economic development of the

Magadan Oblast. (Also, of course, I wanted to travel around Kolyma as much as possible.)

Shaidurov said there was "nothing objectionable in taking advantage" of my suggestion "in order to benefit the cause" and asked that it be cleared with the CC CPSU and the KGB. (Incidentally, "benefit" is a favorite Soviet word. When I told Academician Shilo that I followed the Jewish ethical rule, "Do not do unto another person what you would not want him to do unto you," he replied, "Our rule is to benefit society and thereby to receive benefits from society.")

It took a month to get the clearance from Moscow. They decided, as Comrade Stalin taught, "not to neglect little things." I was to begin with one article for the local paper, *Magadan pravda,* and then they would see. Choosing a subject for that article was something that occupied Kolomiychenko and me for a long time. Gold could not be discussed because information about it was "classified." Fishing was a hazardous subject (he was always complaining about Japanese fishermen). Finally we settled on energy. At that point I recalled that the KGB had "coded" my trial as a "conference of power engineers."

We decided I should visit the construction of the Kolyma dam, the Bilibino nuclear plant, the Magadan Thermoelectric Power Station, and the Magadan Energy Administration's offices. On paper, my trip was designated as a field assignment for the institute, which paid the expenses. The UVD gave me permission to "leave his place of exile," and even authorized a flight to Chukotka, which was off limits as a border region.

Early in July, accompanied by a gebist energy engineer assigned to "help me," I flew to the settlement for the workers building the Kolyma dam.

The chief of the KGB's local department, who had spent his whole life in one god-forsaken hole after another, told me: "The great thing about Kolyma is that there are music schools in every raion."

His daughter was attending a music school, his wife had been graduated from one, and he himself had studied at one for a year or two. I don't know whether he played the flute, but he could have organized a family orchestra. I remember his telling me how to trap chipmunks. You put some nuts into a cage with an open door. The chipmunk goes into the cage, fills both cheeks with nuts, and then can't get out because he doesn't want to let go of the nuts. In underworld slang this would be expressed as: "Greed killed the pigeon."

Yury Frishter, construction superintendent for the dam, was quick of movement, with the kind of manners one necessarily acquires when he has to boss twenty-five hundred people.

He was a good specialist, but as a hard-driving Soviet manager, he had only the vaguest notion of economics. I seriously doubt whether the Soviet economy would be restored to health if the managers were allowed a completely free hand. They are unhappy about Party tutelage. But the Party relieves them of the problem of dealing with workers and of the necessity of thinking about economic feasibility. Thus Frishter, as a great believer in hydroelectric stations, was of the opinion that "the production of electric power is as cheap as the production of vodka."

To get to the site of the future dam, we took a motor-launch up the Kolyma River, so that I not only saw the Kolyma, I dipped my hand in it. Whoever has been in the Soviet North will never forget its incomparable beauty. There is, indeed, something exciting about pioneering these tremendous wide-open spaces.

From Magadan we flew to Bilibino, the center of the gold-mining industry in Chukotka, to inspect a nuclear power plant. After the long flight, I asked the chief of the KGB's *raiotdel* where I could find a toilet. With an understanding smile he led me out of the building. We crossed the street and walked for two or three blocks, then made a turn, and he pointed to a tumbledown hut. Inside, it was even more horrible than the privy at the penal camp. Colonel Tarasov told me that Chukotka was called "the land of eternal half-crapping." Year after year, the local inhabitants use outhouses in the below-zero weather, and the incidence of disease is very high, especially among the women. A friend of mine was telling some Siberians on a kolkhoz that in Moscow there are buildings thirty stories high. They listened, all ears, until finally a shrewd peasant said: "The way I figure it, you're feeding us a line, buddy. If people live thirty stories up, how do they get outside in a hurry when they have to shit?"

In any case, the architects' plans for the apartment buildings intended to house the workers at the Kolyma dam project included electric heating but no indoor toilets, so Frishter ordered his own chief engineer to provide a toilet for each apartment.

The settlement of Bilibino, which lies within the Arctic Circle, had a depressing effect on me. It was hard to believe that it had been founded only fifteen years before. Filth, barracks, bunk beds—no wonder a local bum was able to sell a morgue with a corpse in it to a man who needed a house. The five-story apartment houses erected on the permafrost had round foundations instead of being built on pilings. As a result, they have begun to sink, and the cracks in the walls are big enough to see through.

The power plant itself is of small capacity, and was built primarily for purposes of prestige. The "technological heat"—i.e., 80 per cent of the output—is wasted, although it could be used to heat homes and greenhouses.

I gave my article a journalistic title, "From Wood to the Uranium Nucleus" and sent it to two experts: Serov, chief engineer of the Kolyma project, and Kolomiychenko, chief of the Magadan UKGB.

"I liked your article," Serov told me. "It's written in an interesting way; it makes sense; and it shows an understanding of the subject, as if it had been written by a power engineer. I think it will be very useful to executives at all levels, and to the workers in this area."

Kolomiychenko gave the article an even higher rating and had no criticisms to offer. He did suggest mentioning the fact that the Kolyma project was built in accordance with a resolution passed at the 24th Congress of the CPSU. "If," he said, "you don't want to mention the CPSU on your own, you can put the words into the mouth of one of your characters. You can have Frishter say, for example, 'Our construction project was initiated in accordance with a directive from . . .,' etc."

Such was the artistic approach suggested by Kolomiychenko, and I saw no objection to it.

The offices of *Magadan pravda,* located in the *obkom* building, were very modest. Bogdanov, the chief of the newspaper's ideological section, greeted me cautiously. My general impression was that I had passed from the realm of the living into the realm of the dead. The construction workers constructed, the power plant workers produced power, and the gebists sniffed out sedition—all of them were in contact with reality. But the people in the newspaper office lived in a world of imaginary numbers. They seriously debated such questions as to whether to call a column "Pathfinders of the Line of Defense" or "The Line of Defense—Pathfinders." Ideology is ballast—not only ideological ballast but that of the human variety as well. If, for example, the Soviet Union were to throw off the shackles of totalitarianism, the Communist Frishter would go on building dams, the Communist Shilo would go on with his geology, and the Communist Kolomiychenko, when passions had cooled, would find something to do with the police or in an intelligence service. But who would need the millions of Communist ideologues, and what would they need them for? They, more than anyone else, have an interest in seeing that a dead calm prevails, that nothing changes.

When Bogdanov returned the edited article to me, I clutched my head in my hands in sheer desperation: the editors had almost completely rewritten it in their own style. We quarreled for several days, until finally I slammed the door and left. Then Kolomiychenko sent Eliseyev to push the article through, and to keep me in check.

The people on the newspaper were not happy about the fact that I kept mentioning Frishter: there was some friction between him and the *raikom,* and besides, Frishter was a Jew. In two passages I agreed to change "Frishter pointed out to me" to "it was pointed out to me." But with respect to another personage, I refused to yield. Nor was there any suspicion that the other person was Jewish: she was the Kievan Princess Olga, one of the first Russian saints. About her I had written: "Because as early as the 10th century, Saint Olga had ordered the construction of dams, she can rightfully be called a patron of hydroelectric power stations."

"We can't print that in a Party newspaper!" Bogdanov shouted.

The acting editor-in-chief, Sorokoumov, mumbled like Demosthenes with too many stones in his mouth. As an experienced bureaucrat, he had long avoided meeting me, until finally I said I wondered what kind of person the editor was, since every toad (as in the fable) wants to swell up until he becomes the size of an ox.

When the first part of the article was already in pageproofs, I noticed the whole thing was signed not "Andrei Amalrik" but "A. Amalrik."

"We print the full name only when the author is a member of the Writers' Union," Bogdanov told me. "Even articles by the first secretary of the *obkom* are signed 'S. A. Shaidurov' and not 'Sergei Afanasyevich Shaidurov.'"

"I don't care how Shaidurov signs his articles," I said. "I sign all my articles and books 'Andrei Amalrik.'"

They let me have my "Andrei," deferring the matter of Olga and other questions. Meantime, the moment for putting the pageproofs on Shaidurov's desk was drawing near, and Sorokoumov was frantic. I made no more concessions, and at the last minute the article was killed. Or at any rate it was killed "temporarily," since it was sent "for clearance" to the *obkom* secretaries for industry and ideology, and then to Moscow. It was plain to see, however, that the "Party press" had won this battle with the "glorious organs" and that the article would not be printed.

In the fall of 1974 there was a shift at the top toward a harsher policy. About this time, Kolomiychenko told me that the article could be published only if prefaced by an editor's note saying that I had repudiated all my former views. I replied that I wouldn't authorize anyone to write such a prefatory note, and for the first time in any of our talks we grew irritated with each other. As he said later, I produced two weapons that I had been concealing. First, I reminded him that the KGB had not kept its promise to release me. Second, it had shown that it lacked clout, since it hadn't managed to get the article published. Kolomiychenko, very upset, tried to explain that away by saying that neither Shaidurov nor the editor-in-chief had been in Magadan at the time.

I had heard on the Voice of America that Brezhnev had been ill. And so, toward the end of our talk, I said boastfully that Brezhnev would soon die, and then the people who had been forcing others to repent would have to do some repenting themselves. A few days later Kolomiychenko triumphantly showed me a report that Brezhnev, in good health, had appeared at a reception.

"And do you know who spread those dirty rumors about the illness of the much-respected Leonid Ilich?" I asked. As Kolomiychenko hung on my every word, I said, "It was your former chief, Shelepin. How nasty people can be!" I concluded, using Zverev's tactic.

Kolomiychenko gave Eliseyev the unpleasant job of "pressuring" me. And once Eliseyev went so far as to promise that he would get down on his knees before me if I could "find the courage" to repudiate my books. However much as I was tempted by the prospect of a KGB officer genuflecting before me, I refused.

In January 1975, four months before the end of my term of exile, Kolomiychenko proposed that I request an exit visa for Israel. He said that if I did, I could take a plane for there directly from Magadan within two weeks.

"In the first place," I told him, "I have no intention of going there. In the second place, my wife is a Moslem who even has some Arab blood. So at the very least, we have to wait until Yasir Arafat conquers Palestine."

"But the trip to Israel would be only for the sake of appearances," he said. "It's easier for the MVD to get you an exit visa that way. Later on, you can go wherever you want to. Why waste your time here? You can buy a couple of cars, and go to nightclubs."

Kolomiychenko's pet fantasy was obvious. In retrospect, I find that conversation amusing, because when I left Russia I did in fact buy two cars. And I even went to a nightclub in Frankfurt that featured striptease dancers. Not only that, but following the example of Dmitry Karamazov, I bought champagne for the whores and we drank a toast to the health of the chief of the Magadan KGB—I imagine Kolomiychenko will be pleased to learn that.

As for the striptease itself, it had a demoralizing effect on me. When a woman on a stage shows you her G-string with pubic hairs sticking out, it destroys not only the element of human relations but any trace of mystery. That striptease act reminded me of nothing so much as American TV commercials and Soviet Socialist Realism; and the impersonality of both corresponds very well to the spirit of communism.

Kolomiychenko made it sufficiently plain that if I did not agree either to leave the country or to repudiate my books, I would get a third sentence.

When I was already halfway out the door, I said, "Oh, yes. I have a favor to ask of you. I'd like to see a film called 'The Spiderweb.'"

"Has it been screened for our colleagues?" Kolomiychenko asked Eliseyev. "Then let's arrange for a screening and invite Andrei Alekseyevich."

"I think it will be most edifying," I said.

This KGB film about ideological saboteurs had been shown at meetings of Party activists from Magadan to Moscow, and I played one of the leading roles in it. It included clips from Cole's interview with me, the visit from Bernard Gwertzman, myself at my trial, and the French journalist showing me his car. Eliseyev said later, however, that as an unrepentant person I was not worthy of seeing such a fine film.

"You never had such a tranquil life before," Boris Tarasov once said to me, and he was right. But as the end of my term of exile drew near, I became more and more nervous. I wasn't ruling out the possibility of a third sentence, and I realized that even if I were released, my troubles wouldn't be over.

I was told I wouldn't get an internal passport right away; that the UVD's administrative section would give me back the document certifying that I had been released, which I would then turn in to the passport section, after which I would have to wait "for a few days." This meant that my exile would be extended for an indefinite length of time, and there would be new opportunities to "pressure" me. Kolomiychenko tried to reassure me, saying that it was an unimportant bureaucratic problem and that after five years, five days was nothing. But, as he himself said, "the burnt child fears the fire." So I decided not to pick up my passport in Magadan.

A week before the end of my term, Gusel flew to Moscow so as to be able to stir up some activity in the unlikely event that I was arrested, or in the very likely event that I was detained because I didn't have a passport.

On May 6, 1975, my first day of "freedom," I refused to accept the document certifying that I had been released and had served out my term of exile, and I turned in the document issued me in lieu of a passport. Thus I became, in all likelihood, the only person in the USSR with no papers.

"It wasn't enough that they dumped you into our laps," MVD Colonel Pomykalkin said to me. "Now you're giving us trouble even after your release. I don't know how you're going to fly to Moscow without a passport."

The way things turned out, I would guess that Kolomiychenko wanted to get rid of me as quickly as possible and not stir up unnecessary trouble. In any case, on May 7, I had my last talk with him.

"Andrei Alekseyevich," he said, "May 12 is your birthday, isn't it? I wish you a happy birthday in advance and promise you that on that day you will be home in Moscow."

CHAPTER 24

Moscow

Early on the morning of May 12, my plane landed at the same airport near Moscow, Domodedovo, to which I had been taken under guard two years and eight months before. Now I was returning as a free man.

En route we had touched down at Krasnoyarsk, where I saw a group of men I took to be zeks: shaven heads, poorly dressed, with haunted eyes and a look of exhaustion and resignation. But except for two officers, there were no guards.

"Are they 'chemists'?" I asked.

"No, they're army recruits on their way to duty in Siberia."

Moscow greeted me with a marvelous scent: the grass was coming up in all the meadows. But when we went through the empty streets in a taxi, I felt only once or twice that excitement one usually feels when coming home. And when we drove along Okhotnyi Row, past the ugly Stalinesque buildings, I felt only hostility.

Scarcely had I sat down to breakfast, after catching a bit of sleep, when in came a tearful old woman. I didn't recognize her, and yet I had a vague recollection of having seen her somewhere. Then I remembered Ubozhko's mother, who had once advised her son to "get all that rubbish out of your head." She told me Ubozhko had been transferred from a prison psychiatric hospital to a regular one in western Siberia and that he had been placed on work gangs with psychotics at a macaroni factory. Once, when there was an urgent need for someone to give lectures on the international situation, the factory director asked Ubozhko, as a former lecturer, to take on the assignment. Despite his status as an antisovetchik and a madman, he did the job very well, until a new case was brought against him—under Article 190-1, as before. When he protested that he had been found mentally incompetent, the investigator told him he had feigned insanity so that he could infiltrate the hospital and stir up trouble among the patients.

In July I had word that Ubozhko was in Moscow; that just before his trial was to take place, he had escaped from the hospital and had been in hiding for a month. But I was afraid to meet with him: I had reason to fear that the KGB had planned his escape. He was soon rearrested, and I heard no more of him.

"How long are you going to keep leading us around by the nose?" KGB Major Pustyakov, whom I had already met in Magadan, asked me. "We'll give you a month to think it over. Either write a repudiation of your books, and we'll publish it in *Trud* along with your article, or request an exit visa for Israel, and we'll get you out of the country in two weeks, or . . ." At this point he spread his hands and looked at me: what would happen in the third case was too obvious to require an explanation.

The KGB now had a new weapon: the "residence permit," or authorization by the police to reside in one place or another. I had been counting on getting one, since all residents of Moscow convicted under Article 190-1 had, upon their return from camp or exile, been given temporary residence permits, and some had even obtained permanent ones. But what I received instead, shortly after my return, was a notification from the local police station that I was to leave the city within three days.

But it was with a view to just such a decree that Gusel and I had bought our house in the country back in 1968 and had had our belongings sent there from Magadan. So we went to Ryazan to pick up the crate containing our things and have it transported to Akulovo, where I could register as a resident. We had trouble from the beginning: I had a receipt in my name, but I didn't possess a passport. Not only that, but there were no trucks available at the transportation office. But I had my Polaroid as an aid in smoothing out human relations. And the sight of the instantly produced snapshots so amazed the clerks at the office that they found a truck and let me have my crate even without a passport.

Once in the truck, we drove for a long time, taking one wrong side road after another, and the driver began to get nervous. Then, as night started to fall, we saw some familiar fields, with trees along the stream, in the distance; in a surge of joy and excitement, I caught sight of our home.

"I must say, that's a strange-looking house," said the driver of the truck.

But it was no longer a house—only four brick walls. Everything else was gone: the roof, the floor, the beams and rafters and window frames, the lean-to, and the stove. No furniture was left. There was no sign of a fire, and robbery was out of the question, since a thief wouldn't have taken the roof away with him, ripped up the half-rotten floorboards, or made off with the stove. Someone had done a long, thorough job of wrecking our home so as to make it quite unhabitable, and it wasn't hard to guess who that someone was. (Not long afterward, the home of the friends with whom we had stayed in June was burned to the ground.)

Since we couldn't very well just spread out a rug under the nearest bush, Gusel suggested we give everything to the truck driver. "After all," she said, "we can't live here any longer."

The young driver, who apparently had never been involved in such a transaction before, was frightened by the gift. "But where am I going to put everything? My room isn't as big as this container."

On our way to Mikhailova, I threw the keys to the house in the ditch. In Mikhailova we boarded that same slow night train that had brought us there from Moscow seven years before. A certain cycle in our life had been completed.

Gusel saw the hand of God in everything that had happened to us: it was His Will that we leave the country. I realized that sooner or later I'd be sent back to prison; and in the meantime, life on the outside was being made unbearable. We wanted to work in peace on our books and paintings. We wanted to see the world, to go abroad. And yet it is very painful to leave one's own country—if not forever, then for a long, indefinite period. And for a writer it is especially hard.

In 1976, in Amsterdam, my old acquaintance Leonid Chertkov reminded me that ten years before, everyone had laughed at my prediction that the authorities would soon be sending people not only to Siberia but out of the country. Deportation is one of the oldest forms of political punishment. It was not in vogue in the USSR during the period when millions were being repressed, since the authorities wanted to conceal that fact from the rest of the world. But in a period of selective repressions and public protest within the country, a return to the use of expulsion made sense. It did not contravene the principles of the closed society, since a deported person, although he could stir up trouble abroad, could not do so in the USSR. After a quarter-century, a balance had been reached at the top between the neo-Stalinists and the moderates. The top people like to feel secure, and it is better to tolerate a certain amount of opposition within the country than to be sucked again into the maelstrom of terror. The thing to do, then, is to combat the opposition by means of selective methods: by frightening some of them, by locking up others in prisons and psychiatric hospitals, by killing and beating up others, by getting others fired from their jobs, and by expelling still others from the country. There was an element of chance in all this; but then not everyone could be expelled. Indeed, the idea of deportation did not catch on quickly among the seventy-year-old dullards at the top. ("*What*? Let that enemy get away from us?'') But they were finally persuaded by those who realized that it was essential to have a safety valve if the regime wanted to avoid an increase in protests on the one hand, or a return to the Stalinist meat grinder on the other.

But the regime would not have been true to itself if it had started deporting its opponents in the same way as any authoritarian regime. A regime that elects a deputy from a list of one candidate, that compels prisoners to "thank" it for their arrest, that calls the occupation of an allied country "brotherly aid" and, when it raises prices, rationalizes that move as a "request" from the consumers—such a regime must necessarily package expulsion so that it appears to be voluntary departure.

To the bureaucratic mind, two options seemed open: the dissident could leave the country in response to an invitation from abroad, with subsequent "deprivation of citizenship for actions incompatible with the title of Soviet citizen"; or he could go abroad "for permanent residence."

The first option, however, had two shortcomings in the eyes of the authorities. Sometimes it meant that the expellee was accorded the status of a writer, a scientist, or an artist, whereas the regime wanted the dissident regarded as "a person without a definite occupation." And in each individual case, deprivation of citizenship required a decree from the Presidium of the USSR Supreme Soviet. Now, there is a certain quota for everything (even on black caviar for covert distributors), and apparently the KGB had a specific quota on those it could deport in that way.

The second way, whereby a person's expulsion was camouflaged as voluntary emigration, was much more convenient for the KGB. Indeed, the very fact of deportation is obscured by the circumstance that hundreds of thousands of Soviet citizens desire to emigrate (although most of them cannot), so that expulsion seems not so much a punishment as a humanitarian act—even a concession on the part of the regime. The criteria for authorizing emigration are based on ethnicity and kinship: Jews are allowed to emigrate to Israel, and Germans to Germany. It is Jewish emigration that provides the most convenient cover for expulsion: Israel immediately grants citizenship to new repatriates, so that they are automatically deprived of Soviet citizenship. Also, dissidents who emigrate—and, thus, dissidents in general—can be characterized within the country as Jews.

I had no objection to an exit visa for Israel and would have been grateful to Israel for such a visa, if I had wanted to leave the USSR for good. But, as I have already said, I wished to leave under circumstances that would not rule out the possibility of returning, rather than under those proposed by the KGB—in any case, not within a month. I had received invitations from three universities: Harvard, George Washington, and Utrecht. So I wrote OVIR asking what documents my wife and I would need to go abroad for a year. In response, I was told that OVIR did not consider any invitations from instititions to a Soviet citizen—only requests for visas based on invitations from private persons—and that the universities should send their invitations via the appropriate Soviet organizations. I even paid a visit to the foreign section of the USSR Ministry of Higher Education. But all these demarches proved to be as senseless as my talks with bureaucrats about money six years before. I wrote to the U.S. President and the Prime Minister of Holland, saying that a refusal to consider an invitation to a Soviet citizen was a violation of the Helsinki accords. Prime Minister Iop Den Uyl mentioned the matter in parliament, but I had no hope for response from President Ford.

My disenchantment with détente was severely aggravated during my first months in Moscow. Of course, the growth of military technology and of instability throughout the world were incentives for both the West and the USSR (with one foot in "the rich men's club," while making friendly gestures toward the poor) to seek agreement. It seems to me, however, that for the U.S. the chief motive for détente was frustration after the defeat in Vietnam, while for Western Europe it was fear arising from the Soviet occupation of Czechoslovakia. Among politicians, the type who became most popular in those days was the "realist" whose creed was, "If you can't lick 'em, join 'em." (My own belief, though, is that accommodation is the lowest form of realism and that changing reality to fit one's own goals is the highest form. When in the West, I am reproached with being unrealistic, I remember that "fink" who said of me, "He doesn't know the realities of life; he doesn't want to cooperate with the bosses.") But if the West was motivated by fear, the USSR—the initiator of "the peace offensive"—was nudged toward détente by something more than the fear of China. The West has always been a stabilizing factor for the Soviet system: the existence of an ideological enemy has justified the former's aggressiveness and repressions, while the West's technological achievements have served as a stimulus to Soviet economic development: the USSR had to "overtake and surpass," as the Stalinist slogan had it. If the West reaches a point of technological stagnation, development in the USSR will come to a halt. The idea of socialism involves the cessation of development, since the goal will have been achieved. In détente, the USSR saw not only an opportunity to avoid internal reforms with the help of Western credits, technology, and grain, but a chance to weaken the ties among the Western countries.

It would be trite to say that the will to victory is stronger than a will to maintain the status quo. It is plain to see how a strong "policy of will" drives Soviet military technology forward, whereas in the U.S. the military-industrial complex has to drag politicians along behind it. Although Henry Kissinger underestimated the importance of ideology, as far back as twenty years ago he understood very well the military and political factors accounting for the USSR's advantage over the West. Yet it was he who became the most consistent in personifying the West's will (which might rather be called a lack of will) to preserve the status quo. And what détente boiled down to was that the USSR had to be bought off so that it would not aggravate the world situation.

But if the West undertook not to cause trouble within the Soviet bloc, the USSR took no corresponding obligation upon itself. This led to a sequence of situations, each of which was recognized by the West as the status quo but was, even more than the situation that had preceded it, favorable to the USSR. For example, Kissinger did some loud saber-rattling in opposing any accession to power by the Italian Communists. But if they should come into power, he would of course avoid conflict with them, since that would be a violation of the new status quo. It is no wonder that he is so hostile toward the dissidents, who in fact offer the West a chance to change Soviet policies. The democratization of the Soviet system is the only guarantee of security for the West. So long as questions of war and peace are decided by ten men who are not accountable to anyone, no accords, however favorable on paper, will allow the Americans and Europeans a good night's sleep.

Kissinger has been compared to Metternich, the ideal practitioner of a policy aimed at preventing any change whatsoever. As Danilevsky wrote in *Russia and Europe,* in the nineteenth century Austria-Hungary had become a political corpse; and the only way to prevent its rapid decomposition was not to allow the slightest breeze to stir. Metternich did prolong the existence of Austria-Hungary, but with the result that its final fall was a most frightful one. But is the West so much of a corpse that Kissinger must use an undertaker's skill to preserve it? There is something childish in the Americans' attitude toward the USSR, although there is something senile in the attitude of the Western Europeans. I'm not at all sure that this military alliance between a kindergarten and an old folks' home could restrain the Soviet Union if the latter did not have grave domestic problems and China behind its back.

Détente is helping to determine what values will prevail in the world order now taking shape, and it frightens me to see how easily the USSR has managed to impose on the West its way of conducting relations. The most dramatic example of this was President Ford's unwillingness to invite Solzhenitsyn to the White House for fear of angering Brezhnev. At the time of his expulsion, Solzhenitsyn symbolized freedom and human dignity; yet the president of a great country was afraid to meet with him in his own home. President Carter, on the other hand, did decide to invite Vladimir Bukovsky, only just released from a Soviet prison, to the White House. He did not, however, invite him personally, but delegated that duty to the vice-president. And he permitted no photographs to be taken, as if the meeting were one among conspirators. What had been conceived as symbolic thus symbolized nothing more than the president's indecisiveness.

I read in *Izvestiya* that my friend Jack Madlock had been reassigned to the American Embassy in Moscow. I had made his acquaintance fifteen years before, when he was on the staff of the consular section of the embassy. Six months later I was picked up by KGB agents near his home and taken to the Lubyanka, where two investigators began to question me: "On such and such a date you left Madlock's home in the company of the hardened American intelligence agent Kerst. What did you talk about?"

I remember I had once walked a short distance with Mr. and Mrs. Kerst, and they complained that their bulldog was always urinating on the floor. Not wanting to conceal anything from our "glorious organs," I replied that we had talked about a dog that urinated on the floor.

"*What?* Do you think you can get by with insulting the organs?" both of them shouted at once.

They concluded the interrogation by suggesting I give them a statement saying that I had been subjected to "subversive brainwashing" by Madlock. That would have been sufficient grounds for expelling him from the country, which would have ended his career as a diplomat in the USSR. I won't pretend that I wasn't afraid. There was not yet any dissident movement or public exposure of illegality; everyone still had vivid memories of the days when, if you were taken to a KGB office, you might not come out. And yet I did not inform on Madlock, and told him the whole story.

He was frightened when I phoned him—now perhaps even more frightened than I had been that day fifteen years ago when I was picked up by the KGB. And he refused to meet with me. If I had followed the remarkable logic of "national interests," I should have written a denunciation on him at the very beginning.

The journalists were more independent, although you could see that they, too, were afraid of accidentally offending the Soviet government. In a few of them, that feeling of compassion that enables one human being to understand the pain of another was well developed. And those reporters, setting aside their political preferences and never losing their critical sense, had a better understanding of the dissidents' problems than did their colleagues with a cynical or purely speculative approach.

After he met us, Peter Osnos of the Washington *Post* graciously said that he wanted to invite us to dinner. Since I was in hiding from the authorities and making only quick dashes into Moscow, we agreed that I would phone him when I was in town. The first time he told me that their housemaid's son had died. The second time he said that the printers at the *Post* were on strike, so that it was not a suitable time for the projected dinner. And the third time he was entertaining an important person from the U.S. Department of Agriculture who might be distressed if a Russian were among the guests. I decided that if Osnos ever invited me again, I would refuse. But I must give him credit: he never did.

He was forever saying, in person and in print, that the dissidents were indebted for their influence solely to the communications media, which exaggerated their importance. The amount of space given to them in Western newspapers, he said, should be proportionate to the space they occupied in Soviet society. But I don't know how he defined that space. If his premise was arithmetical, then in view of the fact that out of 250 million Soviet citizens there were only 250 known dissidents, the American press should devote to them only one-millionth of the information they published on the USSR. On the other hand, considering that the dissidents constituted one of the chief indicators of the ferment in Soviet society, and also one of the fermentation agents, I could have told Osnos what I once told Podolsky: "Lots of flour, and only a little yeast; but it's the yeast that makes the dough rise."

Osnos believed that the information the dissidents furnished on the USSR was of the kind that "the most disillusioned and persecuted" citizens of the U.S. would furnish on that country. But it was thanks to the dissidents that foreign correspondents were able to make the acquaintance of other segments of Soviet society. And it is hard to compare Andrei Sakharov or Yury Orlov with, say, the "American dissident" Johnny Harris, whom the Soviet press calls "a fighter for human rights" and who was indicted for rape, armed robbery, and murder.

I don't mean to say that in taking an "antidissident" stance, Osnos was guided by bad motives. Indeed, he even helped some dissidents. I suppose that, as an ambitious young journalist, he wanted to find his own approach to the Soviet scene and not follow a stereotype. But I believe he lacked faith in the individual and showed deference to organizations. This trait ran like a thread through his writings, beginning with his amazement that "such a small number of obscure private citizens in the most powerful totalitarian state" could have any influence at all, and ending with his preferring to dine with an official representing an organization than with a writer representing only himself. The dissidents, however, are inspired precisely by a belief in the ability of the individual to oppose the system. And we have seen how the fate of Anatoly Shcharansky, a "private citizen," aroused world public opinion, whereas the dismissal of Podgorny, the president of the most powerful totalitarian state, was forgotten in less than a month.

On August 15, 1973, on the twenty-sixth day of my hunger strike, *Literaturnaya gazeta* had published an article titled: "What Was Mr. Shaw Trying to Get?" John Shaw, a *Time* correspondent, had tried to obtain the details of my second trial. A TASS editor, Yury Kornilov, had explained to him—and to all of the paper's readers—that "a certain Amalrik . . . a dropout . . . engaged in speculation . . . sent anti-Soviet materials abroad at the request of the reactionary press . . . and during his sentence, continued to fabricate anti-Soviet falsifications and, through his wife, tried to send them abroad."

After I had returned to Moscow, I went to the offices of the *Literaturnaya gazeta* and asked Mikhail Maksimov, the editor in charge of the foreign department, why he printed such lies. I had not been charged with speculation, and I did not get my second term for "falsifications" sent abroad by my wife. I asked him to read the judgment in my case and then print a retraction. Maksimov said he had received the article from TASS, and he had complete faith in that organization. It would be better, he said, if I talked to Kornilov. He played the fox with me, and at the end of our conversation he asked, "What are *you* trying to get?" I replied that I was making the rounds of Soviet institutions and talking with functionaries so that later, when I wrote about them, I could make them look as idiotic as possible.

At the TASS offices, the guards wouldn't let me in. Kornilov was upset by my phone call. After checking with his bosses, he told me over the phone that it would make no sense for him to meet with me, and besides he didn't have the time for it.

"And yet you have time to write all kinds of rubbish, don't you?"

"It doesn't make sense. It doesn't make sense," Kornilov kept repeating, like a wound-up toy.

Yury Emanuilovich Kornilov, fifty years old, one of the few Jews publishing in top-level periodicals, is the Soviet government's mouthpiece for its most vicious attacks: on Academician Sakharov and on President Carter. I gathered information on Kornilov, but I managed only to file charges of libel against him and *Literaturnaya gazeta,* as codefendants, in the People's Court of Moscow's Dzerzhinski Raion. The bureaucratic machine spent ten weeks ingesting my complaint, and on December 26, 1975, I received the reply that "such action must be preceded by a preliminary investigation carried out by organs of the Prosecutor's Office."

I didn't have time to undertake all that; but I'm sure that if I had, the Prosecutor's Office would have replied, "There are no grounds for instituting proceedings against Comrade Kornilov."

The authorities' campaign against the dissidents had been preceded by the signing in Helsinki, on August 1, 1975, of the Final Act of the Conference on Security and Cooperation in Europe, which included articles dealing with human contacts and improvement in the dissemination, accessibility, and exchange of information. At this historic conference Prime Minister Den Uyl asked Brezhnev to let me come to Holland. He asked if they could have a ten-minute talk. Brezhnev replied that he was very tired, he was old, he had no time, and that there was no sense in having such a talk, but then he agreed to speak to Den Uyl the next day during the break. Since no break had been planned, Den Uyl asked the chairman to declare one. Brezhnev, however, said that he and Den Uyl had already had a talk, but if the Russians were known for their rudeness, the Dutch were known for stubbornness. Den Uyl persisted and began to discuss me, as Brezhnev grimaced. At this point Gromyko came up and began to explain to Den Uyl, in an affable way, that he was familiar with my case and knew that the Dutch thought it important. He said he would keep it under personal observation. Whereupon Brezhnev, furious, called Gromyko away.

I found out what "personal observation" by VIPs meant when I was routed out of my bed half-dressed; then dragged along our long hallway, just as I had once dragged a half-drunk painter along that same hallway; then down the stairs, as I had once been dragged in Magadan Prison; and finally hauled outside. Of course it wasn't Brezhnev and Gromyko who did this to me: it was some policemen and *druzhinniks* under the supervision of the district police inspector, Zabudryacv. I had known him when he was only a sergeant, but now he was a captain. He was not a bad person, and the necessity of having to harass people had worn him down: in ten years he had grown twenty years older. He was most unwilling to deal with my case, and people had even come from headquarters to make sure he was not avoiding his duty to expel me from Moscow. As a result, he was handling me very roughly.

As I waited at the precinct station, wearing only pajamas and socks, I realized bitterly that if there had been any changes during the years of my incarceration, they had been for the worse. The police brought in an old woman in black who had been arrested outside the Sierra Leone Embassy, where she had wanted to send letters on the subject of religious persecution; I can imagine how the Sierra Leoneans would have gaped at her if she had gone there. A doctor had been summoned to conduct the body search. (According to the regulations, male policemen are not supposed to search females, but there seems to be an assumption that a doctor is sexless.) Soon a doctor and two orderlies showed up and pounced on the woman, extracting from her bosom a letter and some printed prayers. She was put in a cell where, in an astoundingly beautiful voice, she began to chant prayers, as the policemen guffawed.

What a horrible country! I thought. And how desperate people are if their only way of seeking help is to go to a foreign embassy. And the kind of policemen we have! Jailing an old woman as a dangerous criminal. And the kind of doctors! Perfectly willing to play the role of prison warders. I would have to leave.

"Treat him a little rougher, so he'll ask to be sent to Israel sooner," the desk sergeant said to a fat-faced man in civilian clothes. I don't know whether I heard this by accident, or whether I was supposed to hear it; but hear it I did.

I refused to sign the notification that I was to leave the city, and they kept me in jail overnight. The next time I could be arrested and sentenced to one year. Henceforth it would be dangerous to lack a passport and to stay on at our place on Vakhtangov Street. (I had resided there up to that point only because of my faith in Gromyko's good intentions.) We had rented a separate apartment on the outskirts of Moscow where we could live secretly; and now I had to get a passport and register as a resident of a neighboring oblast. On a map I found the nearest railroad station outside Moscow, and I went there.

Vorsino Station was empty of people. To the left, black plowed fields, already damp from the autumn rains, stretched away as far as the eye could see. To the right were the station barracks and a small stand of stunted trees along the embankment. After some hesitation, I turned and went in that direction, hoping that the path along the edge of the grove would lead to a village. I had not even gone two miles when I came upon a big village. Sitting in front of her house, and watching the road curiously, was a fat peasant woman in a shawl.

"Do you know anyone who could rent me a room with a residence permit?"

"With a permit?" She understood right away: I wasn't "the first, or the last." There are many Muscovite ex-convicts in all the oblasts around Moscow, and a kind of underground has developed in those regions. People who actually work in Moscow and live there in concealment with their wives or mothers rent rooms in those outlying villages and procure fictitious residence permits. On the average, such a permit costs ten rubles a month. The owner of the house nearest the station charged me fifteen rubles. Moreover, he turned out to be a retired policeman. I must say, though, that he, his wife, his son, their two dogs, and their three cats treated Gusel and me kindly, especially when we actually had to live there for a certain length of time.

For a passport, I went to the raion center of Borovsk, a town in the Kaluga Oblast. Borovsk still has something of Old Russia about it. The Archpriest Avvakum was once imprisoned in shackles in the nearby monastery; and later the town was one of the centers of the Old Believers' movement.† The biggest of the Old Believers' churches is now a garage, and the monastery is used as a school of agricultural science. The condition of the

---

†The Archpriest Avvakum was the chief leader of the Old Believers (or Old Ritualists) during the Great Schism in the Russian Orthodox Church in the seventeenth century, and the author of the first (and perhaps the best) full-length autobiography in Russian, *A Life*. He was burned at the stake in 1675.

old churches in towns off limits to foreign tourists exceeds my powers of description.

I was given a passport right away, but the chairman of the Vorsino Rural Soviet rudely refused to issue me a residence permit; and in the *raiotdel* the police advised me to obtain one in another raion. At the Kaluga UVD I was told they had to have instructions from the USSR MVD. I went to the MVD office in Moscow, and everything began to unwind like a reel of film going backwards. Armed with one slip of paper from the Moscow MVD, I went to the Kaluga UVD; armed with a slip of paper from there, I went to the Borovsk *raiotdel*; armed with still another slip of paper I went to Vorsino, where they affixed a stamp authorizing me to reside there for one year. When I told a police officer in Borovsk that in sending me from pillar to post and back again over such a simple matter they were giving themselves needless work, he answered in the words of Zoya Kosmodemyanskaya: "That's all right. There are lots of us."

As soon as I heard about Den Uyl's talk with Brezhnev, I wrote the latter that the second case against me was "not only a frame-up but sense-less," and that since I was not being allowed to live in Moscow with my wife, I wanted permission to leave the country. Six weeks later I received an unexpected request that I bring to the Moscow GUVD's* passport section the documents required for a residence permit. I was given a courteous reception (unlike the last time I had been there) and told that I would get an answer within ten days. I had no doubt but what my letter had produced an effect and that I would receive a temporary residence permit. On October 30, however, I got a flat turn-down; they detained me that day and again in December. Gusel and I were coming home from a visit with Alfred Friendly, who had just interviewed me for *Newsweek*; hardly had we left the bus when someone tapped me on the shoulder and said, "Papers, please." I had no passport with me, but the two young policemen knew who I was, because they took me to our local precinct station. (Fortunately I managed to slip to Gusel the bag of books I was carrying, which included a copy of *The Gulag Archipelago*.)

Our arrival stirred up no great enthusiasm. "You didn't pick him up in our precinct," the desk sergeant told the policemen, "so take him to your own."

At the other precinct an inspector from the Criminal Investigation Department fingered my lapel. "That's a dandy suit you're wearing," he said. "We're going to find out where your money's coming from."

"It's our job," his assistant told me. "You must understand that that's what we're paid for."

"Don't count on my understanding," I replied, throwing him into a rage.

In the duty room on the floor below, where—in the familiar company of policemen, dope addicts, and petty thieves—I was waiting to learn what my fate would be, the talk was about how the Jews were to blame for everything. The duty officer opined that in the U.S. I would be welcomed with cheers and would live off the fat of the land. He simply couldn't believe that there was no such thing as a residence permit in the U.S. To him, living with such a paper was as inconceivable as living without air.

I was detained until late at night, when the psychiatrist on duty came to see me. I was extremely cautious in talking to him, saying that I simply wanted to live in peace. When he asked me about Solzhenitsyn, I replied I didn't know him and hadn't read his books. Nonetheless, he told his colleagues, "This is the first time I've met a real dissident." When the talk was over, I was released without even having been given a formal warning.

It isn't always easy to tell what the rank and file are doing on orders from above, what they are doing on their own, and what is simply a result of routine. But it was plain that the KGB had a plan to drive me out of the country by constantly detaining me with the threat of arrest, and now with the threat of psychiatric repression. I believe that in October they actually had decided to give me a residence permit for Moscow. But by the time I submitted the required documents, two events had occurred that changed that decision: on October 22, an article of mine on détente was published in the *New York Times*; and on October 27, I joined other dissidents in acclaiming the awarding of the Nobel Peace Prize to Andrei Sakharov.

C H A P T E R 2 5

Toward the
Helsinki Watch Group

In the first draft of my article for the *Times*, I led off with a quotation from Hegel. Then, thinking that might be too much for the Americans, I switched to Franklin Delano Roosevelt. The *Times* editors called the article "Evaluating the Advantages of Détente." I very much fear it was the longest ever published in that paper. But the fee of $150 struck me as too small. So I wrote the editor that although it was an honor for me to be published in the *Times*, the merely symbolic fee obliged me to make a symbolic gesture in return and donate the money to retired employees of the newspaper. I later found out, however, that the fee was the usual one, and hence I had not been discriminated against. A person with a zek's mentality ("Give me what's due me") tends to take umbrage when there is no reason to.

Marshal Shulman wrote a reply. At first I wondered whether it wasn't the same Shulman who had written of me to his nephew: "Is that villain still at large?" But it proved to be someone else. I met Professor Shulman a year later in New York, and he struck me as a nice person, although I was surprised that a specialist on the Soviet Union could hardly speak Russian. Shulman hoped that through concessions and its own example, the West could gradually "educate" the Soviet Union. In his professional way, he constructed abstract schemata of the Soviet system without understanding the Soviet way of thinking. Apparently he assumed that a method that had proven successful in American academic circles would also enable the U.S. to achieve its ends vis-à-vis the USSR. If you take the "mirror image" theory seriously, what you see in place of the U.S. is a crafty, uncompromising gangster. And what you see in place of the USSR is a well-intentioned but misunderstood gentleman. Neither Americans nor Europeans realize that the Soviet leaders have the mentality of thugs. The saying "Nerve is an extra dose of luck" is a basic part of the Leninist doctrine. I now see that after opposing that system for fifteen years—being jolted around in police vans and living on thin gruel—I have much clearer political ideas than if I had spent all those years in university classrooms studying political science.

In the *Times* article I wrote that American politicians are conditioned to the idea of compromise, whereas for Soviet politicians, "compromise" is an abusive term, and that for all its inevitability, the difference in approach plays an important role. I pointed out that while in both countries most of the politicians are men, there is a great difference between their position in the U.S. and the USSR. The Russian ideal of a man is that of a person able to rule his family with a firm hand. But the American, in the eyes of Russians, is something of a "milquetoast." It seems to me that the way husbands behave toward their wives, which justifies itself at home, is unconsciously brought into play in relations between the U.S. and the USSR. It would be a good idea to choose a team of ambitious, vigorous American women to conduct talks with the USSR. This would scarcely make for a complete turnaround, but the U.S. would make some considerable gains.

On October 9, I heard on the BBC evening news broadcast that Andrei Sakharov had been awarded the Nobel Peace Prize. In the tragic figure of Sakharov one finds most fully expressed both the strong and weak sides of the Human Rights Movement. He has left his imprint on the Movement, although he is not a charismatic figure like Solzhenitsyn, and has rejected the role virtually imposed upon him by history. Although they are the two most prominent figures in the opposition, neither has become an actual leader— Solzhenitsyn because he disbanded his army, and Sakharov because he didn't want to command one. Sakharov has even expressed doubts as to the existence of the Movement. He wanted to be, as Mao Zedong might have said, "a solitary monk under a leaky umbrella" whose voice in defense of the oppressed would be heard because of his moral prestige. But the Movement did exist, and Sakharov was nudged into being its leader, both from without the country and from within—from without, not only by the foreign press and radio, whose attention was concentrated on him, but by thousands of Soviet citizens who heard and read about him and wanted him to represent them; from within, by the dissidents ourselves. Whenever we were drafting a statement or setting up a committee, the first thing we asked ourselves was whether Sakharov would sign the statement or head up the committee. If he didn't, everyone would wonder: Could he be opposed to it? This contradiction led to compromises, occasionally to hurt feelings, and when the independent trade union was founded, even to attacks on Sakharov by the union members.

A second contradiction arose from the wish to preserve a purely moral position, which conflicted with the need to propose political solutions. Sakharov wanted to criticize society from the position of a scientist; his first article resembled a memorandum to a superior. But the more clearly he saw that trying to "persuade" the authorities was fruitless, the more critical became his judgments, and the more evident became the weakness of the political thought in those judgments—that, and the lack of interest in seeking a feasible way to change society.

I agree with Solzhenitsyn that Sakharov is a poor tactician—though God forbid he should follow the tactics of Solzhenitsyn. But Sakharov is a great strategist, and that cancels out his weakness as a tactician. His strategy involves an infallible understanding of good and a constant readiness to oppose evil. There is something of the saint in him. The fact that there is in Russia a man like Sakharov, who to some extent is even an eccentric but who is not infected by the prevailing falsehood, has struck millions of people as important. In this there is something of the traditional Russian view that only a "fool of God" can speak the truth to tsars. When I heard, in Magadan, that Sakharov might go to the U.S., I was frightened at the notion that he wouldn't be with us, although I realized he deserved a rest and the opportunity to work at physics. And in Moscow a cab driver told me he didn't believe what was being said in the newspapers about Solzhenitsyn.

"Why not?" I asked him.

"Why, because Sakharov spoke out for him," the cabbie replied. "If he'd been a traitor, Sakharov wouldn't've taken his side."

The inability of most people to feel the pain of others as if it were their own is what makes evil possible. But it is not hard to understand how trying life is for those who do have such an ability. The authorities, not yet having decided to touch Sakharov himself, tried to take it out on his dear ones. They threatened to imprison his stepchildren and kill his wife's four-year-old grandson, and they spread rumors about her. On the other hand, a man is very lucky to be married to a woman he loves and who shares his way of thinking.

The grandson is much like Sakharov himself. When Gusel and I visited the Sakharovs at their dacha in Zhukovka, he came running to meet us, smiling, with outstretched arms. In the same way he ran to meet Brezhnev, when the latter came to Zhukovka to see his son. No one had ever welcomed Brezhnev so sincerely. The old man, deeply touched, smiled and asked, "Who is this lovable little kid?"

Someone in his retinue whispered in fright: "Leonid Ilich, that's Sakharov's grandson!" Whereupon Ginzburg, who was taking care of the boy, was warned that he had to leave Zhukovka within twenty-four hours.

The newspaper campaign against Sakharov was launched two days after the news of the Nobel Prize. It began with quotations from Western Communist newspapers. Then came "letters from the workers" in which the prize was compared to Judas's thirty pieces of silver. There was a statement from members of the Academy of Sciences saying that the prize was an "unworthy and provocative" act. Seventy-two persons—scientists who knew very well about Sakharov and what was taking place—had found it possible to sign that statement.

I started thinking about a counterstatement: one that would not necessarily bear a large number of signatures but that would come from people of differing viewpoints. I began my draft by congratulating Sakharov. I said his activities were based on the premise that genuine peace was impossible without the government's recognition of human rights, and I added that violence directed inward will sooner or later be directed outward. Recalling the pact between Stalin and Hitler, I observed that "it would have been tragic if in 1939 the peace prize had been given to Stalin and Hitler, while those who said anything about their victims were condemned as 'enemies of détente' . . . ," and concluded by saying that the statement issued by the seventy-two scientists had caused "grief and amazement."

Yury Orlov suggested that we get together with Valentin Turchin and Roy Medvedev so that we could read the draft together. I had met Orlov at Ginzburg's place shortly after my return to Moscow. A rather short man with reddish, somewhat curly hair, he looked younger than his fifty years, and at first he seemed to be a mild person. I soon learned, however, that he could be firm when necessary. He was perhaps the only person I knew who combined sophisticated scientific thought with broad life experience.

Orlov grew up in the country, worked in a factory, and was an artillery officer during the war. Later he went to a university and became a professor of theoretical physics. During the war he joined the Communist party, but in 1956 he was expelled. He was repeatedly dismissed from employment because of his views, and when he came to Moscow in the early 1970s he joined the Movement. With a capacity for political thinking that was rare among dissidents, he realized the necessity for a political alternative in a country where stability was based on force. He realized (and now I am quoting from a letter he wrote me) that "the Democratic Movement must, in a cautious way, come closer to the blue-collar workers if it doesn't want to be swamped by nationalism and hatred toward the intelligentsia." Although his attitude toward Marxism was even more negative than my own, he felt that the "liberal Marxists" were important both for ideological balance within the country and for establishing contacts with Western leftists. He once said that if the world could not avoid communism, it was our task to humanize it a little.

Valentin Turchin was chairman of the Soviet group of Amnesty International. There was something Greek in his facial features, or perhaps he had forebears among the peoples of the Caucasus. As compared to Orlov, he was more of the ivory-tower scientist, and his political leanings were more to the left. Both he and Orlov belonged to "the generation of 1966"; my meeting with them, as with many others, made it plain to me that the Movement had passed through its crisis. When they joined it, the atmosphere became cleaner than it had been in the days of Yakir and Krasin.

I had come to know about Roy Medvedev through his book on Stalin. When we met, I sensed in him something pedantic and lukewarm. (I told him that his brother Zhores had a womanish face, which was not really very polite, since they are twins.) It was important to me to get his signature on our statement for two reasons: his brother had come out against the award of the Nobel Prize to Sakharov, and his own views were often opposed to those of Sakharov.

Medvedev favored "purging" Marxism of Stalinism; his declarations (so I firmly believe) expressed the unarticulated opinion of some workers in the Party apparatus. But he had no real following. His approach was aimed at persuading the regime, and even Sakharov seemed to him a radical. He gauged the ideas and activities of the dissidents with the yardstick of Marxist pedantry, and there was something arrogant in his attitude toward them. He judged me as if from an historical distance, forgetting that he was dealing with contemporaries who were vulnerable vis-à-vis the regime.

As might have been expected in our unfortunate country, it was soon rumored that the Medvedev brothers were KGB agents. In my view, their tragedy lies in the fact that, partly out of ideological considerations, and partly out of tactical ones, they clung to the ideas of 1956 in the hope that Khrushchev's unstable anti-Stalinism would prove to be organic. But the regime retrogressed and had no further need of the Medvedevs' "best wishes"; society moved forward, and Solzhenitsyn, Sakharov, and Turchin left behind the phase of fascination with the Medvedevs' ideas.

In the course of our meeting, Medvedev (seconded by Turchin) demanded that the adjective "great," as applied to Sakharov, be replaced by "outstanding." I didn't argue with them, although I saw no good reason to deprive Sakharov of greatness.

It seemed important to me that a member of the Jewish Emigration Movement sign our statement. During the years I had spent behind bars and barbed-wire fences, my old friend Vitaly Rubin had changed a great deal—something that reflected a shift in the status of Jews. He had always been helpful to the Democratic Movement, but he had been cautious. He was afraid to visit our homes, saying he wanted to leave for Israel, but there was a risk of losing his job and not getting permission to emigrate. Now, however, I found a man who couldn't care less. He was a "refusenik" who had been turned down for an exit visa to Israel because he was privy to classified government information. (He was a specialist in ancient Chinese philosophy.) Along with other Jews, he had signed declarations, taken part in demonstrations, and been detained by the police—and all this was the stuff of life to him. (The upsurge of Jewish nationalism among formerly assimilated Jews also had its comic aspects. When someone once called a certain Jew stupid, Rubin frowned: "*What*? A Jew and stupid?") Rubin had done time behind bars in his youth, and had got tuberculosis. Of the two of us, he looked more like a man who has just been released from a prison camp.

In 1968–69 the Jewish Emigration Movement was just taking its first, timid, toddling steps; but by 1974–75 it had considerably more influence than the Democratic Movement, its model. The Democratic Movement had passed through several crises and had lost many members. The authorities looked upon us as the most dangerous of the oppositionists, since we wanted to change things within the country, and not simply leave it. No political forces outside the USSR had an interest in supporting us. But the Jewish Movement was backed by Israel, Zionists all over the world, and (most important) several million American voters—and hence the U.S. Congress and Administration. Moreover, quite apart from whether one was or was not Jewish, it was easier for the West to support the idea of emigration than to back changes within the USSR.

All the national movements in the USSR have two factions: one emphasizes their own ethnic problems, while avoiding conflict with the authorities as much as possible; the other considers that without democratic changes within the USSR, there can be no solution to ethnic problems, that the struggle for the rights of national minorities is part and parcel of the Human Rights Movement. For Soviet Jews, the switch from Russian culture to identification with Israeli culture has necessarily involved an internal constraint. And by way of a natural justification, it has been suggested that Russia is a hopeless case and that there is no future for the dissident Movement. Indeed, some of the Russian intelligentsia, in order to justify their own misfortune, have said the same thing. All this has tended to reinforce the Western view that the problem of human rights in the USSR is exclusively one of emigration. Henry Kissinger, for example, based his assessment of human rights only on the number of Jewish émigrés, something that corresponded fully to the interests of the Soviet authorities in representing all opposition as "Jewish" and then fanning the flames of anti-Semitism. Orlov and Sakharov defended the rights of Jews to emigrate. But Jewish organizations in the West, with few exceptions, have not defended Orlov, and I don't know whether they will defend Sakharov. As for Rubin, he promptly signed our statement.

It turned out that my friends the novelists Vladimir Voinovich and Vladimir Kornilov had themselves drafted a statement. We argued as to which statement was the better and tempers flared. But finally they agreed to sign our statement. Osip Cherny and Father Sergei Zheludkov also signed.

I had known Voinovich for a long time. When interrogated in connection with my case, he had said that my plays were written in a style that was foreign to him. That was true, but he later regretted saying it, just as Pasternak had regretted his judgment of Mandelstam in his talk with Stalin. I had always considered Voinovich a good writer, but his *Adventures of Ivan Chonkin* struck me as distinctly superior to his other books. He had been expelled from the writers' union; Kornilov was expecting expulsion. His novel *Demobilization,* which very accurately conveys the atmosphere in the Soviet Union in the early 1950s, had just been published abroad. Neither of them was a political dissident; their break with the system had been dictated by the logic of their creativity. Gusel and I had often visited their homes, which bore the imprint, still, of the privileged life led by "official" Soviet writers and, at the same time, of the unstable life of dissidents.

Kornilov had conceived the idea of organizing a Moscow Center of the PEN Club, in which case International PEN would not admit the official Writers' Union. A minimum of eighteen persons was required to establish the PEN Center, and we spent a long time taking head counts, but we didn't make out very well. Also, those who were already honorary members of foreign PEN centers probably sized the situation up as follows: We are already PEN members; if a Moscow PEN Center is organized, all kinds of riff-raff will join, and before you know it we'll be lost in the crowd (like Shilo among other academicians).

I wanted two artists, Ernst Neizvestny and Oskar Rabin, to sign the statement. I had known both of them for some fifteen years, though we saw Neizvestny only occasionally, whereas Rabin had been a close friend. In 1962, during the "rotten thaw," when not even all of the corrupt bureaucrats knew which way the wind was going to blow, Ely Belyutin, an artist, art critic, and adventurer, sent a memorandum to the authorities. He said that since our society, having completed the construction of socialism, was now undertaking the expanded construction of communism, and since art, as is generally known, always takes the lead, the time had come to replace Socialist Realism with Communist Realism. In order that he might present some specimens of Communist Realism, Belyutin was authorized to display paintings by his students and some of Neizvestny's sculptures. The exhibit was set up on the mezzanine of the gallery where works by members of the Moscow artists' union, the domain of the senile Socialist Realists, were being shown. Khrushchev called Belyutin's students "faggots" (to the accompaniment of approving guffaws from the Socialist Realists, who had taken heart), and with that, "Communist Realism" was finished. Meantime, Neizvestny's star rose very high—not because Khrushchev had praised him but because he had got into an argument with Khrushchev and had promptly achieved world fame.

Belyutin did not lose heart. He disappeared for a month and then assembled a group of artists and poets at his home. He told them he had been to Cuba and that Castro had promised him full support, while at the same time praising highly those same artists who had come to Belyutin's home that evening. "My friends, Castro is with us!" he exclaimed, running his hands through his long hair as he stood before a painting by Canaletto (Lord only knows whether it was authentic or a fake). Later, it turned out he had spent that month in the Crimea.

The paintings by Belyutin's students were pale imitations of the surrealists and the abstract expressionists. But Neizvestny is a real artist. When I returned from my exile I found him in a new role: not an official (although rebellious) sculptor but expelled from the artists' union as a renegade and seeking permission to emigrate. During my last year in the USSR, I often visited his studio on the first floor of a half-decayed building, where his electric power or his water supply was intermittently cut off. And I often drank with him (not water, of course) under the reproachful glance of a plaster-cast Khrushchev. (Ernst had been commissioned by Khrushchev's family to create a bust of him for his grave.) At fifty, Ernst gave the impression of being a worldly-wise man, with a way about him that was suggestive, at the same time, of a *mafioso* and a "butter-and-egg man" out on a spree. He was capable of pulling out a fat roll of bills with a gesture that seemed to say, "Don't you try to change my way of living."

The tone he used toward lower-class people was firm. Once there was a knock on the door, and in came a humble-looking woman. As she stood looking down at the floor, Ernst said to his guests, "That's my stoolie. She's come to keep an eye on us." Then, to the woman: "Well, what do you want? Do you need five rubles?"

"Five rubles," the woman said. And when she had got them she left, closing the door quietly.

Yet for all this, I believe he lacked self-confidence and had never really found himself. In him, as in so many Soviet artists, there was a deep internal fissure between inculcated Soviet artistic culture on the one hand and his God-given talent on the other. This was complicated by the fact that, having rid himself of the Communist ideals, he wanted to embody *some* ideals. Thus the metaphysical aspect of his art emerged from the depths to the foreground, burdening the pure plastic image. Nor could he find his own place in society. He had broken with a system in which, for better or for worse, he was nonetheless still included. And in coexisting with that system, he had elaborated a complex set of compromises so that he simultaneously played the role of cynic and hero.

While Ernst was talking about something, he would constantly be asking, with his lack of self-confidence, "Do you find that interesting? Really interesting?"

"I never heard anything more uninteresting," he was once told by Benedict Erofeyev, whom he had met at Gusel's birthday party.

Erofeyev was a drunk and something of a bum whom the irritated Neizvestny called a *raznochinets*.† He had attracted attention with a novella titled *Moscow-Petushki*, recounting the insane travels of a man who kept trying to get a look at the Kremlin but always ended up at Kursk Station on a train headed for Petushki.

Erofeyev and Neizvestny belonged to two different subcultures: that of the dissidents and that of the "referents."‡ This dichotomy is somewhat arbitrary, especially in the arts, but a rough distinction between the two can be made nonetheless. The individual personality of the dissident is formed in the course of opposing the system, while that of the "referent" is formed while serving it, although inwardly he has not accepted it. If he is an honest person, he will try to improve the system from within. If he is a careerist, he will try to improve his own position. When the people at the top reverted to Stalinism and those below began to get tough, the most independent spirits among the referents started dropping out of the system, one after another, becoming dissidents in spite of themselves. And then there was a new option: leaving the country. Among Soviet émigrés in the West, the dissidents can be clearly distinguished from the referents. The dissidents stress their opposition to the Soviet regime as the chief reason the West should pay heed to their homilies, while the referents say the West should follow their advice because of their closeness to the regime and their knowledge of its mechanisms. In general, the referents are more professional than the dissidents, but their moral thrust is much weaker.

Ernst signed the statement in defense of Sakharov with no hesitation.

Unfortunately, I did not have time to see Oskar Rabin, although I had no doubts about his support. He was the first painter I met in my youth; and it was my acquaintance with unofficial artists that showed me I was not alone in my rejection of the system, that some kind of opposition was possible. Rabin was ten years older than I, but because of his baldness and sad face, he seemed even older.

I very much liked his paintings, in which one finds a certain distancing

---

†An archaism (widely used in the nineteenth century) meaning "an intellectual who does not belong to the upper classes."—TRANS.

‡The usual sense of this word is "adviser" (for a publisher).—TRANS.

from Soviet life, so wretched and yet so touching. His firmness, decency, and common sense made him a leading figure among those artists who were striving for the right to an independent existence.

When an exhibit being held in a vacant lot on the outskirts of Moscow was broken up by bulldozers, the event made such an impression on the West that the authorities decided to sanction some "free" exhibits. I went to one of them with Oskar in the summer of 1975. One of his paintings showed a "nest" in which live human beings were sitting on eggs like setting hens. Nearby stood a policeman wearing an indulgent smile (although those young people should have been promptly locked up for fifteen days). The only painting found to be subversive was *Down with National Borders!* It was removed; on the spot where it had been, the artists who had painted it sat down and declared a hunger strike by way of protest. After my experience in Magadan I was amazed. And yet there was not a single work that was really moving. Isolation had made it impossible to restore the continuity not only of Russian art in the twentieth century but of unofficial art during the twenty years of its existence.

The authorities made no further concessions. They began to cut off the artists and to isolate Rabin. After an exhausting struggle, he emigrated in 1978, and was deprived of his Soviet citizenship.

Petr Grigorenko signed our statement immediately, and Reshat Dzhemilev, who was at his place, signed it as a representative of the Crimean Tatars. But two of those we approached refused to sign: Nadezhda Mandelstam and Igor Shafarevich.

I had met Nadezhda Mandelstam, the widow of the poet, fifteen years earlier. She had looked like a little gray mouse who wanted to scurry into a hole without being noticed. At that time she was worried about the same thing that was now worrying me: the lack of a residence permit for Moscow. This time, when I saw her in her Moscow apartment, I could hardly recognize her: what I saw was a general on a white horse. During those intervening years, the two volumes of her memoirs had been published in the West, and this had given her the status of an "outstanding" (Roy Medvedev's word) Russian writer. The opportunity to express herself and (most important) her success and the fact that she was looked upon not as an unfortunate widow but as a person who has something to say had changed her completely. I had read her first book in manuscript before my arrest. It explained much to me, and many of her judgments coincided with my own. I read her second book seven years later, and it too was remarkable. But it was spoiled by a kind of senile spitefulness, by settling little accounts dating back a half-century, by distortions and injustices. A strong personality will not let years of humiliation go unavenged; and apparently her need to get back at everybody for everything had broken the floodgates. It all surged out in a wild torrent, carrying mud and chips of wood along with it, and never passing through the filter that separates the important things from the unimportant ones.

She received me courteously, and we had a long talk about the regime and about artists. She displayed a lively mind, but also the partiality of one who reigns over a small circle of people. She refused to sign the statement, saying that she agreed with it entirely, but that she was quite simply afraid. As she was seeing me out, she nodded toward a door in the entrance hallway: "For the first time in my life, I have a bathroom of my own." After the death of her husband she had lived in one small town after another; the problem of the outhouses in such towns is one that I have already described.

I don't think that Igor Shafarevich, associate member of the Academy of Sciences, ever ran into such a problem, nor do I believe he was afraid. He explained that he didn't want to sign because the award of the Nobel Prize might serve as a pretext for letting Sakharov leave the country to attend the award ceremonies and then refusing to let him back in. He was opposed to Sakharov's departing the country, just as he was opposed to emigration in general.

I thought Shafarevich's signature was important for two reasons: he was a colleague of Sakharov's in the Academy, and his views were those of a Russian nationalist. Since there was no logic in the reasoning of this specialist in mathematical logic—I was asking for approval of the award of the prize, not of Sakharov's emigration—I abandoned logical arguments in favor of an emotional appeal. He wavered for a moment but still didn't sign.

If one were to compare my travels among the dissidents in search of signatures with Chichikov's travels among the landowners in Gogol's *Dead Souls*, it would be most appropriate to liken Shafarevich to Sobakevich. There was something bearlike about him—something crushing. His book on socialism is interesting, with some unexpected *éclairs en profondeur*; but it is a caricature, not a serious analysis; the author sees nothing but what he himself has come to believe. Like Solzhenitsyn, Shafarevich lectures the intelligentsia on not giving children an education, which is linked to falsehood, and on not leaving the country.

Getting an education in the USSR (especially a higher education) involves the necessity of lying. I was expelled from the university for refusing to lie; it was in that sense that I told Shilo I had the tremendous advantage of not having spent much time on university studies. Shilo, Brezhnev, Kolomiychenko, Medvedev, Sakharov, Solzhenitsyn, Shafarevich, and millions of others spent long years as university students. And in order to procure their diplomas, they had to take exams on Marxism-Leninism, showing that they believed in it (whether they sincerely believed in it or not, I won't presume to say); but afterward they made very different choices. I could count on the fingers of one hand those people who have broken with the regime before managing to get an education and have yet made something of themselves. For a person without an education, the opportunities are very limited, even the opportunities to oppose falsehood. Apparently the only feasible way is to keep falsehood within minimum boundaries, recognizing it as an evil and preparing to redeem it. People with a strong enough moral imperative can serve as a kind of reference point for taking the reading from the dial.

The absolute moral demand "not to leave"—since whenever a person leaves the country it means a break with his native land and his culture—soon engendered an equally absolute requirement that one "leave," since staying in the country means cooperating with the totalitarian regime in one way or another. I once got into an argument with an outstanding scientist, the linguistics expert Yury Melchuk, on that subject, an argument so heated that our eyes were bulging and our voices were strained to the point of hoarseness. I already had in my pocket the documents required for an exit visa, but I didn't see emigration as the fulfillment of a moral duty. Instead, I incline toward Shafarevich's view: there is a deep bond between a person and his country, and a duty toward the latter. But a country also has a duty toward its "children"; sometimes, when that duty is not fulfilled, one has no choice but to leave. For far too long, Russia has been, and still remains, not a mother but a stepmother—not only to the Jews and Crimean Tatars but to a great number of Russians. To explain away that pernicious influence as the fault of "Lettish sharpshooters," "German money," "Jewish commissars," and "Western ideology" is to behave like an ostrich hiding its head in the sand. Marxist ideology came from the West, but so did the idea of the legacy. Why did the former strike root and triumph, while the latter failed to?

I am against absolutizing the problem of leaving the country. One can live like a foreigner in a dacha near Moscow, and one can feel like a Russian while living in Vermont. A person who has opposed the Soviet system while residing in the USSR can continue to oppose it from abroad. Involuntary emigration is preferable to long years in prison. Whoever really wants to leave a country has every right to do so.

Sakharov's Nobel award gave new impetus to the Movement, and in the winter of 1975–76, Yury Orlov and I often discussed what should be done to get the Movement out of the vicious circle of "arrest—protest—arrest" and to achieve greater influence. We both thought that the matter of having a name was important, and we drew up a draft Declaration for the Human Rights Movement in the USSR.[*] We came out for human rights throughout the world and warned against the dangerous tendency to fight for them in some countries while opposing that struggle in others. Whoever fights for human rights in his own country is fighting for them everywhere, since violence "from the left" serves to justify violence "from the right," and vice versa. A halt to repressions in the USSR would have a beneficial effect in both pro-Soviet and anti-Soviet countries. We proposed putting faith in human dignity—a value that had gone out of fashion but has returned to favor.

Sakharov would not sign the declaration, and it was the same with other human rights activists. It would have been easy to get their signatures on a protest against this or that trial, but not on a straightforward declaration of what they wanted.

Orlov and I then proposed an appeal to the Politburo that had been newly elected at the 25th Congress of the CPSU. We wrote:

> In many countries the Communist parties are switching from confrontation to a dialogue with other social groups. In awareness of that fact, we extend a hand to you, and suggest that we begin a dialogue about the future of the country. We propose that representatives of the CPSU leadership meet with representatives of the Democratic Movement.

Our plan was that the proposal should be signed by Petr Grigorenko as a "Eurocommunist," Valentin Turchin as a Socialist, Andrei Sakharov as the nucleus of our political coalition, Yury Orlov as a liberal democrat, and myself as an extreme Rightist.

Sakharov, however, shot down that proposal too, because of his dislike for declarations that had even the slightest political coloration. Instead, he suggested a routine appeal for amnesty. Naturally, we all signed it, but it went unnoticed.

We realized that we had to stop spinning our wheels. The preceding autumn I had met, at the Rubins', a man who outwardly resembled Ubozhko, being young, prematurely balding, and short but powerful. Anatoly Shcharansky was an electronics engineer, a refusenik, and a Jewish activist who had repeatedly been detained for fifteen days in jail, had been fired from his job, and was picking up work here and there, giving English lessons to refuseniks and dissidents. (He had taught himself English, but at least he knew it better than his students.) Yury Orlov and I had attended one of his classes.

On one occasion, Shcharansky told Yury and me that it would make sense to appeal to the public in those countries signatory to the Helsinki accords, suggesting a discussion as to how to promote observance of the humanitarian articles of the accords. The idea opened up opportunities to make use of the accords, which we had previously regarded as a Western concession to the USSR; in particular, the "third basket," which we thought was nothing more than an attempt by the West to save face. It was plain that the USSR was not going to honor its obligations, and that the West would not insist they be honored.

After talking with Yury, I wrote an appeal that "we propose founding national committees independent of governments, and forming an international committee from representatives of the former." I added that "since the Soviet Union was the initiator of the Helsinki conference, we feel that the Soviet public should take the initiative in founding the first national committee."

Again, the chief obstacle was Sakharov's refusal to sign the statement, even though we had wanted him to head the committee. Our first reaction was to abandon the idea. But then I told Orlov it would be best if he chaired the committee; and if Sakharov's wife, Elena Bonner, joined, it would show that Sakharov was not against it. I hoped that Orlov would thus become well known—something that would help him in his work and would protect him against harassment by the authorities.

Orlov and I didn't know Shcharansky very well, and we decided that if he had merely passed on someone else's idea about the Helsinki accords, it would be preferable, instead of asking him to join the committee, to invite Rubin, who was better known. Also, we didn't want a disproportionate number of Jewish activists, since that would give a distorted idea of the committee's aims. But Shcharansky had conceived the idea in the first place. And as a person with common sense, good political judgment, a strong will, and nobility of character, he not only became an irreplaceable member of the Helsinki Watch Group but withstood face-to-face encounters with the KGB. In July 1978, he was sentenced to three years in prison and ten years of exile for "high treason." In his final speech he said, "I am proud to have known, and worked with, such honest, daring, and courageous men as Sakharov, Orlov and Ginzburg."

Orlov began to figure out how best to formulate our program and the conditions under which one could become a member of the committee. (As for me, I disengaged myself from the project; by March 30 it had become clear that my days in the Soviet Union were numbered.) Orlov proved to be a first-rate leader: he was tolerant of others' views and knew how to bring people together without imposing his own will on them. I was not mistaken in thinking that his heading the Helsinki Watch Group would make him well known, but my hopes that this would provide him with protection were not realized. In May 1978, he was sentenced to seven years of prison camp and five years of exile for that activity.

In the USSR the Helsinki Watch Group served as a bridge between segments of the opposition with differing orientations (human rights, nationalist, economic) and between the intelligentsia and blue-collar workers. And in the West it provoked a reaction against Soviet violations of the Helsinki accords. The Soviet government responded with repressions that were essentially due to instability at the top in anticipation of a "biological" replacement of leaders. (The same thing had happened, but in an even more frightful way, on the eve of Stalin's death.) The Soviet authorities had been frightened and angered by President Carter's condemnation of repression in the USSR; but his human rights policy proved to be inconsistent and was not supported by specific actions. Carter began to tone down his statements, and the Soviet leaders realized they could ignore him.

In early 1977, there were three important arrests: Ginzburg and Orlov in February, and Shcharansky in March. Not a single one of them pleaded guilty.

Alexander Ginzburg was not only a member of the Helsinki Watch Group, he had also been director of the Fund to Assist Political Prisoners. The collecting of money for such assistance had begun in 1968. (I knew a girl who gave five rubles every month, out of her wages of 100 rubles.) Then, in 1974, Solzhenitsyn donated to the fund a considerable part of his royalties. In July 1978, Ginzburg was sentenced to eight years in labor camp for having assisted prisoners and their families. At his trial he looked like an old man.

Shcharansky's arrest was preceded by a press campaign in the same spirit as the "Doctors' Case"† in 1953. Thus *Izvestiya* published an "open letter" from Alexander Lipavsky, who acknowledged that he had been a CIA agent and accused Shcharansky, Rubin, and other Jews of also having been CIA agents. Earlier, the CIA bogeyman had been used against American journalists in Moscow; now the KGB was trying to make one single package out of the dissidents, the Jews, the journalists, and the American intelligence service. This was dramatized in President Carter's statement that Shcharansky was not a CIA agent and that to try him for that would be to spit in the face of the President. The Soviet authorities did precisely that.

Jews who have worked at institutes with American equipment are denied exit visas to Israel on the grounds of "secrecy" or access to classified material. This means that either the rationale of "secrecy" is untrue or else the Americans are supplying equipment for Soviet military research. Shcharansky was one of the Jewish refuseniks who helped to compile a list of such institutes. As soon as Lipavsky's letter was printed, a UPI correspondent in Bonn asked me about it. I told him that I thought Lipavsky was a KGB agent who had first infiltrated the Jewish Movement so as to make contact with the Americans through the Jews and then compromise all of them. I said that the

---

†When a group of Kremlin doctors, primarily Jewish, were charged with conspiring to kill Stalin and other members of the Politburo.

fact that Lipavsky was "exposed" by the KGB showed how very necessary the case was to the authorities. Not everybody agreed with me at the time, but my interpretation was later confirmed.

Lipavsky wore a mustache and (always) a smile, and was the best-natured person imaginable. A neurosurgeon by profession, he had advised Gusel on my treatment when I was in the camp hospital with meningitis. I had seen him several times at the Rubins' without feeling the slightest suspicion. Indeed, he did not try to worm his way into my confidence. He never claimed he was a dissident or a Jewish activist. He seemed to be just an ordinary Jew patiently waiting for an opportunity to emigrate. But he was always ready to help others: he would give one person a lift in his car, bring medication to another. And he rented an apartment in Moscow for Shcharansky. Since he was a warmhearted man, doing good deeds came easily to him. He was the kind of informer who takes the bait through weakness and feels guilty toward his victims, so that he is glad to do them favors.

Just before the arrests of Ginzburg and Orlov, the *Literaturnaya gazeta* printed an article by another provocateur, Alexander Petrov-Agatov. I had seen him once at Orlov's home; in his interview with the Soviet reporters he had referred to that occasion, rather squeamishly, as "my last meeting with Amalrik." He had spent many years in prison camps, both as a regular criminal and as a political prisoner, and had been taken under Ginzburg's protection as a former prisoner. He had "writers' itch" and, despite his sixty years, a young man's yearning to see his name in print. It is possible that that was one of the reasons (although not the main one) for Petrov-Agatov's slandering people to whom he owed debts of gratitude. There was, after all, no other way for him to get published in the USSR. I thought he was unpleasant and sensed something false in whatever he said. Sad to say, every social movement must have its traitors, just as it must have its heroes and martyrs.

The Group to Promote Observance of the Helsinki Accords in the USSR was founded in Moscow on May 12, 1976. Later, other groups were founded: in Kiev, Vilnius, Tbilisi, and Yerevan. At this writing more than forty of their members have been arrested. But their places have been taken by others, and the groups continue their work.

CHAPTER 26

The KGB
vs. Disa the Cat

On the night of February 20, when Gusel and I were leaving the home of a friend, four men in civilian clothes hustled me into a car. They didn't show me any credentials; if we had been in Italy, I would have thought I was being kidnapped by the Red Brigade. In Moscow, however, it was merely "our glorious organs."

A Congress of the CPSU was scheduled to begin four days later, and the authorities were getting nervous. Day after day, the police had broken into our empty apartment on Vakhtangov Street. Then, having bugged telephone conversations among diplomats, they discovered on that particular evening we would be at the home of our friend Joseph Presel, an American foreign service officer.

First they took me to a police station. Then they put me in another car, and I thought perhaps I was going to the Lubyanka. But they drove in the other direction, toward Lefortovo. We went on past Lefortovo, however, and I noticed, terrified, that we were heading toward our secret apartment. I thought to myself: they've found us out, and we're in for a search. But the driver went right across the boulevard that encircles Moscow, and it turned out they were taking me to Kaluga.

I spent the rest of that night and the following morning in the local jail, with no explanation as to why I had been detained. The next afternoon, two polite civilians took me to Borovsk. There I was greeted by a police officer whom I already knew, and the raion prosecutor, who complained it was all my fault that he had to work on a Saturday. He said I had been registered as a resident of their raion for four months but had not been working, so they had to send me a summons. The summons was for the 26th, and I received it two days after they picked me up—on the 22nd. In other words, since I had not responded to the summons on the 26th, the "organs" detained me on the 20th—which proves that time is relative.

When I realized that I was not under threat of arrest, I began to relax and enjoy myself a little. I said I had been working—at my desk. And I even mentioned the International Convention on the Abolition of Forced Labor, which had been signed by the Soviet Union. The prosecutor replied, quite reasonably, "It wasn't for your sake that we signed it." And in the presence of two witnesses, who seemed above all else to fear that they themselves would be put behind bars, I was given a formal warning that I must find regular employment within a month. The KGB was repeating the tricks it had used in 1965 and 1968. That was understandable. What was not understandable was that they neither detained me for fifteen days nor advised me to stay in Vorsino. Instead, they told me to go to Moscow right away and consult with my wife. I thought that perhaps they wanted to cool things down. It turned out that Lyuda Alekseyeva, a founding member of the Moscow Helsinki Watch Group, had already phoned Andropov, chief of the KGB, and Gusel had called various foreign correspondents, who notified their newspapers every time I was detained. (Andropov's secretary replied evasively: "We're not involved in this. Blame it on the police.")

It wasn't until I rode the subway in Moscow that I noticed my tail: a young man in a red scarf. When he realized I had noticed him, he came up to me and said, "How much longer are you going to go on playing hide-and-go-seek with us, you bastard? Get your ass on home! We won't bother you there." He added that if I went to see any friends, I'd have to pay dearly for it.

Gusel wasn't at our place on Vakhtangov Street, so I went to see friends anyway. But I stopped off at the KGB office on Kuznetsky Most. Because of the late hour, there was no one present except the duty officer, a lieutenant, and a second lieutenant. I told them I was being threatened by their colleagues who had been assigned to tail me.

The lieutenant, discountenanced, made a call and then said to me: "Either give us a statement right now, or else come in on Monday. Some of our people will be here to help you."

"Help" is their favorite word. Like the tsarist secret police, the KGB is ever eager to dry the tears of widows and orphans. Even people who have served time claim that KGB agents often say they "helped" them so as to restrain them from committing even more dangerous deeds, or to protect them against the wrath of the people.

"What kind of help can I expect on Monday," I asked, "if on Saturday they've broken my head?"

I was really nervous as I walked along the dark, deserted side street and heard footsteps and heavy breathing behind me, getting closer and closer. The same thing happened in the dark woods near Vorsino. On the way to Kaluga, I had been threatened with seven years of strict regimen; now I was under the threat of either being beaten up or murdered. On one occasion in Magadan KGB officers had hinted they might kill me, and I didn't take it as an empty threat. Vladimir Voinovich, who had been invited in for "help" in getting his books published, had been poisoned (although not fatally) by two KGB agents. Several painters had their skins burned with mustard gas, and KGB officers had fractured the skull of the translator Konstantin Bogatyrev in front of his own door. Plainly, they wanted to frighten writers; in the case of Bogatyrev they had old accounts to settle, since he was a former zek and had been a friend of Pasternak's. When he was in the hospital after the assault, the gebists supposedly told the doctor: "If he survives, you'll get the same thing." But Bogatyrev did not survive.

Wherever Gusel and I went, we were always followed by two cars with four men in each. Of course, we had had the experience of being tailed well before that. I didn't always notice when somebody was following us, but Gusel was more observant. One night the previous summer, after dinner with Abraham Brumberg, the editor of *Problems of Communism,* we were passing through Red Square on our way home, and Gusel pointed to an agent who was shadowing us in the deserted square. The poor guy! He had to find a policeman right away to check our papers, since a tail doesn't have the right to do so. But there were no policemen around: only the motionless sentries at Lenin's Tomb. As the agent rushed toward a police telephone, we ran through the courtyards behind the university, familiar to us from our student days. Gusel removed her blond wig and her long dress, and I emerged onto the street arm-in-arm with a brunette in a miniskirt. We made our way home undisturbed.

By this time, however, I no longer called it "tailing" but out-and-out harassment. The agents made no pretense that they were not following us, although sometimes they played the game of "not noticing us"—rather like the game played by the court in a judicial investigation. I have mentioned my poor memory for faces, but once in the subway, when I noticed that one of the passengers was sitting there with an air of paying no attention to what was going on around him, I asked Gusel: "One of our boys?"

The agents all bear the imprint of what might be called "the presumption of mistreatment." One senses that they hold a grudge against the whole world, and especially against their victims, because they have to practice such a loathsome trade. If you stare at them, they really hate it and become noticeably nervous.

Our tails were especially unhappy about having to keep watch on us in

Vorsino, far from Moscow. Once when I was boarding a train for Kaluga, one stupid-looking agent complained to another: "I'm really fed up with that bastard!"

By this time they were equipped with radios (thanks to the West); and whenever we went on the subway, we would find their cars waiting for us when we emerged onto the street. Sometimes one of the drivers, letting go of the wheel, would spread his hands as if to say to us: "What can I do? I have to follow you—it's my job."

Once when Ira Orlov, Yury's wife, noticed a fellow with an indifferent expression sitting on a bench near the entrance to their apartment building, she went up to him and asked in exasperation, "How much do they pay you for this?"

"Enough to buy vodka," the man replied, quite unperturbed.

We could not return to our "secret apartment," or the KGB would have discovered it. We remembered the time we had spent there as a happy one. There were woods nearby, and we often went skiing, sometimes with the Orlovs.

One day in the fall, a gray cat came confidently into our apartment. He had a rather pointed face and looked like a judge. In fact, he reminded me of Rybachuk, who tried me in Talaya. He crapped wherever he happened to be at the time; but his favorite place was the bathtub, which was not an easy place for a cat to get into. Yury Orlov called him "the heir of our revolutionary traditions," because after the Winter Palace was stormed in October 1917, the insurgents crapped in the bathtubs. Washing out the tub was no great task. But the cat's revolutionary spirit was so strong that once when we were not at home, he crawled under the blanket on the bed and crapped on the sheets. For that, I gave him a beating and put him outside. When I wanted to let him back in, he was nowhere around, and all our efforts to find him were in vain.

One day a kitten showed up at our door. She was a Siamese, which was unusual and mysterious, since in Moscow, Siamese are very expensive. We called her Disa. She made herself perfectly at home with us, and never once did she "violate discipline," as they say in camp. She would run along with us when we went walking in the woods. She even tried to play with the dogs, but not with dogs that were too big. Just before the Party Congress, when we were being tailed, Disa once had to stay home alone for two days, until a friend of ours in secret took her to the Orlovs'. (Yury said she had the mind of a scientist: she would see a picture on the wall and try to get it off so as to find out what was on the back.) From then on, we always took Disa with us in case we couldn't get back home. She nestled very comfortably in my arms and was all curiosity when we were riding in the subway or in a taxi. When we were walking down the street, it was like a carnival procession. At the head of it marched Gusel, in her white fur coat, and I with a seal-point Siamese in my arms. On both sides of us, two cars would be cruising along, and behind us were the tails.

Tailing, an effective method of harassment, is ordinarily used on someone about to be arrested. Our friends recommended that we leave the country. Elena Bonner, Sakharov's wife, was especially insistent, saying that as a former zek I would be one of the first to be arrested. For that matter, I myself realized that it was time to choose between prison and leaving the country.

Back in July our friend Prof. Richard Pipes had issued us a personal invitation to come to Cambridge, Massachusetts, in view of the fact that the authorities had refused to consider invitations from the universities. When it came to filing for an exit visa, it turned out that although Gusel and I were man and wife, we had to apply separately, since we were registered residents of different places. Merely to get a slip of paper certifying that I was registered as a resident of Vorsino and wasn't employed anywhere, I had to go first to the Vorsino Village Soviet, then to the passport section of the Borovsk Police *Raiotdel*, then to the deputy chairman of the raion soviet, and back to the Vorsino Village Soviet. Everyone was frightened by the word "abroad." As for certifying the fact that I wasn't employed, who knew but what I was working for American intelligence? Finally, Gusel's application was turned down in Moscow. Since in any case I wouldn't have left without Gusel, I demanded the return of my documents and the customs fee I had paid. But, as might have been expected, I got nothing.

In early March another private invitation was sent to us, this time from Holland. The invitation from Amsterdam had reached Vorsino in only three days, whereas under Soviet conditions it would usually have required two weeks; I took this to be a good sign. But the invitation sent to Gusel in Moscow never arrived at all. Mail for Vorsino was screened in Kaluga, where the censors don't have such a heavy workload and where they had no special instructions with respect to me.

At this point we even entertained the idea of asking for an invitation from Anwar Sadat, since Gusel's great-grandmother had been born in Cairo. But in order to find out what had been going on in the matter of our applications, I decided to phone someone upon whom our departure depended more than it did upon Sadat.

But when I tried to call Major Pustyakov, who in June of the year before had told me I had just one month "to think things over," someone with a pleasant voice told me: "Andrei Vasilyevich is no longer working here. He has, as we say, 'gone into reserve.' But I can give you his home phone number."

"No, thank you. If he is no longer working there, I no longer have any need of him."

"I have replaced him," the voice said, as pleasantly as before. "Can I help you in any way?"

"My name is Amalrik," I said.

There was some static on the phone, and then the voice said quickly: "Andrei Alekseyevich, please let's get together and have a talk."

The pleasant voice proved to belong to Yury Belov, a young man whose feelings were easily hurt. He wanted me to like him and emphasized that he had joined the KGB during the period of de-Stalinization and that he had his own convictions. He claimed he had asked his superiors to let him handle my case. (KGB officers usually say this in order to "smooth out relations.") He said I would have made a first-rate physician. He also remarked, however, that I was too opinionated, to which I replied that a person who wasn't opinionated would have a hard time struggling with such a powerful regime. Belov said that the only way for us to get out of the country was via Israel and advised me to exercise that option "before it was too late." I think it quite possible that the authorities, even though they were very put out with me, might have let me out of the country on the basis of the invitation to Holland, with subsequent loss of citizenship. But they wouldn't have done so for another year, and by then it would indeed have been too late: I would have been arrested along with Ginzburg, Orlov, and Shcharansky. (For that matter, there was no guarantee that the emigration policy would last very long.) So I told Belov it didn't matter to me how my emigration was packaged, but that I did not want to seek out imaginary relatives in Israel and then catch a plane for Vienna rather than for Amsterdam. He replied he would report my sentiments to his superiors.

Four days later we had another talk and agreed on the following: (1) I would apply to the Dutch Embassy for permission to go to Israel (Holland looked after Israel's diplomatic interests in the USSR), and I would submit that permission to the OVIR; (2) once I had received the exit visas, I would get visas for Holland, and we would fly directly to Amsterdam; (3) I would be allowed, without paying customs duties, to take along my personal belongings, pictures, and books; (4) during the three weeks between filing the application with the OVIR and receipt of the exit visas, we would be permitted, without being tailed, to travel through the country by way of bidding farewell to Mother Russia.

We had to have another meeting, since the KGB was at first unwilling to agree on the last point: they thought I wanted to travel around "in order to gather material." For my part, I raised a question about government bonds. In Stalin's day, everyone was obliged to buy government bonds, in an amount equivalent to at least one month's pay, every year. Then a moratorium was declared. My parents had left me bonds in the amount of 1,200 rubles. Since the redemption date had been deferred and taking bonds out of the country was forbidden, I suggested that the KGB buy them from me before maturity. At first they hesitated. Then Belov said that if they bought them from me, I would make a laughingstock of the KGB everywhere.

Scarcely had Gusel and I come out of the building, however, when we had another encounter. Coming toward us with a smile in the spring sunshine, was Boris Tarasov, the same Tarasov who once talked with me about my release and had summoned me forth from Magadan Prison and who had later been transferred to Moscow.

"Boris Vasilyevich!" I shouted gladly, and Disa stared at him with bulging eyes.

The smile vanished from his face and, looking off to one side, he started walking faster.

"Boris Vasilyevich!" Gusel shouted in her turn.

At this, Tarasov did not so much run away from us (neither his fat belly nor his rank as colonel would have permitted that) as mince along with unusual celerity.

I thought to myself: the poor guy! All that rank, and yet he's afraid to talk to anybody without special permission. If he had stopped to greet us in front of the KGB headquarters where everyone could see us, he would later have had to write up an explanation of what he had (or had not) talked to Amalrik about in secret. No wonder the police officials who had dragged me out of my bed behaved so strangely when they met up with me on the street afterward. One would cast his eyes heavenward, another would look down at the ground, and still another would look into his own soul: but none of them stared straight at me. They didn't have orders to pick me up, so why give themselves extra trouble?

From KGB headquarters I went directly to the Dutch Embassy. I was stopped at the gate by police, because I arrived before the bureaucratic machine had started to function, and a senseless conversation ensued. Why had I come there? For a visa? Get a Soviet visa first! One of the two officers, a captain who was not too bright, began to lecture me about the obligations of Soviet citizens. The other, who was more clever, having noticed that I was behaving with a good deal of self-assurance, phoned for instructions. Finally I was allowed into the consular section.

As I was going back home along the Arbat I experienced a strange sensation, like a man who has always carried a heavy knapsack on his back and then suddenly thrown it off. At first I couldn't understand the reason for it, and then suddenly I saw why: there was nobody tailing me. There had been some tails lounging on the other side of the street while I was arguing with the police officers at the gates of the embassy. But the moment I left the embassy, they stopped shadowing me. It often happens the other way around, but in my case the tails had done their job: I had asked for a visa. It is interesting, by the way, that after having urged me to leave voluntarily, the authorities continued to insist that I be referred to, in the newspapers, as someone who had been thrown out of the USSR—a belated acknowledgment of the truth.

A few days later the Dutch consul gave me the following document:

> March 30, 1976
> The Embassy of the Kingdom of the Netherlands, representing the interests of the State of Israel in the Soviet Union, hereby confirms that Andrei Alekseyevich Amalrik . . . and Gusel Kavylevna Makudinova . . . have requested that the Embassy issue them visas for Israel, which will be furnished them when they receive Soviet exit visas.

The submission of documents to the OVIR, and of one's belongings to the customs, is designed as the last and really quite effective humiliation of "Soviet man"—especially for those who are leaving the country for good.

The KGB, however, did want us to leave: they now issued us the certifying documents without delay. They even suggested that we could do without the permission of Gusel's parents, but her parents gladly gave permission, figuring that as proletarians they had nothing to lose but their chains. Our questionnaires were issued to us and our documents accepted by the central office of the OVIR, though we had to wait in line for two hours to get everything. Gusel was taking Disa to her parents' home and had asked me to get some sand for her, just in case. I found a satchel lying on the balcony and filled it with Disa's sand. But in the subway I noticed that it was giving forth the unbearable stink of cat piss, and since I didn't dare bring the satchel into the OVIR, where even without such an annoyance everyone was scowling at everyone else, I left it outside. While Gusel and I were waiting in line, I would go outside from time to time, to see whether the satchel had been stolen. Ultimately it was. I have no way of knowing whether the person who lifted it was disappointed at finding that it contained stinking sand or whether he thought to himself: How sly those Jews are!—and then began washing out the sand to find the gold someone intended to smuggle out of the country.†

---

†With this transformation of piss into gold, like water into wine, the flashes of scatology in this book (I refrain from saying "like gold dust in the sand") come to an end. One American professor who read this manuscript remarked cautiously that perhaps I had overworked the theme: Americans, he said, are eager to find Freudian complexes in everything. I replied that if those psychoanalysts had squatted out in the freezing cold with a bare ass, as the great Russian people do, they would have found a simpler explanation. My own inclination is to seek, in Freud's writings, an explanation for the Americans' preoccupation with toilets. In America the number of bathrooms in a home determines its desirability; I have seen a house that had seven toilets for one married couple.

By the morning of April 10, we had two plane tickets. The evening before I had again been picked up by the police, who told me their orders were to take me to Borovsk, since the deadline for my finding employment had long since expired. After keeping me in detention until midnight, they released me, but only after warning me, in the presence of two witnesses, that I must report to the prosecutor's office in Borovsk within two days. Belov later assured me that the prosecutor, when I did not report in accordance with the earlier warning, had wanted to send out a nationwide bulletin about me and that the KGB had restrained him. Imprisoning unemployed persons, or sending them to Siberia, is the Soviet equivalent of the unemployment compensation paid in Western countries. Neither the first time I was warned nor the second did I see the decree of the Presidium of the RSFSR Supreme Soviet dated August 8, 1975, on which the warning was based. It has not been published, and law enforcement officers are scarcely familiar with it.

At first I thought that the KGB and the police had simply failed to coordinate their moves, although I was surprised that I was given a warning only about finding employment and not about leaving Moscow. But I soon saw what the KGB had been up to; that same night I wrote a letter to Belov, that

I have, most regretfully, reached the conclusion that both you and your superiors are very stupid. A preplanned, idiotic action was carried out against me, involving my detention and warning on finding employment. It is perfectly plain to me that you are doing this so as to have another means of pressuring me in case I refuse, at the last moment, to leave the country. By way of consolation, I might add that I too am stupid, since to a certain extent I believed I could take seriously what you told me.

Early the next morning we set out for Central Asia. Neither checks nor credit cards exist in the USSR, so I always carried a few thousand rubles around with me, not bothering to thread them on a string, as I had once advised Akhnazarov to do. Sometimes at a railroad station or airport, well-intentioned people who noticed I was carrying a thick roll of bills would say: "Careful you don't get robbed!" But God was good to me. For that matter, I trusted pickpockets far more than I did the State, which stole lots of money from me and which I would not trust with a single kopeck.

C H A P T E R   2 7

Finale

Our travels began in Tashkent. Rebuilt after the earthquake, that city has a beauty all its own, since "local color" (in the ethnic sense) is the only way to escape Socialist Realism in architecture. Samarkand produced an entirely different impression on us. For the first time we saw an authentically Asiatic city. In the teahouses of the Old Quarter, aged Uzbeks were sitting, tailor-fashion, on rugs. In the streets, where burros mixed with the automobile traffic, they were cooking *shurpu* and selling *vavash*—unleavened bread the taste of which I can still remember. (There is no comparison between it and bread baked in electric ovens.) The bazaars offered a greater variety than those in Russia; the shops were more exotic; and the people more hospitable. And yet one sensed—strongly in the new sections of the city—that one was in a Soviet provincial town.

In Tbilisi we were invited to the house of Merab Kostava, a musician and an "anthroposophist" with a piercing gaze, a loud voice, and incisive gestures. We had intended to spend four days in Georgia; we stayed for four weeks. Among our hosts were Kostava, the poet Zviad Gamsakhurdia, and the historian Victor Rtskhlladze.

Despite the protection he gave me by "hiring" me as a gardener, there was something about Gamsakhurdia that rubbed me the wrong way. According to his friends, he had in the past been a mirthful man of radiant personality; but constant harassment had made him gloomy and hysterical. He was moody in the extreme and thought he saw KGB agents and provocations around every corner, something that became completely pathological, although it must be said that there actually were attempts to frame him.

During the period when Orlov, Ginzburg, and Shcharansky were arrested, Gamsakhurdia and Kostava were also detained. A few months later,

Rtskhiladze was apprehended. After spending more than a year in prison, Gamsakhurdia "repented" at his trial, just as Krasin and Yakir had done earlier; he even appeared on television.

For Georgians, it is important to preserve their language, their culture, and at least some degree of independence from Moscow in their life-style. They often complained that the churches were being destroyed, and the David Goredzhi Monastery was even being used as an artillery proving ground. I asked whether it was right to criticize the Russians for that, since our own churches are in much more frightful condition. The Russians are destroying their own culture, I was told, but we Georgians want to preserve ours; and we would do so except for interference from the outside. (In all the union republics, "the Soviet regime" is called "the Russian regime.")

The process of Russification is carried on cautiously but unremittingly; during our visit, there were protests against the requirement that dissertations be written in Russian, and two years later, thousands of people demonstrated against the fact that the new Constitution did not mention Georgian as the official state language. In Tbilisi there was much talk about arson and explosions. Before we arrived, there was an explosion in the reception room of the Council of Ministers. According to the official version, it was the work of black-market businessmen and followers of the former secretary of the Georgian Central Committee, Mzhavanadze—people whom the new secretary, Shevardnadze, had begun to purge. I doubt, however, that the purge put an end to the corruption. More likely, it merely made the bribes bigger. For example, the Prosecutor of the Republic was getting 30,000 rubles for dropping charges in criminal cases, and the chief of the MVD's medical department was getting 60,000 rubles—as much as a top engineer makes in forty years—for releasing prisoners on medical grounds.

In taxicabs, shoemakers' shops, offices, and stores we saw many portraits and photos of Stalin. There is a black market in postcards bearing his likeness. The most highly prized photos are those in which he is wearing his generalissimo's uniform, especially those that include Churchill and Roosevelt. This "cult of Stalin" does not mean that the Georgians favor Stalinism as a political doctrine. It is simply that, to their misfortune, Stalin is the most famous Georgian, and Southerners are especially fond of fame. On every other building in Tbilisi there is a memorial plaque stating that such and such a writer, general, or scientist once lived here. So what can you expect in the case of Stalin? (It is true, however, that there is no plaque on the building that once housed the theological seminary he attended, which has been converted to a fine arts museum.) The "cult of Stalin" is a way of taunting Moscow. If a policy of out-and-out Stalinization were to be adopted, the photos of Stalin would disappear in Georgia (I saw almost no photos of Brezhnev there).

Finally, the Georgians are pleased at the fact that not too long ago the Russians were trembling before a Georgian, just as Gusel, a Tatar, finds pleasure in the fact that Genghis Khan terrified the Russians seven hundred years ago.

The famous Georgian hospitality, which corresponds to the Georgians' feudal and chivalric spirit, is unique. During our month there, we had almost no occasion to spend our own money. Naturally, the desire to put one's best foot forward plays a large part in this; and the numerous—and obligatory—banquets are sometimes hard to survive. The banquets have a definite ritual; there is a toastmaster, and a prescribed sequence for the toasts: to this house, to one's parents, to one's friends, to "our long-suffering Georgia," and so on, for each person at the table. But the toastmaster not only proposes toasts, he addressed compliments to one of the guests; then, with the words "*alla verdy*," he yields the floor to the next guest, who yields to the next, until everyone has had his say. The guests start drinking from goblets, then metal-encased "drinking horns" may make their appearance.

We took a plane to Kutaisi, and then we went by car to Svanetia, on the slopes of the Caucasus Mountains. The Svany constitute one of the Georgian tribes, but both in language and in anthropological type they differ from the Georgians living in the valleys. The higher up we went in the mountains, the more hazardous the road became; sometimes we had to get out of the car and check the obstacles ahead. The ascent from Lower Svanetia to Upper Svanetia cannot be negotiated even on horseback. We covered thirteen miles on foot (one third of the way over the snow), along a narrow path that skirted an abyss. The snowstorm made it hard to see, but I don't think sunshine would have been better: it would have blinded us. One of the people in our company fainted. Gusel bore up better than the rest of us, and she was the first to enter Ushguli, situated at a higher altitude than any other village in Georgia. The villagers were amazed to see us. In July, a good many people climb through the pass; but almost no one does it in the spring.

Ushguli has a large number of stone towers that rise to a height of sixty-five feet, with thick walls and narrow loopholes. In the era of blood feuds, the Svany could remain in their towers for years, exchanging rifle fire with their neighbors. The women were never touched: they worked in the fields and at home; their husbands used pulleys to hoist up food for themselves in the towers. The most recent time these towers were put to use was during the period of collectivization; and the kolkhozes in Upper Svanetia are more fictitious than real. Although there is an abundance of stone, the streets are not paved, and the stone fences have stiles—almost no gates. Most of the houses in Georgia have two stories; but the proud Svany have no indulgence for human weaknesses: their toilet is a rickety outhouse, often situated in the middle of the street. When the cattle herds come down the street, mooing as they trample their way through the mud, they pass by it on either side. And I, sitting inside it and watching through a chink in the wall, feared above all else that a bull would hook the outhouse with one horn, and bring it down along with me.

I saw a peasant bringing in soil for his garden on a sledge pulled by an ox, just as was done in Egypt five thousand years ago. Almost all the women in Svanetia wear black; after the death of a relative, whether a near or distant one, they must wear mourning until they themselves die. If a woman wants to drink with guests, she must ask her husband's permission. Nonetheless, women are highly respected.

In Mestia, the capital of Svanetia, we were invited to a banquet. The guest list even included the secretaries of the *raikom*, and I was asked to act as toastmaster—a great honor. When it came time to offer a toast to friends, I proposed that we drink to our friend Yury Orlov, a fighter for human rights, who had only recently organized the Group to Promote Observance of the Helsinki Accords. All of the Svany who were Party members warmly approved the founding of the group. Then I concluded: "Please allow me to send Orlov a congratulatory telegram in the name of all those assembled here." There was loud applause.

Later, Yury told me that the day before the founding of the group was announced, he was detained and given a warning at the prosecutor's office. His apartment building was surrounded by KGB agents, and no one was allowed to enter or leave. Then, at the height of the siege, a telegram, opened and crumpled, was brought to him: "ALL SVANETIA DRINKS TO YOUR HEALTH. VICTORY WILL BE OURS!"

From Mestia we took a plane back to Kutaisi. But we couldn't get tickets for Tbilisi right away; so our guide took us to a restaurant in a park to eat. There we saw something most unusual for Georgia: the restaurant was empty, except for a few men sitting at two tables that had been moved close together. It seems that two warring criminal gangs, after each had killed a few of the other gang's men, had decided to make peace. We had arrived right in the middle of the peace talks. Our guide, who was from Kutaisi, knew somebody or other; and the gang leaders had heard about me. So they promptly sent the manager of the State-owned restaurant to the market to buy some meat. We soon had a splendid feast on the table, and the two Mafiosi paid courtesy visits, so to speak. They dispatched two young men to the airport, where they had no trouble getting tickets for us right away. (If one is to compare Georgia to Italy, the Svany are like the Sicilians: all their business connections are based on kinship, and betrayal is severely punished.)

Whereas Georgia is a Mediterranean-type country, Armenia lacks access to the sea. It is hard to imagine a people with a more tragic fate than that of the Armenians, hemmed in by the crescent of the Moslem Levant. From Yerevan one can see Mount Ararat, which ornaments the state seal of Armenia—but it is in the hands of the Turks. While the Georgians have a feudal cast of mind, the Armenians are bourgeois: they have a fondness for work and trading and are skillful at it. I would not say that relations between the Georgians and Armenians are actually hostile: they are, rather, like two brothers who have been quarreling all their lives. And it is difficult to imagine one without the other.

"Well, did the Armenians bad-mouth us?" we were asked in Tbilisi when we returned from a week in Armenia.

"No, they didn't say anything bad about Georgians to us."

"See what I mean? It's like we told you. The Armenians are crafty. We bad-mouth them, but they don't bad-mouth us."

The Armenian landscape is one of sun-baked hills with no stands of trees. Only to the north of Sevan do you begin to see forests. And wherever we visited, our guide would tell us in great agitation that although Armenia had been converted to Christianity five centuries before Russia, a Russian had tried to prove to him that the Russian churches were older than the Armenian ones. I told him there was a Russian proverb: "Get your sleigh ready in the summer, and your carriage ready in the winter." The Russians, I said, are a farsighted people: they built churches long before they became Christian, just in case that might happen.

Another part of Georgia we visited was Abkhazia. But the Abkhazians spoke of the Georgians in about the same terms as the Georgians use when talking about the Russians. The sense of national pride is strong in both Central Asia and the Trans-Caucasus. Russification is encountering resistance, though we didn't notice any overt anti-Russian feeling. In Latvia, however, where we had gone for a seaside vacation in the summer of 1975, we would occasionally sense a hostility toward us as Russians. Thinking back on my trips to the Baltic countries in 1964 and 1970, I would say that the hostility has increased.

What I was most interested in seeing in Odessa was the famous flight of steps down which the baby carriage rolled in the film *The Battleship Potemkin*, a scene I had remembered since childhood. Kiev struck us as very beautiful. It was for a paper on Kievan Russia that I was expelled from the university; and now for the first time I saw the Monastery of the Caves and the Cathedral of St. Sophia. Thanks to the kindness of the attendants, reinforced by a bribe, we were able to visit the cathedral almost alone.

We were demoralized, however, by the sight of children doing sentinel duty at the monument to the heroes of World War II. Twelve-year-old girls with braids, who were carrying carbines, goose-stepped back and forth or stood stock-still, their faces tense. A wish to preserve the memory of those who perished is understandable, but an overtly militaristic upbringing is hardly calculated to avoid wars in the future. As for the monument at Babi-Yar, it is a group of men and women with Slavic faces; the inscription contains not a word about the Jews.

On June 7, we returned to Moscow, where we found awaiting us a postcard dated April 29: "Report promptly to the OVIR, Room No. 22, to get your visas. Kosheleva."

Remembering the bureaucrat's sullen face, I wrote back: "We shall go to the OVIR when we get a polite invitation from you."

I don't know what effect our reply produced at the OVIR; but among Moscow Jews, who are used to such rudeness, it produced a "malodorous sensation," as the Soviet journalists like to say. In my memory, a "malodorous sensation" is associated with the no less foul, stale smell of barracks and the pungent smell of cheap perfume. (The officers and warders, when going on duty, would douse themselves with perfume so they wouldn't take on the smell of the prison or camp. I very much fear, however, that the result was a mixture that was even worse.)

In Moscow we were in time to say good-bye to Ina and Vitaly Rubin. The authorities had denied Vitaly an exit visa for several years, but as soon as he joined the Helsinki Watch Group, he got his visa.

The first crisis in the Helsinki Group—one that, fortunately, was rather comical—occurred just at that time. One member, the historian Mikhail Bernshtam, a Jew converted to Russian Orthodoxy, addressed two grievances to the editors of the samizdat magazine, *Jews in the USSR*: (1) they had distorted certain things in an article of his that they had published; and (2) (and more important) they had compelled his wife to leave him and emigrate to Israel. In his letter to the editors, he first put "Jews in the USSR" in quotes, then dropped the quotes in further mentions of it, so that one didn't know whether he was blaming just the magazine or all of the Jews in the USSR. Mark Azbel, editor in chief of the magazine, demanded that Orlov censure Bernshtam and expel him from the group. Orlov was unwilling to make any public declarations, because he didn't want to draw undue attention to the incident. And the problem solved itself. As often happens in Mother Russia, Bernshtam, after having solemnly declared that he would never emigrate (thereby fulfilling his duty toward Orthodoxy), left on an Israeli visa and ceased to be a member of the group.

Gusel was very tired after our traveling, so I went north alone: before leaving the USSR, I absolutely had to visit that part of this country where, after the fall of Kievan Russia, the future Russia had taken shape. From Vologda I took a bus to Kirillov to see the Monastery of St. Cyril of the

White Lake and the nearby St. Therapont Monastery, with its wonderful wall paintings by Dionysius.[18] (Those paintings give one the feeling that the great wave from the Mediterranean, in a final surge, had washed up on the plains of northern Russia.)

It was raining heavily, and the church with the frescoes was closed. I looked for the director of the museum, to ask him to let me in the church. In the cell formerly occupied by the gatekeeper, where it was warm and dry, I saw a man in a steaming cloak sitting in front of the stove drinking tea.

"Why, it's Amalrik!" he exclaimed. He was an old schoolmate I had not seen for twenty years who had come to the monastery as an architect specializing in restoration. It was as if my youth, rather a sad one, had wanted to remind me of itself before I went away. Later, in Moscow, I visited the building on Suvorov Boulevard where I had lived from the day I was born until my first exile. The broad, grim-looking cement stairway, without banisters, ascended directly from the doorway. In the dim light, the dirty-looking light blue paint on the walls was depressing, as if in a nightmare. And in fact I had dreamed of it often. Everything was so demoralizing that I didn't even go up to the apartment where we used to live. But then, could I indeed have gone up those stairs for a quarter-century?

There were no rooms available at the hotel in Kirillov, but a citizen who was very friendly, if not very steady on his feet, invited me to spend the night at his place. His family, however, would not let me in—nor would they let him in. My friend the bum (the last bum I saw in Russia) then took me to a hostel, where they allowed me to spend the night, more or less illegally.

I took the hydrofoil up the Volga-Baltic Canal via Belozersk and Vyterga to Petrozavodsk; on Lake Onega I saw Kizhi, an amazing complex of wooden churches. I kept wondering how the same nation that had created these churches, frescoes, icons, and tapestries could suddenly have started destroying them in a blind rage. What, I wondered, would the Georgians have said if they had seen the decaying sixteenth- and seventeenth-century churches of Vologda converted into warehouses? Of course, Kizhi has been preserved, while Kirillov and Therapont are museums; but they are so little compared to the treasures that are being irretrievably lost.

From Petrozavodsk I took the train to Kem: I remember the gray boulders and the sudden spectacle of the White Sea. I wanted to take a boat up to the Solovki Islands with their monastery, now famous not so much for the eight-year "Siege of Solovki" during the schism of the seventeenth century as for the prison camps created there after the Revolution. (The name "Solovki" calls up the same kind of associations as "Lubyanka" and "Kolyma.") Kem was the transfer point for the prisoners, and I wanted to follow the same route they had taken. But I couldn't. A military unit was stationed on the Solovki

Islands, and only tourist groups coming via Arkhangelsk were allowed to visit the area. I sought out a boat anyway and almost made a deal with the captain. But at the last minute he refused to take me, hinting broadly that I would give him away if I were asked how I managed to get to Solovki.

After strolling around Kem and admiring the White Sea—so different from the Black Sea, where I had been only ten days before—I boarded a train for Leningrad. On the way there I made the acquaintance of two officers. One of them, a young woman who was a police lieutenant, told me that her chief, just before he retired, had suddenly confided in her how much he hated the system he served and how much effort it had cost him to conceal that hatred. "It was all so unexpected," she said. "I had known him for several years, and I never could have imagined anything like that. He got a bit frightened afterward and asked me to promise not to tell anyone what he had said."

A person can't go on forever keeping bottled up all the things he has never said. That young woman was glad to talk openly with me, and I suspect it was the first time she had told anyone about her former chief. (In Moscow, Orlov and I had a chat with a reporter on a very orthodox Party magazine. When he found out that he was talking to Orlov and Amalrik, he experienced, perhaps for the first time, the luxury of talking freely and told us that he was writing articles on Marxism in secret. How many such articles are being written today in Russia?)

The other officer was an army lieutenant, and the stories he had to tell differed little from those of the writers Evgeny Zamyatin and Alexander Kuprin: "It's so sickening that booze is the only salvation. The wives hold out longer than the rest; they subscribe to magazines and organize concerts. But more than two years even gets to them." From morning on, he was plainly drunk.

I spent most of my time in the company of some young Pioneer girls who were being taken from Murmansk to spend a summer vaction. They wept and they sang; and some of them obviously wanted to become movie stars.

Awaiting me in Moscow was a postcard saying that we were "requested" to come for our visas. The visas were dated May 17 but had been extended to June 30. In exchange for them we turned in our Soviet passports. The OVIR inspector explained to us that we would lose our Soviet citizenship the moment we crossed the border. Also, that we had been granted the right to become Soviet citizens gratis, but that giving up that citizenship would cost each of us 900 rubles. The "regular visa" that each of us got was a long sheet of paper, with photographs, a seal, and space overleaf for an entry visa. At the Dutch Embassy we were given visas to Israel and Holland, and at the Aeroflot ticket office we had no difficulty in buying tickets for Amsterdam.

A decent zek, when about to be released from a prison camp, distributes his belongings among others. So we gave ours—including the piano—to friends. Two trunks were sufficient for the clothing we were taking with us: the real problem was the books and pictures. Upon receiving our visas, I had called Belov, who was deeply offended by the fact that I had called him "stupid." He told me, however, that I could get permission at the Lenin Library to take my books with me duty-free; as for the paintings, I could get the same kind of authorization from the Cultural Department of the Moscow City Executive Committee.

In order to take any books published before 1947 out of the country, one must obtain special authorization and pay customs duties equivalent to their value. However, the woman at the Lenin Library (who looked more like a gebistka than a librarian), returned my list to me after a few days, with duty-free authorization. It later turned out that my victory was illusory: when I unpacked the cartons in Amsterdam, I discovered that the most valuable books had been stolen by the customs agents.

"I simply can't understand why your wife wants to leave her own country," the woman at customs said, in a hostile tone. The fact that I wanted to leave it meant that I was, in her words, "a typical Jew." What triggers this hostility is the feeling that "you, you shits, are going away, while we are stuck here." This explains why the authorities tolerate theft and graft on the part of customs agents: both are a kind of compensation. Ernst Neizvestny once told me that he gave a customs officer 300 rubles when he was having his sculptures sent abroad.

"Ernst!" exclaimed the officer, putting the money in his pocket. "Does this come from your heart?"

There you have Dostoyevsky's "magnanimous Russian man": it wasn't enough that he got a bribe—it had to come from the heart.

"I would have told him," I said to Neizvestny, "that I was giving him three rubles from my heart, and the rest out of practical considerations."

I had informed the KGB people that I wouldn't give the customs people a single kopeck—so customs had punished me by stealing my books. The matter of the paintings was more complicated. Despite the KGB's assurances, I was supposed to have the paintings evaluated by a committee. Belov moaned when he heard that I had included an icon and a samovar in the list: he had wanted to make a deal with the customs people to let my things go through without an authorization. Along with me, there were a few Jews and Armenians with wretched paintings: they were rejected. While the committee was in session, an old Armenian woman complained to me that when she and her husband had come to Russia from Lebanon twenty years before, the Soviet officials had said to them—and in particular, to their gold—"Welcome!" But now, although they were letting them leave the country, they weren't allowing them to take the gold with them. "Is that fair?" she asked me.

"Of course it's fair," I replied. "When you came to the Soviet Union, were you stupid?"

"Yes, we were stupid," she agreed.

"And now you're leaving. Doesn't that mean that you've become sensible?"

"Yes, we've become sensible."

"Well, that's why they're taking your gold—because they made you fools into sensible people."

The Armenians had a good laugh. But I'm still not convinced that the old couple put up with the loss of their gold; just as I'm not convinced that all of it was left in the USSR. I myself did not submit all of our art objects to the committee: ultimately, some of them—including the samovar and the icon—"went by another route."

The next day I was told that I had to pay 6,ooo rubles to take the paintings out of the country. As for the icon, the samovar, and two spinning wheels, regulations forbade their removal. But in view of their artistic value, the Ministry of Culture offered to buy them, citing "Lenin's decree on preserving things of artistic value." I replied that I would rather demolish the icon with an ax, which would be in full conformity with Lenin's policy toward the arts, than sell it to a mangy State.

The paintings were the work of artists whom the State did not recognize as artists. Only a short time ago those artists' paintings had been razed by bulldozers, and they themselves had been punched in the face by "friends of the arts." One might think that the authorities would have been only too glad that I was taking "ideologically harmful rubbish" out of the country and that they would not have required duties amounting to five years' wages for the average "Soviet man." The main thing, however, was not that: it was our agreement with the KGB, which I figured they were obliged to honor. To persuade Popov, the Deputy Minister of Culture, to overrule the decision would have required intervention by high KGB officials, and that was not to the liking of those who were handling my case. They were hoping that, since I already had our plane tickets, since the deadline was running out on our visas, and since we had already said good-bye to our friends and given away our things, we would be inclined to forget about the paintings. Belov hinted to me several times that since I had friends among the diplomats, it might be simpler to send the things out through their good offices. Unlike the Mafiosi of Svanetia, whose word you can count on, the gebists are the kind of Mafiosi for whom a promise is as straight as a marked card. The KGB people had not kept their promise as to my farewell trip, since they had detained me on the eve of my departure; and now they were trying to wriggle out of their promise about our paintings.

I went to the Aeroflot office and canceled our reservations. "And the third party isn't going either?'' asked the clerk, as she crossed out Gusel's name and my own.

I didn't know whom she meant by "the third party." But later it occurred to me that someone from "the organs" was scheduled to accompany us and that we had wrecked his field trip to Amsterdam.

With much gnashing of teeth, the OVIR people extended our visa until July 15. From time to time I would call the Ministry of Culture, and each time I would get the same answer. "In a few days."

Our refusal to leave for Amsterdam caused a small sensation, and we began to get phone calls from journalists. I would always say that our departure depended on the outcome of the battle between the KGB and the Ministry of Culture; that so far the Ministry had been dancing on the corpse of the KGB and that I hoped world public opinion would support the KGB in this noble struggle.

Foreign reporters asked me whether I considered my emigration a victory or a defeat, and I told them that since I was leaving my own country under pressure, it was certainly not a victory for me, but that it was hardly a victory for the authorities, either, since I had not repudiated my books. Our Movement had what might be called three lines of defense or attack: (1) those who were carrying on the fight in prison or penal camps; (2) those who were at liberty in the USSR—"in the big camp," as the zeks say; (3) those who have emigrated and are continuing the struggle from abroad. I thought then, and I still think, that what a person does is more important than where he is, and my two years abroad have confirmed this. When asked whether I intended to return to Russia, I would always say that the USSR was in for either a bad crisis or radical reform, and that in both cases a return was possible.

In late June, before our departure had been postponed, we had invited friends to a farewell party at the home of Yury and Irina Orlov. The affair had been planned on a grand scale, and we had even ordered two cases of Bohemian glassware so the guests could break their goblets on the floor for good luck. Andrei Sakharov, after drinking his champagne, was the first to do so. A few of the dissidents' wives thought that was a bit too "dashing" and cautiously set their goblets aside. But the majority of the guests smashed theirs.

The rooms were full of people, producing a constant hum that could be heard outside the building, and KGB officers were posted at the entrance, endowing the party with an air of official ceremony. At one point the door was flung open and, led by a girl with magnificent breasts, in came five men marching in Indian file—all wearing boots and Russian peasant blouses—looking at no one and not saying hello to Gusel, the Orlovs, or me. As though guided by infallible instinct, however, they headed for the table with the vodka. In time their identity was revealed: they were "Russites," bearers of "the Russian national spirit" who gravitated around the magazines *Veche* and *Zemlya*. I was even glad that they had come to say a last word of forgiveness to the "prodigal son." But then two of them started to attack Sakharov so rudely that Gusel had to show them the door.

Another uninvited guest showed up even before Gusel and me. This was the poet Lev Khalif, a man of impressive appearance whom I had never seen before. Khalif had been expelled from the Writers' Union and figured that this entitled him to attend every party given by dissidents. While he himself didn't do anything objectionable, he had brought along with him a young fellow and a strumpet who spent the entire evening sitting on a sofa saying nothing but looking at everyone—and especially at me—with undisguised hatred. I am convinced the KGB shamelessly sent that couple to the party, and now I'm sorry that I didn't throw them out. (My good-heartedness has often served me ill.)

A few days later I was awakened by a telephone call from Khalif. Taking the kind of liberty that is allowed only to an old friend, he asked if I could get him an invitation to the U.S. Embassy.

"Listen," I said with considerable irritation, "you've already come to a party of mine without an invitation. And now you want me to get you an invitation to the Fourth of July celebration. Well, I'm not the ambassador."

When Yury Orlov and I went to the Fourth of July reception at the American Embassy, marking the 200th anniversary of the U.S., the first person we saw, standing by a table laden with bottles, was Khalif. I'm not sure whether he saw us, because he seemed to be directing his gaze right over our heads—something not hard to do, considering his height.

I don't know how Khalif got his invitation, but Yury and I procured ours only after some adroit diplomatic skirmishing. The spirit of détente was very much in the air, and the Americans would not have invited me on their own initiative. I wanted them to invite Orlov as leader of the Helsinki Group. I said that he and I represented something closer to the spirit of the American Revolution than did the several dozen KGB agents, both secret and undisguised, who had already been invited and that I would raise the question in the American press. The embassy people called the State Department and sent us our invitations on July 3. Later, though, they blamed us (half in jest) for the fact that when Gromyko saw us, he promptly left the festivities. That was too bad, because I had wanted to thank him for "personally keeping an eye on" my case.

Along with Gromyko, there were a good many other Soviet officials at the reception, and they could be divided into two groups. Those who were not from the KGB talked only to one another and gradually moved off into one of the smaller rooms, where the atmosphere of a Russian beer parlor soon prevailed. By contrast, the KGB officials nosed about all over the place with the most worldly air; they talked to everyone, even me. I caught glimpses of faces familiar to me from my days with Novosti, and I saw the poet Andrei Voznesensky, who at the going-away party for Ernst Neizvestny had shaken my hand warmly and spoken of his respect and fellow-feeling for me. Now, however, with his Soviet colleagues looking on, he responded to my greeting in a rather sour manner. Just you wait, buddy, I thought. And, taking him by the arm, I led him over to where Yury was standing. "This is Professor Orlov, the leader of the Helsinki Watch Group," I said. "If you ever have any trouble getting your poems published, get in touch with him right away." Poor Voznesensky! He shook us off as fast as he could. Later I ran across him in Washington, D.C., and once again he behaved in a way that did him credit. He and several other writers and directors have inherited a strange role: that of serving as a kind of "credit card for Soviet liberalism" that the regime pulls out of its pocket from time to time to show to the West.

At some point in the proceedings I was approached by an individual whom Gogol would have called a gentleman of middle years. He was not exactly thin, nor was he fat, and there was something very judicious about his facial features. "Hello, there," he said, extending his hand and smiling at me. "Don't you recognize me? I'm Victor Louis."

Of course! The Soviet citizen and (at the same time) British journalist with a reputation as "the KGB's special envoy"—my old, although not close, acquaintance. I hadn't seen him for ten years, which was why I hadn't recognized him right away. Once he had asked me why, as a capable person, I didn't set my sights on the same kind of prosperity that he himself enjoyed. Now, however, he said that he respected me for not having repudiated my views, although they were nonsense, because the USSR would survive for another thousand years. (These were the same words I had heard from Nadezhda Mandelstam.) I replied that, to the contrary, I anticipated a serious crisis and that for me the last symptom of its onset would be Louis's own break with the system and flight to the West. "Provided," I added, "such a break is still possible."

I wanted to see members of the Helsinki Watch Group invited to other embassies as well, especially the British, French, and West German. Two years later, however, not even the Americans invited dissidents—not a single one. I wouldn't attempt to say whether this was in accordance with their general policy, or merely with the approach taken by Ambassador Malcolm Toon. The wife of a former British ambassador told me that they (the English) do not frequent foreign embassies. That is not true: many Englishmen frequent the

Soviet Embassy in London—even members of Parliament. And the broader an embassy's contacts, the better it understands the situation in a particular country. Also, there is a great difference between the USSR and England—a difference the ambassador's wife either didn't understand or understood too well.

On July 11, the Ministry of Culture informed me that I had been authorized to take my paintings out of the country duty-free.

"A flight to *Amsterdam?*" exclaimed a depressed-looking woman at the Aeroflot office. "But you have an exit visa for Israel. You have to take a flight to Vienna." And with that, she tore up our tickets.

I don't know whether she did it on her own initiative or whether the KGB had decided to violate the last point in our agreement. At any rate, we now had to make more telephone calls. The next day we were told at Aeroflot that they would give us tickets for Amsterdam for July 15, the day our visas expired, but that since they would have to make out new tickets, I would have to pay an additional seventy kopecks.

"But I wasn't the one who tore up the tickets," I said, "and I'm not going to pay anything."

"*What?*" asked the same woman we had dealt with the day before. "Are you trying to say that I should pay the fee?"

"Of course," I replied.

Quite unexpectedly, the woman started sobbing. Meanwhile, I sat down, waiting to see how things would turn out. The head of the agency, when he saw that my heart of stone was invulnerable to tears, finally issued the tickets to me.

Because of the KGB tricks, our departure had been delayed for two months, and that fact played a decisive role in the fate of our cat, Disa. When we returned from our travels, we learned that in early May she had run away from Gusel's parents' home and was lost. Then, four days before we were to leave, Gusel's sister called to say that not far from the apartment building a cat much like Disa had been found. We went there immediately, and indeed the cat did look like Disa. But she was so ragged-looking and so easily frightened. Back at our place, she crawled under the bed and didn't come out until night. Then she curled up in my arms, as she had when she was a kitten, so there was no longer any doubt about it: this was our Disa.

Early on the morning of July 15, 1976, our friend Dick Coombs from the U.S. Embassy picked us up. I have always found leave-takings hard, especially that moment of unsteadiness when you are still there, but you already feel detached. As I looked into the faces of the friends who had come to Sheremetevo Airport to see us off, I felt guilty: I was leaving them at a bad time.

The customs agents went through our things rather cursorily, not subjecting us to a body search. But it would have been strange if they had let everything through; later they seized the clock that had belonged to my grandparents—the same clock I had so often, and so agonizingly, thought about in the early part of my second term of confinement. (It has now been returned to us.)

We were taken aboard after the other passengers were already on the plane, by a roundabout—or, as the gebist who was accompanying us said, a "direct"—way. The night before we had wondered whether we should eat on the plane. What if they should poison us? But that struck me as very unlikely.

We didn't sleep that night, nor did we eat anything. I was apprehensive, however, that we might have to cope with a press conference in Amsterdam the moment we got there; for that we needed some energy. So after carefully observing to whom, and how, the trays of food were served, we ate. Mother Russia gave us black caviar as a going-away present.

Gusel dropped off to sleep with her head on my shoulder; Disa quieted down and crawled into my lap. As for crossing the border, I didn't give it a thought. All that was visible through the porthole was a layer of white clouds beneath us. Then suddenly, to my own surprise, I started to weep, though I remained silent as the tears ran down my cheeks. We had left a great country that we both loved and hated. Could it really be that we would never return?

Genthod, Switzerland
Utrecht, Holland
New York; Washington, D.C.; Cambridge, Mass., United States
1977–78

Translator's Notes

1. From Lermontov's narrative poem, *The Demon*.

2. The reference is to a famous quatrain written by Fyodor Tyutchev.

3. Lines from another famous poem by Tyutchev.

4. From a Cossack marching song.

5. A memorable scene from *War and Peace*.

6. The reference is to Lenin's famous pamphlet.

7. In Gogol's *The Inspector General*, the mayor (town governor), in a famous scene, reprimands one of his subordinates, not for taking bribes but for taking bigger bribes than his position warrants ("not in accordance with your rank").

8. Cf. the oft-quoted remark by Napoleon: "Every French soldier carries in his knapsack the baton of a Marshal of France."

9. A quote from a Radio Liberty broadcast.

10. Julius Margolin, *Journey to the Land of the Zeks* (New York: Chekhov Press, 1952). This book, published at the height of the anti-Semitic campaign in the USSR, attracted almost no attention in the West. And Margolin's lectures in Tel Aviv, which at the time was full of placards and greetings to Stalin, didn't draw more than ten people.

11. From Gogol's play.

12. Vasiliy Chapayev, a hero of the Russian Civil War. (He commanded an infantry division of the Red Army.)

13. Data from a questionnaire distributed to 2,500 prisoners in various camps. *Toward a New Life*, no. 2 (1978), p. 56.

14. In Krylov's fable, "The Elephant as Governor" (which may or may not be the one Kolomiychenko is misquoting), the Elephant issues a ruling that the Wolves can take as much of the Sheeps' hides as they need, but that otherwise they mustn't touch a single hair of a Sheep.

15. Letter to the editors of *L'Unità* (*Kontinent*, no. 10).

16. A character in Dostoyevsky's early novel, *The Village of Stephanchikovo*

and Its Inhabitants (best-known English-language title: *The Friend of the Family*). Opiskin, a kind of Russian Tartuffe, is generally thought to be a caricature of Gogol.

17. From Boris Pasternak's poem "The Old Park."

18. Dionysius, a Muscovite, was perhaps the greatest Russian painter of his day. The frescoes in the St. Therapont Monastery were painted in 1500.

Glossary

In translating Andrei Amalrik's book, I have left in the Russian spelling a number of words that are customarily rendered into English. They fall roughly into three categories: (1) recent loan words, or loan words *ferendo;* (2) names of territorial administrative divisions; (3) acronyms of frequent occurrence.

Loan words. Just as "samizdat" and "kolkhoz" are now to be found in English-language dictionaries, so "zek" is well on its way there too. And it *will* arrive, despite some translators' insistence on rendering it as "con," for the simple reason that it has very different *con*notations, owing to the large number of law-abiding political prisoners in the USSR. Finally, lagging not far behind words like "zek" are such terms as *gebist* (a KGB officer or agent) and *antisovetchik* (an anti-Soviet person). In the text, I have italicized these newly naturalized words only on their first occurrence and have used English plural endings for them; e.g., "one zek," "two zeks."

Words denoting territorial administrative divisions. Of these, I have kept two common ones, *oblast* and *raion,* in the Russian form, because the attempt to find English equivalents for them (which, for that matter, don't exist) leads to utter confusion. Thus, most Russian-English dictionaries give "district" as an equivalent for both *oblast* and *raion.* But those same dictionaries also give "district" as an (or the) equivalent for three other Russian words: *uchastok, okrug,* and *kvartal,* making "district" do duty for *five* delineations of space on earth that in Russian are quite distinct. Also, there is a very practical consideration here. *Raion* is almost invariably used in specifying an address (usually along with *oblast*), the same way "arrondissement" is used in France; and surely *raion* has as much *droit de cité* in an English-language dictionary as does the already naturalized "arrondissement." (*Oblast* and *raion* have not been italicized in the text.)

High-frequency acronyms. In the language used by Soviet bureaucrats—and, necessarily, in books about Soviet bureaucracies—there is always a dense underbrush of acronyms and abbreviations. If all of these were to be translated in full, it would clutter up the text (not to mention the reader's ear) to an unbearable degree. In order to avoid this kind of agony, I have in most cases left the acronyms "as is."

Activist To be taken in the English sense (e.g., "an activist in the Human Rights Movement"), and *not* to be confused with the *aktiv* (below).

Agitator Usually translated as "propagandist" or "electioneer." But I have preserved it (in quotes) in English quite literally, since it is such an excellent specimen of Soviet "doublethink." (In the USSR, "agitators" don't agitate *against* the system: they propagandize *for* it.)

Aktiv More doublethink. Unlike most Western "activists," those who belong to the *aktiv* in a Soviet penal institution, as in any Soviet institution on the outside, collaborate closely with the higher-ups.

Aktivst A member of an *aktiv*.

Antisovetchik A person opposed to the Soviet regime.

CC Central Committee

CPSU Communist Party of the Soviet Union

DPNK Acting Deputy Chief of (Penal) Colony

Druzhinnik Member of voluntary auxiliary police force.

Gebist (fem., *gebistka*) KGB officer or agent.

GUVD Main Administration of Internal Affairs

KGB Committee of State Security

Kolkhoz A collective farm.

Komsomol The Young Communists' League

MGB Ministry of State Security

MID Ministry of Foreign Affairs

Muzhik In prison camp parlance, an inmate (usually a workingman, and neither a regular criminal nor a political prisoner) who tends to steer a middle course between the "finks" (members of the *aktiv*) and the "refusers."

MVD Formerly Ministry of Internal Affairs; now Ministry of Public Order.

NTS Originally the National Labor Union, now called the People's Labor Union.

Obkom Oblast committee.

Oblast A large territorial administrative division of the USSR, roughly equivalent to the former provinces of Russia.

Organs *Organy:* applied indiscriminately to all Soviet security forces (KGB, MVD, etc.), the word most frequently occurs in the phrase "our glorious organs."

OVIR   Visa and Foreign Registration Office

Partorg   Party organizer (secretary)

Raikom   Raion committee.

Raion   The basic territorial administrative division in the USSR. Oblasts and other large territorial units are divided into raions, as are all cities with a population of at least 100,000.

Raiotdel   Raion Department.

Refusenik   A Jew who is refused an exit visa to Israel.

Refuser   In a penal camp, a member of the "opposition" (*otritsalovka* or *otritsalovo*), those who generally refuse to cooperate with the camp administration.

Remand prison   A place where anyone undergoing pretrial investigation is held.

Samizdat   Self-published, underground literature.

SKK   Council of the Colony Collective: equivalent to the *aktiv* ("finks") in a penal colony.

Sovkhoz   A State farm.

SVP   Section for Internal Security: the nucleus of the *aktiv* in a penal colony.

UKGB   Administration of the KGB

UVD   Administration of Internal Affairs

Vneshposyltorg   Office in Charge of Postal Exchanges with Foreign Countries

VSKhSON   All-Russian Christian-Social Union for the People's Liberation

Zampolit   Deputy camp commandant for political matters.

Zek   Prison slang for *zaklyuchennyi* (a prisoner)—given wide currency in translations of Solzhenitsyn's novels.

Zone   Zone (*zona*) has a wide number of meanings in prison camp parlance, ranging from "area" or "strip" (as in *zapretnaya zona*: "forbidden strip") to the entire compound or camp itself.

A Note on the Type

The text of this book was set via computer-driven Cathode Ray Tube in a face called Times Roman, originally designed by Stanley Morison for The Times (London) and first introduced by that newspaper in 1932.

Among typographers and designers of the twentieth century, Stanley Morison has been a strong forming influence, as a typographical adviser to the English Monotype Corporation, as a director of two distinguished English publishing houses, and as a writer of sensibility, erudition, and keen practical sense.

Composed by Centennial Graphics, Ephrata, Pennsylvania.
Printed and bound by R.R. Donnelly & Sons, Co.,
Harrisonburg, Virginia.
Designed by Virginia Tan.